# Radical Politics and Governance in India's North East

Tripura in India's North East remains the only region in the world which has sustained a strong Left radical political tradition for more than a century, in a context not usually congenial for Left politics. Tripura is one of the 29 States in India which has returned the Communist Party of India (Marxist) led Left Front repeatedly to power. By contrast, radical ethnic politics dot the political scenario in the rest of the region.

This book examines the roots, nature, governmental performance, and theoretical and policy implications of Left radicalism in Tripura. The case of Tripura is placed in comparison with her neighbours in the region, and in some cases with India's advanced States in governance matters. Based on original archival and the very recent empirical and documentary sources on the subject, the author shows that the Left in Tripura is well-entrenched, and that it has sustained itself compared to other parts of India, despite deeply rooted ethnic tensions between the aboriginal peoples (tribes) and immigrant Bengalis. The book explains how the Left sustains itself in the social and economic contexts of persistent ethnic conflicts, which are, rarely, if ever, punctuated by incipient class conflicts in a predominantly rural society in Tripura. It argues that shorn of the Indian Marxism's 'theoretical' shibboleths, the Left in Tripura, which is part of the Indian Left, has learned to accommodate non-class tribal ethnicity within their own discourse and practices of government. This study demolishes the so-called 'durable disorder' hypothesis in the existing knowledge on India's North East.

A useful contribution to the study of radical Left politics in India in general and state politics in particular, this book will be of interest to researchers of modern Indian history, India's North East, and South Asian Politics.

**Harihar Bhattacharyya** is Professor of Political Science, University of Burdwan, India. He has published extensively on aspects of Indian political processes and institutions, comparative federalism, social exclusion, citizenship, ethnicity and nationhood. His recent publications by Routledge include *Federalism in Asia: India, Pakistan and Malaysia* (2010), *The Politics of Social Exclusion in India: Democracy at the Crossroads* (co-edited, 2010) and *Globalization and Governance in India: New Challenges to Society and Institutions* (co-edited, 2015).

# Routledge Studies in South Asian Politics

6 **US-Pakistan Relations**
   Pakistan's Strategic Choices in the 1990s
   *Nasra Talat Farooq*

7 **Public Policy and Governance in Bangladesh**
   Forty Years of Experience
   *Nizam Ahmed*

8 **Separatist Violence in South Asia**
   A Comparative Study
   *Matthew J. Webb*

9 **Pakistan's Democratic Transition**
   Change and Persistence
   *Edited by Ishtiaq Ahmad and Adnan Rafiq*

10 **Localizing Governance in India**
   *Bidyut Chakrabarty*

11 **Government and Politics in Sri Lanka**
   Biopolitics and Security
   *A. R. Sriskanda Rajah*

12 **Politics and Governance in Bangladesh**
   Uncertain Landscapes
   *Edited by Ipshita Basu, Joe Devine and Geoffrey Wood*

13 **Constitutional Democracy in India**
   *Bidyut Chakrabarty*

14 **Radical Politics and Governance in India's North East**
   The Case of Tripura
   *Harihar Bhattacharyya*

# Radical Politics and Governance in India's North East

The Case of Tripura

Harihar Bhattacharyya

LONDON AND NEW YORK

First published 2018
by Routledge
2 Park Square, Milton Park, Abingdon, Oxon OX14 4RN

and by Routledge
711 Third Avenue, New York, NY 10017

*Routledge is an imprint of the Taylor & Francis Group, an informa business*

© 2018 Harihar Bhattacharyya

The right of Harihar Bhattacharyya to be identified as author of this work has been asserted by him in accordance with sections 77 and 78 of the Copyright, Designs and Patents Act 1988.

All rights reserved. No part of this book may be reprinted or reproduced or utilised in any form or by any electronic, mechanical, or other means, now known or hereafter invented, including photocopying and recording, or in any information storage or retrieval system, without permission in writing from the publishers.

*Trademark notice*: Product or corporate names may be trademarks or registered trademarks, and are used only for identification and explanation without intent to infringe.

*British Library Cataloguing-in-Publication Data*
A catalogue record for this book is available from the British Library

*Library of Congress Cataloging-in-Publication Data*
A catalog record for this book has been requested

ISBN: 978-1-138-66872-0 (hbk)
ISBN: 978-1-315-61851-7 (ebk)

Typeset in Times
by Apex CoVantage, LLC

**Dedicated to Prof (retd.) Kalayan K. Bhattacharyya who initiated me into learning about politics**

# Contents

*List of figures* ix
*List of tables* x
*Preface and acknowledgements* xii
*Glossary* xiv

Introduction: radical politics and governance in
India's North East  1

1 Marxism and the national/ethnic question: theory
and practice in India  17

2 Ethnic diversity and ethnic radicalism in India's North East  36

3 Institutionalization of ethnic radicalism in India's
North East: power-sharing, participation and governance  52

4 Roots of radical politics in Tripura: princely State;
demographic, social and economic transformations  72

5 The ethnic radicalism in Tripura: Reang rebellion 1943–45
and the birth of an ethnic identity  88

6 Origins of the communist movement in Tripura: Jana Mongal
Samity, Jana Shiksha Samity and Paraja Mondal  102

7 Dialectics of radical ethnic nationalism and left radicalism
in Tripura, 1948–51: communist influence over the tribal
mass mobilization  117

8 Radical ethno-nationalism in Tripura, 1948–50  141

9  Left radicalism turned parliamentary and institutionalized in Tripura: appropriation of tribal ethno-nationalism  159

10  The rise and decline of the TUJS in Tripura: radical ethnic challenge to the left  182

11  Marxists in power in Tripura: sub-State-level institutionalization of tribal identity  197

12  Marxists in power in Tripura: dilemmas of governance since the 1990s  214

Conclusion  233

*Bibliography*  239
*Index*  247

# Figures

| | | |
|---|---|---|
| 3.1 | Number of deaths in violent conflicts in the States of India's North East (1992–2015) | 62 |
| 3.2 | Public Policy Effectiveness Index in India's North East (1981–2011) | 64 |
| 3.3 | Policy Effectiveness Index in India's advanced States (1981–2011) | 64 |
| 3.4 | Rule of Law Index in India's North East (1981–2011) | 65 |
| 3.5 | Rule of Law Index in India's advanced States (1981–2011) | 66 |
| 12.1 | Public Policy Effectiveness Index in Tripura compared to some Forward States in India (1981–2011) | 226 |
| 12.2 | Rule of Law Index in Tripura compared to India's Forward States (1981–2011) | 227 |
| 12.3 | Physical Infrastructure Development Index (PIDI) in Tripura compared to India's Forward States (1981–2011) | 228 |
| 12.4 | Social Opportunity Index in Tripura compared to India's Forward States (1981–2011) | 228 |
| 12.5 | Livelihood Opportunity Index in Tripura compared to India's Forward States (1981–2011) | 229 |

# Tables

| | | |
|---|---|---|
| 2.1 | Army deployed in aid to civil order in the North East, 1973–83 | 38 |
| 2.2 | Population and areas of States in NE and India, 2011 | 39 |
| 2.3 | Tribes and their percentage to population in the North East (2001) | 39 |
| 2.4 | Economic activities of the people in the North East (2011) | 46 |
| 3.1 | Ethnic peace accords in India's North East (1947–2015) | 56 |
| 3.2 | Popular participation in Lok Sabha elections in the North East (1951–2014) | 60 |
| 3.3 | Incidence of riots (IPC defined): North East and (all) India (1959–93) | 62 |
| 3.4 | Scheduled caste households without electricity, safe drinking water and sanitation (1991–2011) in India's North East | 67 |
| 3.5 | Scheduled tribe households without electricity, safe drinking water and sanitation in India's North East (1991–2011) | 68 |
| 3.6 | Literacy rate among the scheduled castes in North East India (1981–2011) | 68 |
| 3.7 | Literacy rate among the scheduled tribes in India's North East (1981–2011) | 69 |
| 4.1 | Decadal growth of population in Tripura (1881–2011) | 76 |
| 4.2 | Ethnic composition of population of Tripura (total = 3,671,032) (2011) | 78 |
| 4.3 | Percentage of different tribes to total tribal population in Tripura (2001) | 78 |
| 4.4 | Decadal growth of literacy in Tripura (1931–2011) | 79 |
| 4.5 | Schools in minority languages in Tripura (2010) | 81 |
| 4.6 | Religious composition of population in Tripura (2001) | 83 |
| 4.7 | Land tenures among the tribals and non-tribals in Tripura (1964) | 84 |
| 4.8 | Workforce participation in Tripura (2015) | 84 |
| 5.1 | Discriminatory rates of family tax among tribes | 91 |
| 5.2 | Rice prices 1937–8 and 1942–5 | 92 |
| 8.1 | Tripura's rural class structure (1931–51) | 146 |
| 8.2 | Percentage distribution of literacy in Tripura (1911–51) | 147 |
| 9.1 | Ethnic composition of UF candidates in the Tripura Electoral College elections 1952 | 174 |

| | | |
|---|---|---|
| 9.2 | Performance of political parties in EC (1952) | 175 |
| 9.3 | Performance of political parties in Lok Sabha elections 1952 | 175 |
| 9.4 | CPI's comparative electoral strength in the State-level elections in India, 1952 | 175 |
| 10.1 | Performance of political parties in the State Assembly elections in Tripura in 1988 | 192 |
| 10.2 | Electoral performance of political parties in the State Assembly elections in Tripura in 1993 | 193 |
| 10.3 | Electoral performance of political parties in the State Assembly elections in Tripura in 1998 | 193 |
| 10.4 | Political party performance in the Tripura State Assembly elections in 2003 | 194 |
| 10.5 | Political party electoral performance in Tripura in the State Assembly elections in 2008 | 194 |
| 10.6 | Political party performance in the State Assembly elections in Tripura in 2013 | 195 |
| 11.1 | Party performance in the elections to the ADC in Tripura (1982–5) | 206 |
| 11.2 | Performance of political parties in elections to the ADC (2010, May 3) | 206 |
| 11.3 | Public expenditure on tribal welfare (2011–12) | 208 |
| 11.4 | Governmental performances in implementation of MNREGA (2006–7 to 2014–15) | 208 |
| 11.5 | Tripura's performance in implementing MNREGA in FY 2015–16 until 28th March 2016 | 208 |
| 11.6 | Benefits to tribal families under the Forest Act 2006 (up to 31 December 2014) | 209 |
| 11.7 | State's sharing of taxes with the ADC Plans (2011–12) | 210 |
| 11.8 | Satisfaction over the ADC's role | 211 |
| 12.1 | Performance of political parties in State Assembly elections in Tripura in 1977 | 219 |
| 12.2 | Political party performance in the State Assembly elections in Tripura in 2013 | 221 |
| 12.3 | Grants released (and utilized) under BRGF to the States in the North East | 223 |
| 12.4 | Tripura's growth of GSDP (2004–5 to 2013–14) | 225 |
| 12.5 | Per capita income in Tripura (2004–5 to 2013–14) | 225 |

# Preface and acknowledgements

India's North East comprising eight States of the Indian Federation are conventionally understood as the 'insurgent country' and security region ridden with ethnic militancy and the breakdown of law and order. Arguing against the conventional wisdom, this study shows how radical politics, ethnic and Left, when institutionalized, produces better rule of law, and governance not simply in terms of the law and order, but the fulfillment of identity needs and delivery of a set of public goods and services that include better physical infrastructure, social and livelihood opportunity and social inclusion. On the basis of the first ever detailed, empirically based, and comparative study of the States in the North East, with particular reference to Tripura, this book examines the roots, nature and institutionalization of both ethnic and Left radicalism in the North East, examines the processes of their institutionalization for participation for power-sharing and governance. As a study in the dynamics of Indian federal politics at the State level, hitherto not adequately dealt with, it shows how India's federation building determined the contour of ethnic and Left politics in the region, and how the creation of new States on the basis of some ethnic markers has served to prevent the spillover effects of ethnic conflicts through territorialization, which has transformed yesterday's rebels into tomorrow's (and the days after) stakeholders in the region. The region, as a result, does not represent any more the typical case of 'durable disorder' but more enduring order and political stability, and governance.

This study grows out of my decades long research on Tripura's Left politics and the more recent research engagement with the rest of the region in connection with a collaborative international research project on 'Continuity and Change in Indian Federalism in the Age of Coalition Government' (2014–17) funded by the Leverhulme Trust UK and based in the University of Edinburgh, UK. My association with this research project as a Lead Partner responsible for 'Ethnic Conflict Managements in India's North East' helped me in generating a lot of detailed empirical data on the basis of elite interviews and field surveys. The research for the book has also been enriched further by my detailed case study of the working of the Tripura Tribal Autonomous District Council during 2011–13 funded the Indian Council of Social Science Research (ICSSR). I wish to record my sincere thanks and gratitude to the Leverhulme Trust, UK and the ICSSR New Delhi. I record also my thanks to the field investigators in the States of the region who helped collect data and conduct interviews. I sincerely record my thanks and gratitude to many political elites in the North East who kindly shared their knowledge in the interviews which facilitated the research for the book. In the penultimate days of drafting the book, Abhishek Karmakar and Monohar Karmakar offered technical support for which thanks are due. Sahon, my son, has jumped in whenever needed for technical issues. I wish to record my thanks to Koteswar Prasad for sending me a material on the communist movement in Madras.

Three published articles have been included here with suitable revisions. I record my acknowledgement to *South Asia Research* (vol. 9, No. 1 1989); *The Indian Economic and Social History Review* (Vol. XXXII, No. 3 (1995); and *The Socialist Perspective* (Vol. 19, No. 3 1993).

The anonymous referees of the project deserve thanks for consenting to my proposal. Dorothea and Lily (of Routledge) have stood by with their kind patience with my changing deadlines. Lisa Salonen, my project manager, was very encouraging in the final stage of publication.

I wish to record my sincere thanks and gratitude to Subrata K. Mitra for his unending encouragement and support. Marie-Paule (Boudi) has always bestowed her blessings on me. I wish also to record my sincere thanks and gratitude to Sudipta Kaviraj and Gurharpal Singh for reading the draft and their endorsements.

Drafting a book-length manuscript sitting for long hours 'upstairs' has been made easier when the family has been under the good care of Saswati, my wife, who perhaps does not always realize how much this has meant to me.

The views expressed in this book are my sole responsibility.

Harihar Bhattacharyya
Department of Political Science
Golapbag, Burdwan University

# Glossary

| | |
|---|---|
| *Adhibhag* | share cropper with half-share |
| *Adhi-bhagi* | share cropper with half the share of the crops |
| *Adivasi* | Aboriginal people |
| *Amlatantra* | (in Bengali) bureaucracy |
| *Bhadralok* | higher caste Hindu educated middle class |
| *Baideshik amla* | foreign bureaucracy |
| *Bangal kheda* | drive out the Bengalis |
| *Bibarani* | description |
| *Barta* | messages |
| *Bubagra* | a Tripuri word for the divine right of kings |
| *Chowkidars* | village guards |
| *Chukti Bhagi* | share as per the contract in share cropping system |
| *Dadan* | loan |
| *Dalits* | lower castes in India |
| *Dewanti rule* | rule by the civil servants |
| *Falgun* | a month in the Tripura calendar; also a month in Bengali calendar (covering February and March) |
| *Gharchukti* | family-wise fixation of tax |
| *Hartal* | total strike |
| *Jatiyo monobhav* | national consciousness |
| *Jhum* | slash and burn method of cultivation |
| *Jotedar* | holder of a small estate |
| *Kok-Borok* | lingua franca of the tribes in Tripura and second official language in the State |
| *Kshatriya Mondalies* | political organization of the Tripura kshatriyas |
| *Lok Sabha* | lower house of Indian Parliament |
| *Mahajans* | money lenders |
| *Operation Rhino* | Indian Army code for anti-insurgency operation in Assam |
| *Oproja* | non-subjects; settler Bengalis in Tripura |
| *Prodhan* | village headman among the tribes |
| *Puran Tripuras* | original Tripuris |
| *Proja* | subjects |

| | |
|---|---|
| *Praja Mondal* | political organization of the subjects in Tripura |
| *Rajya Sabha* | upper house of Indian Parliament |
| *Sardar* | village headman |
| *Swadhihar* | (in Assamese) self-determination |
| *Taluk* | small estate |
| *Talukdar* | holder of small estate |
| *Tebhaga* | share cropper with ¾ share |
| *Udayachal* | a separate State out of Assam in the North East of Assam on the northern side of the river Brahmaputra |
| *Zamindary* | holder of a large estate |

# Introduction
## Radical politics and governance in India's North East

**Introduction**

As a contribution to the study of radical Left and ethnic politics in India in general and State politics in particular, the book examines, in detail, the roots, nature, governmental performance and theoretical and policy implications of Left radicalism in Tripura within the broader regional context of the North East. India's North East now comprising eight States – Arunachal Pradesh, Assam, Manipur, Meghalaya, Mizoram, Nagaland, Sikkim and Tripura – is India's strategic and security region bordered as they are with Bangladesh on the West and Myanmar, Bhutan and China on the east, North East and the north. The region contains a significant concentration of tribal population so that five of the eight States are inhabited predominantly by the tribes of many different groups and sub-groups. No wonder the region remains for many decades since India's independence in 1947, the 'insurgent country' – now much dissipated – with hundreds of militant ethnic groups. As a result of manifold rounds of negotiations and power-sharing, many ethnic rebels and their next generations are now elected to government and the ruling parties, and have proved themselves effective in governance in ensuring durable ethnic peace and some growth too. This explains that today's ethnic radicals, when accommodated and transformed into stakeholders, can become tomorrow's (and the day after) defenders of law and order, and the responsible rulers. This offers a scope of comparative assessment in terms of public policy effectiveness of the State governments run by the Left radical (in Tripura), and those in the region run by various ethnic parties.

As far as our specific focus is concerned, we will explain how the Left sustains itself in the social and economic contexts of persistent ethnic conflicts, which are, rarely, if ever, punctuated by incipient class conflicts in a predominantly rural society in Tripura. Based on years of research stretching over decades and the use of original archival and the very recent empirical and documentary sources on the subject, the book seeks to show that the Left is well-entrenched in Tripura, a peripheral State in the Indian Federation, has sustained itself compared to other parts of North East, despite deeply rooted ethnic tensions between the aboriginal peoples (tribes), on the one hand, and the settlers Bengalis, on the other hand. It is argued here that shorn of the Indian Marxism's 'theoretical' shibboleths, the Left in Tripura, which is part of the Indian Left, has learned to accommodate non-class tribal ethnicity within their own discourse and practices of government. This has required not only much modification of the received knowledge of Marxism but also allowing the space for tradition too. No wonder, unlike her North Eastern neighbours, Tripura is the most successful state in ensuring durable ethnic peace and political order. Neither class struggles nor a revolution are any longer the immediate agenda of the Left in Tripura or in India. These are not the near or even the distant vision either. Given the space and context, as a landlocked border state, pursuing a typical Marxist line of class action for the Left was, arguably, not the viable option. The Left gradually cut down the edge of its radicalism, and settled down in government for governance once it came to power in 1978. However, they developed some innovative methods and institutional mechanisms that served them to strike a tricky but critically stable balance between otherwise warring ethnic groups. As a result, the space, if any, of moorings of Left extremism, such as Maoism, on the one hand, and ethnic sub nationalism (tribal and Bengali), on the other, has been occupied within the Left discourse and governmental practices, and the ethnic identity issues have been quite successfully accommodated by institutionalization of autonomy. As a result, a reformist and pragmatist Left in the State has been able to hold on to enduring mass bases. The State has witnessed, as a result, ethnic peace and relatively durable political order in India's 'security region', not known as such for ethnic peace and order.

Tripura in India's North East remains the lone region not only in South Asia but also in the world which sustains for more than a century a strong Left radical political tradition in a context not usually congenial for Left politics. Tripura is one of the 29 States in India which has returned since 1978, except 1988–1993, the Communist Party of India (Marxist) led Left Front repeatedly to power. In the study of parliamentary Left in India Tripura has been less known than West Bengal and Kerala. But while the Left failed in 2011 after 34 years of ruling over West Bengal, and Kerala too in 2011, (it was regained in 2016) Tripura Left's experiment in government, even as a parliamentary, liberal democratic force, is a case apart. Tripura's Left are well-entrenched in the State, as well as at the sub-State-level governing institutions evident in its successive electoral victories at Panchayats (rural self-governing bodies), urban local bodies and the elections to Tripura Tribal Autonomous District Council (ADC) – a 28-member elected tribal governing body governed by the 6th Schedule of the Indian Constitution. The Left is well entrenched further down at the Village Committee level of the ADC too. While the LF has failed in West Bengal, Tripura retains the mass bases in the face of the new forces of globalization. Most remarkably, while in the rest of India's North East, ethnic conflicts verging on militancy, often of longer duration, has defined the stuff of politics, Tripura offers an exception. In Tripura it is not class struggles that serve, arguably, to sustain the Left; the State was not, however, free of ethnic conflicts. Compared to other States in the region, Tripura was the most vulnerable case of persistent ethnic conflict rooted in widespread frustration among the original tribesmen who witnessed their kingdom been swamped by the influx of Bengali refugees from across the border since the Partition (1947) and before. The demographic upheaval in the State was revolutionary so that the immigrants turned an original tribal majority State into one in which the tribals found themselves in a minority in their own land and marginalized. No wonder, Tripura encountered ethnic conflicts and riots resulting in the death of thousands in 1980–81. In the late 1980s and early 1990s ethnic militancy was also rather rampant in the State encouraged by some political parties within the State and outside. But Tripura has since the mid-1990s remains the most militancy-free and is the best governed state in India's North East by any reckoning.

This book proposes to examine closely the following:

- First, it provides a broad outline of the regional context of North East India in order to highlight the roots of radical ethnic politics, and the extent of management of ethnic conflict in favour of durable ethnic peace and political order;
- Second, it examines the historical roots of Left radical politics in Tripura, and the development of a radical tribal nationalist discourse of self-determination against the growing Bengali ethnic domination in the State.
- Third, it pays serious attention to the State's societal complexities and conflicts arising out of the revolutionary transformation in its demography due to successive influx of Bengali refugees from across the border particularly since India's Partition that overnight transformed a tribal majority State into a Bengali dominated one
- Fourth, since ethnic identity, especially of the tribesmen, remains an important issue in Tripura politics, this book proposes to show how the Tripura Left banked on the tribal question; how the tribal identity question was accommodated within the discourse of the Communist Party and the institutionalization of tribal ethnic nationalism at the sub-State level
- Fifth, the book examines in detail, the cultural diversity of North East, that was the roots of radical ethnic politics and also the mechanisms responsible for transforming the rebels into the stake holders.
- Finally, this books seeks to assess, in comparison with other States in the region, the effectiveness of the Marxist led State government in Tripura over the decades since 1978 in maintaining ethnic balance, curbing ethnic militancy, ensuring a modicum of development, banking on social welfare programmes and policies, land reforms and rehabilitation of the landless tribes and sharing powers and responsibilities with the sub-State-level governments, tribal and non-tribals for better governance. The well-built party organization of the Marxists and the GMP (still with family based membership) will also be taken up for discussion because in Tripura's framework of governance party organization has mattered for governmental performance. In this context, the dialectic between Left radical politics in Tripura and India's ongoing reforms will also be taken for detailed discussion. How does Left radicalism survive facing up the forces of reforms in India? Has there been a discursive shift in Left politics in Tripura? What does it mean to be radical/Left in Tripura today? The last chapter of the book will seek to answer those questions.

- Thematically, the work will be centrally concerned with the intricate and complex transactions between radical Left and ethnicity (tribal and Bengali), something missing in the mainstream Marxist writings in India, and the impact of the latter on the former in Tripura. The work is also concerned with the dilemmas Left radicalism in Tripura, ethnic identity and the Marxists' approach to ethnicity in Tripura, theoretically and practically, limits of radical Left politics in Tripura stemming largely from the State's dependence on the Centre, the constraints of Indian federalism and the Constitution of India, and the compulsions of electoral politics that appear to blunt the ideological edge of Left radicalism. Radicalism par se implies anti-systemic perspective and approach. This works seeks to delineate the contours of Left radicalism in Tripura vis-à-vis ethnic radicalism in the region and the problems that arise from its adaptation to the local social and political environment.

The history of Left radical politics in Tripura is now over more than five decades old, and a Left coalition (effectively a CPI-M led) government has been governing the State since 1978 except a brief interlude of five years from 1988–93. Like the rest of the region, insurgency also gripped Tripura for a considerable period of time, but since the early 1990s – the same time when India embraced neo-liberal reform – insurgency in Tripura dipped, law and order improved, ethnic conflicts managed, and the State registered growth. The rate of popular participation in the electoral process at several levels of the polity in the State is also very high not comparable with the relatively poorer records in her neighbours. Tripura's Left radicalism is much moderated since the Left in the State like elsewhere in India has fully immersed itself in the parliamentary politics since the early 1950s but has sustained its mass bases among the Bengalis and the tribals for decades. While ethnic radicalism has occupied the political space in the rest of the region, it is alone in Tripura that Left led by the CPI-M remains the most powerful force and occupies the political space in the midst of ethnic divisions and conflicts in society.

## Radicalism: left and right

The dictionary meaning of the term 'radical' suggests something 'innovative or progressive', positions that advocate 'thorough political or social reforms'. A 'politically extreme' position is also included in the meaning of the term radical (COD 2011). Radicalism could thus be understood in the sense of an individual's attitude or frame of mind when she/he takes a particular position on social and political issues, or on some particular aspect (s) of society and politics against existing social and political arrangements; when it is so done then the latter is considered an unjust, untrue, unfair and so on (Kallen 1959: 52). When seen as a distinct philosophy, the term refers to a programme of social change that entails 'systematic destruction' of existing social order to be replaced by one which is 'true, good, beautiful and just' (Kallen 1959: 52). Since radicalism as an attitude or a distinct philosophical position or sides with the unprivileged, propertyless and majority, it is inherently democratic and humanitarian. Since radicalism *per se* would entail positions that seek total alteration of the existing social and political order that is hated, the term may cover, on the face of it, Nazism, Fascism and Leninism. But then in terms of usage, the term has been accepted more for Leninism than Nazism or Fascism (Kallen 1959: 53).[1] Econ Bitner (1968) has pointed out one major dilemma that radicalism faces: between an activist's ethical principle defending radicalism, and the 'exigencies of existence. Calhoun (2009: 845–6) would argue that the varied usages of the term suggest the lower case use of the term, when it is used to refer to various actual political orientations and political mobilizations (Calhoun 2009: 846).[2] Historical usages of the term 'radical' or radicalism have also varied depending upon the context. In England, for example, those who advocated for reform of Parliament in 1769 were called radicals (Kallen 1959: 52). Also, Jeremy Bentham who advocated the philosophy of the 'greatest good of the greatest number' was known as the philosophical radical. John Maynard Keynes who advocated for a welfare State of high order was the Left radical at the close of the World War ll while Margaret Thatcher, the Conservative Prime Minister of Britain in the late 1980s, who was mainly responsible for the whole-scale dismantling of the social welfare State was known as the 'Right radical'. In fact, in this period of neo-liberalism and free market, all neo-Right writers and thinkers including invariably (late) Friedrich Hayek are all known as the Right radicals. Since the term 'radicalism' is suggestive of an anti-Establishment stance, much care is needed to specify the context that explains what constitutes the 'establishment' and what it is replaced by. Once the specific context is known it is better to understand the true value of radicalism in politics. The Nazis and the Fascists were Right radicals but that was condemned and had to be rejected whole some. In a capitalist State, if the social welfare programmes/policies are under virulent attack, the Left's fight for conserving welfare programmes and policies would also be termed 'radical' because the struggle here is for policies that benefit larger sections of society. Such a position will be accepted as legitimate given the specific context.[3]

The term 'radical' has also been used to describe such extreme tendencies in religious movements such as 'radical Islam', 'radical Hinduism' and 'Christian radicalism', 'radical spirituality' and so on. Of the above three, only Hinduism, whether understood as a culture or a religion, is not global; the so-called radical Hindus can only be found in the shape of the Hindu Right in India exemplified by the rise to power of the BJP with absolute majority in Lok Sabha (2014-), the RSS and other Hindu extremist outfits as the VHP, and the Bajrang Dal. Such radical movements are very important to understand contemporary movements in social and also political life of the people but beyond the purview of our investigations. In discussions on patriarchy and gender, the term 'radical feminism' is also in vogue in the feminist debates since the late 1960s, which is based on the assumption, among others, that gender discrimination is the most fundamental and deepest form of social discrimination.

Karl Marx (1818–83) and Friedrich Engels (1820–95), the founders of Marxism, were the most radical of their time. Marxism that the founders developed as a revolutionary theory of and guide to revolutionary political action for bringing about fundamental social and political change in capitalism in favour of socialism was the doctrine that the founders and their followers stood for. Marxism's radical revolutionary *élan vitae* consisted among others in the propositions that an intransigent critique of the existing order (read capitalism), and the doctrines and philosophies that seek to defend capitalism, is to be pursued, along with a determined Marxist self-criticism of actions and understanding. Despite the Stalinist aberrations, until the breakup of the Soviet Union and its East European neighbours in the early 1990s, Marxism, or to be precise, Marxist socialism as an ideology, theory and doctrine was considered as the most radical political position against capitalism although there were radical critiques of Soviet Marxism and Stalinism from the early 1920s by the 'Western' Marxists (Anderson 1979).

But after the fall of the Soviet Union and its East European neighbours in the early 1990s and the concomitant resurgence of neo-Right intellectual and political waves across the world, the position of the Left radicals has turned 'conservative', not in the sense of defending capitalism but in respect of defending the remains of the social welfare State under severe attack by the neo-Right radicals. Anthony Giddens (Giddens 1994: 9) noted the radical processes of change 'stimulated by the incessant expansion of markets'. As a result, 'the Right here turned radical, while the Left seeks mainly to conserve – trying to protect, for example, what remains of the welfare State'. (Giddens 1994: 9). For him, this is a 'retreat' of socialism from radicalism. (Giddens 1994: 51–77). In the face of the retreat of socialism/communism and the onslaught of free market globalization, Giddens himself has asked the question: 'What can it mean to be politically radical today?' (Giddens 1994: 1). He says that political radicalism associated with socialism – the determined struggle for progress, radical social change and a new social order which would provide for the conditions for human beings to be 'truly free' – seems to be in tatters. Where socialism has suffered most is the loss of credibility of the socialist 'project' (Giddens 1994: 1).

## Indian left radicalism: conceptual issues

In exploring the critical space of radical politics in India's North East, or for that matter, in India, as a whole now, this global intellectual-ideological shift is to be understood in the proper perspective. A context-free examination of the gamut of radical politics will not be of help because Left radicalism cannot have an absolute or fixed meaning. Left radical politics is and should be seen as relative to context and time. The terms' 'radical', 'radicalism' and 'radical politics' thus have implied meanings which are context-bound. If some political groups are engaged in political activity of violent nature for fundamental alteration of the existing order, they are termed 'extreme radical'. If there is a movement for destruction of the existing system, say, welfare State, that is also called radical, but Right radical, to be exact. If there are political groups based on some ethnic identity, but which seek to change the existing ethnic distribution of powers in favour of them, they would be called *ethnic radical*. But it is doubtful if the category of *ethnic radicalism* would be termed 'radical' in the true sense of the term because even if such radicals have some redistributive content in their programme and policies, they are inherently limited to their ethnic brethren or constituency. Such politics are by nature segmental, and not universal. But in the given context of multi-ethnic social and cultural mosaic, they appear to be radical in seeking to change the existing pattern of distribution of powers in society. They often resort to violent means to achieve their goals and come to be known as ethnic militants. By contrast, the Marxist and Left parties of different ideological hues would be termed Left radical for espousing the secular causes of the vast majority of people irrespective of caste, ethnicity, colour or creed.

In multi-ethnic societies which are also capitalist, an examination of radicalism has also to address itself to the relation between ethnicity and Left radical politics. In pure theory, ethnicity and Left radical politics would conjure up two diametrically opposed spaces – an ethnic space (a non-class community space), and a class space of secular character. In such contexts, economic inequalities take also on ethnic character so that a space is created for contestation not only against inequalities *per se* but also how such economic inequalities have impinged upon ethnic distribution of powers. In other words, in capitalism, some ethnic groups are better empowered than the others so that the subordinate and subjugated ethnic groups engage themselves in struggles for redistribution of ethnic powers in their favour. Wallerstein (1991) called it 'ethnicization of the work force' globally speaking and found a strong correlation between ethnicity and occupation in capitalism (Wallerstein 1991: 83) that benefits unequally the groups. Wallerstein wrote: Ethnicization, or peoplehood, resolves one of the basic contradictions of historical capitalism – its simultaneous thrust for theoretical equality and practical inequality – and it does so by utilizing the mentalities of the working strata. (Wallerstein 1991: 84). If that is a global reality, the colonial and post-colonial India is no exception. Typically, in all colonial countries the extreme ethnic division of work/occupation is a stark reality. In India with manifold social and cultural diversity, ethnic divisions of work/occupation in various regions of the country have provided the solid material bases for persistent ethnic conflicts and political extremism. The ethnic division of work/occupation has also meant a particular pattern of distribution of powers between ethnic groups. The above has been aggravated by large-scale migration of groups from one region to another in search of better jobs and work. Such in-migration has most often upset the local demographic balance which has meant a near total loss of livelihood for the local inhabitants, their eviction from land and habitat creating in its wake a permanent conflict space between ethnic groups. For the colonial masters, such ethnic divisions of work facilitated the continuation of colonial exploitation and subjugation. It has produced an ever-present conflict between the locals and the outsiders; tribals and the non-tribals; and between the tribes themselves. Needless to point out, the above does not augur well for cultivation of Left radicalism; on the contrary, *ethnic radicalism* gains greater sway in such contexts. The space for articulation of secular economic interests and grievances, if any, by the radical Left is highly circumscribed here. One of the reasons why the incipient Left radicalism in different parts of North East India (and also in other parts of India) failed to hold on to the mantle was this: *ethnic radicalism* has overwhelmed the space of Left radicalism. If it has happened otherwise, as in Tripura, as we shall explore in greater detail, it was because of the Left's relative success in appropriately defining the terms of engagement with ethnicity.

In conventional Marxism, the space of the non-class identity is nearly absent. For the founders of Marxism, the more homogeneous and industrialized West provided for the space in which class struggles took place and on which the Marxist doctrine was formulated and reformulated. In Marx's *The Class Struggle in France (1848–50) (1860)* or *the Civil War in France (1871)* let alone *Capital* (1867, Vol.1) non-class ethnic identity had no place.[4] However, in practical Left radical politics, as exemplified by Lenin's accommodation of the cause of self-determination of the nationalities in pre-revolutionary Russia, or for that matter, by Ho Chi Min in the Vietnamese revolution in his successful attempt to combine communism with Vietnamese nationalism, co-existence of Marxism and non-class identity issues was allowed. The traditions of analytical Marxism post-1980s have variously highlighted the need to accommodate non-class including individual identity within the parameters of Marxism as a non-Hegelian endeavour (Callinicos 1989). Be that as it may, theoretically the relation between the two remains still uncertain (Connor 1984). This unresolved relation between Marxism and non-class identity (nations, nationalism, ethnicity and other such identity) allowed space for mutual co-existence between class and non-class identity, and their combination in the realm of practical Left radical politics. (This will be examined in greater detail in chapter 1.) However, for a variety of reasons, the success in achieving such a symbiosis in various regions in India has rather been limited.

Sudipta Kaviraj (2009: 172–99) in an original argument has drawn our attention to what he calls a 'translation' problem in Marxism and radical politics in India. He argues that the language of radical politics in India has remained far removed from the practical social and cultural reality of India because the language used by the Marxist radicals and communists are universalistic (and context less), the one coined by the founders of Marxism to describe and explain the Western contexts. Marx's terms, he says, were contextual but when the same terms came to be used by the Indian Marxists, practitioners as well as academics, they became 'context-free'. He says: 'Radical politics implied taking part in social conflict in favour of egalitarianism, while conflicts themselves occur around fundamental divide between social groups specific to a given social form' (Kaviraj 2009: 180). Following Kaviranj then, the so-called successes or failures of egalitarian politics in India, and its various regions, produced what he calls 'strange practices' (Kaviraj 2009: 172). As the actual empirical stories of the region-based experiments of Indian communism suggest, the communists (parties and movements) succeeded in the regions where they were also successful in creatively adapting (or failure to do so) themselves to local reality of regional identity, ethnicity, sub-nationalist moorings etc. This adaptation did not entail any original coinage or recreation of context-specific fundamental categories but combination of class categories with the non-class categories in practical political persuasion while the overarching theoretical universe remains context-free universalistic idioms of

Marxism as derived from the West. On the top of that a commitment to equality and exploitation less society in future did always ring hollow in the society of manifold inequalities and discrimination. The result has been a series of what Kaviraj (2009: 172) calls 'strange practices'. The examples are: in Punjab the CPI failed to accommodate in the post-independence periods, the Lal Party, (as the Communist Party was then known in pre-Partition Punjab), the radical political vehicle of Sikh ethno-nationalism (Singh 1994); in Telangana, in the erstwhile princely State of Hyderabad, the CPI led the radical movement of the rich peasants in 1950–51 against the Nizams (Dhanagore 1983), while in Bengal the same party was leading the movement for *tebhaga* for the share-croppers and poor farmers during 1946–47 (Dhanagore 1983); in Tripura (then a tribal princely kingdom) in India's North East now, the CPI was successfully leading a movement of radical tribal nationalism against the princely regime and the Indian State in the late 1940s and came to establish hegemony in the post-independence period over an indigenous radical tribal nationalist movement by providing for a space of accommodation of the same within the discourse of universalist and context less Marxist categories. Given the time and space, Tripura remains a 'success story' (more in the electoral sense and governance of a State within Indian federalism) while Punjab and Telangana remained failed cases. All remain though 'strange practices' as far radical Marxist politics are concerned.

## *Tribal ethnicity and radical politics in India's North East*

India's North East now comprising eight States was not, on the face of it, a natural case to be easily mobilized for Left radicalism. A land of tribal ethnicity of varied kinds with manifold diversity in languages, and religion, the region is also not a natural case for Left radicalism. On the contrary, varied brands of ethnic radicalism, as we examine in chapter 2 the book, have filled up the political space in the region – whether ethnic rebel space or ethnic democratic space. But attempts have been made by the Left radical since pre-independence days (prior to 1947) in Assam, Manipur and Tripura in particular for control over the political space. In the rest of the region, *ethnic radicalism* has held sway over anything else, however.

The question then arises: how does one mobilize tribal ethnicity? This question assumes added significance because while ethnicity or ethnic identity is non-class, it is not as homogeneous as it is thought out to be. Tribal ethnicity in the North East, as perhaps elsewhere too, is differentiated, internally extremely heterogeneous, and politically very fractious – the reason why there is proliferation of ethnic political parties and groups, and a continuous counter-mobilizations. One of the reasons why this happens in a democracy as India's is due to the fact that the ethnic ruling parties in power at the State or sub-State levels of the polity are limited in their redistributive programmes, limited as they are to the particular ethnic constituency(-ies). Why is ethnic identity so easily to be mobilized? What are its political resources? Of course, beyond doubt, ethnic markers and symbols are emotional and more vulnerable to mobilization. Late Eric Hobsbawm (1992), famous British historian, specifically focused on the political dimension of

10  *Introduction*

'tribal ethnicity' which he believes is most powerful and lasting. The political dimension of 'tribal ethnicity', he says, is to be seen not so much in its programme of a polity, but in its *resistance to the imposition of the modern nation-state*, to be precise, any State (Hobsbawm 1992: 64). Tribal ethnicity may involve an alternative political programme of a polity which is fundamentally different from the existing arrangements of the State. It may also so happen that 'tribal ethnicity' expresses itself, in the absence of its own appropriate idioms, in the terms of its adversary, in terms of the (modern) nationalist discourse which signifies partial defeat on its part.

## *A study in State politics*

The genre of State politics in India today is well grounded. The States today receive grater academic and policy attention than in the period until the 1990s. In the long period of command economy and public welfare State the States were not seriously considered. There was such contemptuous reference to the States as 'glorified municipalities'; as agents for implementing the development objectives of the Centre and so on. In the heyday of the Congress party in power in the Centre until about the 1980s barring a few years, the States were, as it were, at the mercy of the Centre, which took not infrequently recourse to Article 356 to dismiss the duly elected State governments and placed the States under Central rule. The Sarkaria Commission on the Centre State Relations (1983) (1987) admitted that in most cases Article 356 was misused. The States thus were made heavily dependent on the Centre, not only financially but politically too. There were many cases when late Indira Gandhi (the Prime Minister) dismissed State governments run by her own party on the flimsy grounds that perhaps she did not like the Chief Ministers. This has been well-researched (Dua 1979; Dua 2005; Maheswari 1977). In the first 16 years of the federal republic (1950–66) President's Rule was imposed for a total of ten times and between 1966–86 seventy times (Khilnani 2004: 51). During the two terms of Prime Ministers, late Indira Gandhi had had the credit of imposing it for as many as forty-two times, most often on partisan grounds (Hardgrave and Kochanek 2000: 76). Hardgrave and Kochanek said that the trend continued until 1991, covering the period even of the Minority governments in New Delhi (Hardgrave and Kochanek 2000: 76). In the period of India Gandhi's rule, political loyalty was on a high premium, and sycophancy as a result skirted the political space. Consider the frank admission of a sycophant Chief Minister of Andhra Pradesh on the hit list in the 1980s after Indira Gandhi's return to power in 1980: 'I came in because of Madam, and I am going because of her. I do not even know how I came' (Khilnani 2004: 51).

Quite predictably, there were from the very inauguration of the Constitution demands for more powers and autonomy to the States; such movements by the State Chief Ministers belonging to the opposition to Congress particularly after 1967, and more sharply in the post-Emergency period held Conclave, mass demonstrations and submitted Memoranda suggesting revision of Centre–State relations and for restricting the use of Article 356, if not, abolishing it. Elsewhere (Bhattacharyya 2009: 99–112) I have examined the various phases of such assertions by the States I have termed 'States rights'. From the onset of India's neo-liberal reforms in 1991, the situation, however, changed completely when the States did not have to fight any more for more autonomy and powers; the States came be considered free to invite FDI, and to attract more business, trade and commerce in their realms. Per capita FDI became a unit of measurement of development of the States. Without changing the Constitution, the States found themselves autonomous, with very little Central control. Thus, the time-honoured complaint by the States of the Centre's step-motherly approach to the States became passé. In other words, the States were invited (often cajoled and coerced) to become partners in implementing the SAP.

As far as the specific focus in this study is concerned it is a contribution to State politics in India. Although located within the broad regional context of North East India, the case of Left radical politics in Tripura is examined, in detail, in this study. In this respect it takes as unit of analysis the State of Tripura as a territorial and constituent unit of Indian Federation. The advantages of studying the States of India as units of analysis are many: they are easily identifiable sub national units; they are autonomous units for electoral purposes; they are by and large distinct sociocultural units; and they have distinct regional identity of their own which do not arguably always accord well with the national identity of the pan-Indian variety.

A long time back the study of State politics was pioneered by Myron Weiner (Weiner 1968) with special attention to certain dimensions and variables. The dimensions covered by Weiner (1968) included: social and economic environment of the State; and the treatment of the State as a constituent of the larger Indian polity as well as a separate political system itself (Weiner 1968: 7). Within those broad dimensions, the specific variables considered were: social configuration in each State; description of the political process; party system; political participation; political integration in the States; levels of institutionalization in the State; social and economic basis of conflict; and governmental performance (Weiner 1968: 3–56). But the central objective of this pioneering effort was political stability with particular reference to governmental performance at the State level. In the 1980s, John Wood reflected in the post-Emergency period upon the 'crisis' in State politics and its continuity within the overall national context of the Indian polity as re-emerging from the dark days of the Emergency (1975–77). In 1990, Atul Kohli updated on Weiner's studies and moved down to the district level to inquire about the roots, if any, of the overall *governability crisis* that seemed to have gripped India. Post-1991, to be exact from the mid-1990s, the States came to be recognized as very important factors and actors in the new emerging political economy of India.

It is therefore important to specify the reasons of studying State politics in India for underlining the special relevance of such study now. In the era of India's globalization since the 1990s the State in India have become unusually important not as just units of academic study but as the real vectors of implementing India's reforms. Scholars (e.g. Tillin et al. eds. 2015; Manor 2016; Mitra and Bhattacharyya 2018) highlight the role of the States in carrying out even in the days of reforms many social welfare programmes in the changed context of 'rights-based approach'. The States today are, arguably, the centre stage of India's political economy and political process; the fragmentation and regionalization of the party system and the polity has added further strength to the States in the sense that now the State-based regional parties are playing active role in the making-unmaking of the coalition government at the national level, and policymaking for domestic and even foreign affairs. Who does not know the Tamil factors in India's policy to Sri Lanka, or the role of the TMC President and Chief Minister of West Bengal, Mamata Bandopadhyay in the Centre's conduct of foreign policy with Bangladesh with regard to issues affecting West Bengal (the river Tista water distribution and the Land border agreements)? However, the newly found autonomous role of the units of Indian Federation for attracting FDI in their realms and for promoting more trade and commerce are encouraged by the successive governments at the Centre and allowed not by any constitutional change but by the fiat of executive federalism. The official commission set up by the central government in 2008 (known as the Punchi Commission[5]) and mandated to recommend the measures to be taken that reflect the changed role of the States in the vastly changed context of globalization in India submitted its 10-volume report to the central government in 2010 in which there is a strong emphasis on the more autonomous role of the States in the period of globalization. However, as I have argued elsewhere (Bhattacharyya 2009: 99–112; Bhattacharyya and Koenig eds. 2016), the process has already produced some ill effects as all the States in the Union are not equally placed and capable of attracting FDI, and also that regional underdevelopment and disparity has risen many fold giving birth to two categories of States in India: *forward* and *backward* States (Tremblay 2003: 335–50). Some time back Lawrence Saez (2002) noted that due to reforms in India the inter-State relations in India have transformed from inter-governmental cooperation envisioned in the co-operative federalism of India into 'inter-jurisdictional competition' (Saez 2002: 7). That was a very early statement on the reforms. Things have changed significantly since.

The outstanding importance of the States today in India for reasons stated above has attracted serious intellectual attention to State politics not seen before. The States today are very important for the citizens within their realms as well as in national politics co-existent with a fragmented political party system. Yadav and Palishikar (2008) in their 'ten theses on state politics in India' thus observed:

> Clearly when we talk about the autonomy of state politics, we are talking about autonomy from national politics. In the last two decades, state politics has broken free of the logic of national politics and has acquired a rhythm and logic of its own.
>
> (Yadav and Palshikar 2008)

The observation they made of the renewed strategic significance of the States are worth-quoting:

> First, the States have emerged as the effective arena of political choice. If the people voted in state assembly elections in held the 1970s and 1980s, as if they were choosing the prime minister, they now vote in the parliamentary elections as if they are choosing their chief minister. I their eyes an individual constituency is too small and the country is too big; it is at the level of their State that the voters make their choice.
>
> (Yadav and Palshikar 2008)

We will provide empirical data on reforms in the North East, the elite perceptions of reforms and the impact of the same in the respective States in the region. In our specific and detailed account of Tripura, we will take into consideration the variables identified by Weiner plus more and seek to bring out the role of the State government under the Marxists vis-à-vis India's globalization. We will examine the nature of Left radicalism in Tripura in the period of globalization.

## Research methods and sources

Many years of research and collection of hard empirical and archival data have gone into the making of this book. While some published but updated materials of the author particularly on Tripura will be utilized, the author's completed and ongoing researches (funded by the Indian Council of social Science Research, New Delhi) on Tripura in 2013, and the collaborative international research project on 'Continuity and Change in Indian Federalism in the Era of Coalition Governments' (Centered in the University of Edinburgh and funded by the Leverhulme Trust, UK) (2014–17) in which the author was a lead partner responsible for 'ethnic conflict management in North East India' respectively, are utilized here. Archival research materials, parliamentary proceedings, newspaper briefs, inner-party documents, elite interview materials for the region as well as Tripura (total respondents were 80) and official sources are utilized in this study for providing a comprehensive understanding of the subject. The quantitative and qualitative techniques of interview have been used, and the data collected have been processed to buttress arguments wherever made. The necessary ethnographic materials from the official sources have been used for providing the relevant social, economic and demographic backdrop of the region in general and Tripura in particular.

## Chapterization

Since Tripura is the only success story of Left radicalism in the North East – although there were some beginnings made in other parts of the region – a theoretical understanding of the relation between Marxism and the ethno-national question was called for. Tripura's success has combined a Marxist class perspective with tribal nationalism. This was important also to place the Left's experiments with the ethno-national questions in building mass bases in comparison with other parts of India such as Telangana, Punjab and Kerala. Chapter 1 examines the above issues and shows that Marxism, so far, has remained, theoretically, incompatible with the issues of non-class identity such as nation and ethnic identity although the ethno-national factors have played important role in the success of the socialist revolution in Russia in 1917 (as well as in its break down in 1991); in the Chinese revolution in 1949 and in Vietnam in 1967. The Indian Left's identification with the ethno-national cause and its effects on the movement has been examined. This chapter explains why the Left failed in India, and what explains the relative success of the Left in Tripura, and Kerala. This chapter raises the question of any theoretical contributions the Indian Marxists' made, in adaptation of Marxism to the local environment and or the creation of political categories, as suggested by the founders of Marxism and their sincere followers.

Chapter 2 provides a detailed account of the very complex and diverse ethnic mosaic of the North East with particular references to tribal affiliations, language and religion, and the complex territorial issues that do not correspond with the former. It highlights the roots of what I have termed 'ethnic radicalism' in the region, and explains the interplay of ethnic radicalism, struggle for territory and power-sharing. This chapter also shows that the weight of class divisions in the region has been no match for the heavy weight of ethnic divisions. With the use of the very recent elite survey data it is shown in this chapter that the region's elites are no longer particularly concerned about insurgency, or the law and order but about the implications of India's neo-liberal shift since the early 1990s for this region. This chapter shows also that while the ethnic rebels have caused persistent violence and crisis in governance for over three decades since the 1960s (not in all States though), things improved considerably since the 1990s and few unresolved territorial issues remain. This region can no longer be described as India's 'insurgent country'.

As a sequel to the above, the subject of matter of Chapter 3 is the detailed examination of the transformation of the ethnic rebels in the region into the stakeholders – yesterday's rebel into tomorrow's defenders of law and order – though ethnic peace negotiations, institutionalization of power-sharing, territorial concessions and participation. A detailed comparative analysis is provided on the governance records of the States in the region from the early 1980s to 2011 and beyond. The region's records are then placed in comparative perspective in relation to other more advanced States of India. The tenor of the chapter is the process of institutionalization of ethnic radicalism in the North East that has moderated the sharp edge of radicalism so that a number of ethnic parties (formerly militants) have been, or are now in power in most of the States in the region. The former militants have reconciled themselves to democratic transfer of power from one ethnic party to another, or to a State unit of the national parties, or by joining a coalition government led by a national party.

Chapters 4–12 that follow deal with, in greater detail, the case study of Left radicalism in Tripura and its institutionalization into a liberal democratic force, not in name, but in effect, and the comparative records of governance in Tripura relative to the North East, India's advanced States as well as the all-India macro level. Chapter 4 provides a critical historical and sociological analysis of the roots of radicalism, Left and ethnic, in Tripura and traced it to a set of major demographics, social and economic changes in Tripura in late colonial India and more particularly in the wake of India's Partition which brought millions of Hindu Bengali refugees from across the border, and which upset the demographic balance of the State. The tribals, the original residents of this erstwhile princely State, were reduced to a minority in their own land. The settlers, as a result, came to dominate all aspects of public life in Tripura.

Chapter 5 provides a detailed account of the first major ethnic tribal rebellion in Tripura during 1943–45 led by the Reangs, the second largest tribes in the State but much discriminated by the then monarchy which belong the Tripura or Tripur tribes, the majority tribes in the States. It explains with detailed statistical and archival records the cause of the rebellion, its nature and impact, and points out how ethic identity formation took place in and though a rebellion rather than an 'elite manipulation' as many theoreticians would have us believe. However, this rebellion exemplified an autonomous political action at a time when the urban based political movements in the States led by some communist leaders and other progressive persons were pursuing a constitutional method of agitation.

Chapter 6 examines the origin and very limited growth of the communist movement in Tripura through the agency of a number of semi-political associations such as the Jana Mongal Samity, Jana Shiksha Samilty and the Porja Mondal engaged in mass welfare and literacy and for responsible government since the 1940s. Chapter 7 explores the radical turn in Tripura communist movement in 1948–51 in symbiosis with the Tripuri tribal radical nationalist movement and provides the detailed account, on the basis of secret police and military intelligence files and confidential communist sources, the rise of the rebellion, its course, its ideology and leadership and the nature and functioning of an alternative government formed by the rebels in large parts of Tripura. This was the most strategic phase in the development of radical Left in Tripura when its mass bases were exclusively tribals. This chapter also points out how the shifts in the national and international communist policy produced its effects in Tripura; in particular during 1948–51 when two successive policies of the method of armed struggle were applied to the ongoing indigenously developed radical tribal nationalism.

Chapter 8 analyses the development of a radical doctrine of ethno-nationalism during 1948–50 formulated and propagated by two leading Tripuri elites called '*thakurs*' who sought to articulate a Tripuri nationalist identity in opposition to the growing dominance of the settlers Bengali called '*aproja*' (non-subjects).

Chapter 9 provides a critical account of a radical ethnic challenge to the Left in Tripura in the form of the TUJS (now defunct) since 1967 which sought to capture the tribal ethnic space by projecting itself as the party of the tribals. This party rose to power in an alliance with Congress during 1988–93 but with the recovery of the political space by the CPI-M since 1993 the TUJS increasingly lost ground.

16  *Introduction*

Chapter 10 examines the process of institutionalization of the Left radical in Tripura and is metamorphosis into as an electoral party – a liberal democratic force – since the early 1950s and its participation for power-sharing. It also examines how the State Unit of the then CPI appropriated tribal ethno-nationalism, its original support, in the wake of its transformation into a parliamentary party. Tribal nationalism was retained along with all the tribal associations and mass front but only as a secondary force subordinated to the authority of the all-India party.

Chapters 11 and 12 provide critical accounts of the Marxists in power in Tripura, and their records of governance. Chapter 11 focuses on the sub-State-level institutionalization of tribal autonomy in Tripura and examines the role of the agency of the ADC in protecting tribal identity – a tribal self-governing body under the 6th Schedule of the Constitution of India. Chapter 12 analyses the role of the CPI-M in power in the State since the 1978 except 1988–93 and assesses their governance records since the early 1980s in comparative perspective. This chapter shows that Tripura under the Marxists has scaled remarkable height in maintain the rule of law, and delivery of public goods, social inclusion and growth. The critical role of the CPI-M as an organization and the very positive image of the Chief Minister Manik Sarkar is also pointed out here.

**Notes**

1 But nonetheless, radicalism is problematic.
2 Bartoszewicz, M. G. (2015) has found out '50 shades of radicalism' in the case of political parties in Europe.
3 The term 'eco-terrorism' is nowadays considered as an example of radicalism. See Loadenthal, M. (2017).
4 As pointed out by Jyotirindra Das Gupta (2001) the fact that the non-class ethnic identity remains neglected in Marxism is proven by the absence of the term 'ethnicity' in the index of the large volume *A Dictionary of Marxist Thought* edited by late Tom Bottomore et al. (1983). One needs of course to qualify this by stressing that for the founders, class identity and class conflicts were more real than any ethnic conflicts in the context in which they formulated their theory.
5 This was the second Commission on Centre State relations (2008–10), after the Sarkaria, commission on Centre–State Relations.

# 1 Marxism and the national/ethnic question

## Theory and practice in India

### Introduction

The national question has been very challenging to the Left radical politics in India's North East since pre-independence days. Given the very different and somewhat underdeveloped economic structure in the region, class was not and is still not the defining category of social and economic relations. In most States in the region, tribal ethnic identity, most often formulated as a national question, or what is most commonly known as the ethnic question nowadays, and inter-tribal and intra-tribal as well as tribal and non-tribal ethnic conflicts, have tended to define the space of politics. In such predominantly tribal inhabited States as Mizoram, Meghalaya, Nagaland and Arunachal Pradesh, Left radical politics has failed to make any inroads. In Assam, and Manipur, Left radical politics had had a significant beginning and still retains some areas of influence, most notably in Assam, but in Manipur the Left lost all its bases in the face of the more powerful and belligerent ethnic challenge and insurgency. In Assam, although the Left, particularly the CPI-M, maintains a level of influence, the very powerful surges of national/ethnic political mobilizations since the 1960s have tended to occupy most space rendering the Left to marginality. Therefore, the success of the Left in Tripura in the midst of severe ethnic conflicts, on the one hand, and the failure of the Left in the rest of the region, on the other hand, raises the important question about the strategic success and failure of the Left in building bases in ethnically sharply divided society. Why it failed in most States in the region and also why it succeeded in others are bogged down to the Left's strategic understanding and handling of the national/ethnic situation. The categories that the Left (parties) theoretically adhered to were universal and secular (mostly derived from the external international environment); but the actual context within which they had to operate defies the application of such universal categories. In the actual context, class conflicts, if there were any, arguably, played little role in the development of Left politics. This is not to underplay the role of class and class conflicts, but to suggest the very complex social and economic reality in which class elements were intertwined with ethnic elements. The national/ethnic question remains the most challenging for the Marxist Left in the region as much as in the rest of India.

## 18  Marxism and the national/ethnic question

A brief theoretical analysis of the relation between Marxism, on the one hand, and the national/ethnic question, on the other, is called for putting in place the Marxist positions on the national/ethnic issues. The Left mobilizations and explanation, what Kaviraj would call 'strange practices' need to be placed in reference to the theoretical position left behind by the founders of Marxism. Can Marxism have a 'theoretical' position on nation and nationalism? Can one bank upon Marxism for finding solutions to the ethnic problems the world over today? How does an ongoing radical Left politics grapple with the national or the ethnic question? Can the former overcome the latter? Or, else does radical politics itself becomes ethnified in the course of hobnobbing with ethnic politics? The following brief exploration seeks to address some of those issues.

If the national question has proved very challenging to Marxism from its very inception through to the Russian revolution (1917) and the revolutions in China (1949) and Vietnam (1967), the ethnic question has emerged since the 1970s and early 1980s as equally challenging to Marxism. This does not mean of course that the ethnic question has replaced the national question although there are considerable overlaps between the two in actual political practices. In the non-Western and multi-ethnic countries with lesser industrialization and without clear cut (industrial) class divisions in societies, the issues of national/ethnic question remain perplexing for the Marxists engaged in movements for major social transformation. However, the historical evidences from across the world suggest that this perplexing reality has proved to be resourceful to political parties and movements with profound ethnic orientation. For sub-nationalist and ethnic elites, the growing awareness of sub national deprivation and the sharp ethnic divisions in society are a minefield for political mobilization and power. The legitimacy that many such sub nationalist movements and parties acquired in decades of struggle has been quite stable and deeply rooted. The Parti Quebacois (PQ), the Basque, the Catalan and the Scottish nationalists and others, for example, are well established as the legitimate partners in power-sharing and self-governance (Gagnon and Tully 2001). In fact, the communities they represent are accepted as 'nationalist' rather than 'sub-nationalist'; the nationalist space involved is recognized as a distinct society. In Canada, for example, even the aboriginal peoples are now constitutionally recognized (1992) as the *First Nations* with their right to land and self-determination (Tully 2001: 23). While the liberal democratic States the world over have rather successfully grappled with the questions of ethno-nationalist forces and agreed to the mutually acceptable *terms of engagement* with the latter, the mighty and multiethnic former Soviet Union and Yugoslavia broke into pieces in the early 1990s by the heavy weight of ethno-nationalist forces. Late Eric Hobsbawm (1992: 163–92), in an early statement on the breakup of the USSR argues that although nationalism was not the factor in the breakup of the USSR, the Soviet Union disintegrated into many 'nation-states' for the ethno-national identity proved attractive to the peoples in time of disintegration, something to cling to in times of crisis. If the national, or the ethno-national question proved very challenging to classical Marxism, theoretically as well as practically, the post-Soviet and post-Yugoslav nationalisms proved as problematic to Marxism.[1]

## Categorical imperatives: class, nation and ethnic identity

Classical Marxism remains philosophically incompatible with the categories of nation, nationalism or the national question. This incompatibility is categorical rather than ideological. Classical Marxism is based on the assumptions that the most fundamental human divisions are horizontal class divisions that cut across ethnic or ethno-national divisions. Class here is understood as an economic category with a particular location in the mode of production, and secular in nature. Marx defined classes in relation to their location within the given mode of production. Classes are economic, secular and rational categories; class action, if any, therefore would be inclusive of all persons belonging to that class irrespective of any non-class character of the people. The category of class is divisive but would imply unity (class unity) of the particular class concerned. The question of class leadership and the ideological basis of class action, if any, would follow from the above basic premises of class. Classes in Marxism are seen as trans-ethnic, as nations are trans-class in nationalism. Nationalism, on the contrary, is based on the assumptions that human societies are fundamentally divided along many vertical cleavages of ethno-national groups (Connor 1984: 5). Nation and ethnic groupings, on the other hand, are trans-class categories; they centre on identity markers which are emotive, sentimental and exclusive. The leadership and ideology of nationalism and ethnic mobilization therefore appeal typically to the emotions and sentiments, and the attendant loyalties of the ethnic brethren for consciousness and action. In actual political mobilizations, nationalist and ethnic actions prove more effective than class actions. When translated into subjective dimensions and political actions, the nationalist would argue that national consciousness, or nationalism would prove more powerful than class consciousness. The Marxist, on the other hand, would argue that just the opposite will happen: in a test of loyalties, class consciousness would prevail upon national consciousness (Connor 1984: 5). That is an ideal typical position. In actual practice, workers may be gravitated more towards national and ethnic loyalties than class movements. In pre-revolutionary Russia, Lenin had to adjust his strategies by promising political democracy (national self-determination) in the future to the warring nationalities if they joined the revolutionary movements.

Marxists consider nations and nationalism as part of the superstructure of the capitalist base which is economic and which sustains and determines the superstructure. The latter is secondary to the base which is primary. Therefore, nations and nationalism are epiphenomena which will not survive capitalism. Since such non-class categories include identities such as religion, ethnicity, tribe and so on, the questions relating to them are subjugated to the class or the labour question. In the post-Napoleonic Europe Marx and Engels, as pointed out by Hobsbawm (1992), nationalism was no less powerful than class struggle as the vector of social change. The founder themselves were witnesses to what role nationalism was playing in the making of modern Europe; in the consolidation of the capitalist order in the continent. And yet, they diagnosed that class struggle as the motor of history, and that the recorded history of mankind was but a history of class struggles (*The*

*Communist Manifesto 1848*). This theoretical incompatibility between the two is intelligible. Classes are related to the mode of production either as the owners of the means of production, or the non-owners i.e, the workers irrespective of the national or ethnic character of either. For reasons of political mobilization, the class space and the ethno-national space are also very different from each other. The class space is homogeneous, equal, universal and secular admitting of no ethnic, linguistic or religious borders. The ethno-national space is segmental and exclusive; it excludes those who are non-nations, and who do not belong to the same ethnic category. For the Marxists, the capitalists as capitalist do not exploit less their ethnic brothers; the workers' struggle will not compromise because the capitalists belong to the same ethnic group. In nationalist or ethnic mobilizations, the internal differentiation along class lines are deliberately underplayed in order to present a cohesive unity among all members of the nation or the ethnic groups. In this case, the intra-ethnic emotional and other cultural bonds are highlighted for unity and power. Therefore, the categorical differences between Marxism and nationalism are irreconcilable.

## Categorical imperative: ethnic identity

The world which has experienced a high degree of 'ethnicization' witnesses, quite naturally, proliferation of studies on ethnicity. As a result, the current literature on ethnicity is too vast. In this small section; we will attempt to find a workable definition of ethnicity for our purpose. The term 'ethnicity' is derived from the Greek term '*Ethnos*' which has two basic elements: the idea of living together, and being alike in culture.[2] The English language possesses no term for the concept of an ethnic group or ethnic community, and that is cited as one of the reasons for the wide spread neglect of ethnicity. The foremost sociologist of ethnicity, Anthony Smith, has listed a number of usages of the Greek term: a band of comrades; a host of men, e.g. the tribes of Achaeans or Hycians (as in Homer's Iliad); the race of men and women, e.g. the Median people or nation, (as in Herodotus); the casts of heralds (as in Plato), and so on.[3] Smith believes that the Greeks have not made any distinction between tribes and nations: 'it is the similarity of cultural attributes in a group that attracts the term '*ethnos*'.[4] In his famous book the *Ethnic Origins of Nations* (1986), Smith has strongly argued that ethnic roots have provided the 'constant elements of nationhood': ethnicity has provided, in a very general manner, a potent model for human association which has been adapted and transformed, but not obliterated in the formations of modern nations (Smith 1986).

Smith's definition of 'ethnicity' is sociological in the sense that it overemphasizes the social-cultural dimensions of ethnicity, and this is where it is to be modified to incorporate the political dimension of ethnicity. One major conclusion of Smith's great study of the origins of nations (1986) that the ethnic elements have never disappeared from history and remained a constant factor in the making and unmaking of nations (Smith 1986: 209–27).

Any serious student of modern affairs knows that the development of nationhood involves political mobilization. Another interesting aspect (and which is quite relevant for our purpose) of the Smithian definition is that the Greeks did not make any distinction between nation and tribes. This is significant for the modern period not only because the tribals justify and rationalize their claim for nationhood on the criterion of their being tribes, but also because the real world is faced with a mixed situation where tribes and nations may appear to be synonymous, not objectively, but in terms of the deliberate constructions that are undertaken.

## Marxism's opposition to ethnicity

Unavoidably then, Marxism, theoretically, is, in fact, more opposed to ethnicity than the national question. Ethnicity is a lower order phenomenon than nationality, or nationhood. In the broader framework of the classical Marxist understanding, as above, a nation (such as the German, the French and the Italian) may consist of *ethnie* but then the founders would not consider them separately. Ethnicity implies an identity and a movement which contradict the basic Marxist assumptions. True, what we today mean by the term 'ethnicity' was unknown at the time of Marx and Engels or even Lenin. Ethnicity is, as Wallerstein wrote,[5] a very recent phenomenon connected with a distinct identity. The non-class identities, movements and ideologies that baffled Marx, Engels and Lenin, and also Stalin, were mostly 'nationalist' in character. It was the question of nationalism that seemed to puzzle Marx and the Marxists. It was the force of nationalism that was challenging to the Marxists; it was the nationality question that appeared as a rival to the class question. The nineteenth century and most of the twentieth century have known the nationality question', 'nationalism' and 'nationalist movement'. It is only since the bread-up of the USSR that scholars, especially those who specialized in the study of nationalism, have noticed the decline of nationalism.[6] What has emerged out of the break-up of the USSR, and the forms this break-up has taken eventually, is not nationalism, at least, not in the classical sense, but precisely ethnicity.[7] The end of the Cold War and the decline of the USSR have strengthened the question of 'ethnicity' which has found favour with the post-modern political theorists. This post-Cold War era believes in as much globalization as ethnicization.[8]

How then to conceptualize the relationship between Marxism and ethnicity? The question is important, for theoretical as well as practical purposes. Sociologically-oriented studies of ethnicity emphasize the 'social identity' dimension of ethnicity: 'ethnic identity is to be understood and theorized as an example of social identity in general'.[9] While Anthony Smith considers ethnic communities and identities as 'pre-modern'(Smith 1994: 376), Wallerstein under Marxist inspiration sees it as a 'peoplehood' which is a 'major institutional construct of historical capitalism':

> Ethnicization or peoplehood resolves one of the basic contradictions of historical capitalism – its simultaneous thrust for theoretical equality and practical inequality and it does so by utilizing the mentalities of the world's working strata.
>
> (Wallerstein 1991: 84)

The working people, depressed and marginalized all over the world, have organized themselves in 'people' terms. This has been a dilemma for the world's proletariat. Wallerstein makes sense when he says that class-based activities are not divorced from 'people-based activity',[10] but his assertion that this is not a dilemma resolvable within capitalism, and by implication resolvable only in socialism, is too far-fetched a hypothesis that sounds idealistic. While Weber saw 'ethnic groups' as 'status groups',[11] Marxists, historically, were not at ease grappling with the problem known today as 'ethnic'. The reason why Marxism and ethnicity do not go together, or cannot co-exist, is categorical. Ethnicity or ethnic identity suggests a community space and is trans-class; it also sustains itself on horizontal communal feeling and sentiments which admits of no internal divisions along classes. Class space, by contrast, is egalitarian, secular and universal, which admits of no non-class markers of unity. Classes are economic categories directly related to the prevailing mode of production. While an ethnic zealot would look at society in terms of ethnic distribution of powers and resources, Marxists would argue along the class lines and explain society in terms of classes. Thus, it is found that class and ethnicity are diametrically opposed categories. In practical political mobilizations, ethnic and class movements would be mutually exclusive; the ethnic leaders would not allow class dimensions to be brought in the ethnic mobilizations; class-based communist movements would prevent an effort to ethnicize the working class; ethnicization of the working classes would greatly harm the movements. The working classes may have some ethnic identity, linguistic, religious and others; the ethnic movements necessarily include people who are working classes. But in both cases, ethnic and class elements are not allowed to loom large at all.

## Marxism and the national question

The Marxist approach to the national question provides the route to the ethnic question because what is understood as the ethnic question was not considered as such during Marx's time, and secondly, because the founders' overall approach to the national question, ideologically as well as strategically, remains the key to later day Marxist approach to the question. The second approach above applies with full force to the ethnic question of today. Although the founders were deeply committed to class analysis and involved themselves in political movements for class struggles in Europe, their writings show that they were persistently preoccupied with the national questions of their times. To begin with, the national questions were those of the people of a country as a whole such as the Irish, the Polish and others, and their role in national self-determination from alien rule, or colonialism in favour of capitalist progress and development. In this respect we find the intellectual engagement of the founders with the national liberation movements of the Irish and the Polish. However, their differential assessments of the two cases at different times, often at odds with each other, do suggest that there was no theoretic explanation of the issue involved. The reason, to follow Connor (1984), was strategic: the 'ostensible commitment to the principle of self-determination in the abstract, while concomitantly reserving to themselves as to whether a particular movement was to be supported or opposed' (Connor 1984: 12). Their stereotypical remarks on the 'lazy Mexicans', or the *wild, headstrong, cheerful, light hearted, corruptible sensuous* Irish people were symptomatic not of theoretic explanation but very casual, if not, condescending allusions. Those remarks were made by Marx and Engels in the mid-1840s. In their subsequent private correspondence, which was more frank, the same Irish question received serious attention: 'not merely a simple *economic question* but at the same time a *national question*'[12] (emphasis in the original).

In Marx and Engels there were two perspectives on the national question. First, the most importantly, they wrote and commented upon the broader nationhood meaning the whole citizenry of a nation-state such as the German, the British, the Polish and the French. The nationality involved here was based on nationalism as articulated by the victorious bourgeoisie against feudalism. Nation and nationalism that the bourgeoisie upheld was, for them, artificial constructions designed to cover, ideologically, the capitalist domination. Tribes, clan and peoples in this perspective are pre-capitalist in form and character. Nations and States in this Marxist perspective have been used interchangeably; the term 'nation' has often been used to refer to the total population within the boundary of the States regardless of their ethnic complexion. Connor (1984) has observed some terminological confusion, or conceptual imprecision in the perspective of Marx and Engels with regard to their use of nationality to mean as ethno-national groups, or often as a synonym for nationalism; they used the term sometimes as referring to the legal definition of citizenship (Connor 1984: 9). Be that as it may, it was the firmed belief of the founders that national differences and antagonisms would disappear along the path of the further development of the bourgeoisie, of commerce and trade, and the world market (Marx and Engels 1848). This overall perspective suggests that the national characteristics of citizens were transient, and the loyalties of nationalism determined by economy and not by ethno-national factors will not survive the demise of capitalism.

The relative theoretical neglect of nations and nationalism in Marx and Engels prior to 1848 was rectified, as it were, in their writings post-1848 in the wake of the uprisings of many ethno-national groups in Europe. But then, as Connor pointed out, the greater attention to nations and nationalism in the writings of the founders was paid not for any new theoretical consideration; from now on their thought on the subject assumed a profoundly strategic consideration (Connor 1984: 11). As we have indicated above, from the beginning Marx and Engels were found to be grappling with the theoretical implications of nations and nationalism, offered no place of them in their theoretical scheme, held a negative attitude to the issues and settled down to strategic considerations while affirming their ideological support to the cause of nationalism, to the idea of self-determination, in the abstract, if they found the latter to be progressive. This strategic outlook was not simple an expression of intent on the part of Marx and Engels but confirmed in the political revolutionary activities they were involved as leading elements. For example, the *Proclamation on the Polish Question* (1865) drafted by Karl Marx and endorsed by the London Conference of the First International in 1965 noted the need 'to annihilate the growing influence of Russia in Europe by assuring Poland the right of self-determination which belong to every nation and by giving to this country once more a social and democratic foundation' (Connor 1984: 11). And yet, in 1866 Engels (with Marx's urging) disclaimed the universality of the principle reserving this for a few select people (Connor 1984: 12). In many other writings, Engels confirmed the ambivalence maintained by the founders with regard to the question of self-determination of nations. In all cases, Engels would support the self-determination of large nations such as the German, the Italian and the French but would not concede the same to the nationalities such as the Germans in France, and the Basque in Spain. In other words, he would not concede Statehood to the small nationalities; those ethno-national sentiments would not be supported for Statehood (Connor 1984: 12). The above only confirms the *strategic flexibility* of classical Marxism with regard to the vexed national question so as even to take precedence over ideological purity and consistency.

## Strategic considerations: post-Marxist positions

After Marx the major theoretical explorations on the national question, nation and nationalism were made by the Austro-Marxists, most notably Auto Bauer and Karl Renner (Nin 1935), but then the theoretical attempts were motivated to understand the relation between capitalism and nationalism, and finally to show how nationalism gave way to imperialism, ideologically speaking. While Bauer underlined the connection between the rise of capitalism and the nation-state, Renner sought to show how the once progressive, revolutionary principle of nationality gave way to imperialism. According to him, as 'capitalism is now passing from its industrial to its finance-capitalist stage' so the old principle of nationality which was democratic, revolutionary around the goals of unity, freedom, and self-determination, is over and done away with, paving the way for rise of 'social imperialism', or the 'imperialism of the whole people' (quoted in Bottomore 1979: 101).

Most significant strategic contribution to the issue was made by Lenin and Stalin, who developed the strategic angle in classical Marxism with regard to nationalism and the nationality questions to suit a different revolutionary situation in Russia before 1917. However, we seek to argue here that Lenin's immensely strategic approach to the national question in pre-revolutionary Russia was not something universally accepted among the leading Marxist thinkers of the time. Rosa Luxemburg, for example, raised a fundamental question here by arguing that the Marxist can never uphold any right to self-determination of nations because that would be akin to taking a bourgeois standpoint. As a Marxist, she defended the self-determination of the working people alone (Davis 1978: 54–5).[13]

The Leninist formulation of the question has been known for its strategic implications. Lenin proposed a three-pronged strategy for harnessing nationalism to the cause of scientific socialism in which the manipulation of the national aspirations of peoples, especially minorities, is a key element.

Lenin's first injunction was: *prior to the assumption of power, promise all national groups the right of self-determination (including the right to secede) while proffering national equality to those who wish to remain within the state* (Connor 1984: 580).

The second injunction was: *following the assumption of power, terminate the fact (though not necessarily the fiction) of a right to secession and begin the lengthy process of assimilation via the dialectical route of territorial autonomy for all compact groups* (Connor 1984: 583).

The third injunction was: *keep the party of all national proclivities* (Connor 1984: 584). The party here means of course the Communist Party.

In the first socialist State, immediately after the revolution, the Bolsheviks' commitment to the national question was honoured only in its breach. The national question was now re-interpreted as the self-determination of the toiling masses; the national question now came to be subordinated to the class question; actual self-determination of any nationalities was made impossible by hedging around the theoretical possibility with a lot of conditions including the willingness of the Communist Party. The preservation of socialism in the USSR was to take precedence over any other questions; any question of secession came to be defined as going against socialism.

This manipulative Leninist 'strategy' on the national question, though having seen both successes and failures, has informed many communist movements and parties throughout the world in their dealing with the national question. The brief outline, given above on the relation between nationalism and Marxism, may be concluded with a few observations. First, the philosophical and theoretical incompatibility between Marxism and nationalism has not stood in the way of the Marxists' 'manipulation', 'utilizations' and adaptation of nationalism in the cause of socialism in many parts of the world. Second, communist movements scored greatest success in countries where communism and nationalism were wedded in the popular imagination because that ensured broad-based acceptability for communism in the colonial and post-colonial societies. Third, communists make nation and nationalism subservient to class and class-struggles. Last, in grappling with the national question, communists adopt an instrumentalist attitude and consider ethno-national groups and identities as pre-modern and regressive. Marx's attitude of condescension towards such 'pre-modern' issues and identities is intelligible.

The relation, then, between Marxism and nationalism remains unresolved, and little ground has yet been broken in this regard in conventional Marxism. Practically, this gives rise to a host of tensions, since Marxists are inclined to treat nationalism, the nationality question and national identities from a typically negative perspective.

Stalin's 'theory' of the national question is worth considering here, at some length, not for its 'derivative' intellectual merits, but for its subsequent political influence (Hobsbawm 1992: 1). Stalin's 'theory' of nationalism and the national question has remained the 'operational' model for practicing Marxists all over the world until the breakup of the Soviet Union. Although

Stalin wrote altogether twelve pieces on the question,[14] his *Marxism and the National Question* (1913) remains the central text. The political need for such a tract on the national question was more motivated by the political considerations then prevailing in Russia and the dangers of nationalism gripping the ongoing working-class movements in Russia, especially in the border areas. As Stalin said:

> From this it follows that the views of Russian Social-Democracy (read the Bolshevik party) on the national question are not yet clear to all Social-Democrats.
> "Consistent Social-Democrats must work solidly and indefatigably the fog of nationalism, no matter from what quarter it proceeds".
> (Stalin 1913: 2)

For a Marxist leader engaged in a revolutionary struggle, class struggle and class consciousness are the *sine qua non*, and hence an opposite consciousness is therefore to be condemned. In *Marxism and the National Question*, Stalin gave not one but two definitions of what constitutes a nation:

> A nation is a historically constituted stable community of people formed on the basis of a common language, territory, economic life and psychological make-up manifested in a common culture.
> (Stalin 1913: 5)

> None of the above characteristics taken separately is sufficient to define a nation [...] it is sufficient for a single one of those characteristics to be lacking and the nation ceases to be a nation. It is when all these characteristics are present together that we have a nation.
> (Stalin 1913: 5)

The 'people' mentioned in Stalin's definition of the nation rules out the tribes, which is not a historical but an 'ethnographic' category (Stalin 1913: 8); hence it does not qualify as a nation, for Stalin.

A close and critical look at the definition suggests that first, his first definition does not mention at all the State as any element of the nation; apparently his is a cultural definition of the nation. But when one read the whole text and understand the background of his writing one will not miss the reason as to why he did not mention the State, which was a deliberate omission. Stalin was aware of the phenomenon of the State, and of the nation-states in the West. In his brief reference to what happened in the West he made a distinction between what he called a 'national community' and a 'state community' and said that the national communities developed into State communities in the West (Stalin 1913: 3, 9). But in his definition he abjured the issue of the State, which was contrary to the modern lesson about State formation in the world. Max Weber, the famous German political sociologist, famous for his definition of the nation-state emphasized that a nation becomes truly a nation when it has got a State of its own (Weber 1948). Stalin here made an interesting distinction between the West and the East:

*Whereas in the West nations developed into states, in the East multi-national states were formed, states consisting of several nationalities* (Stalin 1913: 9) (emphasis is added).

That is historical fact but when providing a definition which is a scientific exercise and which should command universality, one cannot have two different definitions one pertaining to the West and the other to the East. Horace Davis (1978) raised a different question here concerning whether a Marxist should at all attempt a definition and fixing up factors for all times to come. When things are always in a flux, and changing how can we fix up the factors as permanent in the definition of the nation? This way explaining nationhood is fragmentary in the sense that on the one hand, nations are considered by Stalin as sovereign and on the other hand, Statehood is not ascribed to the nation: 'Social-Democracy in all countries, therefore, proclaims the right of nations to self-determination. [. . . . .] Nations are sovereign, and all nations have equal rights'.

(Stalin 1913: 14)

In support of the above claim, the right to secede is accepted by Stalin (Lenin also accepted it on strategic considerations!) but it implies that the nations first have to come under the control of a multi-national State, and then they may demand the right to secede in favour of a separate State. In his tract Stalin mentioned again and again the right of nations to self-determination but does not support any programme of recognition to nationalities that gives birth to nationalism. So Stalin had two solutions to the national question: first, one of course is self-determination; and second, regional autonomy as the 'essential element to the solution of the national question' (Stalin 1913: 48). However, one is not sure how one can prevent a community demanding self-determination from developing nationalism among them as the precondition for such a demand?

## Analytical Marxism and ethnic identity

Dissatisfied with the wisdom of conventional Marxism, the 'Analytical Marxists' have since the late 1970s, but more prominently since the 1980s, expressed a positive attitude to the ties of nationality (Chohen in Callinicos 1989: 69). The foremost analytical Marxist G.A. Cohen argues that Marx and his followers 'have underestimated the importance of phenomena, such as religion and nationalism which satisfy the need for self-identity'.[15] As he wrote:

It is the need to be able to say . . . who I am, satisfaction of which has historically been found in identification with others in a shared culture based on nationality, race of religion. They generate or at least sustain ethnic and other bonds whose strength Marxist systematically undervalue, because they neglect the need for self-identity satisfied by them.

(Cohen 1989: 157)

One of the fundamental traits of this new tradition of Marxism is that it expels Hegelian modes of thinking from Marxism (which implies that the State is a good medium for the embodiment of nationality), which according to this Marxism, stands in the way of developing a positive attitude towards such identities. The full implications of such assertion by analytical Marxists are yet to be assessed, but one thing can be said with certainty is that analytical Marxism by questioning the embedded Hegelianism in Marxism has cleared the deck for rethinking anew non-class identities without the State. But then it begs a whole lot of questions about the relation between nationality and political power; religious identity in a situation of Statelessness; and ethnic identity apolitically.

Sudipta Kaviraj has approached the question from a different but very interesting theoretical angle worth considering. For him, two interlinked issues are involved here: the State, and nationality Kaviraj (1992: 173). has argued that Marxism as a form of modernity, as a political theory and as a movement, is statist in orientation. For Marx, the market and the State were the two instruments of 'rational' allocation of resources which capitalist utilization had slowly brought into being.[16] The Marxists beginning with Marx have not been able to visualize alternative agents of rationality in socialism beyond the State. Thus, when those non-class identities, especially 'nationalist', assume distinctly political forms, often demanding a State of their own, Marxists face a real challenge. Marxism shares a common ground with bourgeois political theory so far as it visualizes a centralized (nation) State as the political framework for socialism. It is statist to the same extent as it is centralist. The non-class movement and identities, such as nationalist and ethnic ones, are a challenge to the 'centralized' authority of the nation-state. The Hegelianism embedded in Marxism, that analytical Marxists want to remove, may be a reason why Marxism tends to be statist. But it is today a big question about Marxism: how much of Marxism remains when it is truly divested of Hegelianism?

## Adaptation to local environment: recreating political categories?

The founders of Marxism reiterated that while the general principles of their theory remained, but the (successful) application of the same would depend on the particular historical contexts concerned. What did they imply by that? One aspect of the implications of what they said was the need for proper understanding of the particular social, economic, cultural and historical reality of the context concerned. The second aspect would entail formulation of the appropriate strategy of revolution: organization, leadership, objectives and goals. But in both cases, the central question remains the formulation of the most appropriate categories and idioms to address the specific contexts. Late E. P. Thompson, renowned British Marxist historian, dismissed the attempt made by the Marxists worldwide to imitate in the name of 'internationalism' the discourse of Western Marxism:

> But internationalism, in this sense, ought not to consist in lying prostrate before the ("Western Marxist") theorists of our choice, or in seeking to imitate

their modes of discourse. The reasons why this kind of imitation can never produce more than a sickly native are complex. Mimesis, for some reasons, can copy but cannot originate or create. The "adoption" of other traditions – that is, adoption which has not fully worked through, interrogated, and translated into the terms of our own traditions – can very often mean more than the evacuation of the real place of conflict within our own intellectual culture, as well as the loss of real political relations with our own people.

(Thompson 1987: iv)

Therefore, a certain translation of Marxism is unavoidable when applying Marxism to different traditions not simply the non-Western world but even in the Western context itself. But as Thompson argues, this translation has to be creative into the terms of each tradition. Mechanical imitation of what others have done, or adoption of the terms and categories derived from other sources but not interrogated or worked through, is a very poor recipe, and it dilutes the real conflicts by the imposition of terms and concepts alien to the contexts but superimposed on the same. This practice serves to establish ideological-political hegemony over the indigenous theatre of conflicts but remain alien to the former.

## A brief overview of Marxism and the national question/ethnic in India

A brief and cursory glance at the intermeshing of Marxism and varied non-class categories (nationalism, ethnicity and regional identity) in India is in order to buttress the point made above about the mechanical translation of Marxist categories to varied contexts even within India. The way the radical Left movements has been carried out in different regions of India suggest the possibility of an ethnic history of Indian communism or radical Left politics. To place it a comparative perspective from Asia, the political adaptation to local environment took place where the theatre of conflict remained more around ethnic, or nationalist and less obviously around classes. The challenge of conflicts around non-class identities was quite strong and daunting even to the Bolsheviks. Lenin faced this in the making of the Bolshevik revolution in 1917 with regard to the acute nationalities problem confronted in pre-revolutionary Russia. Lenin and his party comrades had to concede some ground to the cause of the nationalities in his famous pledge to the right of nations to self-determination as a tactic to mobilize the nationalities in the process of revolution. The strategic implications of Lenin's formulation of political democracy have been explained by scholars (Hill 1947; Connor 1984). Immediately after the Revolution, Lenin's advice to the people of the East on 12 November 1919 was that the Asian parties would have to adapt themselves to 'peculiar forms' of waging the revolutionary struggle. A. Doak Barnett, who had studied the varied radical Left in Asia, emphasized the need to study 'local applications and adaptation of the so-called "universals" of Marxism and Leninism' (Barnett 1963: 4). Her study suggests how the indigenous factors became important in communist politics in Asia and the problems that arose out of such adaptation to indigenous factors and forces. In Turley's study (Turley 1980) on Vietnam, it is shown how the Vietnamese revolution reconciled the borrowed doctrine with indigenous nationalism and social conditions, and pointed out also how the ideological conformity and creative adaptations co-existed in the making of the Vietnamese revolution (Turley 1980: 1). He made the methodological suggestions that the adaptation to local cultural-historical factors had meant the 'marks of compromise with ethnic and religious identity' (Turley 1980: 1).

What then happened to Indian communism? What was the ethnic history of Indian communism, if any? How did the communists in India adapt themselves to local indigenous factors and contexts? What was the diagnosis of the communist parties of the Indian situation? The Communist Party of India (CPI) as the most radical political organization of the time was painfully aware of the local contexts of India and the difficulty it confronted. In an inner-party document (1952) it was stated:

> Inevitably in a vast country like India where the conditions are different in different parts, where the popular movement is marked by its extremely uneven development, no generalization can be made which would hold true for all areas.
>
> (quoted in Bhattacharyya 1999: 5–6)

This serves to show that from early on the CPI conceded to the forces of regional/local factors and foreclosed any possibility of generalization. However, if one reads carefully the overall policy directions of the party it will be obvious that when its regional units were grappling with the indigenous factors, the party had adopted a global perspective, or the 'universal' derived either from Moscow or Beijing, or Moscow again depending upon the inclination of leadership of the party as well as the international political line then in vogue, either dictated by Moscow or Beijing (Overstreet and Windmiller 1959: Vic 1958). In other words, the party's global shifts in policy were far removed from the specificity of the local situations, or the character of class conflict at the ground level. There was thus a great gulf between the party's so-called universal approach, or theory, on the one hand, and the specifics of mobilizing the different sections of society in highly regionally-based social, economic and cultural environment, on the other. At the same time, the Left radical intellectual exercise was undertaken by some left-wing scholars for recovering Indian history in the image of the West as identified by the founders of Marxism. For example, the late S. A. Dange's attempt in his *India from Primitive Communism to Slavery* (1949) was to show that India had also passed through the same stage of history as identified by Marx and Engels in the *Communist Manifesto* (1848), and, therefore, India had also had a slave society before passing on to what Kaviraj terms 'mandatory' evolution into 'feudalism' (Kaviraj 2009: 181–2).[17] And yet, when it was so done, the overall policy directions of the party widely diverged from any theoretical seriousness whatsoever. What passed on as 'theory' was but the particular strategy of revolution dictated either by either Moscow or Beijing. The absence of any theoretical seriousness and the mechanical imitation of some international line allowed a lot of space for practical purposes. Each regional units of the party, predictably, followed its local considerations often paying only a lip-service to the general line; often the local situations were forced, intellectually speaking, to toe the overall policy line of the party, as if, the received 'theory' was always right; the particular practice had only to confirm and re-confirm it. The late E. M. S. Namboodripad, the former general secretary of the CPI-M who headed the Ministry in 1957 of the world's first democratically elected Marxist government in Kerala, quoted in his 10-page *Preface* to an odd 900-page volume a long passage from Karl Marx's *Class Struggle in France from 1848 to 1850* in order to underline the absence of dogmatism and the emphasis on the interactions of non-economic with economic factors in Marx and Engels, without bothering about the gap in a century between when Marx and Engels postulated in the above and Namboodripad's uncritical reference to the founders' understanding. This is an instance of theoretical short-circuiting.[18]

On the basis of the detailed empirical case studies of region-based communist movements in different parts of India, it is possible to provide a brief summary of the same. Andhra Pradesh was until the early 1950s a stronghold of the CPI. In this region, there was a strong affinity between communist politics and the Telegu ethnic identity. Mohan Ram (1973) who observed the movement from inside argued that the communist movement in Andhra was so powerfully regionally rooted that it gave the movement a character of a regional nationalist movement. Sen Gupta (Sen Gupta 1972: 136–7) believes that the Communist Party was able to mobilize peasant nationalism against the oppressive rule of the feudal Nizam of Hyderabad; this also implied, he says, the communist identification with linguistic nationalism of the middle-class elite because the CPI unit spearheaded the struggle for a separate Telegu-speaking State. The following passage from P. Sundarayya's *Visalandhrala Praja Rajyam* (1946) is strongly evocative of the Andhra nationalist fervor under the leadership of the CPI in the late 1940s:

> We are three crores of Telegu people, living in the same or only one area; our history is very ancient. We have our own language, culture and tradition. Our political and economic future will be bright if all our Telegu people, belonging to one race, have a right to decide freely independently whether to join an Indian federation or not.
>
> (quoted in Bhattacharyya 1999: 9)

Ram said that the Andhra communists who had a stronghold in Andhra region since the late 1920s exhibited some 'creativity' in associating themselves with the movement for a separate language based State of Andhra going somewhat against the then international lines (Ram 1973: 281). At about the same period (1946–51), the CPI in Telangana (then under the princely regime of Hyderabad), now a State within Indian Federation since 2014, led the movement for the rich peasants against the feudal Nizam rulers, a movement launched as an application of the Maoist experiment in peasant revolution.[19] Beyond doubt, the Andhra case was adaptation certainly to local conditions, but no creative conceptual categories emerged. The way the movement was simply cancelled out in 1951 under directions from the 'authority' of the international communist movements was something to be desired.

In Kerala, formed in 1956 out of three distinct territories of Malabar, Travancore and Cochin, the case of communist adaptation to regional environment was very complex because of the complexity of caste, class and communities that made up the sub-national identity. But, as Nossiter (1982: 38, 366, 1988: 194–6) argues with detailed case studies, the communist success in Kerala lay in their identification with Malayali sub-national moorings that transcended caste, class, village, community and party. And yet, the process of this identification with a very complex regional environment was facilitated by such factors as the breakdown of the joint family system, the intensity of caste discrimination, the changing agrarian system and the diffuse impact of high level literacy. The CPI and later CPI-M and other Left parties have retained subsequently a strong support base among the property less and underprivileged although their bases of support dwindled in electoral politics due to highly institutionalized competition in a fragmented political system. The Kerala communists could not recreate any original categories of understanding and mobilization that has comparative significance beyond Kerala. The niceties of electoral politics in which the communists have since been fully immersed have demanded class compromise rather than class struggle in the sense that in an election the communists have to appeal to the cross-sections of society. Bhabani Sen Gupta (1972) argued that the CPI in Kerala was most successful in mobilizing the untouchable and the lower castes; the party sought to secularize the castes but 'became exposed to caste influences' (Sen Gupta 1972: 181).

One of the other regions in South India where the CPI built some support was in Maharashtra. The communists here built two types of support corresponding to two types of movement with which they identified themselves and fought for the same. In the formerly bilingual State of Bombay, the CPI identified itself with the middle classes who were engaged in a movement for a Marathi-speaking State (Maharashtra) for the Marathas (Sen Gupta 1972: 137). The party's support for Marathi self-determination was anchored in the 'political thesis' of the Second Congress of the CPI (1948) in Calcutta when the party's General Secretary was late B. T. Ranadive, himself a Marathi. The thesis in fact criticized both the Congress Party and the Socialists for not incorporating in their demands the cause of self-determination movements in Tamilnand, Andhra or Maharashtra in the late 1940s (Sen Gupta 1972: 137). In the estimate of the party those movements were 'directed against the imperialist feudal big bourgeois combine' (Sen Gupta 1972: 157). However, the Communist Party lost ground after the creation of Maharashtra by the Government of India in 1956 on the basis of the recommendations of the State Reorganization Commiseration. The other type of movement that the CPI led was that of the tribals in the Worli region of Maharashtra since the early 1940s for a decade. The movement of the *adivasis* (i.e. India's aboriginal peoples) was directed against the prevailing system of bonded labour and the marriage of serfs. It was a successful movement which resulted in the end of the dreaded and brutal feudal system of bonded labour. Godavari Parulekar, one of the leaders of the movement, said that the communist identification with the movement was not to be seen as identification with the tribals *per se* but with the tribal peasants (Parulekar 1978: 422–53). Awfully with the change of guards in the leadership of the CPI the movement came to receive only a negative assessment (Rao ed. 1976: 81–2). There is no detailed study of what happened to the movement afterwards. From a report of Hare Krishna Koner (1970) to the Central Kisan Council (quoted in Sen Gupta 1972: 302–6) it is recorded that due to the 'powerful peasant struggles of Thane district' in Maharashtra, the government had to retreat from evicting the peasants from about 48,000 acres of land. Peasants' occupation of land of 5,000 acres in Wardha and 1500 acres in Chandrapur was recorded too (Sen Gupta 1972: 204–6). This small piece of information is an indication that the communist movement in the State subsequently has engaged in class struggles among the rural poor. But the party membership figures of the CPI-M of the very recent years show that the communist influence in the State is rather minimal: 12,051 in 2007 to 12,586 in 2011 (CPI-M 2012: 173). The figures are meagre given the large population of Maharashtra. This is in a State which is most industrialized with Mumbai (Bombay), the State capital and India's commercial capital.

The communist influence (beginning in the early 1920s) in Tamil Nadu (formerly Madras province) was very limited; the CPI made very limited headway in the pre-independence period and immediately after. As shown by Padmanavian (1987: 225–50), the small unit was subjected to all the shifts and turns in the all-India movement and was hardly able to withstand such changes. The only success that the party unit scored in the post-independence period was in the first general elections in 1951, and that too, by joining a United Front with the Tamil regional party DMK. Padmanavian (1987) says that the CPI candidates won in 13 out of 16 seats to the Madras Legislative Assembly and that was solely because in those seats the communist candidates were supported by the DMK (Padmanavian 1987: 233). The CPI took the leadership in forming a United Front with T Prakashan as the Chief Minister, but the Governor did not allow that to happen, and invited C. Rajagoplachary (Congress) to form the Ministry (Padmanavian 1987: 234). Unlike Maharashtra and Andhra, the Communist Party in Madras/Tamil Nadu could not make any headway in an ethno-regional movement of the Tamils because the space, if any, was fully occupied by the Tamil regional party DMK. And the CPI's refusal to support any secessionism of the Tamils from the Indian Union meant loss of further ground. The CPI-M, the major communist force after the CPI split in 1964 in Tamil Nadu, was found to have achieved as many as 11 seats (on 3.89 per cent votes) in the fourth general elections in 1967 and became part of the United Front ministry with the DMK voted to power. Subsequently, the CPI-M in Tamil Nadu fully engaged in parliamentary politics and mobilizing the industrial and rural agricultural labourers has increasingly been marginalized in the State politics although the party maintains a regular organization and its mass fronts with decent levels of membership. The party membership figures at 94,472 in 2007 in such a large populous State is not much but in the various mass fronts membership figures are quite satisfactory (CPI-M 2012: 173–7).

Left politics *per se* have remained marginalized, if not, non-existent, in most parts of the North East except Tripura. In Manipur, an erstwhile princely State, there was a beginning of radical Left since the late 1940s under the leadership of Irabot Singh who led the Praja Mondal movement against princely autocracy, was influenced by the CPI and the AIKS but preferred to form the Manipur Communist Party by resisting to transform his party into the Manipur State Council/Committee of the CPI. This resistance reflected the overall public mood in the State against integration with India in 1949. With his death in 1951 the communist movement, however, dissipated in the State. Of late some underground communist organizations have been formed in the State such as the Maoist Armed Revolutionary Party (formed in 2011) (banned), the Kangleipak Communist Party (KCP) (formed in 1980) (banned) and the Maoist Communist Party (banned), which are all based in armed struggle; the KCP above believes in restoring the sovereignty of Manipur from the Union of India. But then since they are all underground and banned, it is difficult to guage their real influence in society. We find that the territorial sovereignty of Manipur in this case was a bone of contention, although the movement by the Praja Mondal against feudal autocracy was genuine.

On ethno-territorial issues emerging in the areas of Assam, now carved up as Meghalaya, Mizoram and Nagaland, the scope of action of the CPI, the undivided Communist Party (until 1964) was limited. The CPI and its trade unions organized strike actions in tea gardens and oil refineries, and among the peasants (Sen Gupta 2009: 22–30) with limited success, but on the thorny issue of language and ethnic identity, the party's ambiguous approach was the cause for alienation of the party from the masses. On the burning issue of the land question in Assam, aggravated by the incessant migration from the former East Pakistan and (now) Bangladesh, the party sided with the Assamese nationality with its understanding of the 'very question of self-existence of the Assamese people as distinct and growing nationalities' (quoted in Sen Gupta 2009: 27–8). When the Statehood for Meghalaya to be carved out of Assam was becoming a reality, the party supported the move although the leadership in the struggle for Meghalaya was in the hands of the tribal ethnic organizations such as the APHLC and the Hills State People's Democratic Party, the more radical wing which split out of the former, the CPI only passed resolutions to welcome the formation of Meghalaya in 1972, a position which was at variance with the party's positive approach to an 'integrated Assam' espoused in the late 1960s (Sen Gupta 2009: 82–3, 86). The point that is made here is that as ethno-territorial issues arose one after another for the separate Hill States of Meghalaya, or Nagaland, the Left parties found themselves increasingly isolated as they could not, for 'theoretical' reasons, offer leadership to those movements. At party CPI split in 1964 nearly the entire party went over to the CPI-M but the latter along with other Left parties failed to make an enduring mass bases in the State except the State Assembly elections in 1978 – which brought some surprises to the CPI-M itself.[20] The mass bases of the Left as such dwindled, and the Left as a whole paled into insignificance in the face of the growing strength of ethno-national questions. The questions of 'nationalism' and 'nationality' has stood strongly in the way of any mass building efforts by the

CPI-M and other Left parties in the State – the former always loomed large over any class perspective. In the last State Assembly elections held in 2016, the CPI and the CPI-M drew a blank with 0.22 per cent and 0.55 per cent popular vote share respectively.

## Notes

1 Hobsbawm (1992) made a distinction between classical Mazzinian nationalism premised on the principle of one nation, one state, and the notion of nationhood as nation-building by 'nations uniting, one the one hand, and nation-building by nation-splitting of the post-Soviet variety, on the other'.
2 Avineri, S. and de Shalit OP. cit. esp. 'Community and Citizenship' by David Miller, pp. 85–101.
3 Smith, A. D. *The Ethnic Origins of Nations* p. 21.
4 See for an instance of the Marxist neglect of ethnicity, see, Bottomore et al. (1983) (eds.), *A Dictionary of Marxist Thought* in which the term 'ethnicity' does not occur at all.
5 Wallerstein (1994).
6 Hobsbawm (1992), esp. chapter 6 'Nationalism in the Late twentieth century' (pp. 162–192). See also, Paul Brass (1990) provides an opposing view.
7 Ibid.
8 Winter (1992).
9 See, for instance, Jenkin (1984); P.I: Banton (1994); and Smith (1994).
10 Wallerstein (1991: 85).
11 From Weber (1948), Chapter VIII.
12 Marx's *Letter to Ludwig Kugelmann* dated 29 November 1869 in Marx and Engels (1975: 216–17). The founders' serious engagement with the Irish question was not to be doubted given the large extent of their writings on the subject. Marx and Engels (1972).
13 Rosa Luxemburg's fundamental disagreement would be that to defend the right of self-determination of nations would mean an absolute right for all people. The Marxists, she argued, can only defend the specific right of the working class. (Davis 1978: 58).
14 *Selections from Lenin and Stalin on the national Colonial Question* (1975) for details.
15 Callinicos (1989), especially, G.A. Gohen, 'Reconsidering Historical Materialism'.
16 Kaviraj (1992).
17 Kaviraj (2009) pointed out that Indian historians followed suit by uncritically applying Marx's categorization to Indian context.
18 Namboodripad (1989).
19 Interestingly, the movement had to be abandoned in 1951 at the instance of the international intervention by the Cominform. (Ram 1973: 282), 1.
20 In this election, the CPI-M got 11 seats and emerged as the second largest party in the Assam State Assembly in the post-Emergency elections. See Sen Gupta (1979: 187–97).

# 2 Ethnic diversity and ethnic radicalism in India's North East

## Introduction

While in the rest of India, ethnic diversity and the resultant conflicts have since the early 1950s (in staged processes) been accommodated and managed by a set of institutional strategies, both non-territorial and, most importantly, territorial, this has not so happened in the North East of India which is perhaps more diverse than the rest of India, and whose territorial trajectories were more complex. A strategic and security region of India with long international borders, demands for identity, autonomy and power in this region have invited more frequently State violence which resulted in an unending war like situation between the security forces of India, on the one hand, and those on the other side of the fence, the ethnic rebels, on the other hand. In other words, ethnic diversity of the region has provided for a fertile ground for ethnic radicalism. In post-Statehood situation in the rest of India, radical ethno-nationalism – whether the Tamils, the Telegus, the Marathas, Gujarathis or the Sikh (post-1966) – subsided. In those cases, the territorial solution in the form of Statehood has worked. In the late 1950s and 1960s, territorial strategies for Statehood with autonomous powers accompanying the non-territorial but symbolic recognition of identity turned the Tamil secessionists into the defenders of Indian sovereignty and law and order. In the case of Punjab, the radical Sikh ethno-nationalists were accommodated within even a truncated and shorter Punjab (post-1966) (Singh 1994). By contrast, in India's North East the same strategies have not worked to ensure durable ethnic peace and political stability. Unlike other regions of India, ethnicity and territory do not match with each other neatly in the North East. In the more improved political situation in the region since the 1990s, the militants surrendering arms to join the 'mainstream' looks like a routine affair.[1]

This chapter seeks to answer the above question by examining the significance of social, economic and cultural diversity in the North East for radical politics in the region and explain why territorial solutions to ethnic conflicts have most often resulted in more conflicts, and also sometimes worked here. The complex territorial trajectories of the region vis-à-vis ethnic diversity and identity are explored to show that there were objective imperatives that stood in the way of durable solutions to ethic conflict. Overall this chapter seeks to provide an answer to why ethnic mobilizations take on more frequently political and militant forms in the North East. The secondary texts on the politics and ethnic conflicts in the region apart, we will use official and other reliable unofficial statistical data, and supplement them with detailed elite interviews on the States carried out during 2015–17.[2]

## Demographics: ethnicity and diversity

India's North East comprising today eight States of the federation – Arunachal Pradesh, Assam, Manipur, Meghalaya, Mizoram, Nagaland, Sikkim (added in 2012) and Tripura – remains a very diverse, ethnically speaking, strategically significant and the hotbed of varieties of ethnic radical politics. Das (2010: 45–7) offered an inventory of 77 armed militant ethnic outfits still operative in the region (except Sikkim). The number of such organizations has of course dwindled over the decades since the 1950s in consonance with the changes in the outer political environment. This region shares India's international borders with Bangladesh, on the west, (and south and east too for Tripura) and Myanmar, China and Bhutan, on the east and North East. The so-called 'North East' is a post-colonial construction, as Bhaumik (Bhaumik 1996: 310–27)[3] has rightly pointed out. Of the units, Sikkim is the latest entrant. The trajectories of territorial 'integration' of the units with the Indian Federation are chequered and complex. During the British colonial rule in India, the region comprised of four territorial units: Assam (as a directly governed province), NEFA (today's Arunachal Pradesh), Manipur and Tripura as two princely kingdoms (with indirect British control) and Sikkim as a British 'Protectorate'. Today's Meghalaya, Mizoram and Nagaland were the Hill Districts (predominantly tribal inhabited) within Assam. During colonialism, the Hill Districts were 'excluded' and 'partially excluded' (Chaube 1999) so that people from other parts of India could not access those regions. After India's independence (1947) the Nagas rebelled and declared independence – pioneering the tradition of ethnic radicalism in the region – but eventually after a long period of rebellion and war with the Indian armed forces, settled down for a separate State (1963) with special rights.[4] Political insurgency, ethnic conflicts and violence vis-à-vis the heavy hand of the Indian security forces have most often served to mark the region out as not 'normal', and added a blot on the process of democracy, participation and development in the region. Given the special territorial trajectory of Sikkim which was added to the region as late 2012, Sikkim would not fit with the rest of the region in matters of the common problems afflicting it. No wonder, a kind of insurgency framework of understanding has dominated the discourse on the region. (Bhaumik 2009; Baruah 2005, ed. 2009; Chaube 1999) Baruah (2005) made an interesting point when he argues that some States such as Arunachal Pradesh may not have ethnic militias but nonetheless are not immune from them. He adds that since there are Nagas inhabited areas in Arunachal Pradesh, Manipur and Assam, the Naga militancy has spread over to these States (Baruah 2005: 5). The Naga insurgent groups, most notably the Naga Socialist Council (NSC)

38  *Ethnic diversity and ethnic radicalism*

*Table 2.1* Army deployed in aid to civil order in the North East, 1973–83

| Year | Place | Reason | Duration |
|---|---|---|---|
| 1973 | Assam | Language riots | 13 Apr.-17 May |
| 1973 | Arunachal Pradesh | Tribal violence | 13–18 June |
| 1973 | Imphal, Manipur | Riots | 13–21 September |
| 1980 | Assam | Anti-foreigner's stir | February (continuously) |
| 1980 | Tripura | Tribal violence | 7 June-14 Nov |
| 1980 | Meghalaya | Tribal Unrest | 17 Apr.-17 May |
| 1980 | Nagaland | Tribal violence | 23–30 July/15 Nov-* |
| 1981 | Assam | Anti-foreigner's stir | Continuously for 1 year |
| 1982 | As above | As above | As above |
| 1982 | Arunachal Pradesh | Tribal unrest | 17 July-21 Aug |
| 1983 | North East | Anti-insurgency | Continuously |

Source: S.P. Cohen (1988)

(Issak-Muivah) demand inclusion of such areas in their proposed *Nagalim*, the greater Nagaland.

The deployment of military and para-military forces in the region, only second after Kashmir (Bhaumik 1996), was more frequent as an aid to civil order (Table 2.1). Civil order was difficult to obtain despite the introduction of democracy based on adult suffrage in the region since 1950. No wonder, various repressive laws of the Indian State, most notably, the Armed Forces (Special Powers) Act (1958), have been imposed on the States on various occasions.[5]

Sharing the country's international border with Bhutan, Nepal, China, Myanmar and Bangladesh, the region is marked by the extreme diversity of social structures, languages, religions and ethnic groupings, a large presence of immigrants, the single largest concentration of tribals, the lack of development (until about the 1980s), and relative deprivation, on the one hand, and the persistent sub-nationalism and political extremism, on the other. The region's population is estimated to be 45,587,982 (2011) which was around 3.76 per cent of the total population of India.

As evident from Table 2.2, the region is still sparsely populated; of them, Arunachal Pradesh and Mizoram are still more sparsely populated compared to India as a whole. The region's current level of decadal growth of population is rather stable but historically that was not the case. Due to India's Partition (1947), the region, particularly Assam and Tripura, received millions of refugees from across the border from East Bengal (pre-1947), which became East Pakistan (1947–71) and now Bangladesh. In the wake of the Bangladesh war of independence further migration took place disturbing and upsetting the demographic balance in the region. In Assam, the rate of decadal growth of population during 1951–61 and 1961–71 was very high –35 per cent and 34.7 per cent respectively compared to the all-India average of 21.6 per cent and 24.6 per cent respectively. (Weiner 1978: 82) Weiner (1978: 75–143) shows in greater detail how this huge demographic transformation became the roots of ethnic conflicts in the State

*Ethnic diversity and ethnic radicalism* 39

*Table 2.2* Population and Areas of States in NE and India, 2011

| State | Area (Sq. Km) | Population | Density (per sq. km) | Growth Rate * |
|---|---|---|---|---|
| Arunachal Pradesh | 83,743 | 1,383,727 | 17 | 26% |
| Assam | 78,438 | 31,205,576 | 398 | 17.1% |
| Manipur | 22,327 | 2,570,390 | 115 | 18.6% |
| Meghalaya | 22,429 | 2,966,889 | 132 | 27.9% |
| Mizoram | 21,081 | 1,097,206 | 52 | 23.5% |
| Nagaland | 16,579 | 1,978,502 | 119 | −0.6% |
| Sikkim | 7,096 | 610,577 | 86 | 12.9% |
| Tripura | 10,486 | 3,673,917 | 350 | 14.8% |
| NE total | 255,083 | 45,587,982 | 174 | – |
| All-India | 3,287,263 | 1,210,193,422 | 382 | 17.64% |

Sources: Basic Statistics of North Eastern Region 2015, North Eastern Council Secretariat, Shillong, pp. 1–4

Note: * indicates the decennial growth rate during 2001–2011.

*Table 2.3* Tribes and their percentage to population in the North East (2001)

| States | Number of Tribes | Percentage to population |
|---|---|---|
| Arunachal Pradesh | 101 | 68.8 |
| Assam | 23 | 12.4 |
| Manipur | 28 | 35.1 |
| Meghalaya | 14 | 86.1 |
| Mizoram | 5 | 94.4 |
| Nagaland | 20 | 86.5 |
| Sikkim | 6 | 33.8 |
| Tripura | 18 | 31.8 |

Source: Basic Statistics of North East India (2015), p. 7

subsequently. As we will see in Chapter 4, in Tripura, the migration of Bengalis from East Bengal and later East Pakistan reduced the local population (aboriginal peoples) during 1941–51, and later in 1951–61 to a small minority in their own State. The resultant loss of land and habitat to the settler Bengalis in Tripura was to become the roots of radical ethnic politics in the State.

This region is reported to have as many as 215 Scheduled (constitutionally recognized) Tribes (said to be the aboriginal peoples) and many more which are not yet recognized as such to be entitled to constitutional special protection and privileges. Of the eight States of the region, four are predominantly tribal (aboriginal) inhabited, (of them three are predominantly Christian)[6] and there are significant proportions of them in the rest (Table 2.3).

The data offered in columns second and third in Table 2.3 merits some explanation for adequate understanding the depth of ethnic diversity in each State in the region. The percentage figure in the third column is very broad which is to be qualified by the data in column first. For example, while it is true that 68.8 per cent of the population in Arunachal Pradesh are tribal but then they are 101 tribal groups and sub-groups – each having their own identity and culture (perhaps inhabiting a little territory of their own) and speaking a dialect. In Tripura, 31.8 per cent tribal refers to as many 18 tribal groups and sub-groups; in this case too each of them has its own dialect although *Kok-Borok* is the lingua franca. The intricacies of such diversity are to be read in conjunction with the linguistic diversity in each State. The 50th Report of the Commissioner of Linguistic Minorities, Government of India (2013) contains detailed information of the linguistic diversity in each State.[7]

In Arunachal Pradesh, there is no majority language group, and hence there is no dominant ethnic group. There are significant speakers of three 8th Schedule languages (i.e. Bengali, Hindi and Nepali). The majority speak different tribal dialects lacking in scripts so that the official language of the State is English. The State was created in 1987 without any distinct identity basis.

In Assam, the major State in the region with 68.45 per cent of the region's total population in 2011, the Assamese speakers are found to have lost their majority for the first time. In 1971, the Assamese speakers were some 60.89 per cent of the total population so this loss of majority is likely to create ethnic tensions among the Assamese in days to come. The linguistic diversity in the State is immense because apart from the Assamese, Bengali and Bodo/Boro, the major language speakers, there are a plethora of languages spoken not all of which are officially recognized. The recent decline in percentage of Assamese is due to the relative decline of Assamese speakers and the increase of Bengali speakers in seven districts in the Brahmaputra Valley during 1991–2001. (*The Hindu* 9 October 2016) Assam has experienced territorial contraction since pre-independence days, and more particularly since the 1960s when its Hill Districts were separated, Nagaland was conceded as a State in 1963; and 1972 when Mizoram, Meghalaya were conceded Statehood. This added to greater percentage of Assamese to the total population, but diverse ethnic situation remained. The dwindling demographic numbers of the Assumes gave birth to ethnic militancy arising from the majority community (i.e. the Assamese) in the form of the ULFA and the AGP among others. Ethnic minorities have mobilized themselves in militant forms for protection of their identity. Various Bodo organizations have cropped up for a State of Bodoland in the northern banks of the river Brahmaputra. A Bodoland Territorial Authority has been conceded in 2003 but it has created more problems than resolved any (Bhattacharyya et al. 2017). Beyond them, there are demands for further territorial separation out of Assam by different ethnic minorities group such as the Karbi, Dimasa and the Nagas. Assam and Nagaland share a long 434 km border, east of Assam, and there is a long-drawn dispute (border) between the two States over some territories on the border areas. The *Nagalim* (greater Nagaland) demand of the Naga rebels (NSCN-IM) includes parts of Assam's territory.[8]

In Manipur, the erstwhile princely State like Tripura, although the Manipuri is spoken by the majority this majority is not high. There are a lot of speakers of other tongues which are not all recognized officially. Manipuri is the official language of the State, but English is adopted as an additional official language. There is still controversy about the script to be used for Manipur. The people in Manipur are diverse living in the hills (41.1 per cent) and the valley (58.9 per cent). The people living in the plains are also ethnically divided and profess different faiths. There are Kuki and the Naga settlement in the valley – the Nags comprising the second largest after the Meitei (Manipuri). There are some 29 tribes living in the hills generically grouped into the Naga, the Kuki and the Zo. There are many sub-groups among them too. The *Nagalim* demand of the Naga rebels includes parts of Manipur inhabited by the Nagas.

When the State of Meghalaya was conceded in 1972 it was understood to be the State of the whole people of Meghalaya, and that the ethnic rebels fighting for Statehood were the representatives of the whole people. But it turned out to be otherwise. It turned out that the Khasis, the dominant tribe, got the State, and hence the second largest ethno-linguistic group, i.e. the Garos, were unhappy and began demanding a State of their own, which is yet to be fulfilled. The Khasis and the Garos are the two major linguistic groups but then there is immense ethno-linguistic diversity in the State. It was created as an autonomous State within the State of Assam on April 2, 1969. It comprises of the United Khasi-Jaintia Hills District and the Garo Hills District. It became a fully-fledged State in 1972. And yet, Statehood has not been able to resolve inter-ethnic conflicts in Manipur.

Mizoram is the lone tribal State in the region whose dominant Mizo community speaking Mizo/Lushai constitutes 73.21 per cent of the total population. This has served to ensure enduring ethnic peace in the State although the Hmar tribe has been demanding some territorial autonomy and protection of their identity for long. As we will see in the next chapter, the greater ethnic homogeneity in the State has produced better governance results.

Contrary to all claims for a coherent Naga nationhood and solidarity, Nagaland contains very diverse linguistic groups so that there is no single Naga group as a majority in population. The two largest linguistic groups – Ao and Konyak – constitutes respectively 12.94 per cent and 12.46 per cent of the total population. The various other groups have population which are significant in number in a State with a small population. This ethno-linguistic diversity undercuts the demand for a homogenous Naga identity and has given birth to numerous ethnic rebels.

Sikkim is diverse too although its majority Nepali community has majority (62.61 per cent) The other language groups are smaller in number and proportions. But the State has had a different trajectory, and shared very little with the North East. For a long period, it was a feudal dynasty which the British protected with its indirect control. After 1947 India extended the protection but incorporated it into the Union of India in 1974 and made a State in 1975. In the 1960s and 1970s there were attempts to construct a common Sikkimese (national) identity though it turned out to be fraught with a host of problems stemming from a multicultural social mosaic (Hiltz 2003). But the State has a distinct regional identity, which again is multicultural, which sets it apart from similar identity in the North East.

Tripura's linguistic diversity is not as complex for the Bengalis and the Tripuri/*Kok-Borok* languages cover more than 92 per cent of the population. But there is persistent and long drawn ethnic conflict in the State. As we have examined in greater detail in Chapter 4, the roots of the conflicts lie in the fact that the tribals (Tripuri/*Kok-Borok*) plus others such as the Mogh, Manipuri, Halam and Garo-speaking (together about 31 per cent) who were the original inhabitants of the princely State were reduced in the wake of long-drawn migration of Bengalis to a minority. This entailed loss of land and habitats to the settlers on the part of the tribals. This has complicated the sense of identity both among the tribals and the settlers Bengalis whose territorial loyalty is more to the State, and the areas of East Bengal (East Pakistan) from where they migrated respectively. In a detailed empirical survey, Mitra (2012: 59–61) explained why a quarter of the people had reported (in a national survey) themselves as *not citizens of India* with reference to the regions and localities of their origin.

## Religious diversity in the North East

In terms of religion too, this region is especially very diverse because unlike the rest of India where Hindus are a predominant majority, in the North East, Hindus are a majority in population in only three States – Assam, Sikkim and Tripura. In Manipur, the Hindus are the single largest group (43.21 per cent). The Hindus overall are 54.23 per cent compared to India as a whole where they are about 80 per cent. The Christians here have significant presence in the population. The Muslims are sizeable proportions of the population in Assam, Manipur and Tripura. Nonetheless, religion did not play a determining role in redefining ethnic identity in the North East, a role played rather effectively by other factors such as language and tribal ethnicity. Religion as a symbol of ethnic identity claiming special rights and political unit, or association has had a bad name in India. In the Indian Constitution, caste, tribe, and language are accorded legitimate status, but not religion. Because of the creation of Pakistan on the basis of religion, the movement that seeks to use religion as the basis of politics and Statehood has been derogatorily labeled 'communal', and considered to be illegitimate.[9] Weiner and Katzenstein (1981) reported that in the 1960s, some of the Khasi, Garo and Naga tribesmen had begun to assert their identity as Christians, but then realizing the political unacceptability of a religious claim, switched to tribal loyalties, and identities and successfully demanded the creation of tribal States.[10] It must, however, be acknowledged that Christianity has played a major role in redefining tribal ethnic identity in Nagaland, Meghalaya and Mizoram.[11]

Three States in the region – Meghalaya, Mizoram and Nagaland – are predominantly Christian, and there are a large number of Christian in Assam and Manipur (43.32 per cent and 30.28 per cent respectively). However, the Christian overall in the region are only 17.31 per cent. Arunachal Pradesh is the only State with significant Buddhist population (11.78 per cent). While Christianity has served to articulate tribal identity in Meghalaya, Mizoram and Nagaland, somewhat cutting across linguistic barriers, in Assam linguistic markers have gone above the religious in identity articulations. But at the same time, many militant ethnic organizations such as the AGP and the ULFA are dominated by the caste Hindu Assamese. The Muslims in Assam have mobilized themselves separately as well as within the Congress party. In Tripura because of the impact of Left politics over the decades, communal polarization along religious lines did not take place. On the contrary, the fact that most tribals here are Hindus has added to inter-community amity. In Tripura again, the Muslims have traditionally been the support bases of the Left.

The above analysis suggests that a common identity in each State, let alone in the region, remains a far cry. Each unit of the federation is ethnically heterogeneous, and most often territorially rooted, and provided for fertile grounds for political mobilizations for identity and autonomy. Often one dominant group has claimed power and autonomy for the whole lot of people but once in the corridors of power, it has discriminated against the other groups; or the minorities newly created have expressed grievances against the dominant group in power. The latter has followed suit for further territorial division for protection of their identity.

## Unresolved territorial issues

Statehood and sub-State territorial status conceded to the ethnic groups in the North East have not been able to resolve all territorial issues and hence ethnic conflicts. Territorial solutions in the region have given rise to the demands for further territorial divisions in nearly all States in the region excerpt Sikkim, where the extent is very limited. Such demands are unavoidably linked to complex ethno-linguistic diversity we have examined above. In this section I will present evidences from elite interviews conducted on the States during 2015–16. Ten elites (politicians, MLA and Ministers, including former Chief Minister, senior civil servant, senior journalists and academics) from each were selected on the random basis to provide answer to our question: *Are there demands for territorial restructuring in your State? If so please give some examples?* We take up Arunachal Pradesh, an unlikely case for consideration of further territorial divisions, first. This State was created in 1987 by upgrading it from the status of Union Territory (directly governed by the Central government) (1962) and without there being any strong political movement for Statehood. This small State (1.38 million people) is ethnically extremely diverse, as we have seen above. 59 of 60 Legislative Assembly seats are reserved for the tribes (101 in number) and the State is very sparsely populated. And yet, in answer to our question above, nine out of ten elites responded, and of them, eight reported positive. The elites confirmed that there was no demand for a separate Statehood out of the State, but there were demands for smaller territorial units such as Union Territory and Autonomous District Councils. One well-informed respondent, the sub-editor of the *Arunachal Pradesh Times*, there were demands for Autonomous District Councils in Mon, Patkai and Ziro, and a UT demand for Siang belt (dated 20/9/16 at Itanagar). In the case of Meghalaya, nine out of ten respondents reported positive. In most cases, the demand for a separate State of Garoland for the Garos, the second largest tribes in the State, the demand which was supported by the legendary Garo leader late P. N. Sangma, the former Speaker of Indian Parliament (Lok Sabha). Some respondents did mention also the demands for a separate State for the Khasi-Jaintia where an Autonomous District Council is established. On the basis of the experiences of Statehood in the region it has been found out that the Union Territory status and the Autonomous District Councils have been the stepping stone for demanding Statehood. Assam remains almost perennially the fertile ground for demands for territorial divisions in a State which has bourne the brunt of State contraction most. In the case of Assam, all respondents reported positive and mentioned various cases of territorial restructuring. Mr Prafulla K. Mohanta, the former Chief Minister, a founder of the AGP and powerful student leader in the late 1970s and 1980s,[12] opined: 'Yes, almost all ethnic communities in Assam are demanding Statehood – Boros, Rabhas, Mishing Rajbansis' (dated 22/6/15 Guwahati). The Vice-President of the Assam State unit of the BJP Mr Chandrakant Das was cynical: 'Bodoland, Kamptapuri, Rajbansi . . . . Not in every 50 sq km area in Assam is composed of just one ethnic group' (dated 21/6/15 Guwahati). One top civil servant of Assam opined:

> Yes, the Bodos, the Mishings, Rabhas, all are demanding separate territory for them (30/6/15). The President of the Hind Majoor Sabha, Mr Ajay Dutta saw the tree in the woods:

> Whatever movements are taking place they are benefiting the elites among the ethnic groups. The identities are not asking; it's their leaders who are demanding.
> (Dated 22/6/15)

Mizoram in the North East is considered the most successful tribal ethnic State whose records of enduring peace after Statehood remain remarkable. (We discuss that in the next chapter). It is also the most consolidated tribal State in the sense that the Mizos comprise the overwhelming majority in population. Therefore, on the face of it, Mizoram is an unlikely case of witnessing demands for territorial restructuring. But there are demands for territorial divisions: the Autonomous District Council status under the 6th Schedule of the Constitution for Lai, Chakma, Maro, Bru, Hmar and so on. This is so reported by a majority of respondents. Of the many small tribal communities, the demand of the Hmar tribal community was recognized in a bilateral agreement (Ethnic Peace Accord) between the Hmar People's Convention and the Government of Mizoram in 1993 for more powers and autonomy to the Hmar Autonomous Tribal District Council including their demand for recognizing their language as an official language in the State and a medium of instruction at the primary school level.[13] The case of Nagaland is set apart from the rest. Out of ten respondents, eight reported positive on one point: unification of all Nagas living in the North East under Nagaland. Consider the representative response offered by Mr Z. Lohe, Treasurer, Nagaland Congress

Party, four times MLAs in Nagaland Legislative Assembly and former Speaker of the Assembly:

> No 13 of the 16-Point Agreement[14] is that "the other Naga tribes inhabited in the areas contiguous to Nagaland will be allowed to join, if they so desire, Nagaland".[15] This is to be implemented. The Naga Legislative Assembly passed four Resolutions on Naga integration.
>
> (Dated 2/7/16)

There was, however, a lone exception. One respondent mentioned that there were demands for 'Eastern Nags of Mon, Tuensang, Lenglon and Kiphike districts for a separate state' (a civil servant dated 27/6/16). The unresolved Naga problems today is confined to their demand for Nagalim,[16] a greater Nagaland by incorporating the Naga-inhabited areas in Assam, Arunachal Pradesh and Manipur – which is a difficult demand to fulfill because the affected States would not be willing to part with their territory.

## Ethnicity over class

The region's economy or economies despite some development over the last three decades remains weak. Most of the people in seven States out of eight are dependent population meaning thereby that the work force participation is weaker. Except Nagaland and Sikkim where work force participation is 54 per cent, and 50.5 per cent respectively in the rest it is in the range of 40–49 per cent (Basic Statistics 2015: 8 Note: This is the official data offered by the DoNER—Ministry of Development of the North Eastern Region). In some States it is even lower than that. Because of the hilly terrains and the limited amount of cultivable land, fewer per cent of people are engaged in cultivation (Table 2.4). Except in the Brahmaputra and the Barak Valleys in Assam and the Western part of Tripura, scope of settled cultivation has remained limited. Thus, the growth of a class economy has been very limited. This partly explains why ethnic politics has greater sway over class politics in the region. People are engaged in limited numbers in other kinds of work such as transport, horticulture, shifting cultivation, orchard, tea garden (in Assam), tertiary oil exploration industries and various other tertiary sectors. And yet, the resources are scarce and the scope of control over them by the vast majority is miniscule.

## Conclusion

From the above account it is clear why Statehood and sub-Statehood in the North East do apparently not work in favour of some enduring ethnic peace. The States in the region are small in size and the minority tribal ethnic communities except perhaps the Garos in Meghalaya are still smaller with pockets of territorial concentration. It is also clear from the interviews and the exiting texts on the politics of the region that however small the tribal communities are in size and importance they (i.e. the elites) routinely form militias, articulate their demands in the rhetoric of ethnic self-determination, of which the region, as shown in Baruah (2010), can

Table 2.4 Economic activities of the people in the North East (2011)

| States | CULTIVATORS | % | AGRI LABOUR | % | H. IND. LABOUR | % | OTHER workers | % | TOTAL POP. |
|---|---|---|---|---|---|---|---|---|---|
| AP | 248120 | 17.93% | 20259 | 1.46% | 4723 | 0.34% | 205614 | 14.86% | **1383727** |
| ASSAM | 3138554 | 10.06% | 903294 | 2.89% | 242071 | 0.78% | 4403204 | 14.11% | **31205576** |
| MANIPUR | 365712 | 14.23% | 43774 | 1.70% | 44586 | 1.73% | 40940 | 1.59% | **2570390** |
| MEGHALAYA | 402202 | 13.56% | 114642 | 3.86% | 11969 | 0.40% | 383694 | 12.93% | **2966889** |
| MIZORAM | 202514 | 18.46% | 12448 | 1.13% | 1556 | 0.14% | 33546 | 3.06% | **1097206** |
| NAGALAND | 420369 | 21.25% | 22571 | 1.14% | 9525 | 0.48% | 288704 | 14.59% | **1978502** |
| SIKKIM | 82707 | 13.55% | 11154 | 1.83% | 2888 | 0.47% | 133220 | 21.82% | **610577** |
| TRIPURA | 246707 | 6.72% | 201863 | 5.49% | 19298 | 0.53% | 609153 | 16.58% | **3673917** |
| TOTAL | **5106885** | | **1330005** | | **336616** | | **6098075** | | **45486784** |

Source: Basic Statistics (2015)

boast of producing many, and demand some territory following the provisions of the 6th Schedule of the Indian Constitution, or otherwise. As Baruah (2005: 5) has observed:

> The sheer number of militias in North East is extraordinary. Indeed it might seems appear that any determined young man of the numerous ethnic groups of the region can proclaim the birth of a new militia, raise funds to buy weapons or procure them by aligning with another militia and become an important political player.

Demographically, the region is home to 8.6 per cent of the tribal population of India; four States are predominantly tribal: Arunachal Pradesh, Meghalaya, Mizoram and Nagaland. Of the four, three are Christian dominated. The other States also contain significant numbers of tribals. The total tribal population in the region is approximately 26 per cent of the region. In terms of religion, Hindus are 54.23 per cent, Muslims, as the second largest group, are 25.15 per cent and Christians are 17.31.6 per cent. Buddhists are not dominant in any States (although they have 11.78 per cent of the population of Arunachal Pradesh). Ethnic militancy in the region has been found among the tribals as well as non-tribal, Hindus as well as Muslims and Christians, hill people as well as plains people. Unlike religion, language and tribal ethnicity have (and still do) played powerful determining role in the political processes in this region. Such loyalties and identities have remained very active in political mobilizations for political recognition of identities within Indian federalism. This has called for both the territorial and non-territorial solutions to the categorical problems. Territorially, this had involved different degrees of Statehood (from tribal, district, and regional councils, often through associate Statehood, to finally Statehood as a federal unit with autonomous powers). The non-territorial accommodation, through official recognition of language and its eventual placement in the 8th Schedule of Indian Constitution which entitles the particular linguistic community to certain rights in matters of official communication and instruction etc., symbolic satisfaction of linguistic identity has worked well. As I have argued elsewhere (Bhattacharyya 2008), the ethnic elements of nationhood in the region are very thick, and their civic ties of nationhood are thin comparatively speaking. When the ethnic 'nations' in the region share little with the others in their own State, they hardly share their identity concerns with the others in the other States in the region. The question of common sharing of identity and values with the others in the rest of India thus simply does not arise. Oddly, their incessant demands for identity, (territorial) autonomy and power are at variance with the very poor resources available, given that the region is heavily dependent on the Centre for funding, and the cost of government itself. Emotions born of ethnicity most often does not take care of the practicality in governance.

An important factor that has more easily turned the ethnic groups to take up arms is the deployment of security forces in the region. To the outside world the region has generally been known as India's 'insurgent country' (Bhaumik 1999: 322). The region's ethnic movements and politics, persistent political militancy, ethnic genocides[17] and geographic isolation have made it a 'problem area' of India. The States in the region share India's international borders, particularly with China and Myanmar and hence have witnessed, unavoidably, deployment of security forces on a regular basis. For Indian rulers since independence, the region has remained a major security concern, and many of the policies for 'national integration' have been adopted through a security paradigm. A large number of India's security forces have been deployed in the region, only second to the numbers deployed in Kashmir (Bhaumik 1999: 326),[18] and the AFSPA has regularly been in force. This securitization of the region has failed to quell the large number of ethnic militant and political outfits[19] fighting for autonomy and/or secession. Beyond doubt, this securitization of the region has increased dissatisfaction and the support for movements challenging the writ of the State (although it is important to stress that the intensity of conflict varies markedly across the different States for reasons very specific to the States concerned).

Another reason for the ethnic radicalism lies in the difficulty in accommodating some, although not all, groups because of the presence of groups such as the Nagas across more than one State. India's 2011 census report records some 15 Naga tribes in Manipur (5.7 per cent of Manipur's population), and 3 in Arunachal Pradesh (6978 persons). This diversity has been compounded by high levels of internal and external migration, caused by colonial era migration into the plantations, migration as a result of the Bangladesh war of independence, as well as more recent migration into the agricultural, service and the trading sector (Das 2009: 8).

In economic terms, the region's resource bases are meagre. Historically, about 80 per cent of the region's revenue has come from the Centre. Because of their backwardness, isolation and strategic location, until 2014 all the States of the region were *Special Category States* (SCS) that received (favourable) asymmetric financial treatment from the Centre.[20] The abolition of the Planning Commission in August 2014 raises new questions about the future financing of the region. There is much resentment among the elites of the region against this decision. (Discussed in Chapter 3 next).

Finally, contrary to what Baruah (2005, ed. 2010) would have us believe, the formation of militias in the region is not the entire story. Since the day of the famous Naga-Akbar Hydari Ethnic Peace Accord (26–27 June 1947) with the Naga rebels followed by the '16-Point Agreement' (1960), institutionalization of ethnic radicalism has also taken place in which the ethnic rebels have decided to give up arms in favour of joining the democratic political process, taking part in elections and finally forming the government by them. This has happened in most States, and served to pave the basis for democratic power-sharing and taking part in governance. The ethnic radicals in the region have also learnt that the simply rebellious action does not pay, and for long, and leaves them with little space. The other side of ethnic rebellion in the region since the days of the Nagas in 1947 and then from the 1960s remains negotiation for peace (read power and autonomy) and a share in power. The governments of the days at the State and Central levels have also sought a negotiated settlement, and bipartite and tri-partite peace agreements

(Datta ed. 1995) that have most often worked. This has transformed yesterday's rebels into tomorrow's stake holders (Mitra and Singh 2009). The once militant AGP in Assam of the Assamese (majority), not of the tribals, took part in Ethnic Peace negotiation in 1985, took part in elections, got into State power in 1985 and 1991, and ruled Assam for the next ten years.[21] The other case is the Mizo National Front, one time formidable ethnic rebel organization, entered into the bipartite (The MNF and the Government of India) ethnic agreement known as the Mizo Accord (Memorandum of Agreement) in 1960, (Datta ed. 1995: 146–51) transformed itself into a political party,[22] took part in elections which returned them to power in 1989 and in 1993 as the dominant party (in coalition) and governed the State until on its own from 1998 to 2008 winning successive elections. As a result of this process of institutionalization of ethnic radicalism in North East, the space for ethnic rebellion has been minimized, and that the region has a better record of the management of ethnic conflict and peace since the 1990s has to be explained with reference to the politics of institutionalization of ethnic radicalism and the resultant governance – the subject treated in the next chapter.

## Notes

1 Communist Party, 17 United National Liberation Front, ten People's Revolutionary Party of Kangleipak, eight People's Revolutionary Party of Kangleipak (Pro), seven People's Liberation Army (PLA) and four Kanglei Yawol Kanna Lup (*TheHindustan Times* 14 August 2017).

    In Tripura, four militants (ethnic radicals) belonging to the National Liberation Front of Tripura (NLFT) surrendered before the Border Security Forces (BSF) yesterday at the eastern border of Rajbari under Rashiyabari police station in Dhalai district. According to Border Security Force officials, the militants surrendered without arms, as they confessed that the NLFT had been facing shortage of arms and other resources that compelled them to surrender. The surrenders were identified as Milan Mohan Tripura (38), Niranjoy Tripura (20), Danto Mohan Tripura (24) and Raiya Tripura (37) of the same district (https://theNorth Easttoday.com/4-national-liberation-front-of-tripura-militants-surrender-in-tripura/(sighted on 27 August 2017).

2 I shall utilize the elite interviews data collected in the course of the International Network Research funded by the Leverhulme Trust UK on 'Continuity and Change in Indian Federalism in the Age of Coalition Governments (2014–17)'. The author gratefully acknowledges the funding support extended by the above agency.

3 See also his (2009).

4 Article 371-A of the Indian Constitution says: 'Notwithstanding anything contained in this Constitution –

  a. No Act of Parliament in respect of: (i) religious or social practices of the Nagas; (ii) Naga customary law and procedure; (iii) administration of civil and criminal justice involving decisions according to the Naga customary law; and (iv) ownership and transfer of land and its resources, shall apply to the State of Nagaland unless the Legislative Assembly of Nagaland by a resolution so decides'.

                                                                             (Bakshi 2017: 391–2)

5 On 3 August 2017 the entire State of Assam has been declared as 'disturbed areas' under the above law. Areas near Meghalaya's border areas adjoining Assam and three districts in Arunachal Pradesh have also been declared as 'disturbed' under the AFSPA for two more months with effect from August 3 (The *Hindustan Times* 7 August 2017).

6 These are Meghalaya, Mizoram and Nagaland.
7 See 50th Report of the Commissioner of Linguistic Minorities in India (July 2012–June 2013) (www.nclm.in accessed on 8/8/17).
8 The map of *Nagalim*, released by the NSCN-IM, includes the Karbi Anglong and North Cachar Hills District of Assam as well as parts of the districts of Golaghat, Sibasagar, Dibrugarh, Tinsukia and Jorhat. The unresolved dispute is deeply rooted in the history of British colonialism in the region since the late ninetieth century.
9 See Weiner and Katzenstein (1981: 15).
10 This was an instance of the rational choice on the part of the political actors.
11 See Singh (1987: 51–34–54).
12 He was in the forefront of the campaign against foreigners and the illegal immigrants in the late 1970s and early 1980s. His party the Asom Gana Parishad (AGP) was returned to power in 1985 and again in 1991 and ruled the State for 10 years before conceding defeat to Congress. This party was out of power for a long time since the 19990s but has joined the BJP led State-level coalition government in Assam in 2016 with its 14 Assembly seats.
13 For more details, see Datta (1995: 152).
14 This was signed between the Naga People's Convention and the Government of India in July 1960 (see Datta 1995: 156–61).
15 This statement was under Point 13 was not true. In the actual Agreement, the Government of India did not so commit. (Datta 1995: 159–60).
16 There many such Naga groups, based in the neighbouring countries, especially Myanmar, but six of them are of any significance, and the Government of India is keen on negotiation with them https://theNorth Easttoday.com/naga-accord-nagaland-governor-urges-nscn-k-to-join-peace-talks/ (cited on 28/10/17).
17 Tripura in 1981 (Mandai ethnic riots) see Bhattacharyya (1999) for details, Assam before 1985 and now in the Bodoland areas.
18 These include the BSF and several para-military forces like the Assam Rifles, the Gurkha Regiment and the CRPF.
19 Das (2010) reported that there were some 76 such organizations in the region. (pp. 45–7).
20 These states have traditionally received 90 per cent of India's Planning Commission's disbursement of funds as grants and 10 per cent as loans. In comparison, the general category 'mainstream' states received 70 per cent of central funds as loans and 30 per cent as grants. In addition to the seven states of the North East, Jammu and Kashmir, Uttarakhand, Himachal Pradesh and Sikkim also enjoyed Special Category Status.
21 It is reported that 68 militants (ethnic rebels) along with a huge cache of assorted weapons such as AK series assault rifles, surrendered on Monday 14 August 2017 in Manipur before Manipur Chief Minister N Birendra Singh at the parade ground of the 1st Battalion Manipur Rifles. The ethnic radical groups they represented were as follows: 23 from Kangleipak In Tripura, four militants (ethnic radicals) belonging to the National Liberation Front of Tripura (NLFT) surrendered before the Border Security Forces (BSF) yesterday at eastern border at Rajbari under Rashiyabari police station in Dhalai district. According to Border Security Force officials, the militants surrendered without arms, as they confessed that the NLFT had been facing shortage of arms and other resources that compelled them to surrender. The surrenders were identified as Milan Mohan Tripura (38), Niranjoy Tripura (20), Danto Mohan Tripura (24) and Raiya Tripura (37) of the same district (https://theNorth Easttoday.com/4-national-liberation-front-of-tripura-militants-surrender-in-tripura/ [sighted on 27 August 2017]).

The AGP today is a junior partner in the coalition government in Assam led by the BJY (since 1026). The Bodo People's Front, another ethnic radical party, has also

followed suit. Although AGP has joined the BJP led coalition government in Assam in 2016 it has not given up its regionalism and localism for development, employment and empowerment in government and non-government sectors. The Bodo People's Front came out of the erstwhile militant outfit (Boland Tigers Force) in 2001.
22 The specialized knowledge on Mizo politics suggests that much credit is due to the MNF as a political party and its leadership for far better ethnic peace in Mizoram than elsewhere in the region. (See for details, Hassan 2010).

# 3 Institutionalization of ethnic radicalism in India's North East

Power-sharing, participation and governance

**Introduction**

Institutionalization as a theme has remained neglected in the existing understanding of ethnic politics in the North East of India. 'Institutionalization' does not appear, on the face of it, as the term for understanding the gamut of ethnic politics in India's North East. The terms 'rebellion', 'ethnic violence', 'riots' and 'insurgency' have so far filled up the space of scholarly reflections on the subject. Baruah's famous book 'Durable Disorder: Understanding the Politics of North East India' (2005), or Bhaumik's 'Troubled North East' (2009), or his 'Insurgent Cross-fire' (1996) appear to offer the perspective to the understanding of ethnic politics in the region. To my estimate, these are part of what I have called 'the insurgency approach' (Bhattacharyya 2017) to the North East. This insurgency approach does not hold any more the key to the understanding of politics in the region, not since the late 1990s, if not a little earlier for some States in the region. I argue here that the willingness in entering into negotiations on the part of the ethnic rebels with the State and or Central governments for power-sharing within the overall parameters of the India's constitutional democracy, as a legitimate political party, to participate in the democratic political process for power-sharing and governance have taken place since the 1960s (the Naga case) through to the 1970s, 1980s and 1990s. The above combined together has constituted the process of institutionalization of ethnic radicalism in the North East, and contributed to the regional's political integration with the democratic political process in India. This has facilitated more accommodation of ethnic identity, minimized the scope of ethnic conflicts and ensured more 'durable' ethnic peace and political order in the region.

This chapter seeks to examine the process of political transformation of ethnic radicalism into partners in Indian democracy through the process of institutionalization. This latter process has entailed the willingness of the ethnic rebels to join the democratic political process through ethnic peace accords; their legitimate political participation for power-sharing at the State level and the levels below as well as of at the national level – in the latter realms the scope remains though very limited as the region as a whole sends only 26 members to Lok Sabha, the lower house of Indian parliament and 14 seats to Rajya Sabha (upper house) of which Assam sends seven, and the rest of the States one each. The extent of political participation at the State level is also examined in this chapter to show in particular how in the post-Statehood situation in the region political participation has increased, multi-party competition has become the legitimate methods of power competition and political integration as a result has followed. The last section will examine the governance performance of the States over the three decades between 1981 and 2011 the statistical data on which are systematically available. The period is suggestive also of the effects of the shifts in India's political economy to macroeconomic neo-liberal reforms.

## Ethnic mobilization and ethnic radicalism

First a brief discussion on when the ethnic mobilization turned radical in India's North East is in order. This is to be understood in terms of a conceptual distinction between ethnic mobilizations *per se* and ethnic radicalism. In a multi-ethnic and democratic country it is quite expected that there will be ethnic conflicts, and that some ethnic groups will articulate their identity demands ('diversity-claims'), as I have termed it elsewhere (Bhattacharyya 2015a), in support of their language rights, preferential treatment in jobs and education or the right to education at the primary level in their mother tongue, in protest against discrimination, and or the protection of their culture, as a whole. The Naga Club (born in 1918 in Paris) demanded self-determination vis-a-vis India and submitted a Memorandum in 1932 to the Simon Commission; their demand was favourably considered by the then British rulers by formally making the Naga hills as 'excluded area' (that was how their self-determination was accorded by the British!). But it was then not considered as an example of 'ethnic radicalism'. The Assam Kachari Association submitted a memorandum to the Simon Commission in 1932 for representation, reservation in education and appointment for the Bodo community, which did not make it a radical ethnic organization. The other examples are the All Assam Tribal League (1933) which demanded protection of their land from encroachment by the immigrants. The Bod Sahitya Sabha (The Bodo Literary Association) formed in 1952 was a civil society organization and cultural movement for the protection of the Bodo/Boro language vis-à-vis the imposition of the Assamese; until 1967 it was a democratic and peaceful organization. The Plains Tribal Council of Assam (PTCA) was formed in 1966 – the political wing of the Bodo Sahitya Sabha – with the moderate demands for the use of the Bodo language in the areas they lived, and expressed serious concern in a Memorandum to the Central government in 1972 that the plains tribes, as they were, suffered systematic uprootment 'in their own soil' due to the alleged step-motherly attitude of the State government led by the Assamese (Singh 1987: 102–2). From 1967 the organization began a movement for a separate State of *Udaychal* for all the plains tribes and kept up the demand for the next two decades after which the All Bodo Students Union, a militant organization from its birth took up the cudgel of a separate State but not for all plains tribes but only for the Bodo from the early 1980s. The PTCA was a moderate organization believing in democratic method of struggle. The Bodos for long had demanded their preferred script to be the Roman, rather than the Assamese, which was in vogue. But it gave up this demand on the request of the Prime Minister (late Indira Gandhi) who visited Assam on 12 April 1975 and agreed to use the Assamese script (Singh 1987: 101). But the organization demanded since 1967 a separate State of Udayachal which the Union government was not ready to concede; the Union government's offer of an Autonomous Council was not acceptable to the PTCA (Singh 1987: 101–3). The organization became radicalized not on its own accord but by the forces of circumstances. On grounds of suspicion about the de-limitation of the tribal reserve constituencies for the upcoming State Assembly elections in 1968, the PTCA boycotted the election. The State response was very violent: the President and the Secretary of the PTCA were arrested and the areas of their habitation were brought under the CrPC 144 (commonly known as 'curfew'). Such repressive State action made the organization move to the path of radicalism in its demand for *Udayachal*. With the rise of the All Bodo Students Union (ABSU) on 15 February 2067 and the split in the PTCA the year before the PTCA receded into the background though surviving only as a minor democratic political force until about 1991.[1]

The old and famous Assam Sahitya Sabha (Assam Literary Association) was a civil society association though heavily oriented to 'aggressive cultural nationalism' (Baruah 2005: 138) of the Assamese. So it was and remains an ethnic association. But in the wake of the famous campaign against the illegal immigrants in Assam during 1979–85, it renounced its apolitical stance and became formally part of the Gana Sangram Parishad (a Council for the People's Struggle, and thus became radicalized. The Asom Gana Parishad (AGP) came out of this campaign, and the All Assam Students Union (ASSU), became a political party, entered into political negotiation in 1985, and became a ruling party in the State from 1985–89 and 1996–2001. The AGP is now a junior partner in the coalition government in Assam led by the BJP since 2016. The ASSU was very radical and brought the State to a standstill for long five years from 1979–85. After the so-called Assam Accord (we will examine it soon shortly), the AGP was de-radicalized and institutionalized – remains today a regional political party committed to play by the rules of the game.

The United Liberation Front of Assam (ULFA) (born on 7 April 1979) was formed, interestingly, at around the same time when the anti-immigrant campaign by the ASSU was picking up but then the ULFA's goal was vastly different: its goal was the establishment of a 'sovereign socialist Assam' and it was evidently secessionist. (Baruah 2005: 145–60) This organization merits our attention not because it was a secessionist, or what Baruah called 'independentist' (Baruah 2005: 145), but because of the fact that after the Central government's apparent success in anti-insurgency campaign called *Operation Rhino* during 1992–93 in Assam, the ULFA surrendered weapons and renounced the path of armed struggle as well as the goal of an independent Assam but 'Assamese Swadhikar' (self-determination) (Baruah 2005: 150). In any case, the organization lost much of its force of militancy by the end of the 1990. To cite another grotesque example: the Mizo National Front (MNF) (formed on 22 October 1961) had its goal of 'democracy, secularism, equality and upliftment of the poor' (as per its Constitution), and was a Mizo ethnic party (still it remains so) but it became highly radicalized in the mid-1960s and led to an uprising in 1966 declaring even 'independence'. This attracted a protracted anti-insurgency operation of the Indian security forces. But this 20-year-long insurgency was ended not simply by the forces of the Indian security apparatus. After the Mizor Accord (1986) (Datta ed. 1995), the ground was opened for both accommodation of identity and political incentives to the rebels. The Mizoram was conceded Statehood – an upgradation from the Union Territory status, which was a major political incentive for the ethnic rebels. The then incumbent Chief Minister from the Congress (INC) had to resign at the instance of the then Prime Minister late Rajiv Gandhi (who was desperate to resolve the Mizo insurgency issue) in favour of Laldenga, the legendary Mizo ethnic rebel leader, on 20 August 1986. In the first post-Statehood State Assembly elections in 1987 INC got 13 seats out of 40, and the Independents (MNF in fact) got 24 and with the People Conference party another four. The MNF formed the Government in 1987 but could not continue the full term. In the next elections in 1989, the MNF lost out to the Congress. The MNF got majority of seats in 1998 and 2003 and governed the State between 1998 and 2008; in 2008 it conceded defeat to the INC again which has been governing the State since 2008. The point that is made here is not the issue of victory or defeat in elections but the fundamental question that the MNF has got used to power-sharing and power-transfer by democratic means. The MNF since 1987 has remained a regional political party committed to parliamentary politics. There have been shift and turns in the political fortune of the MNF as well as of the INC in the State but then that has remained the game of electoral politics into which this party (ethnic rebels turned political party i.e., MNF) has institutionalized itself like its counterparts in other States in the region.

## Negotiation for power-sharing: ethnic peace accords and after

The ethnic peace accords, or more formally, 'Memorandum of Settlement', or simply, 'Agreement' have played an important instrumental role in turning the rebels into stake holders in the North East. Such instrumentality has most often been carried out through the appropriate legislation in favour of implementing the objectives in the accords including territorial concessions to the rebels. This has paved the way for power-sharing between the concerned State governments and the ethnic rebels. The tripartite accords (see Table 3.1) has meant that the Union government has got itself involved as an umpire to instill more confidence in the willing rebels to give up arms and to join the democratic political process in India. However, the leadership change at the Centre, in style and approach, was very important in effecting such methods of resolving conflicts in favour of power-sharing and political order. When late Jawaharlal Nehru was the Prime Minister, only one such accord was signed with the Naga rebels in 1960 (see Table 3.1), and by creating the first tribal ethnic State of Nagaland in 1963 – in the aftermath of the Sino-Indian border conflict in 1962 – the basic objective of the agreement was fulfilled.[2] The territorial concession apart, the sovereignty of the Indian State was shared with the Nagas in terms of the provisions of Article 371-A – which constitutionally recognizes the near absolute legislative sovereignty of the Naga

Table 3.1 Ethnic peace accords in India's North East (1947–2015)[5]

| Name of Accord | Date | Nature | Place | Issue |
| --- | --- | --- | --- | --- |
| Naga-Hydari Accord | 26–28 July 1947 | Bipartite | Kohima | Naga Rights |
| 16-Point Agreement (Naga) | 27–28 July 1960 | Bipartite | Shillong | Naga Statehood |
| Shillong Accord (Naga) | 10–11 November 1975 | Bipartite | Shillong | Surrender of arms |
| Suppl. Shillong Accord (Naga) | 5 January 1976 | Bipartite | Shillong | Surrender of arms and rehabilitation |
| Assam Accord | 15 August 1985 | Tripartite | New Delhi | Foreigners' |
| Mizo Accord | 30 January 1986 | Tripartite | New Delhi | Statehood to Mizoram |
| TNV Accord (Tripura) | 4 May 1988 | Tripartite | New Delhi | Tribal causes |
| 1. ATTE Accord (Tripura) | 23 August 1993 | Bipartite | Agartala | Tribal causes |
| Hmar Accord (Mizoram) | 29 September 1993 | Bipartite | Aizawl | Hmar tribal causes |
| Bodo Peace Accord (Assam) | 20 February 1993 | Tripartite | Guwahati | Bodo tribal causes |
| Bodo Peace Accord | 10 February 2003 | Tripartite | New Delhi | Bodo autonomy |
| Framework** Agreement | 3 August 2015 | Bipartite | Nagaland | Nagalim* |

Sources: Datta (1995) and Chakladar (2004: 72–4).

Notes to 1: The full name was Naga Akbar Hydari; Hydari was the Governor of Assam. Bipartite agreement referred to agreement between the State government and the ethnic rebels. Tripartite agreement included the Union government.

* means greater Nagaland including the Nagas living in the neighbouring States of Assam, Arunachal Pradesh and Manipur.

**The details of this agreement are yet to be available in the public domain.

Legislative Assembly in some vital aspects of the Naga life. Consider the *special provision* of Article 371-A:[3]

Notwithstanding anything contained in this Constitution,

No Act of Parliament in respect of:

i. religious or social practices of the Nagas;
ii. Naga customary law and procedure,
iii. Administration of civil and criminal justice involving decisions according to Naga customary law; and
iv. Ownership and transfer of land and its resources,

Shall apply to the State of Nagaland unless the Legislative Assembly of Nagaland by a resolution so decides.[4]

(Bakshi 2017: 391)

Like the Nagas, similar provisions were inserted in the Mizo Accord in 1986, and the same were incorporated in the 53rd Amendment of the Constitution of India 1986 to provide for the Mizo Statehood; and a new Article 371-G was inserted into the Constitution (Datta 1995: 151–2). Mr Laldenga (1927–90), as we have seen above, was made the Chief Minister in 1986–88, and in 1987 State Assembly elections the MNF took part as a legitimate political party.

In other cases of such accords, the appropriate constitutional amendments have followed and the institutional arrangements for power-sharing have been provided for. For some accords, no territorial issues were involved. But the very signing of the accord[6] with the Union government as a party mattered a lot to the rebels who found reasons to give up arms and join the dialogue as a stepping step to participate in the political process. The famous Assam Accord (1985) (see Table 3.1) was a case in point. The ASSU and ASGSP's sustained agitation paralyzed the State administration as long as five years (1979–85) on the issue of illegal immigrants to Assam mostly from Bangladesh (formerly East Pakistan) and felt apprehensive of the loss of the Assamese identity. Statistically, Assam had registered very high decadal growth of population since 1951 which was 34.98 per cent compared to the previous decade (1941–51: 20.40 per cent). This high growth rate was maintained in the next decades too: 34.95 per cent in 1961–71 (Government of Assam 1999). That the Accord accepted 1/1/1966 as the base year of detection of foreigners in Assam and that those entering Assam illegally after 1966 to be deported/expelled, and also that their names would be deleted from the State Electoral Roll were something the ethnic rebels wanted and agreed. The paragraph 6 of the agreement ('Safeguards and Economic Development') is worth quoting for the satisfaction of Assamese identity:

> Constitutional, legal and administrative safeguards, as may be appropriate, shall be provided to protect, preserve and promote the cultural, social, linguistic identity and heritage of the Assamese people.
>
> (Datta 1995: 37)

But it turned out that since the AGP came to power in 1985 the onus of implementing the terms of the accord fell on it; it was found out that the AGP had had a trying time and failed to implement them – the reason for losing out to Congress in the next elections in 1991.

At the same time, not all peace accords resulted in more durable ethnic peace and political order. The Bodo Accord in 2003 (see Table 3.1), for example, remains a case in point. By the terms of the Accord, the Bodos – plains' tribesmen – were to be recognized and considered for the autonomous powers as under the 6th Schedule of the Indian Constitution. As such, the 6th Schedule of the Constitution was amended in 2003 to provide the Bodoland Territorial Council with additional powers (Bakshi 2017: 427). But, as Bhattacharyya et al. (2017) show, this experiment has failed, and paved the way for more ethnic conflicts and persistent violence in the region. The reason was the huge design problem: the Bodos are in a minority (about 30 per cent) of the population in the areas they claim to be their 'homeland'; and, oddly enough, their demographic numerical minority status has been over-compensated by assuring a political majority in the Council by reserving 30 out of 40 seats for the Bodos while leaving only five seats for the vast majority of non-Bodos comprising various ethnic communities.[7] By one account, about one-fourth of the population including the Bodos is now living in relief camps following ethnic riots and pogroms (Bhattacharyya et al. 2017).

Therefore, the positive effects of ethnic peace accords on peace and more durable order in the region are to be squarely balanced with some negative effects. The ethnic peace accords followed by the constitutional amendments and their implementation have not resolved all ethnic conflicts, but they have provided for power-sharing, and minimized the scope of ethnic conflicts, to a large extent, in the region. For example, after the State of Mizoram was created in 1987, the State's ethnic problems have nearly been resolved except the issue of more autonomy to the existing district council for the Hmar tribes (see Table 3.1). In Meghalaya, there are demands though for territorial restructuring by the Garos, the State's second largest tribes who have been demanding a State for them to be called Garoland. But overall much of *diversity-claims* (Bhattacharyya 2015a) have been met, and the detailed elite surveys (see Chapter 2) in the States show that lack of non-fulfillment of *diversity-claims* was not the major concern in the region. The region's elites were found to be more concerned about development in the wake of India's shifts to neo-liberal reforms.

## *Political participation*

Even if we consider voters as rational choosers, in a democracy political participation is nonetheless an important index of political integration. In the specific context of India's North East democratic political participation following the ethnic peace accords has provided for the method of power-sharing in most cases. From the perspective of the Indian State such participation by the former rebels has signified more political integration. In the existing texts (e.g. Baruah 2005; Bhaumik 2009) on the North East, political participation has remained though a neglected subject. This is not surprising given the excessive preoccupation of the North East watchers with the issue of insurgency.

In India, popular political participation in the all-India level has grown since 1951–52. This has attracted limited scholarly attention (e.g. Mitra and Singh 2009). The data from the Election Commission of India show that out of 17 Lok Sabha elections held since 1951, the overall voter turn-out was above 60 per cent in eight, and in the rest it was not below 53.42 per cent. The highest so far remains the Lok Sabha elections in 2014 which brought the BJP led National Democratic Alliance (NDA) to power with the BJP with a very comfortable absolute majority of seats (282 out of 545) in the house on its own. The last time when a single party (INC) got two-thirds of the seats (445 out of 545) was in 1984 when late Rajiv Gandhi, soon of the slain Prime Minister Indira Gandhi, swept the poll mostly on the sympathy wave.

Popular participation in polling is the most important index of assessing the extent of political integration in the State. A separate detailed research, not taken

# Institutionalization of ethnic radicalism 59

up here, on the dynamics of electoral politics in each State in the region will explain the level of institutionalization in the State concerned. In this section we seek to provide statistical data on the percentage of popular votes polled in the State Assembly and Lok Sabha elections in the States in the region in the post-Statehood and post-accord period.

A causal look at the data in Table 3.2 suggests that popular participation in the national level elections has increased over the years since 1951, and the rate is in many cases, higher than that of the all-India average. In the formerly insurgency-infested States such as Nagaland, Mizoram and Manipur, the rate of political participation is found to have increased in the post-Statehood period. The other important finding is that there is symmetry of political participation in State and national level elections. To take the case of Nagaland: starting with 53.77 per cent popular participation in the post-Statehood period, the rate went up very high with 88.32 per cent in 1996, 91.77 per cent in 2004 and 87.91 per cent in 2014.[8] In most cases, the State's rate of popular participation has been higher than that of the all-India average. The data in Table 3.2 strongly suggest that the States in the region or the people of the region are well-integrated with the democratic political process in India.

The select State-level electoral data on popular participation in the elections to the State Assemblies doubly corroborate our argument of political integration of the region into the democratic political process of India. It is found out that in the post-Statehood period, the rate of popular participation has increased at a higher rate in Nagaland, Mizoram, Meghalaya, Manipur and Tripura.

The higher rate of participation has been correlated with the higher level of literacy in the case of Nagaland, Mizoram and Meghalaya and partly in Tripura, but the institutionalized multi-party competition has played the most important part in this. Over the decades since 1951, the presence of Independents as candidates in the electoral fray has been limited so that it is a political competition for power-sharing, wholly or in part (in coalition) among the political parties, national as well as State-based. In Mizoram, the greater ethnic homogeneity coupled with high rate of literacy remains a factor of internal cohesion which is politically reflected in the very high turn-out. But even in an ethnically divided Meghalaya, the rate of popular participation has been high too.

Manipur has experienced ethnic violence to a greater extent than others, but in the post-Statehood period, the popular participation in the State has defied all experience of violence in queuing up for casting their votes in greater numbers. Starting with 75.89 per cent in 1972, the rate went up to 85.87 per cent in 2013.

In Tripura, the sharply ethnically polarized State, the higher popular participation in elections at the State and the national levels is to be explained with reference to the highly institutionalized bi-polar political competition and the hegemony of the Left, to be precise, the CPI-M. The better organized and very disciplined party that the CPI-M is has meant that political mobilization led by the party is not episodic, that is, in times of a particular election, but an ongoing process. Starting with 67.36 per cent in 1972, the rate went up to 91. 82 per cent in 2013.

Table 3.2 Popular participation in Lok Sabha elections in the North East (1951–2014)

| No of Election | Polling Year | Arunachal Pradesh (%) | Assam (%) | Manipur (%) | Meghalaya (%) | Mizoram (%) | Nagaland (%) | Sikkim (%) | Tripura (%) | All-India Turn-out Percentage |
|---|---|---|---|---|---|---|---|---|---|---|
| 1st Lok Sabha Election | 1951 | – | 47.96 | 51.07 | – | – | – | – | – | 44.87 |
| 2nd Lok Sabha Election | 1957 | – | 46.14 | 52.72 | – | – | – | – | 47.72 | 45.44 |
| 3rd Lok Sabha Election | 1962 | – | 52.75 | 65.34 | – | – | – | – | 63.56 | 55.42 |
| 4th Lok Sabha Election | 1967 | – | 54.99 | 67.24 | – | – | – | – | 67.96 | 61.04 |
| 5th Lok Sabha Election | 1971 | – | 50.69 | 48.86 | – | – | 53.77 | – | 74.84 | 55.27 |
| 6th Lok Sabha Election | 1977 | 24.47 | 54.88 | 60.12 | 49.88 | 49.92 | 52.83 | 0.00 | 60.85 | 60.49 |
| 7th Lok Sabha Election | 1980 | 68.60 | 53.37 | 81.65 | 51.23 | 56.12 | 63.9 | 44.47 | 70.07 | 56.92 |
| 8th Lok Sabha Election | 1984 | 75.46 | 77.40 (1985) | 85.75 | 54.47 | 0.00** | 66.46 | 57.64 | 79.97 | 63.56 |
| 9th Lok Sabha Election | 1989 | 59.17 | * | 71.76 | 51.92 | 58.26 | 74.71 | 72.01 | 77.32 | 61.95 |
| 10th Lok Sabha Election | 1991 | 51.28 | 75.25 | 69.65 | 53.75 | 58.64 | 77.07 | 58.75 | 83.89 | 56.73 |
| 11th Lok Sabha Election | 1996 | 55.04 | 78.50 | 75.04 | 61.62 | 73.41 | 88.32 | 77.43 | 67.28 | 57.94 |
| 12th Lok Sabha Election | 1998 | 59.17 | 61.06 | 56.83 | 74.38 | 69.56 | 45.41 | 67.14 | 79.09 | 61.97 |
| 13th Lok Sabha Election | 1999 | 72.15 | 71.26 | 65.67 | 56.16 | 65.31 | 76.25 | 81.71 | 80.86 | 59.99 |
| 14th Lok Sabha Election | 2004 | 56.35 | 69.11 | 67.41 | 52.69 | 63.6 | 91.77 | 77.95 | 68.14 | 58.07 |
| 15th Lok Sabha Election | 2009 | 68.17 | 69.54 | 77.31 | 64.38 | 51.86 | 90 | 83.93 | 67.08 | 58.21 |
| 16th Lok Sabha Election | 2014 | 78.12 | 80.12 | 79.75 | 68.80 | 61.95 | 87.91 | 83.64 | 84.55 | 66.44 |

Source: eci.nic.in/eci_mail/statistical_Reports. (sighted on 4/10/17)

* Ninth Lok Sabha Elections (1989) in Assam were not held. The blank space in the columns mean that the States were not created yet or elections could not be held. Sikkim was incorporated into the Union of India in 1974; it became a State in 1975 and part of the North East in 2012.

Finally, higher level of popular participation in elections at various levels of the polity has provided the political parties with the method available to share power and govern.

## Governance

### Political violence

In the conventional literature on measurement of governance in India the riots and murder per million of population have been used to show the decline in governance, meaning mostly deterioration in law and order (Kohli 1990). These are important components because such occurrences are a serious threat to human life and living as such, and cause for much concern for the politicians facing an election. Thus, the region's (except Sikkim) contribution to the incidence of riots, as defined in the Indian Penal Code (IPC) – implying defiance of law in public – [9] to all India (Table 3.2) remained high and stable with higher picks in the late 1970s and early 1980s. The anti-foreigners' campaign in Assam in the late 1970s and early 1980 contributed a lot to the total amount of riots in the region. Tripura also added to it by the inter-ethnic riots in the State in 1980–81 and the resultant effects (Bhattacharyya 1999).

The data in Figure 3.1 show the number of deaths in violent conflicts in the region since the early 1990s up to 2015 but it shown that most of the deaths took place in Assam, the largest unit in terms of population, and also that from 2000 the trend has been downwards. Manipur scored the second position in terms of the number of deaths; even when the trend went downwards for Assam, in Manipur it went high again during 2006–10. The data from SATP *(Figure 3.1)* do not tell us the optimal level of deaths from violent conflicts to be considered for the measurement of decline in governance. But it makes clear that the decline in the number of deaths from 800 in the late 1979s and early 1980s to less than 200 in the early 2000s is welcome indications for improvement in governance. The rise and decline, and rise again, in the figures of murder due to ethnic conflicts is to read in terms of the specific ethnic conflicts (the anti-foreigners' campaign by the ASSU in the late 1970s and early 1980s, and the Bodoland conflicts since the 1990s). While the former has somewhat been resolved after the Assam Accord in 1985 and the coming to power of the AGP, the Bodoland Accord of 2003 and the application of the 6th Schedule to the Bodos the same year has not brought any solution to the issue but created more ethnic conflicts. However, on the methodological plane, the question remains: first, do such rounded figures of riots, murders and other violent crimes tell us much about the management of crimes, the adequacy or not of the apparatus of the State in dealing with crimes and the deterrents such as the speedy disposal of crimes, and punishment, if any, meted out? Second, the importance of such crime data – very important though they are – is today considered in association with a host of other indices of governance such as the delivery of services and empowerment on a whole set of public goods and facilities.

*Table 3.3* Incidence of riots (IPC defined): North East and (all) India (1959–93)

| Year | North East | All India | NE's % to India |
|---|---|---|---|
| 1959 | 1,294 | 24,992 | 5.7 |
| 1969 | 4,787 | 76,655 | 8.58 |
| 1971 | 3,620 | 64,114 | 5.6 |
| 1972 | 3,544 | 65,781 | 5.38 |
| 1974 | 4,533 | 80,547 | 5.68 |
| 1975 | 4,254 | 67,241 | 6.32 |
| 1977 | 4,425 | 80,449 | 5.5 |
| 1978 | 5,489 | 96,488 | 7.8 |
| 1981 | 6,611 | 110,361 | 5.9 |
| 1982 | 6,846 | 106,511 | 6.42 |
| 1983 | 10,635 | 108,101 | 9.83 |
| 1986 | 4,776 | 94,197 | 5.07 |
| 1988 | 5,546 | 94,587 | 5.86 |
| 1989 | 5,339 | 94,587 | 5.86 |
| 1990 | 5,596 | 102,846 | 0.05 |
| 1991 | 4,786 | 105,309 | 4.54 |
| 1992 | 5,285 | 104,749 | 5.04 |
| 1993 | 5,117 | 93,838 | 5.45 |

Source: *Crime in India* (relevant years) (Ministry of Home Affairs, Govt. of India, New Delhi).

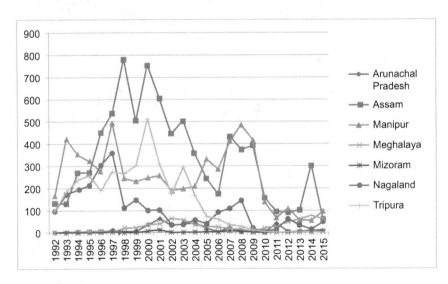

*Figure 3.1* Number of deaths in violent conflicts in the States of India's North East (1992–2015)

Notes: Data adapted from South Asia Terrorism Portal (2015).[10]

Rajeev Malhotra (2014), the statistician, has developed *a set of* better statistical tools to measure 'governance'[11] in terms of four (composite) variables. And he has developed a composite index of what he calls Public Policy Effectiveness Index (PEI for short). In this composite index he has included as a component a broader index of measuring what is conventionally called 'law and order', or crimes, for explaining the decline in governance Kohli's (1990). He calls it the Rule of Law Index (ROLI for short) which entails again a number of sub-variables such as IPC defined crimes, crimes defined as per the State and local laws; police personnel–people ratio; registration and disposal of cases and the crime against women.

Before we proceed further, there is a new methodological point to be highlighted. Generally, there is a correlation between the ROLI and the other indices of governance such as the delivery of services and goods, or the absence of it.[12] In other words, better policy outcomes, on the one hand and better ROLI effects, on the other, can only be presumed as a general inference but may not be directly seen correlated in the short run. That is to say, as it will be evident soon, there can indeed be an inverse relation between the ROLI and better policy outcome in the other realms. Also, there may also be an inverse relation between better 'development' and the ROLI effects.

## *Public policy effectiveness*

In Malhotra's methodological innovation, the individual constituents (four in number) of Public Policy Effectiveness Index (PEI) individually and together show the extent of policy outcome that has taken place in the State in the North East during 1981–2011. Thus, the PEI is proportional to four variables such as Rule of Law Index, Physical Infrastructure Index, Livelihood Opportunity Index (combined) and Social Opportunity Index. Each of them again is composite index comprising a set of sub-variables.

It is seen from (Figure 3.2) that all the States in region show improvement in 2011 over 1981 in PEI which in most cases are better than all-India average. The data in Table 3.9 show that the trend of improvement in PEI was maintained between 2001 and 2011. Malhotra's Public Policy Effectiveness Index suggests human well-being 'collectively secured' (p. 11). The better record of PEI in the North East has helped them score better rank (Table 3). Five out of eight States' records of rank in the PEI are higher than India's advanced States and two Left-run States of Kerala and West Bengal until 2011. Over all Manipur, Meghalaya, Mizoram, Nagaland and Sikkim are the highest scorers. In fact, Sikkim remained the highest of all Indian States and Union Territories during 2001–11. In comparison, the ranks of the so-called 'advanced States' of India such as Tamil Nadu, Maharashtra and Andhra Pradesh (Figure 3.3) are in the range of medium to low performance. Gujarat has done far better than the rest; its rank position improved from 25 in 1981 to 18 in 1991 and 17 in 2001, but it went down to 24 in 2011. Kerala and Wet Bengal fell in the same category, but both went down during 2001–11. But these States except Kerala and West Bengal made remarkable

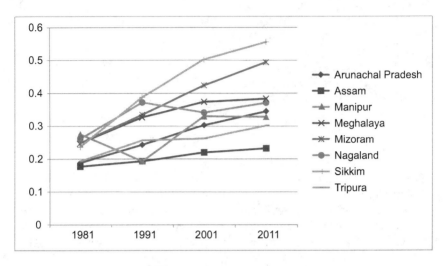

*Figure 3.2* Public policy effectiveness index in India's North East (1981–2011)
Source: Prepared on the basis of data in Malhotra (2014: 148–9).

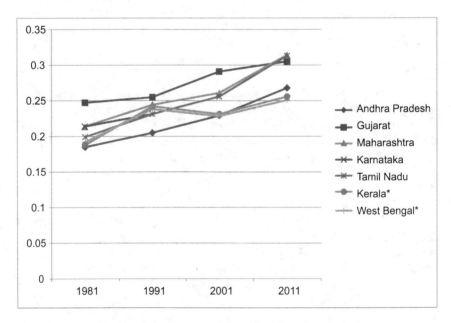

*Figure 3.3* Policy effectiveness index in India's advanced States (1981–2011)
Source: Prepared on the basis of data in Malhotra (2014: 148)

*Institutionalization of ethnic radicalism* 65

improvement in their performance in PEI. The latter two also improved but at a lower rate.

As noted earlier, the PEI gives us an overall perspective of the performance records of the State governments. Since the PEI is a function of four sub-variables (which themselves are composite), the performance of individual variables may be inconsistent with the overall PEI and that of other individual variants.

The dwindling ROLI records of Tripura between 2001 and 2011 are to be explained with particular reference to the State's volatile inter-ethnic relations, which give birth to political insurgency and the resultant violence. Kumar (2016), an experienced top police officer in the State, argues that 'insurgency is never ended in Tripura', and the State experiences the growth in insurgency during election times. The records show that the States had had elections to the tribal council (ADC) in 2000, State Assembly elections in 2004 and again in 2008. Kumar rightly advises us to consider too Tripura's international border with Bangladesh on three sides which facilitates cross-border insurgency.

### Rule of law

It is seen from Figure 3.4 that Mizoram's performance in ROLI improved manifold since Statehood in 1986. Nagaland and Meghalaya performed very well in the post-Statehood period in 1963 and 1972 respectively. Sikkim performed very well all along. Arunachal Pradesh showed improvement in ROLI from 1991

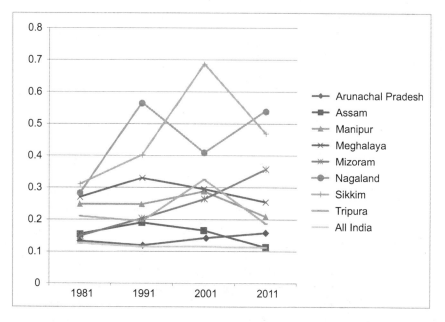

*Figure 3.4* Rule of law index in India's North East (1981–2011)
Source: Malhotra (2014).

66  *Institutionalization of ethnic radicalism*

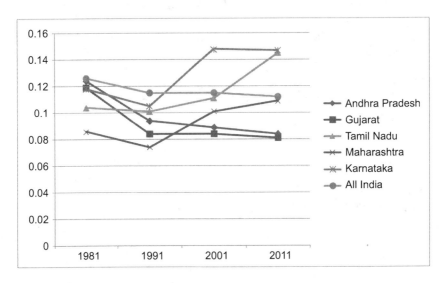

*Figure 3.5* Rule of law index in India's advanced States (1981–2011)

(Statehood accorded in 1987). Assam's story is very interesting: it improved in the post-1985 (Accord) period when the ethnic rebels (AGP) were in power from 1985–1989 but deteriorated since due to the relative failure of the AGP government to implement the very objectives the party had fought for, and the powerful challenge of the Bodoland movement ever since.

Tripura' dwindling records in the ROLI had very little to do with Statehood (in 1972) or accommodation of tribal ethnicity but with the sudden change of government in 1988 (-93) by a coalition of the Congress and the TUJS and the frequent cabinet reshuffle and political chaos following it.[13] With the return of the Left Front in 1993 the situation improved reflected in 2001 (0.325) but it slipped again since 2001. Very interestingly, Tripura's poorest record in the thirty years in 1981–2001 of 0.187 (2011) remained nonetheless the highest of all the so-called advanced States of India. No wonder, the border States are always vulnerable with the ever presence ethnic militants seeking to threaten law and order, and often are being successful in doing so. The persistence of inter-ethnic discord remains the potent source of delivering violence.

The interesting finding is that growth and development in terms of more FDI and other indicators of development in the so-called advanced States in India do not go with better law and order, or what Malhotra calls the rule of law in the same. In the conventional measurement of governance *a la* Kohli (1990), India's so-called advanced States would have been considered as low performers. By contrast, the States in India's North East are better performers both in the conventional and current measurement of governance. Malhotra (2014) has concluded: 'North Eastern states show an overall fall in the IPC crime rates over the period 1981 to 2011, they also have a low SLL crime rate as compared to the national average' (Malhotra 2014: 52). This assessment is corroborated by the official records of the Ministry of Development of North Eastern Region (2012).

## *Social inclusion in India's North East*

Social inclusion is an essential part of democratic governance in a country of manifold discrimination and inequalities (Bhattacharyya et al. 2010). Democracy is nothing if it is not inclusionary. In the specific context of governance in India, social inclusion has entailed a whole set of public policy intervention that is targeted at the socially and economically disadvantaged groups in India such as the Scheduled Castes and Scheduled Tribes. The aim of the policy has been whether the accessibility to such public goods as safe drinking water, sanitation, electricity, literacy and various forms of economic inclusion has increased or not. In this section we will examine the effects of social inclusionary measures in respect of sanitation, safe drinking water, electricity and literacy in the North East. Needless to point out, more social inclusion there is, more empowered the people are. The socially included people are better enabled to take advantage of the opportunities available.

The available data suggest that in the two decades since 1991 a good measure of social inclusion for the Scheduled Castes (*dalits*) has taken place in the States in the North East. The percentage of people without access to electricity, safe drinking water and sanitation has decreased progressively. The people in the rural areas (figures within brackets) too have better access to safe drinking water, electricity and sanitation. The level of performance of the States in the region is comparable to all India; some States such as Tripura and Mizoram are better performer than India as a whole.

The Scheduled Tribes (STs) which predominate in five States out of eight in the region, and with their significant presence in the other (e.g. in Tripura, they constitute about 30 per cent of the total population) have been able to better access

*Table 3.4* Scheduled caste households without electricity, safe drinking water and sanitation (1991–2011) in India's North East (figures within bracket are for rural areas)

| States | 1991 | 2001 | 2011 |
| --- | --- | --- | --- |
| Arunachal Pradesh | 18.9 (20.7) | 9.5 (16.0) | N. A |
| Assam | 35.4 (39.5) | 16.3 (19.2) | 4.7 (5.5) |
| Manipur | 31.6 (37.5) | 6.5 (8.1) | 5.5 (8.5) |
| Meghalaya | 28.7 (41.8) | 13.9 (23.2) | 10.6 (16.2) |
| Mizoram | 11.7 (34.0) | 2.9 (8.8) | 2.6 (5.8) |
| Nagaland | – | – | – |
| Sikkim | 34.2 (40.1) | 20.7 (25.0) | 11.3 (13.5) |
| Tripura | 15.3 (17.7) | 5.3 (6.2) | 0.7 (0.9) |
| All India | 28.7 (32.1) | 13.3 (15.6) | 3.9 (4.7) |

Source: Adapted from the data in Malhotra (2014: 234).

68  Institutionalization of ethnic radicalism

Table 3.5 Scheduled tribe households without electricity, safe drinking water and sanitation in India's North East (1991–2011) (figures within bracket are for rural areas)

| States | 1991 | 2001 | 2011 |
| --- | --- | --- | --- |
| Arunachal Pradesh | 15.7 (16.6) | 10.7 (12.3) | 10.2 (12.5) |
| Assam | 56.2 (58) | 34 (36.8) | 23.2 (25.1) |
| Manipur | 33.5 (36.7) | 19.6 (20.6) | 8.7 (9.8) |
| Meghalaya | 50.9 (57.9) | 32.2 (38.1) | 17.2 (20.6) |
| Mizoram | 19.0 (36.6) | 7.8 (15.1) | 3.8 (4.9) |
| Nagaland | 17 (18.7) | 8.2 (9.2) | 3.8 (4.9) |
| Sikkim | 13.8 (15) | 8.6 (9.5) | 1.9 (2.4) |
| Tripura | 52.3 (53.4) | 34.2 (35.3) | 22.9 (24) |
| All India | 45.3 (48.1) | 31.2 (33.3) | 13.4 (17.4) |

Source: Adapted from Malhotra (2014: 235)

Table 3.6 Literacy rate among the scheduled castes in North East India (1981–2011) (figures are in percentage)

| States | 1981 | 1991 | 2001 | 2011 |
| --- | --- | --- | --- | --- |
| Arunachal Pradesh | 62.3 | 63.59 | 67.64 | NA* |
| Assam | NA^ | 53.94 | 66.78 | 66.76 |
| Manipur | 51.5 | 56.44 | 62.73 | 66.36 |
| Meghalaya | 47.6 | 44.27 | 56.27 | 59.20 |
| Mizoram | 70.8 | 77.92 | 89.20 | 83.25 |
| Nagaland | NA | NA | NA | NA** |
| Sikkim | 60.06 | 61.3 | 63.04 | 67.90 |
| Tripura | 67.1 | 74.7 | 74.68 | 78.92 |
| **All India** | 21.38 | 37.41 | 54.9 | 56.49 |

Sources: Adapted from Malhotra (2014: 174); various census report of India; and the North Eastern Council Secretariat, Shillong, of the DoNER (2012)

\* the Scheduled Caste population in Arunachal Pradesh is very small in number only 6188 persons in 2001.
\*\* There are no Scheduled Castes in Nagaland.
^ No census took place in Assam in 1981.

to safe drinking water, sanitation and electricity during 1991–2011. Only Assam and Tripura a significant percentage of tribes remain still without access to the facilities although these two States registered progressive increase of the tribes to access them. The gap between the urban and rural areas in respect of accessibility has been progressively bridged.

Another marker of social inclusion is literacy. We find that (Table 3.9) during 1981–2011 the SCs in the region with good concentration in Assam, Manipur and Tripura have increased their percentage of literacy progressively since 1981. In this respect, the States have outperformed India as a whole. Tripura is the highest scorer. Assam has remained though a slow performer.

*Table 3.7* Literacy rate among the scheduled tribes in India's North East (1981–2011) (Figures are in percentage.)

| States | 1981 | 1991 | 2001 | 2011 |
| --- | --- | --- | --- | --- |
| Arunachal Pradesh | 14.04 | 34.45 | 49.62 | 54.34 |
| Assam | N. A* | N. A* | 62.52 | 61.69 |
| Manipur | 39.74 | 53.63 | 65.85 | 67.06 |
| Meghalaya | 31.55 | 46.71 | 61.74 | 59.73 |
| Mizoram | 59.63 | 82.73 | 89.34 | 77.33 |
| Nagaland | 40.32 | 60.59 | 65.95 | 68.15 |
| Sikkim | 33.13 | 59.01 | 67.14 | 71.28 |
| Tripura | 23.01 | 40.37 | 56.48 | 63.17 |
| All India | 16.35 | 29.60 | 47.10 | 49.52 |

Source: Adapted from Malhotra (2014: 175).

* No census could be taken in Assam due to political conflict in the 1980s and early 1990s.

In the case of Scheduled Tribes (STs) (Table 3.7) all the State show progressive increase over 1981 although the real push took place since 1991. The better growth in literacy among the STs in Mizoram, Nagaland and Sikkim as against the other tribal dominated States of Meghalaya, and Arunachal Pradesh is to be explained with reference to greater ethnic homogeneity in the States concerned. Inter-ethnic conflicts affect the smooth delivery of services across the people. Arunachal Pradesh is a very sparsely populated State so the delivery of services in this States is more difficult than the other States. And yet, the increase in literacy has taken place among the STs in this State. When placed in relation to the achievement of Statehood, we find that only Mizoram has shown remarkable progress in the level of literacy among the STs from 59.63 per cent to 82.73 per cent in 1991. Arunachal Pradesh has done so but only to a limited scale.

Nagaland achieved Statehood way back in 1963 but the level of literacy among the STs (who are nearly the whole of its population) remained poor at 40.32 per cent until 1981. Tripura received Statehood in 1972 but the STs in the State were only 23.13 per cent literate in 1981. The growth in literacy among the STs in Tripura is a post-1980 development associated with the rise to power of the Left Front (that is, the CPI-M) committed to the tribal cause. But the persistent inter-ethnic conflicts in the State remain a factor in Tripura. Manipur and Meghalaya also have significant areas of ethnic conflicts – the Naga problems in Manipur and the Garos in Meghalaya, for instance. Thus, a case can be made here for the inverse relation between ethnic diversity and conflicts, on the one hand, and efficient service delivery, on the other hand, but this requires more in-depth research and analysis.

## Conclusion

This chapter has argued with detailed data how ethnic radicalism in the North East has been transformed into legitimate stakeholders in India's democratic political process. Compared to other regions of India, most notably the South, an extra mile had to be travelled in the North East to make this transformation possible. The instrumentality of ethnic peace accords preceded by many rounds of 'informal discussion' with the rebels and its subsequent implementation through the appropriate legislation in favour of some territorial concessions and or more powers to the existing ones has most often worked. The non-territorial recognition of identity has gone in tandem. The territorial concession has often to be made for the sub-State-level power-sharing. Thus, there are many Autonomous Tribal District Councils within the tribal ethnic States such as Meghalaya and Mizoram. In Tripura, the ADC has institutionalized tribal ethnic identity since 1985 (under the 6th Schedule) in areas that constitute two-thirds of the territory of Tripura. This has offered a successful solution to tribal ethnic radicalism in the State. The States in the region have demonstrated with remarkable records their ability to govern – maintaining a high level of rule of law; and delivering public goods to the socially disadvantaged so that social inclusion does not remain a mere laudable and hallowed electoral promise but a reality in these, strategically, sensitive border States. Finally, our analysis suggests a major revision of perspective in understanding the North East that abjures the so-called 'durable disorder' hypothesis (Baruah 2005) or the 'insurgency approach' in favour of an alternative radical institutionalization approach through ethnic peace accords, negotiated power-sharing and participation, and governance for more enduring ethnic peace and political order in the midst of democracy and diversity.

## Notes

1 A number of its leaders were assassinated by the extremist wing of the ABSU in 1968. The surviving PTCA took part in elections since 1972 but its support bases were very limited: it got one seat in 1972; four in 1978; three in 1983 and 1985 but drew a blank in 1991 (Election Commission of India website).
2 The issue of incorporation of the contiguous areas inhabited by the Nagas (for example, in Arunachal Pradesh, Assam, and Manipur) was placed as the desire of the Naga leaders but no commitment was made on behalf of the Union government. But it was mentioned that Articles 3 & 4 of the Constitution were designed to address those problem in future. (Datta 1995: 160).
3 Inserted by the appropriate Constitutional amendment (13th Amendment Act 1962 (w.e.f 1/12/1963).
4 This provision was the carbon copy of paragraph 7 of the '16-Point Agreement' with the Nagas in 1960 (see Table 3.1). Going one step backward, this echoes also the spirit of the Naga Akbar Hydari agreement in 1947. (See Table 3.1).
5 It is learnt that many 'informal' meetings with the rebels have preceded the formal signing of the peace accords.
6 They were usually preceded by several rounds of informal discussions with the rebels or their representatives.
7 Five seats are to be filled by nomination by the State Governor.
8 Electoral data used here are from the website of the Election Commission of India of various years.
9 It does not mean *prima facie* any violent clashes but assembly of four persons or more with arms.
10 The SAP data may need to be read cautiously as to its veracity.
11 He prefers though the term 'well-being'.

12 Malhotra has not paid attention to this.
13 The new Congress-TUJS coalition government which took over on 2 February 1988, dissolved on 10 February the Agartala and other Municipalities in which were democratically elected; all elected Panchayats (rural government bodies) were also dissolved the following day. On 18 February the repressive law NASA (detention without trial) was introduced in the State. On 12 October as many as 15 political murders took place in Birchandra Manu in Tripura (Roy 2015: 12).

# 4 Roots of radical politics in Tripura
## Princely State; demographic, social and economic transformations

## Introduction

The roots of radical politics, Left and ethnic, in Tripura need to be traced to the princely regime prior to its accession to the Union of India (15th October 1949), the major demographic and socio-economic changes that took place in the State since the nineteenth century, and more particularly, in the period of the Partition of India and its aftermath, and the resultant new ethnic division of power. While Tripura was a princely State[1] like others numbering about 561 in India, and Manipur in the North East, the State's 'independence' from the British colonial rule in India was only nominal. The princely rulers in Tripura since the late eighteenth century (when Tripura came under the control of the East India Company) had to pay revenues to the Company (and later to the Crown), as the State was brought under the Permanent Settlement Act of 1793, and to cover all maintenance of the British Political Resident in the State. The rulers in turn imposed higher levels of taxation on the peasants and the tribals, and were very oppressive and violent in the event of non-payment of taxes by the poorer peasants and tribals.

This chapter seeks to provide a critical account of the nature of princely regime in Tripura, the demographic and socio-economic changes that took place in the State since the late eighteen century, and the implications of the same for the rise of various brands of radical politics by the different tribal groups in the State. The detailed statistical and updated data provided are meant to cover the period up to the present and explain the implications of the changes since the early 1980s.

## Location

The State of Tripura occupies a narrow strip of land on India's North East, 182 km long and nowhere more than 112 km in width. Its 3.7 million people are slightly higher than the population of Wales in the United Kingdom. It is surrounded on three sides by Bangladesh (formerly East Pakistan, and before that, East Bengal during the British colonial rule in India), with its only geographical link with the rest of India through the Cachar district of Assam in the north. With an area of 10,491 sq. km., it is a small hilly State by Indian standards. It has a small proportion (24.5 per cent) of arable land which is mainly rain-irrigated, and in the hills, exclusively so. Its forest resources, though not negligible, have been affected by the burning associated with age-old shifting cultivation methods of the tribals.

Topographically, the State is similar to the Chittagong Hill Tracts (now in Bangladesh). Tripura's six principal hill ranges increasing in height towards the east, run north to south, with an average interval of 18 km. Along the northwestern and southern boundaries of the State lies a narrow strip of low land differing in no material respects as regards soil, agriculture and population from the adjoining districts of Bangladesh. Along the western border, for some kilometres to the north and south of Agartala, the State capital, the State may be described as a broken ground consisting of hillock and marshy valleys. These hills are utilized for homesteads and the valleys were converted into rice fields long ago. The lowlying plains in the western and southern boundaries of the State are comparatively more fertile and accommodate about two-thirds of the population of the State. This region, geographically, is part of the Brahmaputra-Ganga Plains.

## Princely State and formation of the State

Tripura[2] was an ancient tribal kingdom. The *Rajmala*, the surviving chronicle of the Tripur dynasty, suggests that this tribal kingdom was founded in the fifteenth century. Tripura came under the control of the British East India Company in 1765, but a Political Agent symbolizing imperial control was not appointed until 1871. From 1871 until 1947, Tripura remained a princely State (or what was known derogatorily as 'native State') meaning that there was only indirect British rule over it. From the late nineteenth century onwards, tribal rulers of Tripura incorporated many of the features of the British administrative and legal structures as introduced already in neighbouring Bengal as part of the State formation process, and aimed at modernization in the form of strong internal administration and establishing more control over resources. This process was, however, highly bureaucratic and not accompanied by any mass movement. But despite those changes, the State remained a form of absolute monarchy based on a semi-feudal social structure until 1947 effectively but formally 1949 when it acceded to the Union of India.[3]

Historically, Tripura only very vaguely shared India's culture.[4] It remained a very sparsely tribal society, and its political structure underwent very little change. Elsewhere I have described the administrative structures of the State as well as the hierarchical feudal social structures (Bhattacharyya 1999: 32–5). The high degree of princely repression, and high-handedness (especially in matters of tax collection) coupled with little administrative and social reforms favouring the subjects meant that many tribal-peasants revolts visited Tripura from the second half of the nineteenth century (Bhattacharyya 1999: 35–7). The major such rebellion took place during 1943–45 which dismantled the princely region in parts of the State (discussed at length in Chapter 5).

The Bengali language was adopted as the court language in the nineteenth century, and by 1872 when the first (inexact) official census was taken, the tribal population of Tripura had fallen to 63.76 per cent. The data in Table 4.1 show that due to the policies of the princely rulers of Tripura, the tribal kingdom was already receiving Bengali migrants from across the border (quite porous), and the neighbouring *zamindary*[5] at Chaklarosnabad or simply Rosnabad of the Maharaja of Tripura located within the then neighbouring East Bengal facilitated such migration.

The princely State of Tripura suffered perennially from the lack of effective governance. The State was very repressive, and even the late payment, let alone non-payment, of rent could meet with the severest punishment. The peasant had no rights to the land they tilled, and the issue of individual civil rights was a far cry. The application of armed forces even for the collection of taxes was not uncommon. Tribal revolts and uprisings characterized much of the history of this State for a century and a half since the beginning of the nineteenth century. Alexander Mackenzie (1888), the British colonial official, while commenting on why there were persistent tribal and peasant conflict in the State, wrote:

> The late demand of rent and the manner in which the Raja has set about the collection viz., at the point of bayonet is the only reason for the combination of among the Tipperas.[6] The Raja's conduct in sending out a number of armed officials to collect rent, in afterwards cutting off and hanging up the heads of the murdered men – were sufficient reason accounting for the disturbances.[7]

Nabin Chandra Sen, the famous nineteenth century Bengali novelist and poet who was a sub divisional officer at neighbouring Feni within the British jurisdiction lamented about the state of governance in Tripura as: 'The Tripura State was, as if, fallen from the grace of God. I have never heard of the peace and happiness of this state' (Bhattacharyya 1999: 36). It was a common practice in Tripura that punishment for felling a tree without the ruler's permission could be execution (Bhattacharyya 1999: 34). In his 'Tour Impressions' of the State in the late 1940s, the Political Resident, the high ranking British colonial official wrote rather contemptuously:

> My chief impression in the state is of one of stagnation. This is apparent on all sides and in all branches of the administration, due to inertia at the top. The ruler takes little confirmed interest in anything. And the Chief Minister's guided principle is to do nothing. All subordinate officials follow his example and those who at times may have energy and enthusiasm have eventually been discarded.

The Political Resident for the Eastern States, Mr H. J. Todd found Tripura, a year earlier, in his *Tour Impressions*, to be 'one of the most ramshackle administrations in India', the one which, he believed, 'should be one of the earliest in India for political agitators to topple over' (Bhattacharyya 1999: 36). As British colonialism in India was drawing to a close, large-scale tribal rebellions, first by the Reangs, the second largest tribe in the State, and much oppressed by the rulers dominated by the majority Tripura tribe, and then the Tripuris themselves under the Left-inspired Tripura Upajati Gana Mukti Parishad (GMP) (Tripura Tribal Liberation Council) virtually broke down the princely State. Those uprising were essentially ethnic, or sub nationalist in nature, and acquired mass bases. As we will see, Tripura experienced as series of radical tribal rebellions and mobilizations since the late 1930s which virtually broke down the princely feudal regime. The movement by the GMP during 1948–51, the most critical period in Tripura's accession to India, through a violent mass mobilization against the already disintegrating princely State completed the break-up of the old regime, set up alternative democratic forms of governance in parts of Tripura under its control, advocated strongly in favour a democratic (and multi-ethnic) government in Tripura and paved the way for Tripura's integration with the evolving democratic State in India.[8] Such popular mass mobilizations from below, and the mass bases that they acquired prepared the ground for experimenting with democratic forms of governance. That the India State has remained, more or less, democratic is not because the elites simply chose it that way, but because given the popular democratic pressures from below, the choice was democratically limited. In other words, historically, popular democratic pressures from below in Tripura, as much as in India generally, have meant checks on the development of a centralizing and authoritarian State. Tripura's accession to India in 1949, and then its integration with the Indian Union implied also the democratic transition in Tripura after centuries of autocratic and repressive governance.

## Demographic upheaval and ethnic conflicts

Since the nineteenth century, Tripura has experienced demographic upheavals which resulted in the major transformations in the newly emerging rural class structure. The roots of persistent ethnic conflicts in the State and radical politics lay in those changes. Tripura remains the only State in India and the North East, in particular, where migration of people (mostly land hungry peasants) from neighouring Bengal districts resulted turned the State from a tribal dominated to one in which the original tribal inhabitants found themselves to be reduced to a minority. The growing ethnic conflicts in Tripura have been rooted in the demographic transformation of the State as a result of the migration of the Bengalis to Tripura. The demographic changes in Tripura show a progressive increase of the

With an area of some 10,486 sq km and about 3.7 million (2011) inhabitants, Tripura, is a small State by Indian standards. It is a landlocked region with no access to coastal waters. It has a limited arable land (about 24.5 per cent) with unpromising results. What is of special importance to us here is the demographic transformation of Tripura from the nineteenth century onwards. Although the post-Partition influx of Bengali refugees (Bhattacharyya 1999: 325–47) was a major turning point in upsetting Tripura's demography, the migration of Bengalis into Tripura had been a long-drawn historical process, the one that was partly encouraged by the princely rulers who actively promoted Bengali settlement in their domain, and partly due to heavy pressures of population on land in the erstwhile East Bengal/East Pakistan (now Bangladesh) (Bhattacharyya 1999: 37).

*Table 4.1* Decadal growth of population in Tripura (1881–2011) (census years)

| Year | Total population | Decadal variation (%) | Total tribal population | Percentage of tribal population |
|------|------------------|----------------------|-------------------------|-------------------------------|
| 1881 | 95, 635 | 28.32 | 49, 915 | 52.18% |
| 1891 | 1, 37, 375 | 43.64 | 70, 292 | 51.16% |
| 1901 | 1, 73, 325 | 26.17 | 91, 669 | 52.88% |
| 1911 | 2, 29, 613 | 32.48 | 1, 11, 303 | 48.47% |
| 1921 | 3, 04, 437 | 32.59 | 1, 71, 610 | 52.24% |
| 1931 | 3, 82, 450 | 25.63 | 1, 92, 224 | 50.26% |
| 1941 | 5, 13, 0 10 | 34.14 | 2, 56, 991 | 50.09% |
| 1951 | 6, 89, 029 | 24.56 | 2, 38, 953 | 34.68% |
| 1961 | 11, 42, 005 | 81.71 | 3, 60, 070 | 31.53% |
| 1971 | 15, 56, 342 | 36.28 | 4, 50, 454 | 28.95% |
| 1981 | 20, 53, 058 | 31.91 | 5, 62, 990 | 27.42% |
| 1991 | 27, 57, 205 | 34.30 | 8, 57, 345 | 31.09% |
| 2001 | 31, 91, 168 | 16.03 | 9, 93, 426 | 31.1% |
| 2011 | 36, 71, 032 | 14.75 | 11,7, 935 | 31.13% |

Sources: Various Census Reports of India (1881–2011).

As the data in Table 4.1 show, by the turn of the Partition of India and independence in 1947, Tripura received an abnormally huge number of refugees from Bengal which upset its demographic balance and turned the State into a Bengali (settlers) dominated one. Between 1951 and 1961 the decadal growth in population in Tripura was 81.71 per cent – such an abnormal growth in population was of course related to migration from the then East Pakistan (now Bangladesh). However, the tribals lost their majority in population already in 1951 from 50.09 per cent (1941) to 34.68 per cent in 1951. This created undeniably a very heavy pressure of population on land, particularly in the western part of the State which is fertile and resulted in large-scale and illegal transfer of land from the tribals to the settler Bengalis.

The Tripura's princely rulers were responsible for the Bengali settlement in their domain for higher rent. They gave very liberal land grants to the settlers with the basic motive of increase in land revenue although the apparent approach was a modified laissez-faire policy of development. The Tripura Census *Bibarani* (1931) (in Bengali) recorded:

> The system of settlement should continue. Instead of distributing small pieces of land, large area of 500 drones (1125 Hectares), or more in one block should be given to a number of rich and cultivated persons. And if wealthy and resourceful persons take such *taluks* (estates), then by their endeavour, roads and other means of communication will be built upon which will open the way for the general development and prosperity of the state.
> 
> (quoted in Bhattacharyya 1999: 46–7)

It is further stated in the same official document that there was enough cultivable land in the State, and that the State shall offer adequate facilities (Bhattacharyya 1999: 47). This pro-settlers approach of the princely rulers must have paid off because there was evidence of increases in land revenues from 28.18 per cent in 1939 to 34.29 per cent in 1943 when family taxes imposed on *jhum* cultivation decreased (Bhattacharyya 1999: 47).

Table 4.1 shows that due to the policies of princely rulers of Tripura, the tribal kingdom was already receiving Bengali migrants from across the border (quite porous), and the neighbouring *zamindary*[9] at Chaklarosnabad of the Maharaja of Tripura located within the then-neighbouring province of East Bengal facilitated such migration.

Two other relevant features of the historical transformation of Tripura are to be noted. First, the Bengali migration since the late nineteenth century was quite steady, which is reflected in the higher decadal growth in population. Second, the major demographic transformation took place during 1951–61 so that we find an abnormally high decadal growth of population in 1961 to be 81.71 per cent, over 1951 which surpassed all previous and subsequent records. The proportion of tribals to total population dwindled well into the early 1980s from when the decadal growth became increasingly stable. In fact, during 1985–91, the percentage of tribals to total population began to improve, and from then on, it has remained stable. One would certainly correlate this with the favourable State government and the relative successes of the ADC since 1985[10] in ensuring better protection to tribal identity in Tripura.

The other concluding remark that could be made in this regard is that since the Bengalis had been living in Tripura from the middle of the nineteenth century it may not be appropriate to describe Tripura as the land of the tribes alone, at least not from the nineteenth century. This is, however, not meant to underplay the dwindling demographic position of the tribes in the State, and their marginalized position relative to the Bengalis, but to put things in perspective. Before India's Partition (1947), Tripura was already a State inhabited by the tribals and the Bengalis including some 7 per cent Muslim Bengalis until 1961 (Bhattacharyya 1999: 42). From the perspective of the Bengalis, it is, therefore, hard to deny that Tripura was their home too for about a century even prior to India's Partition. But how can one forget that as a result of this massive demographic transformation in Tripura, the immigrants became the majority and dominant in all aspect of public affairs reducing the original inhabitants to a small minority, which Weiner (1978) would call a case of political core dominating also over the geographic core.

The settler Bengalis today are the vast majority of population in Tripura and also control State administration, and all public affairs. The tribals are only 27 per cent of the population, and mostly concentrated in the hilly eastern areas of the State. Of the Bengalis, the Scheduled Castes (called *dalits*[11]) comprise 17 per cent of the total population. Of the total population, Hindus comprise 85.84 per cent, Muslims (7.97 per cent), Buddhists (3.09 per cent) and the Christians comprise 3.21 per cent. The proportion of Muslims to total population progressively declined since the transfer of population between India and Pakistan in the early

Table 4.2 Ethnic composition of population of Tripura (total = 3,671,032) (2011)

| Ethnic groups | Population | Per cent |
|---|---|---|
| Bengalis | 2677606 | 68.2 |
| Tribes (all tribes) | 993426 | 31.8 |
| Tripuri* | 544298 | 54.79 |
| Reang* | 164909 | 16.6 |

Source: *Tripura at a Glance 2010–11* (Directorate of Economics & Statistics, Government of Tripura).
* denotes two largest tribes out of 19 in Tripura.

Table 4.3 Percentage of different tribes to total tribal population in Tripura (2001) (total population = 3,191,166)

| Tribes | Percentage |
|---|---|
| Tripura | 54.7% |
| Reang | 16.6% |
| Jamatia | 7.5% |
| Chakma | 6.5% |
| Halam | 4.8% |
| Mog | 3.1% |
| Munda | 1.2% |
| Any Kuki | 1.2% |
| Garo | 1.1% |
| Total= | 97.1% |

Source: Census Reports of India (2001).

1960s. Tripuris are overwhelmingly Hindus. However, there are significant followers of Buddhism and Christianity among the minority tribal communities.

Of the tribals in Tripura, the Tripuris are in majority (Table 4.3) followed by the Reangs, who are the second largest tribe in the State. Tripura is a multicultural and a multi-religious society. Apart from the tribals, and the Bengalis, there are small numbers of Biharis, Marathis and others. Although the Hindus constitute about 89 per cent of the total population (most of the tribes, especially the Tripuris, were converted to Hinduism thanks to their rulers' encouragement and special efforts), there are around 7 per cent Muslims, 2.67 per cent Buddhist and 1.21 per cent Christians in Tripura. Unlike the rest of India where 'communalism' has meant conflicts between religious communities, in Tripura, by contrast, religion played no role in the 'communal riots', which often vitiate the civil space.[12] In Tripura, the ethnic conflicts between the tribals and the Bengalis have overshadowed any other conflicts, including class conflicts. The fundamental reason why this has been the case is that the demographic upheaval in the State has resulted in the loss of the tribal control over their land which in an agrarian country is the very basis of livelihood. The large-scale Bengali settlement in Tripura has been unsettling to

*Table 4.4* Decadal growth of literacy in Tripura (1931–2011)

| Year | Total percentage | Male (%) | Female (%) |
|---|---|---|---|
| 1931 | 3.43 | 5.95 | 0.52 |
| 1941 | 7.95 | 12.74 | 2.46 |
| 1951 | 15.61 | 24.63 | 5.58 |
| 1961 | 24.34 | 35.31 | 12.36 |
| 1971 | 30.98 | 40.20 | 21.19 |
| 1981 | 50.10 | 51.05 | 51.60 |
| 1991 | 60.44 | 70.58 | 49.65 |
| 2001 | 73.19 | 91.53 | 87.73 |
| 2011 | 87.75 | 92.18 | 83.15 |

Source: Bhattacharyya (1999: 40), and various census reports of India, and Statistical Abstracts of Tripura (various years).

the lives of the original residents. The tribal people of Tripura felt the loss of their identity in their own land. Agartala, the State capital, remains a predominantly Bengali city with just above 1 per cent tribals residing in the city.

The literacy rate among the tribals was estimated to be 56. 5 per cent (male = 68.0 per cent and female = 44.6 per cent) which was below the State average (85.44 per cent). But even the relatively lower growth of literacy among the tribals has been a factor behind the growth of tribal ethnic consciousness in the State. The literate tribal youths have been in the forefront of several tribal movements fighting for the restoration of their land, and the appropriate recognition of their identity.

Tripura today is a fragmented society in which the Bengalis, the majority, and the tribals, the minorities, vie with each other for scarce resources in this landlocked territory. These communities, despite the 'secular' campaign by the Communist Party of India (Marxist) (CPI-M), the leading political party in the State, and the Left Front Government (LFG) under its leadership, are at loggerheads with each other, and the historic trust built by the communist movement among the tribals, and the Bengalis, which maintained the communal amity and peace for a considerable period of time since independence, was much weakened in the early 1980s after the infamous inter-ethnic riots in 1980 between the tribals and the Bengalis in which more tribal were killed than the Bengalis. The amity has since been restored and the State has not experienced any communal (inter-ethnic) riots ever since. And yet, the maintenance of relative political stability, and a moderate level of governance in this strife-torn State has indeed been remarkable.

The rate of literacy, generally, was abysmally poor in the period between 1931 and 1951 because the rulers of the State took no interest in the matter. Neither did the Congress government in the State do much in this matter which governed the State until 1977. The decent growth in literacy took place after the LFG was installed in Tripura 1978. The rate of literacy in Tripura in 2011 was much higher than the all-India average of 73.04 per cent, and it earned the State 4th rank in the country below Mizoram.

The literacy rate among the tribals was estimated to be around 23 per cent in 1991, which was far below the State average (60.44 per cent). In 2001 it rose to 56 per cent when the State average was 73.1 per cent. The rate of literacy among the Scheduled Castes was 74.70 per cent which was very impressive. The rate of literacy among the Scheduled Tribes in Tripura increased from 1981: 23.07 per cent (181); 40.37 per cent (1991); 56.48 per cent (2001) and 67.17 per cent in 2011 (Malhotra 2014: 175). This is an index of social inclusion of the State's minority tribal communities.

The really demographically upsetting transformation took place during 1951–61 reflected in an abnormally high decadal growth of population in 1961 to be 81.71 per cent, which surpassed all previous and subsequent records. The proportion of tribals to total population dwindled still well into the early 1980s from when the decadal growth became increasingly stable. In fact, during 1981–91, the percentage of tribals to total population began to improve, and from then on, it has remained stable. One would certainly correlate this with the favourable State government and the relative successes of the ADC since 1982 in ensuring better protection to tribal identity in Tripura.

The other concluding remark that could be made in this regard is that since the Bengalis had been living in Tripura from the middle of the nineteenth century it may not be proper to describe Tripura as the land of the tribes alone, at least not from the nineteenth century. This is, however, not meant to underplay the dwindling demographic position of the tribes in the State, and their marginalized position relative to the Bengalis, but to put things in perspective. Before India's Partition (1947), Tripura was already a State inhabited by the tribals and the Bengalis including some 7 per cent Muslims until 1961 (Bhattacharyya 1999: 42). From the perspective of the Bengalis, it is, therefore, hard to deny that Tripura was their home too for about a century even prior to India's Partition.

## Social structure

Tripura, ethnically speaking, is sharply divided between the Bengalis (the overwhelming majority), on the one hand, and the tribes (18 groups), on the other. But it must be stressed here that within the Bengalis as well as the tribes, there are differentiations of many sorts. The 19 tribes are not the same although linguistically they share a lot in common; *Kok-Borok* (literally the language of the people, and the second official language of the State now) is a lingua franca among the tribes). But in terms of social structure, customs, traditions and origins etc., they vary enormously. Tribal society in Tripura thus is not an undifferentiated whole. Beyond those nine tribes, there are nine other tribes of very smaller sizes in Tripura with their distinct cultural traits and customs and traditions. But those mentioned above comprise 97 per cent leaving 3 per cent for the rest. The nine tribes mentioned in Table 4.3 are considered as 'major tribes'.[13] Within this 1 million plus tribal population, there is tremendous diversity. For example, there are as

*Table 4.5* Schools in minority languages in Tripura (2010)

| Languages | Class | No of Schools |
|---|---|---|
| Kok-Borok | I to V | 783 |
| – | VI to XII | 40 |
| Bishnupriya Manipuri | I to V | 36 |
| Chakma | I to V | 58 |
| Halam Kuki | I to V | 17 |
| Manipuri | I to V | 21 |

Source: 47th Report of the Commissioner for Linguistic Minorities (New Delhi: Government of India, 2010), 117.

many as 17 sub-groups among the Kukis who constitute just above 1 per cent of the total tribal population in the State.[14] Linguistically, the tribes in Tripura belong to three distinct categories: the Bodo Language of Tibeto Burman Family, the Kuki Chin and the language of Arakan origin.[15]

The tribal identity in Tripura has been recognized by officially adopting *Kok-Borok* as the second official language of the State; the three-language formula accepted in the State are Bengali, *Kok-Borok* and English. The 47th Report of the Commissioner for Linguistic Minorities in India (2010) recorded satisfaction over the use of minority tribal languages such as *Kok-Borok*, Bishnupri Manipuri, Chakma, Halam Kuki and Manipuri in primary school level of education and levels up.

Thus, at the school levels, as indicated above (Table 4.5), Bengali enjoys the same status as the other minority languages. English is considered as the second language and Hindi as the third language (47th Report 2010: 118). This added strength to the recognition and protection of linguistic identity of the ethnic minorities.

The social organization and self-government systems among the tribes varied a lot. As regards the Tripuris (or Tripura), the majority tribe, the social organization was said to be as follows:

> Each of the Tripuri branches had its own elementary social and administrative organization starting from the village level and up to the chieftainship of the whole tribe. They enjoyed their traditional freedom, which was so essential to tribal society. They kept in touch with their king through their headman or the *Sardars* of their Village Councils.[16]

The Village Council was their self-government body:

> The Village Council was an important organization in the social life of the Tripuris. The Council had the power to resolve serious problems like land disputes, breaches of customs, harassment of women, marriage problems, and so on.[17]

The specific tribe-based empirical researches on other tribes serve to suggest that the traditional tribal life of 'compactness, cooperation, interdependence, exclusiveness, homogeneity and social control' is giving way to disintegration, heterogeneity, indifference and individualism (Gan Choudhury 1983: 2–3).[18] The study of the Jamatia, the third largest tribes, shows that their society is patriarchal and endogamous; and that though there is equality of men and women in respect of work, there is still male domination over women (Bhattacharjee 1983: 19).[19]

As for the Bengali society, divided between the Hindus and the Muslims (about 8 per cent) (2001) (Table 4.5), it is not only proverbially divided along religious (communal) lines, but within the Hindus, there are the usually caste divisions. Broadly, there are about 47 per cent Hindu upper castes, and about 15 per cent lower castes (Bhattacharyya 1999: 42). Linguistically, about 80 per cent of the people of Tripura (that includes tribals as well) speak Bengali; it means that one-third of all tribals speak Bengali, the first official language in the State. The second official language is *Kok-Borok* written in Bengali script. Linguistically, Tripura is a fragmented society. In the official 'Memorandum to the 13th Union Finance Commission' (www.ttaadc.nic.in/13thfinane.pdf (sighted on 29/10/17), the TTA-ADC led by the CPI-M, which also governs at the State level, stated as much:

> Tripura stands on a borderland. It has a dual society, a Borok or Tipra society in the eastern hill and a Bengali society in the western valley. The Borok society consisted of a large number of clans and communities; these people speak various dialects of Kokborok of the Tibeto-Burmese linguistic family.

Speaking in part, the very script in which *Kok-Borok* should be written has remained a matter of controversy in Tripura for long, and a bone of contention among the political parties. Although the Left Front government headed by the CPI-M was the first to recognize *Kok-Borok* as the second official language in the State, it preferred the Bengali script to the Roman script. Books accordingly were translated and published for use in the schools in the tribal inhabited areas particularly in the TTAADC areas. The TTAADC conducts its proceedings in *Kok-Borok* and Bengali, and has made the development of this language as its priority. But the Congress-TUJS-led State government in 1988 (1988–93), through a Committee recommendation in 1990, prescribed the Roman script for use for the Kok-Borok language. This decision was again rescinded by the Left Front led by the CPI-M which was returned again to govern the State in 1993 (and governing since) (after an interlude of five years 1988–93) and at the TTAADC in 1995 in favour of the Bengali script.[20]

## Economic structure

It requires little stress that Tripura's socio-economic structure underwent radical changes thanks to those exogenous factors mentioned above. The new and emerging structure was not also not a simple one but rather very complex. Again, the new agrarian structure that came off became very conflict-ridden because of the

Table 4.6 Religious composition of population in Tripura (2001) (total population = 31, 91, 168)

| Religion | Number | % |
| --- | --- | --- |
| Hindu | 27,39,310 | 85.84% |
| Muslim | 2,54,442 | 7.97% |
| Buddhist | 98,922 | 3.09 |
| Christian | 1,02,489 | 3.21 |
| Sikh | 1182 | 0.03 |
| Jain | 477 | 0.01 |
| Others | 1277 | 0.04 |
| Not Stated | 1104 | 0.03 |

Source: Tripura At a Glance, 2010–11 (Directorate of Economics & Statistics, Govt. of Tripura, Agartala, 2011), p. 7.

lack of arable land and resources in the State, and also because this placed the tribals, quite primitive in their mode of agriculture for a long time since (practicing slash and burn method), in unequal competition with the migrant Bengalis, who were very advanced in all respects.

It was true that Tripura tribals had not taken to settled cultivation. W. W. Hunter (1876) reported that there was very little settled (plough) cultivation in Tripura, and that the largest portion of land remained uncultivated jungle (Bhattacharyya 1999: 44). While this gave birth to a rural class structure with different categories of rural population, the rulers' policy of reserving forests meant that the tribals' customary access to use forests for shifting cultivation and other forest produce came to be restricted. For example, in 1908 only an area of 15 sq. miles was reserved which rose to 1160 sq miles during 1943–44 (Bhattacharyya 1999: 47). This was reflected in the dwindling share of family tax (collected from the tribal for shifting cultivation) relative to land revenues. The share of family tax decreased from 7.79 per cent in 1889 to 3.5 per cent in 1934 (Bhattacharyya 1999: 49). As the data in Table 4.6 show, while proprietary and cultivating peasants grew among the tribals though about 10 per cent lower than that of the Bengalis, there was high proportion of share croppers without tenancy rights more among the tribal (30.08 per cent) to be added with 11.08 per cent (sub-tenants), which together comprise about 42 per cent as well as the Bengalis about 37 per cent. The figures under serial number 1 in Table 3.6 suggest that about 17 per cent of the tribals, and 28 per cent Bengalis together dominated the rural class structure in Tripura within one decade after independence but the process had set in before and was the result of preferential treatment of the rulers to the cultivating and proprietor peasants.

The large percentage of share-cropping among both the tribals and the non-tribals is an indication of large-scale landlessness and the concentration of land in a few hands. Another significant feature of the agrarian structure of Tripura is the predominance of small holdings (below I Hect.): 62 per cent in 1961 and 70 per cent in 1970 (Bhattacharyya 1999: 49). In 1990–91, as per the data offered by the World Agricultural Census, the figure remains 68 per cent (below 1 Hect.)

(*Tripura Human Development Report* 2007: 15) Added to that is further marginalization of the small and marginal farmer (share-croppers) which fell from 54.42 per cent in 1971 to 43.29 per cent in 1981. The State also witnessed, predictably, increase in the number of agricultural labourers from 32,912 in 1961 to 187,537 in 1999 (Bhattacharyya 1999: 49). Of the agricultural labourers, about 50 per cent are tribals and 18.47 per cent belong to Scheduled Castes (Bhattacharyya 1999: 49). As per the Census Report of India 1991, Tripura had as many as 1,898,688 agricultural landless labourers and unemployed youths taken together (Bhattacharyya 1999: 50). Today, the number of agricultural workers has swelled further: 275,132 (9 per cent approx.) (*Tripura At a Glance*, 2010–2011: 19). The above gave enough materials to argue a case for sharp class divisions in agrarian Tripura punctuated by sharp ethnic divisions. According to the Census Report of India (2001), about 64 per cent of the total population in Tripura was dependent population, that is, those who are not 'main workers' in terms of the census definition (*Tripura At a Glance*, 2010–11: 19). This has come down to about 60 per cent in 2011. This is not evidently a healthy sign of an economy. Of the total workers, as per the census definition, about 60 per cent is engaged in agricultural activities as cultivators and as agricultural labourers (*Statistical Abstract*, Tripura, 2014).

Work force participation in various productive activities is an important index of the nature of economic structure. In Tripura (Table 4.7) about 40 per cent of the total population are engaged in work while the rest (60 per cent) are dependent;

*Table 4.7* Land tenures among the tribals and non-tribals in Tripura (1964)

| Nature of Land Ownership | Tribes (%) | Non-tribals (%) |
| --- | --- | --- |
| Ryotwari rights of permanent, transferable and heritable possessions[21] | 16.69 | 28.29 |
| Share-cropping without tenancy rights | 30.08 | 32.29 |
| Sub-tenants | 11.08 | 5.25 |
| Mortgaged in possession | 6.61 | 3.84 |
| Unclassed | 4.37 | 9.89 |

Source: CRI (1961) Census Report of India 1961.

*Table 4.8* Workforce participation in Tripura (2015) (total population of Tripura: 3,673,917)

| Categories | Number | % |
| --- | --- | --- |
| (total) Workers | 1469521 | 39.99* |
| Cultivators | 295947 | 20.14 |
| Agricultural labourers | 353618 | 24.06 |
| Workers in household industries | 41496 | 2.82 |
| Other workers | 778460 | 52.97 |

Source: North Eastern Council Secretariat, Government of India, Shillong) 2015), p. 135.

* denotes per cent of the total population.

this high level of dependent population is a sign of a poor economy, characteristic of Indian economy as a whole, and of its various States. But three features stand out from the data in Table 4.7. First, those who control and cultivate land are only 20.13 per cent while 24.06 per cent are agricultural labourers which are nearly one-fourth of the total work force. This indicates the concentration of land and the landlessness among the sizeable sections of the rural poor. Second, only 2.82 per cent of the work force is engaged in household industries meant that the share of industrial activities is very limited when there are no large industries in the State. Third, the category of 'other workers' comprising 52.90 per cent of the total work force is very significant. Persons employed here refer to the tertiary sectors (white collar jobs including service sector, government employment (in administration), insurance and so on). When placed in comparison with the data in 1992, this is an increase of more than 100 per cent. In 1992, the figure was 20.34 per cent (*Statistical Abstract of Tripura* 1992: 9). This was to do partly with the process of India's neo-liberal reforms.

A predominantly agricultural economy with little industrial base, Tripura's capacity to absorb unemployed people is limited. In 2013, there were as many as 237,902 enterprises in the State which employed in total some 404,215 workers only. The average size of employment per enterprise was only 176 workers. The State had in 2013–14 only five industrial estates and one industrial area whose total export values measured in Indian Rupees was 0.42 crores only (*Tripura At a Glance* 2014–15: 24). However, the employability of the industrial estates was very limited. For instance, during 2007–08, only 98 and 148 candidates belonging respectively to the Scheduled Castes and Scheduled Tribes got employment against 77,430 and 94,609 job seekers respectively during the same period (*Economic Survey* 2008–9, Directorate of Economic and Statistics, Government of Tripura, 2010: 85–6). No wonder, because of the same limitation, work force participation, and that too, in household industry, increased little significantly during 1991–2001: 1.42 per cent to 2.82 per cent (*Economic Survey*, 2010: 87). The Tripura Human Development Report (2007) described Tripura economy as: 'The economy of Tripura is characterized by the near absence of an industrial base, with manufacturing sector accounting for less than 3 per cent of NSDP'. The Report also mentioned that the biggest contribution to SDP comes from the tertiary sector (52. 8 per cent in 2001–02) (Report 2007: 14–15). The primary sector still contributes at 25.4 per cent to SDP during 2001–02 (Report 2007: 15). The contribution of the secondary sector in this respect is weaker (21.8 per cent), but tertiary sector's growth of 52.8 per cent, and that too, mostly in the West District (the flat and most fertile areas), is remarkable, something closely associated with India's globalization too. This sector includes trade, hotels, restaurants, transport and communication, finance, banking and insurance, and social and personal services.

## Conclusion

The above account suggests that there are agrarian class tensions in an agrarian society with good deal of inequalities as a fall out of concentration of lands in a few hands and the large-scale landlessness. Despite long periods of Left rule, the above trend could not be reversed. Coupled with the above are genuine grounds of tensions stemming from landlessness among the marginalized tribesmen most of them are agricultural labourers. Various institutional measures of protection and accommodation of their identity, as indicated above (discussed at length in Chapters 11 and 12) and enabling the latter in taking power at the sub-State levels for self-governance have assuaged their injured feeling and rectified to a large extent their neglect. The latter has served to mitigate a lot of ethnic tensions that may arise from the agrarian economy. The tribals in Tripura have their own organization (GMP) and various mass fronts affiliated to the CPI-M mostly, but they are represented in the main party organizations of the CPI-M in the State in proportions higher than their share in population: 35.68 per cent (CPI-M 2015: 58). The party is multiethnic, multireligious and composed of members 75 per cent of whom belong to the workers, landless peasants agricultural labourers, poor peasants, and middle peasants. The Scheduled Castes are and OBCs are well represented too: 19.33 per cent and 21.98 per cent respectively. This cross-cutting membership in the party has been functional for the party to mobilize a cross sections of society and deliver better governance.

## Notes

1 During British colonial rule in India, the existing feudal monarchies were an important pillar of the British who decided to govern the monarchies indirectly unlike the directly governed provinces. The most of them acceded to the Union of India and a small part went over to Pakistan. For more details, see Jeffrey (1979); Menon (1959); and Copland (2002).
2 The British authorities called it Hill Tipperah as distinguished from Tipperah as a district in the then East Bengal of which the Tripura monarchs were the zamindar.
3 For more details on this aspect, see Bhattacharyya (1999: 28–55).
4 See Datta (1995) for a critical discussion on the extent of cultural sharing between the North East of India and the rest of India.
5 This was a land settlement following the implementation of the Permanent Settlement Act, 1793 of Bengal which gave birth to a new class of landlords in rural Bengal during the Raj.
6 It was so-called during he British colonial rule.
7 Quoted in Bhattacharyya (1999), Op. Cit., p. 35.
8 See, for details, Bhattacharyya (1999: 90–126).
9 This was a land settlement following the implementation of the Permanent Settlement Act, 1793 of Bengal which gave birth to a new class of landlords in rural Bengal during the Raj. The Tripura monarch then enjoyed a double status as a princely ruler and as a landlord post-1793.
10 The ADC was formed in 1982 as per State Law (7th Schedule) but from 1985 it came to be governed under the 6th Schedule of the Constitution with more autonomous powers. The Autonomous Tribal District Council in Tripura which cover about two-thirds of the territory of Tripura has successfully provided self-government to the tribals in the state and helped protect their identity and culture. This asymmetric federal arrangement under the 6th Schedule of the Indian Constitution in Tripura has resulted in the establishment of a 30-member Tripura Tribal Autonomous District Council which remains

like a state within a state. Formed on the basis of universal adult franchise, every five years this experiment in ethnic yet democratic decentralization has added strength to political integration at the bases of the state, and helped contain ethnic conflicts in the state. For further details, see Bhattacharyya (2013: 1–146). The establishment of such a body was a pledge of the Left in Tripura as an institutional guarantee for protecting endangered tribal identity in the State.

11 Significantly, the term '*dalit*' was used for the first time in official document of the Government of Tripura in its Human Development Report (2009), p. 5.
12 The worst such riot took place in June 1980 when some thousand people from both the tribals and the Bengalis were killed. An unofficial estimate said, some 2000 Bengalis were killed in this riot. See Karlekar, 1985: 1428.
13 See, (2010) *A Land of Rich Ethnic Tapestry: Tripura*, Agartala: Government of Tripura. This research-based book contains the details on the each tribe in Tripura today.
14 'A Land of . . .' p. 2.
15 'A Land of . . .', pp. 2–3.
16 'A Land of . . .' p. 6.
17 'A Land of . . .', p. 6.
18 Gan Choudury's is a study of the Reangs. See, for details, (1983).
19 Bhattacharjee (1983). See Saha (1980) for the specific study of the Noatiaa of Tripura.
20 For the ongoing debates among the political parties and linguists on the issue, see Devbarma and Devbarma (2005) (in Bengali) and Dhar (2007).
21 The percentage of this category of owner cultivators has gone down in course of time. In 2001, the cultivators were about 10 per cent of the total population indicating further concentration of land in a fewer hands. (*Tripura At a Glance*, 2010–11, Government of Tripura, 2011: 19).

# 5 The ethnic radicalism in Tripura

Reang rebellion 1943–45 and the birth of an ethnic identity

## Introduction

Tripura (known as Hill Tippera during the Raj in India) now in India's North East experienced traditions of ethnic radical politics since the 1940s up to and beyond Tripura's accession to the Indian Union in 1949. Such ethnic mobilizations took the forms of open armed rebellion first against the feudal princely regime and then against the quasi-civilian regime backed up the heavy handedness military rule in parts of the State during 1948–50. Two tribal ethnic armed rebellions in the early 1940s and the late 1940s effectively dismantled the feudal princely regime and the transitional bureaucratic-military regime. However, organized political movements cropped up in Tripura since the 1920s (Singh 1982: 319), but the visibility of such political activities was dim until the mid-1930s. The social and political history of Tripura, properly so-called, was marked more by such rebellious collective actions than the modernization drives of the (peasant hungry) princely rulers since the nineteenth century which entailed invitation to the Bengali peasants from then and neighbouring East Bengal to come to Tripura, clear the jungle, introduce plough cultivation, and enjoy tax free land for some years. The subsequent Left radicalism in the State built on the anvil of such tribal radicalism.

This chapter analyses the roots, course, character and significance of the Reang rebellion in Tripura (in India's North East) during 1943–45. This was a collective tribal protest movement, violent in form and autonomous in mobilization. This rebellion inaugurated the tradition of radical politics in Tripura. One of the arguments of this chapter is that ethnic identity is not always a matter of elite manipulation of symbols, as some studies (Brass 1990; Alavi 1989; Adas 1979)[1] on ethnicity would suggest, but a product of indigenous mass mobilization. The Reang ethnic identity, now submerged and little known, was born in the Reang rebellion fighting an encroaching State symbolizing modernity. Ethnicity means group assertion of an identity, an attempt of a group to define itself, to make itself heard and attended to. The Reang ethnicity represented a subaltern consciousness, a 'nationalist' urge which met with ruthless State suppression. To be sure, the available sources on the Reang rebellion are thin.[2] The sources used here are not exhaustive. Nevertheless, these official reports failed to conceal the 'truth' even at the margin, of the event. The mentalities of those on the on the other side of the picture, that is, the rebels, are yet to be known properly, but should be explored in writing a total history of the rebellion.

Historically, tribals in India have revolted more violently than any other community (Singh 1982: Vol. 1 and 2). This, of course, does not mean that violence is endemic in their life, and that violence, for them, is the only means for achieving their ends. Ironically, in most cases, violence has seemed to them as the last alternative left for achieving their ends. When the tribals have arisen in revolt they have done so not only for tangible economic demands, but also for the protection of their identity which seemed at stake due to the effects of the forces of change inimical to them. Tripura's history particularly from the second half of the nineteenth century is replete with tribal rebellions and uprisings, such as the Tripura revolt of 1850, the Kuki Disturbances of 1860–61, the Jamatia revolt of 1863 and the Kuki Raids of 1871 (Roy Choudhury 1978). These revolts contributed to the increasing rupture of Tripura's traditional mode of production based on shifting cultivation. The causes of these revolts were complex, but they were launched mainly against the tax collectors of the Tripura rulers, and the local tribal chiefs who also symbolized princedom in Tripura. Also, most of these revolts were violent. The Reang rebellion of 1943–45 represented a major case of indigenous mass protest in modern India.

## Conceptual issues

To be sure, this tradition of mass protest or what Guha calls the 'politics of the people' was not something unique to Tripura. 'There existed', as he argues, 'throughout the colonial period another domain of Indian politics in which the principal actors were not the dominant group of indigenous society, or the colonial authorities, but the subaltern classes and groups. . . . that is the people' (Guha 1982: 1). 'This was', he continues, 'an autonomous domain, for it neither originated from elite politics nor did its existence depend on the latter'.[3] The pattern of mobilization in these revolts essentially involved resistance to elite domination. The Reang rebellion was a powerful protest of subordinate social groups against established princely regime and set up an alternative centre of power in large parts of Tripura. Any understanding of Tripura's social history in this century will remain incomplete without the Reang rebellion. Remarkably, this significant tribal rebellion is *terra incognita* in the existing studies of peasant and tribal revolts and uprisings in India (Singh 1982).

Local writings[4] in Tripura have only added confusion to a proper historical understanding of this tribal rebellion. The local Communist Party has since 1950s tried to explain it away by dubbing it 'spontaneous' and the first local Communist Party interpretation of this revolt was stereotyped:

> The peasant war or rebellion is not something new in Tripura. Recently, we have the Reang rebellion which was also a peasant war. India's past history is full of such revolts but did not succeed. One of the reasons for their failure was the absence of successful leadership by the working class and its party i. e.,

the Communist party. The working class and its party alone can lead successfully peasant rebellions.

(Chanda 1983: 12)[5]

In this chapter we shall be using the term 'rebellion' to refer to 'organized armed resistance to established authority'.[6] We have used the 'Reang rebellion' because the areas encompassed by the rebellion were predominantly inhabited by the Reangs. The Reang rebellion received active support from another subordinate tribal community of Tripura, the Noatias, who participated in the rebellion and added to its mass character.

The objectives of this chapter are three-fold: examination of the roots of the rebellion; analysis of its course and character; and examination of the implications of the same for future radical politics in Tripura.

## Roots of the rebellion

When a peasant rises in revolt he does so necessarily and explicitly in violation of a series of codes which define his existence. The risk in turning things upside down is indeed so great that he could hardly afford to engage in such a project in a state of absent-mindedness. He has far too much at stake and will not launch into it except as a deliberate, even if desperate, way of an intolerable condition of existence.

As Guha says, insurgency is a motivated and conscious undertaking on the part of the rural masses (Guha 1982: 3).[7] The so-called 'spontaneity' of these rebellions is largely a myth. The causes of the Reang rebellion were many and complex. The specific social, economic and political changes are to be understood that triggered the revolt; the consequences of the profound major agrarian changes Tripura, from the late nineteenth century onwards, and the destabilizing effects of the Depression and the Second World War on Tripura. Here we will briefly discuss only the specific factors directly responsible for the outbreak of this rebellion.

The Reangs were (and still are) the second largest tribe in Tripura followed by the Noatias. The *Tripura Census Bibarani* (local census in Bengali) of 1931 put the figure of the Reangs at 35,881 and the Noaties at 27,405 in 1931. These two tribal groups together constituted over 16 per cent of Tripura's population in 1931. They were regionally concentrated in the southern parts of Tripura (over 98 per cent of the Noaties and about 53 per cent of the Reang),[8] the areas, quite remote and inaccessible, where the rebellion was also concentrated. In Tripura society, the Reang and the Noaties, non-ruling tribes, had an inferior sociocultural status. Hunter observes that the Noaties were not regarded as 'true' Tripuris;[9] they were thought to have come from Chittagong and were comparatively of recent origin.[10] The Reangs were ranked lower;[11] they were a hybrid tribe, a racial mixture of the Kukis and the Tripuris.[12] Not surprisingly, these two tribal communities were discriminated against by the Tripura rulers.

In 1931 only 114 Reangs and 244 Noaties managed to have any education at all, in sharp contradistinction to 2,441 Tripuris.[13] Again, in the introduction of settled

*Table 5.1* Discriminatory rates of family tax among tribes

| Tribes | Rates in Rupees (1874–75) |
| --- | --- |
| Tripuris | 3.80 |
| Jamatias | 3.80 |
| Noatias | 10.00 |
| Reangs | 10.00 |
| Kukis | 5.40 |

Source: Hunter (1876: Vol. 6, 505–20).

agriculture, which replaced the prevailing shifting agriculture, the Noatias and more particularly the Reangs, were grossly neglected. For instance, in 1931 out of 27,647 tribals who had adopted plough cultivation, there were only 471 Reang and 2,434 Noatias.[14] These two communities, especially the Reangs, predominantly based themselves on shifting cultivation the land for which was increasingly restricted by the rulers' land reservation policies. By 1943 about one-fourth of the total territory of the State was declared 'reserved' under a process which began from the late nineteenth century, an indication of the tightening of control by the colonial State over forest zones for revenue purposes.

The Reangs and the Noatias were victims of the Tripura rulers' highly discriminatory taxation policy. The shifting cultivation, however primitive, was not a tax-free system. The tribal shifting cultivators produced paddy, cotton, oil-seeds and sesame and added significantly to the State exchequer by paying taxes (locally known as *ghar-chukti*) calculated family-wise. They also paid export duties on cotton, oil-seeds and sesamum. During 1873–74 the revenue collected from the family tax constituted 19 per cent of total revenues. Because of increasing settled cultivation in the State following the Bengali migration to Tripura, the proportion of family tax to total revenues decreased, although the amount of family tax collected increased by and large. Between 1934 and 1943, for instance, revenue collected from family tax increased by 76 per cent.[15] It was the Reangs and the Noaties who shared most of the burden of family tax because they had to pay at a much higher rate than the ruling Tripuris (Table 5.1).

The rates of family tax for the Reangs and the Noaties varied but these two groups always paid the highest rates. In 1913, it was admitted in the State Gazette that these two tribes had been over-taxed, and that the Reangs paid six times the rate of family tax of the Tripuris (that is, Rs.6.00 for the Reangs and Rs.1.00 for the Tripuris).[16] The discriminatory taxation system continued well into the 1940s. In a Government circular in 1940 it was admitted:

> Among the highest tax-paying tribes, the Reangs and the Noaties constituted the greatest number. Previously, the rate was Rs.8.00, and the before that Rs.12.00. For the last two years, the Reangs and the Noaties have been making frequent appeals for the reduction of rates; their appeals were legitimate.

They also pay export duty on bamboo and cane and are over – taxed there too. Their rates of house (family) tax are *quite high* (emphasis added); that should be lowered.[17]

This unequal and discriminatory taxation system was a long-standing grievance of the Reangs and the Noaties, and the most powerful factor in the Reang rebellion.

The Reang social structure like that of other tribes of Tripura was patriarchal and the lineage was traced through the father. Village organizations, cooperation and fellow-feeling among the co-villagers, and the joint ownership of forest lands for shifting cultivation characterized much of Reang life. The Reangs were dominated by the chiefs and the authority of the Tripura monarch over the tribes was 'more nominal then real'. As Alexander Mackenzie wrote in 1884:

> The power or influence of the chiefs of different communities over the vassals within their respective jurisdiction was of the strongest kind. The administration of the state was run through the chiefs who are an intermediate authority and the sole connection between the government and the vassals.[18]

The chiefs of the Reang tribes was called Rai. As Soumendra Chandra Devbarma said, he was like the king of the Reangs, the highest authority; he was a vassal under the Tripura king.[19] Just below the Rai was the Chaudhury, a hereditary title conferred upon the Reangs by the Tripura king. Rais and Chaudhuries were exempted from paying any tax. It was through them that the rulers collected taxes and export duties from the common tribes.

As far as the immediate reasons were concerned, the roots of the rebellion should be traced to famine conditions in Tripura in the late 1930s and early 1940s. Tripura never recovered from the disintegrative effects of the global Depression and the Second World War. The condition of the hill people following the Depression was 'deplorable' with acute scarcity of money and gloomy trade conditions. The effects of the War were destructive on the tribals living in the hills who were 'practically in the throes of famine'. During 1938–43 there took place a high rise of the price of rice which was the main foodgrain and the staple of the people (Table 5.2).

This price rise had a marked impact on the common hill men especially those in the Tripura ruler led to further displacement of the economy. To begin with 'the entire resources of the State and the personal services of the king' were 'placed

*Table 5.2* Rice prices 1937–8 and 1942–5

| Year | Prices in Rupees per quintal |
| --- | --- |
| 1937–38 | 6.25 to 12.50 |
| 1942–45 | 20.00 to 70.00 |

Source: Saigal (1980: 50).

at the disposal of the Crown'.[20] The donations made by the Government to various war funds totalled Rupees 75,000; and the Defence Bonds purchased by the State were Rupees 175, 000, and the total amount of expenditure incurred on the armed forces was over Rs.500,000.[21] It was not easy for the government to fulfill its financial commitments and collect such a huge sum of money, given the disintegrating economy of the State. The government purchased, sometimes by force, all the available paddy and rice to feed the people in the capital and the and the expanding army, including the newly created First Tripura Rifles and the Tripura Mahabir Legion. This led to acute scarcity of food for the common people, and famine prevailed throughout the State but most particularly in the southern parts. One form of political action undertaken by the Reang rebels was the looting of paddy from the granaries of the rich, specially the chiefs, and the way they sought to solve the food crisis was by opening *dharma golas* (grain banks) to distribute food to needy. The government intelligence reports made in the course of counter-insurgency operations repeatedly mention the acute scarcity or famine in the areas of the rebellion:

> While in Kalsi we did not get any rice, lentil etc, even at the cost of lot of money. There is acute scarcity that will lead to famine again. Therefore we are forced to leave the place.[22]

Another report contained a more painful picture of the famine-stricken people of the regions:

> When we captured the area and raided each and every house, we found only some cotton, clothes and utensils without any trace of paddy or rice. In Amarpur and Udaipur, there are no further groups of the "*dacoits* party". In fact, they are passing through acute scarcity. The last group we captured had been starving for the last three days.[23]

## Rise of the rebellion and counter-insurgency operation

The exact beginning of the Reang rebellion is not known. The origins of the supreme leader of this rebellion, Ratan Moni Reang (or Noatia), are also obscure. Local writings based on impressions and memories suggest that the rebellion was preceded by a religious mobilization of the Reangs from the late 1930s by Ratan Moni Reang who was apparently a monk, who lived in Bagafa (south Tripura), and preached a religious doctrine which was a form of Hinduism. The Reang rebellion started in late 1939 as a move against the war effects of the king; the king wanted to raise a band of soldiers from among the Reangs but failed to do so because the Reangs refused to join the armed forces. Ratan Moni Reang was once arrested by the king because he preached against injustice, and also because his disciples disallowed the Bengali Brahmins to perform the annual religious activities of the tribals in Udaipur, and performed them themselves. But Ratan Moni Reang escaped from the prison at Agartala with the help of one of his disciples.

More research needs to be done to corroborate the above facts. The available evidences, however, indicate that Ratan Moni Reang escaped from was a religious leader. The State intelligence reports do not say when the rebellion began,[24] but suggest that by July 1943 the rebellion was at its peak:

> In order to capture and punish the armed "dacoits party" in Amarpur, Udaipur, etc, in accordance with the order of his Highness, the following soldiers under the leadership of Lt. Nagendra Devbarma are leaving today the capital for the disturbed areas: Ramachandra Dev and Bharat Chandra Dev (2 Body Guards Jamadars); 30 Body Guards Other Rank. In addition, the following will also be sent; The Officer of the Rajya Rakhey Bahini (state Security Force), a few Reang Sardars, and some police officers and police forces from the state administration. The following was the order to Lt. Nagendra Devbarma: (a) the captured dacoits must be brought to the capital; (b) the soldiers can open fire in case of self-defence and if faced with resistance from the dacoits; (c) the dacoits arms and ammunition must be captured and sized; (d) if they are not found at home, their houses must be set on fire after removing the properties, women, children and elderly persons from houses, and the relation of the dacoits must be arrested and brought to the capital; and (e) if necessary, the force commander can mobilize more forces from the Amarpur and Udaipur divisional offices.[25]

On the basis of available evidence, the rebellious activities in summary included, looting of properties like rice, money, cattle etc., from the houses of Reang Chiefs; plundering paddy from the granaries of Chiefs and also from their rice fields; kidnapping of tribal Chiefs and inflicting punishment on them which included money and forced indoctrination; opening of *dharma golas* for distributing food grains to the depressed people; setting up an alternative government headed by the religious leader Ratan Moni; massive organized armed resistance to monarchical anti-insurgency operations; snatching of guns; openly engaging in encounters with the military and police forces and so on. (The separate cases of the above activities are documented in the police and Military Intelligence reports of the government of Tripura.)

The secret military correspondence in the second half of 1943 recorded many cases of looting and plundering by what was described as the 'Ratan Moni Party' or '*dacoits* party'. The most important case of '*dacoity*' by the Ratan Party took in Bilonia police station.[26] The diary of the police officer who investigated the case reveals that; (a) those who led the party were mostly Reangs including the brother of Ratan Moni Reang; (b) the act of looting was conducted from a nearby camp the *dacoits* party had set up; and (c) the guns found left in the cam bore the identification numbers of the Tripura Rajya Rakhya Bahini of Udaipur Division.[27] The '*dacoits* party' was sometimes described by the State police as the 'Swadeshi party' against British colonialism. A secret report signed by I. M. Ganguly, Nayeb Dewan, stated that the 'Swadeshi party' (freedom fighters) attacked the house of Tarbang Choudhury, and snatched the guns of his sons Ramananda Reang and

Sricharant Reang who worked in the Rajya Rakhey Bahini, inflicted a financial punishment on the Choudhury of Rupees 20, plundered his house, looted rice, tied these three together and brought them to Ratan Moni at Taichharuha in order to convert them into his disciples.

The administration's response to the rebellion indicated the magnitude of the challenge the rebellion posed to monarchy. Repeated reports from the police and tribal chiefs of Amarpuur and Udaipur that the Reangs had turned violent alarmed the government, which responded by sending the State military and police and tribal chiefs of Amarpur and Udaipur that the Reangs had turned violent alarmed the government, which responded by sending the State military and police forces, the King's Bodyguard Forces, hundreds of armed Jamatias, mercenaries supplied by this community to the service of the king, money, petrol, etc, to put down the revolt. Secret military sources suggest that the government continued to send battalions of armed police and military. P. Bhattacharyya, Chief Secretary to the King, informed the State Commissioner of Police on 26th July 1943:

> A batch of Military Troops will very soon be going to Amarpur area under orders of his Highness the Maharaja Manikya Bahadur. Please depute 2 Constables and I.S.I. or A.S.I. with the party on the date required by Mj. B.L. Devbarma Bahadur who you are requested to consult.

In a letter, Lt. B.L. Devbarma wrote to the Divisional Officer, Bilonia:

> According to H. H's order I am sending one NCO and one BG, two boxes of reserved ammunition containing 1000 (one thousand) rounds in each box containing 300" bore for Bodyguards, and coloured green box 410" bore is for Second Tripura and Armed Police who are in operation in your division. Please hand over to fighting troops if they require; otherwise you can keep in your in your safe custody.[28]

Significantly, the King made a sudden visit to Amarpur on 24 April 1953 Tripura Era.[29] The gravity of the situation led a returning police officer from the rebellion-infested area to wonder 'if Amarpur, Udaipur and Bilonia should be placed under a state of emergency'.[30] The government later launched a violent attack on the rebels' camps, ordered the destruction of camps and a shoot-to-kill policy. There is evidence that tins of petrol were supplied by the government to burn the houses of the Reangs.[31] Hundreds of houses of the Reangs were burnt down.[32]

In the face of such formidable anti-insurgency operations by the State, the rebels offered stiff organized armed resistance. One major aspect of the organized resistance of the rebels was the setting up of camps which provided the bases from which they conducted their operations. Secret military reports suggest that each camp contained about 500 to 700 armed personnel and armed rebels numbering about 150 to 500 would engage in single operations. The rebels often snatched guns which were mostly made locally, and were possessed by the inhabitants.

In many cases the rebels were found to have used such native arms as choppers with a haft, and scissors. Also, guns belonging to the Rajya Rakhya Bahini were snatched by the rebels. From one report, during military combing operations, it was found that out of seven guns seized, four belonged to the Rajya Rakhya Bahini. Dinesh Das, the police officer of Radhakishorepur police station (Udaipur) gives us an idea of the organization of the rebels on the basis of firsthand information. He along with 12 Constables, a few other persons and Rajprosad Choudhury, visited the rebels' area in order to make an investigation; they were kidnapped and beaten up by the armed disciples of Ratan Moni and released later without their guns. Das wrote:

> To get to Ratan Moni one to cross as many as 7 gates encircled by 5 forts; they have a well-built spying system; they were capable of offering resistance to 2000 men at any time; Kumarrai Oghai, Kaliprosad, etc. are now imprisoned in the forts; together they contained 12000 Reangs and 7000 Noaties; if the State Police march towards Udaipur, there is every possibility that they might face encirclement by 500 to 700 rebels from any direction. Situation here is really disturbed.[33]

The same report also indicated that Ratn Moni's headquarters was at Taichhurabuha, 14 miles east of Udaipur and its branches were spread throughout the areas adjoining the town of Udaipur.

There is evidence to suggest that the rebels managed to muster some support among some chiefs of their community and this in particular alarmed the police and military forces: 'We wanted to exorcise ghosts by the mustard seeds, but the ghosts have sheltered in the same seeds'.[34] Several encounters between the military and armed forces, on the one hand, and the rebels, on the other hand, took place. In a 'very urgent' message, P. K. Majumdar, C. L. Bilonia wrote to the Commissioner of Police, Agartala:

> Yesterday about 400 to 500 men of Ratan Moni's party armed with guns, choppers, spears and large falchions arrived in the house of Martha Haria Choudhury of Lakhmipur mouza; they forced him to give Rupees 100.00; then they shouted the pearls of victory of Ratan Moni. At about 4.30 p. m the military and armed forces arrived, but the rebels offered open challenge to them, and opened fires from the top of the hills. Military and armed forces already took positions and began firing from outside the range of the rebels' guns. Two rebels seriously injured fell down the hill but the dacoits were still shouting victory to Ratn Moni. Then the military forces climbed up and encircled the house on the top and captured 5 including 2 injured; one of them died after four hours. After the military has left, we are weakened so we need urgently forces.[35]

In another such encounter[36] in which the rebels put up a powerful defence, it was found that the military's shouting of 'Victory to the King' did not at all move the rebels who countered it by shouting 'Victory to Ratan Moni'. This revealed the strong anti-monarchy feeling amongst the rebels. The same report said that the military and the police forces had arrested 464 persons: 110 men and 354 women.

In the areas of the rebellion, the princely regime virtually broke down. The rebels set up an alternative government of their own: they found a Maharaja in Ratan Moni, and even prepared a chair made up of bamboo as the throne of their king. The monk-turned king, Ratan Moni, had a council of ministers consisting of five ministers who are all Reangs. Ratan Moin had a few commanders-in-chief. The persons in charge of the department were Chitra Sen, Ram Bhadur, and Ratn Moin's brother, Chinta Moni. Ratan Moni tried all cases and delivered judgment. Visitors to the king would have to pay some donation as entrance fee. In the kingdom of Ratan Moni it was obligatory for everybody to address each other by saying '*jai guru*' meaning 'Victory to Ratan Moni'. Ratan Moni kingdom was a moral order where politics was placed under the control of religion with Ratn Moni, the Guru of all the people, at the apex of the political order. But it was also a polity which was based on the denial of sovereignty of the existing Tripuri monarch.

The rebellion was ultimately crushed by the State in 1945, although its aftereffects were the cause of much anxiety to the administration as late as 1948,[37] and large-scale arrests were made. However, it is hard to tell what happened to Ratan Moni whose death remained as obscure as his origins.

## Different assessments and conclusion

The counter-insurgency reports of the government of Tripura mainly described the Reang rebels as '*dacoits*' or '*dacoits* party'. That was the official, negative version of the rebellion. Sometimes, the rebels were described as the 'Swadeshi party' but there was nothing in the rebellion which proved that it was directly aimed at the British. To be sure, the presence of the British in the tribal princely Tripura was negligible and invisible for all practical purposes, but even symbolically the rebels did not reveal anti-British activities. The causes of the rebellion were indigenous: long-drawn neglect, exploitation and deprivation. That does not mean, however, that the rebellion was an event isolated from British rule in Tripura. Tripura was incorporated into the periphery of the British Indian empire in the late eighteenth century, though a British political Agent in Tripura symbolizing imperial control was not appointed until 1871. Tripura underwent major demographic and socio-economic changes from the late nineteenth century – a period, which interestingly, also witnessed the rise of a series of tribal uprisings. The British Political Agent in Tripura, H.J. Todd, in his Resident's Fortnightly Reports,[38] blamed the ruler and provided some indications of the deep-rooted causes of the rebellion and the 'endemic unrest' among the Reangs:

> The aboriginal tribes of Reangs who from time to time have given trouble to the Tripura government usually because of lack of interest the government has taken in their welfare recently approached His Highness for redress of

their grievances and he has decided to set up a committee by a State High Court Judge to enquire into the almost endemic unrest and to suggest measures to ameliorate their conditions generally. The Maharaja has been strongly advised to extend such enquiries into the wellbeing of all his tribesmen.[39]

A special Enquiry Committee was formed in September 1945 with four members – Shri Kumara Nandalal Devbarma, Akhil Chandra Devbarma, Lt. Thakur Hara Chandra Devbarma and Lt. Jitendra Mohun Devbarma – all Tripuris. Jitendra Mohun Devbarma admitted in an interview that the Reang had several times brought to the attention of the king their grievances but with little positive response.[40] We have already seen that the government itself admitted that the Reangs had made several unsuccessful appeals for lowering the rates of taxation. The Reangs had first tried other peaceful means and restored to non-violent mobilization before taking recourse to arms as a means of redressing their grievances.

The Reang rebellion was a minority rebellion within the Tripura tribal-peasant society. It most distinctive feature was that it developed independently of both the Congress and the communist movements in Tripura which represented two major brands of the so-called 'modern' elite mobilization in Tripura. Thus, the mass mobilization in the Reang rebellion was autonomous, and the idioms through which the politics of the rebellion was expressed were indigenous, 'traditional'.

The Reang rebellion, as we have already indicated, represented a powerful indigenous tradition of mass politics with its own mode of mobilization, idioms and methods. While the Reang rebels were engaged in violent anti-monarch activities and virtually broke down princely autocracy in large parts of the State, the urban-based communists as well as Congressman of Tripura (we will discuss them later) experimented with different brands of constitutionalist politics, focusing on the middle class, and cautiously coined 'appropriate' terms to express mild protests against monarchical autocracy. Interestingly, during the Reang rebellion, the Tripura unit of the Communist Party of India[41] had to support the war effects of the monarch who was an ally of the British, and tone down its criticism of the monarchy. The late Biren Dutta, the founding father of Tripura communism said that the Usha Ranjan Devbarma had joined the Tripura Rifles as a captain under the instructions of the party,[42] who was sent to the hills to make the people conscious of the cause of the people War line. Needless to say, the politics of the Reang rebellion was anathema to communist as well as Congress politics[43] in the State.

The State unit of CPI from the early 1950s tried to explain away the Reang rebellion by describing it as 'spontaneous' and therefore doomed to failure in the absence of the leadership of the Communist Party. The late Nripen Chakrabarty the former, long-time Chief Minister of Tripura (1978–88), then at the leadership of the Tripura Communist Party, 'lamented': 'But during the time of the rebellion in Tripura of the Communist Party was too weak to provide leadership to it'.[44] This was a negative attitude to the rebellion. The Communist Party, even if it was then powerful, could not conceivably lead such a rebellion which developed with features fundamentally opposed to the prevailing assumptions of Tripura communism. The communists then did not have the tactics of violence in their agenda. It was doubtful if they were ready to engage in looting and plundering rich people's property. Would they allow religion to have any say in the movement? Such uncomfortable questions are always avoided in the communist assessment of those kinds of rebellion. The Reang rebels did not have as their goal either socialism or any precise class demands. Even though they paralyzed the existing monarchy in parts of the State, they did not want to do away with monarchy generally as a political institution because they eventually set up an alternative monarchy of their own. There were, therefore, fundamental divergences between this rebellion and Tripura communism.

The rebellion was not 'spontaneous' in the sense Chakrabarty 'described'. Our evidences amply showed that the Reang rebellion combined and unified spontaneity and conscious leadership in its practical action. It was 'spontaneous' in so far as those who took part in it were not rebellion by the force of any political party, but drawn into the orbit of the rebellion by the force of circumstances; on the other hand, it was consciously planned, led and disciplined. The defence system of the rebels, their group-based activity and their new setup of government are cases in point.[45] 'Pure spontaneity' Gramsci says, 'does not exist in history'.[46] According to him, the 'unity between spontaneity and conscious leadership or discipline [is] precisely the real political action of the subaltern group claiming to represent the masses'. Gramsci, on the whole, views spontaneity as the 'most marginal and peripheral element of the history of the subaltern classes'.[47] The Reang rebellion, even though it received substantial support of subordinate social groups like the Reangs and the Noaties, did not eventuate in any structural change in Tripura. This was a historic limitation of this mass revolt. It broke down monarchy in parts of the State but replaced it with an alternative which was not qualitatively different from the old one. The rebels set up an alternative monarchy with an additional dimension of religiosity. This revolt was not successful in the sense of achieving some major objective. Such type of mass rebellions rarely has any clearly defined objective. Neither do they have any long-term ideology. The Reang rebellion was millenarian in the same sense as Adas (1979) would have believed; but it was a special type of tribal-peasant protest; it posed a very powerful challenge to Tripura monarchy. The Reang rebellion weakened the princely power in Tripura to a great extent, and added significantly to the disintegration of the existing socio-economic and political structure. It can therefore be said that this rebellion paved the way for major and more powerful political protests in Tripura. The Reang rebellion was in a real sense the precursor to the violent mass mobilization during 1948–51 led by the Tripura Rajya Gana Mukti Parished (Tripuri Nationalist Liberation Organization) which completed the process of disintegration of princedom in Tripura, and through its own integration with Indian communism in the early fifties paved the way for communist hegemony in Tripura. But this is a subject, which is discussed in chapter 6.

*ABBREVIATION*: TE = Tripura Era which falls ten years ahead of the Christian Era.

## Notes

1. See, for instance, Brass (1990); Alavi (1989); and Halliday and Alavi (1988). Adas (1979) defends also the elite thesis in his study of millenarian protest movements on the global scale. His study of the Munda and the Birsa Rising in Chota Nagpur in East-Central India in the late 1890s (19–25) does not seem to establish though that Birsa Munda hailed from an elite background.
2. They include the reports of the Government of Tripura Police and Intelligence (including Military Intelligence) on the course and character of the rebellion available in the Tripura State Civil Secretariat Archive, Agartala (a photocopy under the title 'Records of Ratan Moni Reang Rebellion' is available in the British Library of Economic and Political Sciences, LSE, London), and the Residents' Fortnightly Report, India Office, London. The late Manimay Devbarma of Agartala had a private collection on different aspects of Tripura's modern history including the Reang rebellion which are to be found in the offices of *Daink Sambad* (a Bengali daily, Agartala), and *Daily Desher Katha* (in Bengali; daily news paper of the Tripura State Committee of the CPI-M).
3. See Guha (1982: 1–9).
4. For instance, Devbarma (1974); and Singh (1968).
5. See, Chanda (1983: 12).
6. The Concise Oxford English Dictionary, 7th ed., 1982, p. 863.
7. See Guha (1983: 2).
8. Tripura Census Bibarani, Agartala, 1931, pp. 157–71.
9. Hunter (1909: 62–20).
10. Tripura Census Bibarani, p. 73.
11. Tripura Census Bibarani, p. 73.
12. Karlekar (1985: 1432).
13. Tripura Census Bibarani, p. 73.
14. Tripura Census Bibarani, pp. 157–71.
15. Tripura District Gazetteer, Agartala, 1971.
16. Tripura State Gazettee, 1913 in Tripura State Gazetteer Sanaklan, Agartala, 1971, p. 17.
17. Tripura State Gazettee Sankalan, p. 17.
18. Quoted in The Socialist Perspective, Calcutta (1977: 26).
19. Tripura Census Bibarani, pp. 71–8.
20. 'The State Gazette on War Supplement' (1942), Civil Secretariat Archive, Agartala.
21. Quoted in Dutta (1982: 34).
22. 'A Secret Message' dated 21.4.53 Tripura Era, August 1943.
23. 'A Letter from the Govt. of Tripura', Pol. Dept. Sub: Military Intelligence, No. 1662/P/8142, 1–87 to Martin, O.M., CES, ICS Commissioner, Chittagong Division Comilla, dated 2 August 1942. In this letter the concerned official enquired about the Reangs and the Noatias of the Chittagong Hill Tracts: 'These tribes are more or less allied to the hill people inhabiting the Tripura state . . . I shall be glad you could kindly let me known particulars about the habitats of these tribes as this information will be very useful to us now and may also be utilized in the future for some useful purpose'. This shows that the government of Tripura was concerned about an impending danger arising out of the Reangs and the Noatias, by 1942.
24. 'An Order by the Major of the King's Bodyguards Forces', Memo No. 142/14.4.53 TE, Ujjayanta Palace, Agartala, p. 1–3.
25. Case No. 9 (4) 53, 19.4.53 TE (July 1943).

26 One barrel gun, Camp. No. 8, No. 5 (2072) dated 23.4.53 Te signed by S.L. Bhattacharyya.
27 Message No. 2, Time 1 pm, Place Kurma, No. 1989 dated 20.4.53 TE (Copy to Mj. B.L. Devbarma).
28 Secret Correspondence from Lt B. L. Devbarma to the Divisional Officer Bilonia, No. 4 dated 3 August 1943.
29 Letter from Mj. B.L. Devbarma to Lt. Nagendra Devbarma dated 22.4.53 TE. TE is ten years ahead of the English calendar.
30 Message to Mj. B. L. Devbarma, Camp. Udaipur dated 14 April 1953, TE.
31 Letter to Mj. B. L. Devbarma from the Commissioner of Police, Agartala, No. 2147/29.4.53 TE.
32 Sen (1971: 17).
33 Letter from Lt. Nagendra Devbarma to the Commissioner of Police, Agartala 16.4.53 TE.
34 Message to Mj. B. L. Devbarma Camp: Udaipur 14.4.53 TE.
35 A Message to B. L. Devbarma, Camp: Rajbari, dated 21.4.53 TE.
36 Message No. 1915 received by the Commissioner of Police, Agartala, dated 17.4.53 TE, 'Very Urgent'.
37 'On investigation it is known that the following persons within the jurisdiction of this police station were important leaders of the Ratan Moni party: Chini FA, Dokan Fa, Kanaka Fa, Balaka Fa, Hani Fa, Durgaram Fa and Bidika Fa. At present Ratan Moni's wife is living in Ananda Bazar within our police station. Ratan Moni's followers have high respect for her and care for her a lot. It is said that they are turning towards Christianity; they go th church every Sunday' (Copy of the report of a police officer of Fatikroy, dated 13.4.57 TE (February 1948).
38 'Residents Fortnightly Reports in the second half of September 1945' Ref. 2484/1945 (H.J. Todd), IOL, London.
39 Ibid.
40 Quoted in Das Gupta, *Gomoti*, p. 19.
41 That was the period when the party had to swallow the so-called People's War line (formulated by the then-Communist Party of the Soviet Union) after the German invasion of the Soviet Union in June 1941.
42 Dutta, B. Amar Smritite, pp. 32–3.
43 It was always and still remains a very weak force.
44 Chanda, S. Tripurar Kommunist Party, p. 12.
45 See Das Gupta, *Gomoti*, for details.
46 Gramsci (1971: 199).
47 Gramsci (1971: 199).

# 6 Origins of the communist movement in Tripura

Jana Mongal Samity, Jana Shiksha Samity and Paraja Mondal[1]

## Introduction

This chapter traces the genesis of the communist movement in Tripura in the historical context in which Congress nationalism was nearly non-existent, and the Reang rebellion (Chapter 5) posed a very powerful challenge to the existing State authority. The reason for the very weak position of Congress nationalism in Tripura was to be understood in terms of the Congress policy overall not to initiate any political activities in India's princedom (Jeffrey 1981; Ernst and Pati eds. 2007). The (Congress) INC defended the cause of self-determination of the peoples of the princely States but refrained from taking any active part in the people's movements that were growing there. This was reiterated in the Nagpur Congress (1920), the Karachi Congress (1936) and Haripura (1938) of the Congress. In the princely States, a different brand of anti-colonial and democratic movement took shape under the banner of Praja Mondal (i.e the States' Subject/Peoples' movement) which began to demand from the 1930s responsible government in the princely States. In Tripura, this was an opportunity for the communist group to initiate and intervene in social, cultural and political associations and movements in order to build on them, and occupy any space (limited though it was) available. The initial growth of the communist movement in Tripura developed in symbiosis with various such associations that the communist leaders pioneered and made use of in order to make their presence felt.[2]

## Rise of the communist movement in Tripura

While commenting on the communist movement in Telangana[3] in the late 1940s Morris-Jones said: 'The fact that the communist attempted rising look place in a princely State was not wholly accidental. . . . Congress activity in those units had always been on a reduced scale and its relative advantage over other parries less marked' Morris-Jones 1987: 75). Congress nationalism did not pre-empt Tripura and the communists there did not have to swim against the nationalist tide. Biren Datta (Interview at Agartala on 12 November 1986) the founder of the communist movement in Tripura, pinpointed the 'absence of strong bourgeois nationalist ideas and leaders in Tripura as one of the favourable factors for the development of Tripura communism' (Bhattacharyya 1992).

Communism came very late to Tripura. The communist movement was founded in Tripura in 1938 by a group of former nationalist 'terrorists' of Tripura. mostly Bengalis, with a few tribals who were converted in jail. The birth of communism in Tripura was not preceded by any vigorous peasant or working-class movement in the State. Intellectually, Tripura had no tradition of socialist thought and historically no tradition of a socialist movement. It witnessed very little anti-British nationalist politics. Until the late 1930s, princely Tripura had not even a tradition of a popular movement for 'responsible government', as in other princely States in the country. Tripura did not witness, historically, the rise of any representative political institutions. An absolutist and autocratic monarchy *bubagra* (a Tripuri word for the principle of divine right of the king) reigned supreme in the State as late as 1947 when monarchy ended effectively though not formally by the sudden death of its last monarch. 'Backward', isolated and 'obscure' for centuries, Tripura had hardly heard about the Russian Socialist revolution even in the 1930s. On the face of it Tripura seemed an unlikely part of India to become a communist stronghold.

Geographically located within undivided Bengal, Tripura could hardly remain impervious to rapid political changes taking place in neighbouring Bengal which was the hotbed of radical politics in India during the 1930s and the 1940s. The third Session of the Left-dominated All-India Kisan Sabha (Peasant Organization) was held (May 11–14, 1931) in Comilla which was next door to Tripura. Moreover, the Tripura rulers had a *zamindary*(Rosnabad) within the Bengal district of Tripura whose headquarters town was Comilla. The officials serving in the princely administration at Agartala and those in Rosnabad were overlapping. and there was free movement of people between (Hill) Tripura and Rosnabad (Hill) Tripura, although separate as a political unit was therefore not impregnable to political penetration from outside. The Third Session of the All-India Kisan Sabha passed revolutionary demands like the class struggle as the basis of the Kisan movement and the agrarian revolution as the goal of the peasant movement[4] (Rasul 1974: 33–4). Kaji Samsuddin Kadem, a Congress activist of Tripura (Bengal district and a member of the Bengal Provincial Committee of the INC), argued that the mass movement in Tripura was heavily influenced by the powerful peasant movement in 1930s in the neighbouring (Bengal) district of Tripura.[5] While commenting on the political awareness in the late 1930s among the people of princely Tripura, he said, one bas to begin with the powerful anti-imperialist mass movement in the Maharaja's *zamindary* of Rosnabad which is about 80 miles along the western border of Tripura State. In this area, in every village there was a peasant and a Congress Committee. The mass movement in princely Tripura was part of the mass movement in Rosnabad.[6]

In Tripura, communists emerged out of the disillusionment of a group (in this case the famous Anusilan group) of Bengal terrorists who mainly formed the earlier group of communist leaders. As a princely State, Tripura did not have to fight a liberation movement against British colonial rule. Terrorism or what is usually termed 'revolutionary terrorism' was one of the streams of the Indian freedom movement against the British which sought to liberate India by committing individual acts of terror against colonial officialdom. Terrorism in Tripura was an extension of Bengal terrorism; it was embraced by the urban Tripura youth, mostly Bengalis in the 1920s. Tripura witnessed from the early 1920s the establishment of several indigenous branches of terrorist organization in close proximity with Anusilan and Jugantar. But the Anusilan Samity was much more actively organized in Tripura (Majumdar 1963: 286).[7] One major mode of action of the terrorists was political robbery. In 1932 members of the Anusilan Samity of Tripura robbed a pawnshop near Agartala Municipality on 23 Chaitra 1342 TF (April 1932) and looted money and ornaments (Sen 1971: 57–64). The participation of the Tripuris in the anti-British Indian nationalist-terrorist activities was quite significant. They subscribed, however vaguely, to an all-Indian nationalism, when they joined the terrorist movement. Many of the terrorists were converted to Marxism in jail, although not all of them joined the Tripura unit of the Communist Party of Indian (CPI) subsequently. Those who constituted the CPI unit in Tripura in 1938 were mostly upper-caste Bengalis like Biren Datta, Ananta De, Debaprosad Sen, Nalini Sen Gupta, Santi Datta, Prarnanshu Chaudbury, Kanu Sen, and Rabi Sen. Nimai Devbarma and Usha Ranjan Devbarma were the two notable tribal members in the first unit of the CPI in Tripura. Two prominent Tripuri ex-terrorists, Probhat Roy and Bansi Thakur, the royal notables, who also embraced Marxism in jail and worked with the communists in Tripura in and through different regional political organizations from 1938 onwards, but they never joined the Communist Party. Disillusioned with Tripura communism and with the turn of events in Tripura politics, they turned in the late 1940s to the development and propagation of a radical doctrine of Tripuri nationalism (Chapter 8).

The ex-terrorists constituted part of the earlier group of leaders and provided recruits to the CPI on the national level. In Bengal, as David M. Laushey (1975)[8] has shown, virtually all of the radical parties including the Communist Party drew some or all of their membership from the terrorist groups. In Tripura, the ex-terrorists provided the recruits and leader not only to the Communist Party but also to the State Congress. Most of the Tripura terrorist '*detenus*' were released by the year 1938.[9] Their presence in the State did not escape the attention of the State Commissioner of Police who complacently reported in 1939:

> [t]he only disturbing element was a batch of ex-detenus numbering 22 who were sitting idle in the state. Each considered himself a martyr to the cause of the country and thought it was up to him to redress the grievances of the dumb millions of the land.[10]

In the specific case of Tripura, communists' identification with the regional loyalties was quite problematic. This also raised the question of the applicability of the new mode of politics required a communist movement which was 'Western' and alien to an indigenous tradition, a tradition which espoused a different mode of politics.

At birth, Tripura communism lacked any working-class or peasant elements. It was the local Congress rather than the communists who first attempted to organize

Tripura's proletariat in the tea gardens and among the motor drivers, though with very little success. Beginning in 1916, Tripura witnessed the establishment of a number of tea gardens under State patronage. By 1931 the number of tea gardens went up to 50, covering an area of 3394 Hectare which produced 1,249,374 pounds of tea. By 1950 the number went up to 56 which employed 15,000 workers. Interestingly, both the workers employed in the tea gardens, and the owners appeared to be 'outsiders' – the workers were tribals from other parts of India like Bihar, Madhya Pradesh and Orissa; and the owners were a group of Bengali capitalists who were allowed by the Tripura rulers in 1915 to purchase land in Tripura for a tea plantation.[11] Dutta (1982) recalled that the nationalist-terrorist tradition of politics was a hindrance to class-based mass mobilization. He reminisced:

> The terrorist leaders taught us that for the success of the anti-imperialist struggle and for removing the British from the Indian soil, national unity was of utmost importance. We were taught that class contradictions and class struggles would stand in the way of achieving national freedom. Because of our middle-class origins, and lack of knowledge of Marxism – Leninism, we used to believe that.
>
> (Dutta 1986: 2)

In Tripura the tea garden workers were treated like half-slaves with no labour laws and civil liberties. Leftist-led unions in the tea gardens began to spring up only from the end of 1940s, and the first Left-dominated All Tripura Workers Union was formed as late as 1951.[12]

One all-India-level Communist Party source[13] suggests that the Agartala unit of the CPI was in the late 1930s under the Comilia (now in Bangladesh) District Committee of the CPI which again was under the Bengal District Committee of the CPI. Saroj Mukherjee mentioned that those associated with the Tripura party were Biren Datta, Debaprosad Sen, Kanu Sen, Benu Sen and Captain Usha Ranjan Devbarma. The Agartala unit of the CPI composed of Agartala based Bengali middle-class youths nonetheless was only a tiny cell working secretly. It went neither to the villages nor the hills where most Tripuris lived to launch a movement for their emancipation, nor did it prepare itself for leading any revolt against monarchy. It confined its activities to ideological indoctrination mainly among the students of Umakanta Academy (Boarding High School) at Agartala. Aghore Devbarma who was then a student and convert to communism later recalled that Datta in particular in those small secret meetings would talk about the Russian Socialist Revolution of 1917 led by the workers and peasants.[14] The communists were then an ideological propaganda-group engaged in much abrupt clandestine activity. This did not escape the attention of the British Political Agent who reported:

> Printed leaflets (in Bengali) were distributed in the town by the local communist group preaching communist revolution and exhorting the people to join the Civil Disobedience, Railways and Industrial strike etc. The leaflets

are very anti-British in tone. The leaflets are reported to have been brought in from Camilla.[15]

The local archival records suggest that those leaflets, were entitled '*Asanna Biplab*' (Impending Revolution), '*Lal Nisan*' (Red Star), '*Ingrajer Juddey na ek bhai na ek pai*' (No cooperation with the British war) and so on.[16] Those slogans of revolution sounded hollow in Tripura which was neither confronting a socialist revolution nor seemed ready for one. But one thing that was clear from those slogans was that the local unit was then under the obvious influence of the All-India Party (CPI). At any rate, the Tripura communists made little headway in the State in the early years of its growth.

## Second phase of development of communism in Tripura

The Tripura communist movement developed until 1948 mostly within the frameworks of a series of popular social and cultural associations and movements under the banner of the Jana Mongal Samity (Association for Public Welfare/ JMS), the Jana Shikhya Samitv (Association for Mass Literacy JSS) and the Proja Mondal (Subjects' Association PM). From its birth in the late 1930s until the late 1940s the Tripura communist movement's central concern was survival. During this period the communists were an active element in the regional political movements. They sought to influence the course and character of those movements and to utilize the space available within them in order to build on them. The Tripura communist movement until 1948 cannot be understood without an account of the interaction between Tripura communism and these social and political associations.

### *Jana Mongal Samitv*

As the first 'modem' radical political organization, the Jana Mongal Samity (henceforth JMS) was formed in September 1938 (Bhadra 13. 1348 Tripura Era.). Those actively involved in its establishment were higher caste Bengali professionals and a few ex-Anusilan nationalist-terrorists, mostly Bengalis, with a few (tribal) Tripuris. It was an upper middle-class Bengali organization in the predominantly Bengali city of Agartala, so much that the scope for communist penetration was limited. And yet, the communist utilized even me smallest space available within the JMS.

The rise of the JMS was a significant political development. It introduced what, following Morris-Jones, may be called, the 'modem language of politics' in Tripura. This language 'speaks of policies and interests, programmes and plans'.[17] 'It expresses itself', he says, 'in arguments and representations, discussions and demonstrations, deliberations and decisions' (Morris-Jones 1987: 54). Prior to this, the dominant language of mass politics in Tripura was what the Reang rebellion (Chapter 3) had represented, a language in which violence was the most powerful form.

Dharani Goswami, a Leftist leader in undivided Bengal (now with the CPI) who visited Tripura in 1939 was more optimistic in believing that the JMS had been formed to launch a 'powerful and united struggle against the authoritarian regime'.[18] How far the JMS was able to launch an effective struggle against princedom was debatable, but the existence of popular discontent against the existing regime was clear. This found its first organized expression in the JMS but not until the Royal Proclamation of Constitutional Reforms (1938) which provided the context and an opportunity for expressing limited public opinion.

The Tripura ruler declared on 26.04.48 TE (August 1935) that he was to announce constitutional reforms. The proposed reforms envisaged the establishment of a Raj Sabha – an advisory body to the ruler, the appointment of a Mantri Parishad (Council of ministers), and the establishment of a Legislative Assembly with 'adequate legislative as well as recommendatory powers, comprising of 54 members of whom 29 shall be elected by different groups from constituencies on the basis of broad franchise, territorial and otherwise, representing different interests', and the remaining 25 nominated members including seven non-official to represent the special interests not covered by the territorial electorate. Such an announcement was made on April 16, 1939.[19]

These proposed reforms (which were not implemented) did not aim at any major changes in the State apparatus nor did they curb the powers of the king. They proposed alterations but not substantial changes. The so-called 'broad franchise' was not adult franchise: it was, if at all, a limited adult franchise. But in a State which had only seen stark autocracy for centuries, such limited reforms – even their announcement – were welcome. The Royal announcement was popular and so a framework for the politics of the JMS. Probhat Roy, one of the founders of the JMS, traced the birth of the JMS to the Royal Proclamation. stressing the loyalist character of the association:

> This declaration foreshadowing the introduction of a reform was acclaimed with enthusiasm particularly in those who were interested in the particular standpoint of the state . . . This side of popular feeling led to the birth of the Jana Mangal Samity.[20]

The JMS was initially meant, to be at least, by a section of its leadership, a loyalist association. The Samity declared its aim as the attainment of responsible government under the aegis of the king in all legitimate ways starting on the basis of the reforms, which was comparable to the first phase of the INC in India as a whole when it was constitutionalist.

Roy and Ganga Prosad Sharma (both working in the government Publicity Department) who played the major role in forming the JMS sought to make it an organization . . . with the object of expressing gratitude and unstinted support to the beloved ruler.[21]

Roy later wrote in his private diary that he (and Sharma) had 'to remain responsible to the ruler for acquainting him with the moves and guidance of the organization'. Roy said that he had wanted to make the JMS 'a link between ruler and ruled knocking down the Chinese Wall of vested interests' (the Bengali bureaucrats). Of eight members of the Central Committee, only three were Tripuris. Of the five Bengalis, four were Muslims. The dominance of the Bengali Muslims reflected the peasant element in the JMS. Biren Datta, then a member of the Tripura cell of the CPI, was the Assistant Secretary of the CC and the Secretary of the managing Committee, the editor and publisher of the *Projar Katha*, the mouthpiece of the JMS. Datta used his powerful position within the JMS organizational hierarchy to redefine the JMS movement, and to give it a new orientation. Within a year of its birth, the JMS opened eight branches at the sub-divisional level and its membership grew to 187. The Chief Minister wrote in his secret correspondence with the State Commissioner of Police that the JMS was 'carrying on their organizational work with a new vigour', but in most branches, the Bengalis were predominant. This predominance was, however, no guarantee for the success of communist penetration, as the Agartala-based Bengalis enjoyed royal privilege and patronage.

Another feature of the JMS was its urban (Agartala) base. This was true for most of the Tripuris as well as the Bengalis involved in it. JMS organization did not penetrate beyond the sub-divisional level. In a predominantly tribal society, the JMS incorporated few rural tribal elements. In class terms, the leadership was dominated by the upper class, including landlords and barristers.

*Ideology*

JMS leadership stressed on several occasions that the JMS was 'neither Congress of British India nor a peasant Committee; it was based on royal approval and royalism'. Its objectives were different. The first issue of *Projar Katha* (May 1940, No. 1) which declared the JMS's ideological foundation also revealed the communists' manipulation of space. Datta who edited this issue avoided Marxist idioms in his analysis. Neither socialism nor the abolition of the State was mentioned as a JMS objective. Datta's introduction to *Projar Katha* tactfully redefined JMS aims:

> Achievement of a full responsible government under the aegis of the monarch is the objective of the people of Tripura . . . it is now an important duty of every citizen to restrain oneself from spontaneity and emotion but organize and unite to raise the political consciousness of the people rapidly. In order to achieve this it is necessary to conduct the movement in legitimate ways and peacefully.[22]

Datta could not go beyond this demand when working through the JMS. Neither could he preach violence as a method of agitation. These were the objective constraints. But his message to the 'producing subjects of Tripura to organize and unite' to raise popular political consciousness was clear. That was one instance of how he attempted to put a communist message through to the masses. Another important aspect of the ideology of the JMS was its radical critique of the proposed constitutional reforms. This critique shows strong communist influence.

This was in a sense a critique of the existing system, and expressed the politics of the JMS. The *Projar Katha* pointed out that the proclamation had provided for restricted franchise which entitled only royal notaries, talukdars, businessmen, lawyers, members of the Municipality and Gram Mondalis, and university graduates to vote, and criticized it for not introducing universal suffrage. It also denigrated communal representation. That the women and the propertyless were excluded from the franchise was also pointed out.

The JMS did not simply present itself as a negative force in Tripura politics. Its manifesto contained an alternative programme of action and an alternative framework of polity and society. At a divisional conference (held at Dharmanagar. 16 Chaitra. I34S T.F. April 1(1939) the JMS adopted motions to ensure the democratic foundation of the proposed local self-government: rejection of the communal principle of election and adoption of the principle of free and fair election of members as well as President of the Gram Mondalis; adult franchise; no nomination by the King of any members or President of the Gram Mondalis; freedom of action for the Gram Mondalis; presence of a first class Magistrate at the time of polling; and a secret ballot with the accepted symbols of the contesting candidates.

The JMS's 10-point charter of radical political demands stressed the fundamental need for full responsible government and an alternative structure of power. Its political demands were a fully representative and responsible government: a State Council (Legislature) to be composed of representatives elected by the people: each representative to represent 5000 people; the monarch to call the leader of the majority to form a council of ministers after the conclusion of the election; a chairman of the State Council to be elected by a majority of the members of the house to look after the formal deliberations of the house; a ministerial oath of allegiance and honesty; the State Council to have powers to enact and amend laws and to declare laws null and void, and also powers to prepare the budget and present it for approval to the King. Politically the JMS thus sought to establish, what in Marxist terms, is called, 'bourgeois democracy' under constitutional monarchy.

The JMS's 16-point socio-economic demands included compulsory and free universal education, road and communication facilities; provision for public health; establishment of agricultural banks to offer loans to the peasants in order to rescue them from the clutches of feudal exploitation; abolition of the practice of confiscation of properties of the peasants in case of their failure to repay loans; rent-free leases of land in the inaccessible areas for five years; establishment of industries at State expense; reduction of rent; export duty on cotton paddy and rice, jute and oil seeds; and abolition of road tax. Relative to time and place, these demands were quite radical, but they did not include land reforms, which in a predominantly peasant society was a crucial demand. Roy later provided a clue to this limitation of the JMS. He argued that although the JMS had represented an advance over the *Sabuj Samity*, it could not go beyond the 'dominance of the representatives of the bourgeoisie'.[23]

Even this moderate form of agitation was not tolerable to the princely administration. The administration put most of the JMS leaders into prison by 1941 and expelled others from the State.

## Jana Shiksha Samity (Association for Mass Literacy)

In commenting on the early growth of the communist movement in Tripura, a CPI Central Committee Political Resolution (March 1953) said: 'It is very often forgotten that in Tripura, one of the most powerful bases of the party today, it was on the basis of a literacy campaign that the party grew in the first stage': From the above observation, one should not arrive at any ecological fallacy about Tripura communism. There was no direct causal connection between literacy and communism in Tripura, and yet, the Jana Shiksha Samity (JSS Association for Mass Literacy) played an important role in the development of Tripura communism. To begin with, the local communists supported this movement, maintained close contact with it and influenced it. The JSS provided an organizational framework for the development of communism and also potential recruits to the local unit of the Communist Party.

A sense of Tripura identity provided a powerful ideological impetus for the emergence of this literacy campaign. The founders of the JSS believed that the key to the building of a self-conscious Tripuri identity lay in mass education. A Tripuri ethnic organization, the JSS, was formed on 27 December 1945 and marked a significant political development in post-war Tripura. The initiative to form the JSS came from educated tribal youths. The fundamental goal of the organization, as its very name suggests, was to launch an anti-illiteracy campaign in a State which was about 8 per cent literate in 1941. The hill tribal youths were associated with the formation of the JSS in a two-day long conference in the house of Hemanta Devbarma at Agartala. Illiteracy was considered to be central to Tripura's tribal problems. A Central Committee was formed with Hemanta Devbarma as General Secretary, Sudhanya Devbarma as President, Dasarath Devbarma as Vice-President and Aghore Devbarma as acting Secretary, all founding members of the JSS. The organization was non-political, and meant to be so, and that was why neither Biren Datta (communist) nor Probhat Roy (Leftist) was invited to the conference. Although the basic aim of the organization was to launch an uncompromising struggle to eradicate illiteracy and poverty it had a wider perspective. The objective of the JSS included: literacy through the establishment of State-run and private schools; social reforms to liberate the society from superstitions and corruption, to develop native cottage industries, and to encourage tribal peasants to take up settled cultivation and to discourage them from shifting cultivation. In order to rouse mass consciousness in favour of the JSS, appeals were made to Tripuri ethnic sentiments and emotions.[24]

The JSS ethnicity was understood, by and large. positively as a search for identity of the Tripuris, and not as communally and negatively against the Bengalis. The Bengalis were not viewed as an oppressor nationality although anti-foreigner attitudes were not entirely absent in the JSS thinking. For instance, in, a pamphlet entitled 'To the Hill People of the State', the Secretary of the JSS, Aghore Devbarma, said that to expand higher education, 'we need first of all to expand education, otherwise the money now spent on schools and colleges to the benefit of the foreigners [sic Bengali migrants in the state] would not help our desire for education' 41. In the same document, Devbarma Tripura Communism until 1948 asked the people to mobilize resources for the education of the 'permanent, original subjects of Tripura'.[25]

The opponents of the JSS dubbed the movement 'Bangal Kheda' (Drive away the Bengalis). This view was strongly condemned by the Vice-President, Dasarath Devbarma. In an article 'Bangal Kheda Movement in Tripura State' in April 1948, he defended the non-communal character of the JSS arguing that the JSS had supported the Proja Mondal movement in Tripura, and politically its demands were no different from it. The fundamental demands of the Proja Mondal, Devbarma stressed, were the definition of citizenship in Tripura, the abolition of monopoly dominance of the reactionary exploitative classes of Tripura, Bengali bureaucrats and its replacement by a popular representative government. But the core demand of the JSS remained eradication of illiteracy. Ideologically the JMS was preoccupied with the problem of the internal growth and development of Tripuri nationality:

> *The Tripura Kahatriyas are a nation* but not a developed full-fledged nationality. They wanted to develop it by raising it up to the level of developed nationalities. But there are a number of hindrances: Tripura's feudalism, illiteracy, and monarchy (emphasis added).[26]

The JSS never made any direct attack on the monarchy. Its support for the Proja Mondal Movement and its opposition to monopoly dominance of the reactionary class meant in effect its opposition to upper-class Bengali Hindu dominance because Tripura's feudalism had been mediated by the Bengalis.

## Impact of communism on the JSS

The communist influence in the formation of the non-political JSS was powerful. According to Dasarath Devbarma, the founding Vice-President of the JSS: 'From the very beginning the Communists tried to develop a close relationship with the Jana Shikhya Samity and they spared time to extend their support to the latter's anti-illiteracy drive. Notable among the communist workers who maintained close contact was Biren Dutta'.

In his memoirs, Dutta said that at that time 'the small party group in Tripura was bound with the responsibility to understand the specific problems of the tribals, to develop anti-feudal movements, and to directly intervene in different spontaneous mass movements'. In 1945 open political activity in Tripura was still legally banned. Dutta's advice to utilize non-political organizations reflected his sense of the real situation. As a consequence, he managed to take some JSS leaders to the All-India Kisan Conference in Hasnabad (1946) where they met P. C. Joshi. Joshi apparently advised them to build a movement for literacy which, according to Devbarma, endorsed the stand already arrived at locally. The JSS leadership accepted Dutta as a friend in their fight for tribal interests and was grateful for communist support. Subsequently, this favourable rather pro-communist atmosphere within the JSS facilitated the spread of communism in Tripura's hills.

From its inception the JSS launched a vigorous campaign to establish organizational branches in every sub-division of the State, particularly in Sadar, Khowal and Kamalpur. Each sub-division was under the charge of top ranking leaders; the targeted sub-divisions were to be, within two years, critical bases of Tripura communism. The JSS activists went from door to door in the villages. held mass meetings and organized processions. They focused on the need for mass education and social emancipation, establishment of schools and for financial help to the JSS. Violating the government ban, the JSS held mass meetings even in Agartala. Some influential tribal chiefs extended their moral support for the JSS, and contributed financially to its fund. The JSS Advisory Committee was composed of tribals. The JSS teachers were mostly Bengalis including a few tribals. The medium of instruction was Bengali which was still little known to the hill tribes. The focus in its campaign was the creation of mass awareness of the need for education, and self-reliance in building schools. Within a couple of years, the JSS had established 500 primary and medium-level schools in various parts of rural Tripura and enrolled 50,000 students, both boys and girls – which was the most solid achievement of this movement.

*Assessment*

The JSS was a relatively successful mass organization. Despite the fact that the government was unwilling to recognize most JSS schools, the movement continued its anti-illiteracy drive. The credit for the growth of literacy from 8 to 16 per cent between 1941 and 1951 was largely due to the JSS movement. The JSS was not a communist mass organization, however.

A section of the JSS leadership, Aghore Devbanna said he had 'strong reservations about communism'. Yet the communist association with the JSS movement paved the way for politicizing the JSS, and created a favourable atmosphere for the further growth of communism in the State. Thus, when the Proja Mondal was launched in 1946 as a political movement for achieving a responsible government and for civil rights, with the communists as the major participants, it was at the instance of the communists that the JSS joined the Proja Mondal movement, and some of its leaders became PM leaders.

But the JSS was able, within a year of its formation, to have activists and a committee in each and every village. As Aghore Devbanna said, in the absence of communist organization among the tribals, the communists (himself included) solely based themselves on the JSS in mobilizing the people for their cause. Little wonder, the anti-communist periodical' 'Abhyudai' described the Proja Mondal in Tripura as 'the Communist Party in disguise and the Jana Shikbya Samity as its vehicle'.

### *Tripura Rajya Proja Mondal (Tripura State Subjects' Association)*

Soon after the withdrawal of the legal ban on political activities in January 1946, the Tripura Rajya Proja Mondal (The Tripura State Subjects Association henceforth PM) was formed in May 1946 (25 Baisakh 1356 TE). The PM was a broad-based 'nationalist' political platform in Tripura for a responsible government and for civil rights. Ideologically, it was based on a Tripuri ethnic national identity which demanded a responsible government in Tripura through an end of Bengali domination in the State. The special significance of this organization was that through it the communists began to participate on a significant scale in Tripura politics. The communists participated in the PM as an independent force and decisively influenced its development.

Initially, the PM echoed the Indian National Congress. A substantial number of those who attended its founding meeting of the party were upper-class urban-based people with distinguished social positions: the State's Dewan, Chief Justice and Barristers. Another group associated with its formation comprised of political prisoners of Tripura released in 1945 (Biren Dutta, Ananta Lal De, Sukumar Bhowmik, Sachindra Lal Singha, Umesh Lal Singha, Jiten Dutta, Nalini Sengupta and Dwijen Datta). Those associated with the founding of the PM were Agartala-based, upper-caste Bengalis with only three Tripuris.

The PM platform was broad enough to accommodate many elements from nationalists to communists, and so there were internal divisions on the question of the tactics of agitation and the character of the movement. Roy, one of the founders of the PM, was royalist and constitutionalist. Dutta stressed the popular dimension of the movement and the need for organized protest.

However, the existence of factions within the PM was a serious handicap in the PM's organizational development. The Executive Committee was composed of the leading members of the then-defunct JMS and the local unit of the Communist Party. Jogesh Chandra Devbarma and Bir Chandra Devbarma, both Tripuri tribals, were the President and the Secretary. Debaprosad Sen Gupta, Secretary of the local unit of the Communist Party, represented the communists in the PM. Biren Datta edited and published the *Tripura Rajyer Katha* weekly) mouthpiece of the PM. Apart from the Bengali Hindus, there was a sizeable element of Bengali Muslims in the leadership.

In an article called '*Tripura Rajyey Proja Andoloner Roop*' ('nature of the people's struggle in Tripura State') in the PM organ, Probhat Roy stated the aim of the PM to be a 'full responsible government, and not class struggle'; the attainment of a responsible government under the aegis of the ruler; and non-violent and peaceful means of struggle.[27] Ideologically, the PM was based on kind of Tripuri 'nationalism' against the outsiders' ('*oproja*') domination over Tripura. By 'responsible government' Roy meant a 'democratic parliamentary government' which would mean 'not the dominance of one class over the State, but of all classes (equal partnership) in sharing state power'. He found two historical forces standing in the way of the realization of such a responsible government: the medieval feudal regime and the *Baidesahik Amla* (foreign bureaucracy) that perpetuated the undemocratic regime. He advocated the case for developing economic and democratic consciousness of all classes into a nationalism that would pave the way for establishing a democratic regime. Probhat Roy said that the *Amlatanrra* (bureaucratic regime) which existed in Tripura was not based on the consent of the people.

The 'foreign or alien bureaucracy' referred to above by Roy was a part of (British) Indian bureaucracy, in form, but not in content. As a result of the Tripura rulers' preference for educated Bengalis to man their administration, the princely administration of Tripura came to be entirely dominated by the 'migrated' Bengalis. This added a communal dimension to the pattern of State power in Tripura. Opposition to the alien domination could not avoid this. Bengali domination over Tripura was in a sense total, and so was the PM opposition to it. The Bengali domination in Tripura had a powerful economic dimension which the PM deeply resented: The cultivable land which once the Tripuris prepared by cutting jungles and hills is no longer in their possession, Land, trade, commerce, everything is now owned and controlled by the *oprojas*. The Tripuris have no place in government jobs either; they are now foreigners in their own land.

The PM's two fundamental political demands were: Tripura State for Tripura State subjects and a popular representative government under the aegis of the monarch in which the State subjects alone would have the right to elect representatives, and the *oprojas* would have no rights to vote.[28]

The PM movement thus excluded the Bengalis from sharing political power. It urged the 'pure subjects' of Tripura to join this organization. The leadership of the PM was cautious about being charged with communalism for stressing the above policy. It was asserted:

> The subjects of Tripura are very poor. Communalism is not their problem; their real problem is bread and butter, dominance of *oproja* over *projas*. Abjure all communalism, resolve to end the dominance of *oproja* over *projas*.[29]

In an article called 'Our Problem', Roy added that the PM's anti-Bengali position locally should not be taken to mean that it hated the Bengalis as such; it was only meant to protest against Bengali power in Tripura:

> The alien Bengali presence in all walks of in Tripura is a great hindrance to self-determination of the original subjects of Tripura: their very existence ... is now at stake. It is a problem of minority dominance over majority. The Proja Mondal is in this respect a protest movement. We must end this economic and political.[30]

The PM movement was essentially a Tripuri political movement for self-determination of the Tripuris, but not entirely led by the Tripuris. An important and powerful part of its leadership was the Bengalis. Also, the movement confined itself predominantly to urban areas which had a preponderance of the Bengalis. This had also been the case with the local unit of the Communist Party and the Tripura State Congress. The PM's failure to achieve a responsible government for Tripura was also a failure of the constitutionalist method of struggle, a failure rectified, to a large extent, by the Tripura Jativo Mukiti Parishadi (National Liberation Council of the Tripura State) which, formed in mid-1948, launched a powerful armed struggle during 1948–51 and was strongly influenced by the political thesis of the

Second Congress of the CPI (1948), and led by, to a great extent, the communist leadership in the State. This radical, tribal, ethno-nationalist and violent movement dismantled existing princely and bureaucratic State authority in large parts of the State, and paved the way for the real basis of communism among the tribals in Tripura – a subject treated in the next chapter.

## Conclusion

The materials presented in this chapter offer an early indication that the radical Left, small in strength and organization, was already adapting itself to the local environment and worked through associations and movements that were not neither revolutionary nor very challenging to established authority. The method of movement was constitutionalist to be precise, for eeking out a space for conducting the constitutionalist and peaceful democratic method of struggle. Of the three platforms, the JSS earned them good dividends since it was a campaign for literacy among the largely illiterate masses in the tribal princely regime. The campaign for mass literacy prepared a basis for the subsequent radical, tribal, ethno-nationalist movement led by the Gana Mukti Parishad (GMP) and also the incipient communist movement in the State – a subject treated at length in the next chapter.

## Notes

1 A fuller version of the subject has been treated in Bhattacharyya (1999: 56–89).
2 For an earlier version the subject, see Bhattacharyya (1990).
3 Now a State in the Indian Federation but was part of the princely State of Hyderabad before 1947.
4 Rasul (1974: 33–4). For details. Third Session of the All India Kisan Sabha, May 1938.
5 A press statement by Samsuddin Kadem in Collective Press Cuttings.
6 Ibid. CPC.
7 Majumdar (1963: Vol. 2, 286).
8 Laushey (1975).
9 Das Gupta (1988). B E ((1c)75). p. 40.
10 Report of the Commissioner of Police, Agartala, No. B4 I 6/518. dated April 22, 1939.
11 Sen (1971: 36–8).
12 Das Gupta, P R. ((JC)54) p. 103.
13 Mukherjee, S. *The Communist Party of India and We the Communists* (in Bengali).
14 Devbarma, A. (1986). The Primary Stage of the Communist Party and the Democreatic Movements in Tripura, Agartala: Tripura Darpan, p. 11.
15 *Residents Fortnightly Reports* ended on 30.8. 40.
16 *Chief Minister's Memo*. MNO. 252 – C Dated 9. 10. 40.
17 CPC 'Press statement of Dharani Goswami', Ananda Bazar Patrika dated April 1939 (25 Chaitra 1348 TE), a famous peasant leader of Bengal. In the statement 'The Proja Movement in Tripura: Demand for Democratic Rights', he said: 'Very recently there merged in Tripura a powerful and united struggle of the people of Tripura. Aganst the authoritarian regime. About seven months back the Jana Mongal Samity, has been formed as the sole representative of the people of Tripura. Under its leadership, the people of Tripura are advancing in their fight for democratic rights. The JMS has already been able to exert some pressure on the monarchy'.

18 CPC. Goswamit, op cit.
19 *The Statesman* Calcutta dated 16 April 1939.
20 Roy MSS, p. 18 (Harihar Bhattacharyya Personal Archives) HBPA).
21 Roy MSS, pp. 18–19. (HBPA).
22 *Prajar Katha* (Story of the Subjects of Tripura) (in Bengali) No.1, May 1940, p. 1 (HBPA).
23 *Padatik* (Agartala) 16 November 1986. (HBPA).
24 A JSS pamphlet dated 29 Bhadra 1356 TE (September 1946) (HBPA).
25 'Collected press clippings', *Ananda Bazar Patrika* Calcutta April 25, 1939; and May 11, 1939.
26 Devbarma (1981).
27 Roy (1948).
28 A pamphlet issued by the Proja Mondal (September 1946) (HBPA).
29 A pamphlet issued by the Proja Mondal (1946) (HBPA).
30 Roy (1946). 'Our Problems' (in Bengali), a leaflet. (HBPA).

# 7 Dialectics of radical ethnic nationalism and left radicalism in Tripura, 1948–51

Communist influence over the tribal mass mobilization

**Introduction**

Marxists, as we have seen above (Chapter 1), are opposed, theoretically, to any non-class identity and loyalties. Marxism is considered as opposed to ethnic nationalism and nationalism *per se*. But in Tripura it was in and through the agency of the *Tripura Rajya Jatiyo/Gana Mukti Parishad* (henceforth GMP for short) and its deep engagement in an insurrection during 1948–51 that the Left radicals in the shape of the State unit of the CPI acquired its first ever mass bases and that too among the tribes. It was a watershed in the history of Tripura communism as well as the radical political history of Tripura in days of transitions from a princely regime to a territorial unit in the India Union. The GMP's insurrection and the communist movement then were intertwined. In contrast to other areas of communist penetration in India where communist cadres were decimated during 1948–51(e. g in Telangana region of Hyderabad) in their attempts at insurrection,[1] here it was the communist's class-enemies who bore the brunt of the violence. Tripura was the only area where the Communist Party-led tribal ethnic insurrection proved successful. The key to the subsequent growth and success of Tripura communism lies in this phase of violent tribal mass mobilization.

The armed struggle in Tripura, strictly speaking, was not started by the Communist Party. It originated in armed resistance against government repression of political movements led by the Tripura Jatiyo Mukti Parishad (later known as GMP), essentially a Tripuri ethnic organization under the CPI's influence. In the course of resistance, the GMP combined an indigenous regional ethnic movement with the insurrectionary programme of the Communist Party of India. But it was the local factors which decisively shaped the course and character of this movement.

This chapter analyses the rise and growth of this movement and how the communists established their leadership and control over this ethnic movement, built on it and ultimately appropriated it by converting the GMP into one of its mass (tribal) organizations.

## The rise of the GMP and regional discontent

There lay behind the birth of the GMP a massive tribal regional discontent in Tripura. The end of monarchy in Tripura in 1947 was not followed by the establishment of a responsible government based on poplar consent which had been a fundamental political demand since the late 1930s. Monarchy ended in Tripura but was replaced by bureaucratic political rule of top Indian Civil Servants. On March 21, 1948 the widow Queen took charge of administration as the sole Regent, but the real power came to be exercised by her Bengali Dewan A.B Chatterjee. Tripura came under Congressional rule which effectively meant rule by the Bengalis.

Another powerful root of the discontent was the collapse of administration in the rural areas as a result of the disruption of the link following the end of monarchy. As *The Statesman* (Calcutta, March 3, 1951, 2) reported:

> The Maharaja's rule was autocratic and contact with the people was maintained by him through a system of feudal hierarchy based on racial and economic ties. The village headmen known as Sardar/ Prodhans were social, economic and administrative heads of the villages. The end of that regime disrupted the link without establishing a new one. The administration therefore finds itself virtually isolated from the rural area.

The Tripuris, the dominant dynastic tribe, felt powerless at the changeover from monarchy to Dewani rule and their discontent was utilized by the GMP.

The economic situation of Tripura had not begun to recover from the wartime privations when the dire effects of Partition were visited on the State: a massive influx of refugees from East Pakistan; and an economic blockade by the new Pakistani government. To the dislocation of the market was added an outbreak of a devastating cattle disease. Tripura in 1948 was gripped by an acute food crisis.

The Tripura government had since the late 1930s, suppressed each and every political movement that had tried to mobilize the people against the regime. Nationally, the CPI was banned by the new Indian government in 1948. In Tripura the JSS and the PM were suppressed, though not formally outlawed. The repressive government action against popular movements, particularly, the JSS which was basically a literacy campaign, added fuel to popular anger, and caused desperation among the tribals. As Dasarath Devbarma, the founding President of the GMP, recalled:

> The attack on the Jana Shiksha Samity by the government was taken by the majority of the tribals as an attack on the tribal community as a whole. At this crucial stage the Jana Shiksha Samity leaders along with the communist leader Biren Datta sat in secret consultation to work out the future course of action. The outcome was the Tripura Rajya Gana Mukti Parishad.
>
> (Devbarma 1987: 4)

The Tripura Rajya Mukti Parishad (Liberation Council) was formed in May 1948 secretly in a village called Rajghat in Sadar North. (Devbarma 1987: 17–18) Two (Aghore Devbarma, a Tripuri, and Biren Datta, a Bengali) of the four founding members of the GMP were members of the Tripura unit of the CPI. Both Aghore Devbarma and Biren Datta had been delegates at the CPI Calcutta Congress (February–March, 1948) in which the party had adopted an all-out insurrectionary line premised on the Soviet model: an urban-based attempt to de-stabilize the government through political strikes, leading to a general rising in the countryside. It may be significant that the GMP was formed a couple of months after the Calcutta Congress. But Dasaratha Devbarma has stressed the local, regional roots of the GMP, arguing that it descended directly from the JSS (Devbarma 1987: 101). 'The Congress government attack', he says, 'led to the formation of the GMP which resolved to fight the barbarous onslaught of Congress on the literacy movement of the JSS' (Devbarma 1987: 101). The birth of the GMP rendered superfluous both the JSS and the PM. The Calcutta Congress thus reinforced an existing readiness to launch armed resistance, although the Tripura unit's analysis of its local conditions led to a strategy not similar to that of the Andhra unit, which circulated its dissenting letter three months after the Calcutta Congress. The Andhra line envisaged a quasi-Maoist tactic whereby a prolonged civil war would be fought from liberated villages by a united front of the entire peasantry. Clearly this model was far more relevant to an area where the only town was Agartala and there were neither factories nor trade unions (Bhattacharyya and Nossiter 1988: 156). The local party watched and waited.

## The Golaghati peasant massacre

On October 9, 1948, in an ambush led by the British Inspector Mihir Choudhury, the Tripura police killed seven tribals and two Bengali Muslims at Golaghati near Agartala. One of the most notorious of the money lenders, Hari Chandra Saha, a Bengali merchant, had recently extended his operations to the tribal hamlet at Golaghati. News came that he was preparing to take a large quantity of food grains to the distant Bishalgarh market, so aggravating the local shortage. Negotiations opened between Saha and the tribal and Muslim peasantry to secure local sale on reasonable credit terms but, despite the offer of documented agreement, Saha resigned. On the basis of a secret understanding with the police, an ambush was set up at the site for final talks. This incident convinced the GMP leaders that the Congress government was on a war path, and that the time was ripe to launch a powerful armed resistance' . . . thus the decision to acquire arms, if necessary, by force and to form guerilla squads was taken' (Devbarma 1987: 6). The Golaghati incident gave, wrote Dev, 'a new turn to the peasant movement in Tripura, particularly among the tribals' and the 'resistance movement had taken a militant turn in Khowai and Sadar' (Devbarma 1987: 6).[2] The GMP utilized this incident to justify its resort to arms, and its strategy became a distinctive synthesis of the Tripura experience with the Calcutta line.

## The Calcutta Congress: mass movement in princely States and the Tripura communists

The Political Thesis of the Calcutta Congress argued that princely States of India possessed the most revolutionary potential. While setting down the party's 'Tasks on the People's Fronts', the document said:

> The states with their rotten autocratic and feudal structure and the long oppressed masses awakening to struggle constitute the weakest link in the collapsing imperialist feudal structures.
>
> (Rao 1976: 106)

The Communist Party organizations in different princely States were at different stages of development. In Tripura the party's strength was negligible; but the Calcutta Congress with its own reading of the situation condemned 'excuses for organizational weakness' (Rao 1976: 110).[3] The party at the national level, therefore, asked its cadres to strongly support the people's movement for liberation and democracy in princely States by rapidly rallying round the 'militant elements to form the militant's base of the party there'.

When Datta and Devbarma returned from Calcutta, the local situation seemed anything but propitious for the application of an insurrectionary line. The local communists indeed incurred loss of strength immediately after Calcutta Congress (Devbarma 1986: 68).[4] Nonetheless, the small party unit of Tripura, 'confused and frightened' (Rao 1976: 110–11), held political classes under the leadership of Debaprasad Sengupta, one of the founding members of the CPI in Tripura, on the implications of the newly adopted party line, the history of the Soviet Socialism revolution and dialectical materialism. An underground organizing unit was formed to implement the party programme, and Datta and Devbarma went underground. Yet, the revolutionary situation seemed as much of a mirage as before. The task involved was really difficult: combining the ethno-nationalist GMP and its fears of communism with the party's revolutionary programme. The Golaghati incident provided an opportunity to resort to armed resistance. During the whole period of the underground GMP-communist movement (1948–51), this event was given publicity by the GMP communists.

## Organization

The objective of a social movement determines, to a large extent, its organization. Armed resistance necessitated the formation of a militant organization of the GMP. In the analysis of a social movement, organization may broadly mean two things: organization itself which leads the movement: and the tactics of mass mobilization and the forms of action undertaken. When the GMP was formed, it was a five-member team: president (Dasaratha Devbarma), secretary (Aghore Devbarma), treasurer (Hemanta Devbarma) and two rank and file members including Sudhanya Devbarma. Significantly, Biren Dutta who was one of the founding members of the GMP was not assigned any organizational task. The reasons were the fear of the direct association with the communists and the maintenance of the purely Tripuri (tribal) character of the organization. To begin with, the GMP did not make much organizational advance beyond assigning divisional responsibilities to its top leaders. It built on the existing committees of the JSS which were to be found in almost every village (Devbarma 1987: 40). A Central committee consisting of Dasarath, Aghore, Sudhanya, Hemanta and Rabindra Devbarmas was formed at the final State-level organizational meeting in Kumarbil on 20 Ashar 1358 TE (July 1948) attended by 36 GMP volunteers from the sub-divisions of Khowai, Sadar and Kamalpur. A decision in that meeting was also taken to form Unit Committees at the lowest level of GMP organization, one in each area of the Tripura Kshatriya Mondalis, quasi-Village Councils created by the Tripura monarch in the late 1930s. The GMP decided to build on this legacy of princely Tripura and gave particular instructions to its activists "to recruit the young and energetic tribal chiefs into the Unit Committees" (Devbarma 1986: 42). Attempts were also made to hold political classes with the help of mobile study circles and the basic Marxist texts were distributed among the rank and file (Devbarma 1987: 43).

The Calcutta Congress of the CPI recommended the adoption of 'militant and revolutionary forms of struggle' (political strikes, agrarian struggles, armed conflicts and general strikes) with corresponding forms of organization such as revolutionary peasants strike committees and guerrilla or volunteer squads to conduct the armed struggle (Rao 1976: 127). The Political Thesis showed flexibility with regard to forms of action and also advocated the use of 'elementary forms of protest, agitation and struggle' (Rao 1976: 258).

Real militancy in the GMP was not introduced until the Golaghati incident. Immediately afterwards, says Devbarma, the GMP made preparations for guerilla warfare. It formed five major guerilla units, in Sadar North, Khowai East, Khowai West and Kamalpur. Each squad consisted of 11 members. Devbarma (president) was the supreme commander over the units in Kamalpur, Sadar North and Khowai.

A very important aspect of the organization of the GMP was that it recruited most of the ex-soldiers of the First Tripura Rifles constituted during the war. The total number of ex-soldiers in Tripura was about 4,000, of whom 3000 had been disbanded on February 15, 1945. The exact number of soldiers recruited into the GMP is not known but *The Statesman* (Calcutta), March 3, 1951, 2) reported:

> A leading part in the disturbances is being played by 2000 disbanded soldiers who had training in jungle warfare during the war.

There were also cases of desertion with arms from the Tripura Rifles and police (*The Statesman* Calcutta March 3, 1951, 2). Ex-soldiers imparted guerila training to the GMP activists, in order to keep the guerilla squads under the political control of the GMP, a 20-point Code of conduct was prepared by the CC of the GMP. Each guerilla unit was provided with two political advisers. From

Devbarma's account it is known that the ex-soldiers predominantly belong to the Tripuri community.

The unit Committees of the GMP was later replaced by Village Committees consisting of eight members from one or two villages. Above the village committees were *Anchal* (area or block) Committees comprising a few Village Committees, and above that, the Divisional Committees consisting of members from the Anchal Committees. By 1950, the GMP had had an organizational presence in each locality of the Tripura community, and a Village Committee was to be found in each Tripuri locality (Devbarma 1987: 82, 114).

## Ideology and autonomy

The GMP was not based on a coherently developed ideology of its own. This tribal social movement combined an ill-defined Tripuri nationalism with communism. Its class perspective was derived from the 'Political Thesis' of the Second Congress of the CPI and adapted to incorporate local considerations. The GMP incorporated diverse groups and classes, but it was neither a theory of nationalism nor pure communism which provided the ideological unity among those forces. The *leitmotif* of the GMP movement was a powerful opposition to Congress:

> This anti-Congressism provided the unifying bond among those forces. This ideological focus was significant. The Tripura State Congress had from its birth been anti monarchic. The GMP highlighted this aspect in order to acquire the support of the chiefs who had been one of the powerful social bases of monarchy in Tripura but who became powerless after the end of monarchy. Their grievance was addressed in the GMP slogan:

> *Monarchy ended in Tripura, Congress captured the throne.*[5]

It was this synthesis of a class perspective and local tribal nationalism which characterized much of the ideology of the GMP. This ideology was related to the GMP strategy of mobilizing the tribal chiefs and other notables. The GMP sought to build on the existing structure of dominance of the tribal chiefs. This choice was difficult:

> In Khowai, Thakur Ram Kumar Devbarma was the chief of the Tripuri chiefs, and the most powerful man in the area. It was difficult, if not impossible, to bring the Tripuri chiefs into the orbit of the movement by passing his influence. It was more or less the same in Sadar.[6]

The GMP recruited, therefore, many tribal chiefs into its Unit Committees formed in the *Kshatriya Mondalis*. The underlying assumption was to utilize their knowledge and influence. There was opposition especially from the secretary of the GMP to this move on the grounds that the presence of the reactionary and royalist chiefs in the GMP would be antagonistic to the ideals of the revolutionary GMP. This minority position was however defeated on several tactical grounds put forward by the majority in the GMP including its president (Devbarma 1987: 81–4). The majority position proved effective, and the GMP scored strategic success in acquiring the support of the tribal chiefs who have become the most reliable and powerful sources of GMP finance, and also its support base (Devbarma 1987: 51).

The GMP was not a Communist Party and the CPI originally had control over it. The autonomous development of this movement gave it a secure mass base and protected it from the disorganizing effects of external forces. The GMP then did not readily submit the authority of the CPI. In late October 1949 Aghore Devbarma, founder-secretary of the GMP, proposed to dissolve the GMP into a peasant wing of the Communist Party because it had 'taken a revisionist line and drifted from the path of revolution' (Devbarma 1986: 81).[7] But his proposal was rejected by the majority in the GMP on the grounds that it would be suicidal to impose class struggles on Tripura which had not yet experienced sharp class divisions and contradictions, and that the time was not ripe to persuade the GMP to join the Communist Party. The GMP rejected the communist proposal on the basis of its local strength. It was not the product of the Ranadive Thesis of the CPI, but a specific product of political developments in Tripura from the late 1930s. Regional concerns found expression in the birth of the GMP and moved it on to armed struggle. As Debaprosad Sen Gupta, then Communist Party local secretary, himself opined:

> Such types of armed struggle or resistance took place because of some indigenous factors, and spontaneity of the given situation. Armed struggle would have taken place even in the absence of the Ranadive line.

## The GMP-led armed struggle

The GMP began armed resistance after the Golaghati incident. Prior to that, it had staged on August 15, 1948 a successful illegal massive demonstration in Agartala demanding a popular government, withdrawal of warrants, removal of the Dewani rule, release of political prisoners and an end to police repression. Its fundamental demand was a responsible government which the Ranadive thesis would dismiss as a 'reformist demand'. *The Statesman*, March 3, 1951, 2 summed up the violent activities of the GMP as follows:

> The disturbances in which a section of hill tribes has been involved have taken the forms of violent opposition to procurement of rice and paddy at the prices fixed by the government, clashes between armed bands and police and military personnel, kidnapping of persons suspected of helping the authorities ... Individual policemen are also attacked and their rifles taken away.

This was only a partial reflection of reality. The dimensions of the movement were much wider than this pro-government daily asserted (Devbarma 1987).

### 7.6.1 Armed struggle up to August 1950

The armed struggle began earliest in Khowai in northwest Tripura. The whole sub-division was handed over to a Military Administrator Captain Hredoymoni Devbarma, on 26 Falgun 1356 TE (7 March 1949). Political activities of any sort were banned, and stricter regulations governing people's movement in the area were announced. Captain Devbarma in a 3-page note (in Bengali) addressed to the tribal chiefs explained the nature of the movement:

> *Very recently there has started in this area a wide anti-government movement under the leadership of an illegal party which is urging people to engage in a direct struggle against the government, and imparting military training to its cadres.* Some of the manifestations of this underground movement were "opposition to government's census operations and preparations of the voter's lists, non-cooperation with the government's procurement policy implementation, and the threat to government officials responsible for such policy implementation'. What worried the Military Administrator most was the chiefs' support for the movement, 'even by subscribing to their fund". The military authority asked chiefs to surrender their arms to the government. The GMP was clearly posing a challenge to state authority in this division.[8]

Within a month of its arrival, the military administration in Khowai began large-scale arrests of Tripuris 'suspected to be communists' and seized communist documents and materials. The materials included a copy of *Tripura Rajyer Kotha* (a communist weekly), a handwritten GMP manifesto, several lists of subscriptions, letters calling for public meetings against military rule, petitions, two copies of 'Barta' (the GMP mouthpiece), and a receipt for a subscription of Rupees 36.00 from Hari Chand and others signed by Anand Devbarma which indicated that the GMP movement had started as a regular, organized political movement. The possession of the local Communist Party organ among those arrested suggested a close ideological association between the GMP and the communists. According to military intelligence:

> The documents will show that they are connected with the communist movement, and acted as agents for the collection of subscription, the calling of public meetings, the circulation of literature and manifesto etc. against the government.[9]

The focus of the movement until mid-1949, as the GMP documents, seized by the military, suggest, was resistance to police and military atrocities throughout Khowai. The GMP president Dasarath Devbarma appealed to people of all castes, communities and religions to observe *hartal* from *Jaistha* 6 to 25,1359 TF (June 1949) in their respective areas during *hatbar* (market day) as a mark of protest against military oppression.[10] This indigenous form of popular protest was widely used by the GMP during its armed struggle in Tripura. The police and military intelligence reports on the GMP movement in Khowai in the first half of 1949 contained several GMP notices calling for *hartal* in different places, which the State secret police recorded as successful:

> Today, no hill people (*Puran* Tripura) had turned up in the Maharajgonj Bazar in the Khowai town. The anti-government communist movement of Dasarath and his followers is increasingly gaining ground.[11]

For unknown reasons, the southern part of Khowai division seemed a more powerful stronghold of the GMP movement. This part was declared a 'disturbed area' by the military. Despite the military rule the popular allegiance to the GMP was hardly eroded, and this baffled the authorities. An intelligence Branch officer on the basis of an extension tour of the area found to his dismay:

> The attitude of the *Puran* Tripura (Tripuris/Devbarmas) has not undergone any change, and still they appear to be affected by Dasarath's movement. The Puran Tripuras who are believed to have known the whereabouts of Dasarath do not answer any question.[12]

The military rule was not able to contain the growing GMP movement in this division and came in for much public criticism particularly from the local Congress which questioned the very basis of military rule.[13] The commandant of the first Tripura Rifles found no basis for the Congress complaints: for him there was real cause to fear communism. He suspected that the congress complaints might have been affected by the communists under the cover of the Congress. Whether the GMP was acting through Congress in Khowai is not known, but what made the government anxious was that it monopolized all political activity, and that Congress did not help or cooperate with the administrations. The GMP very often worked under the name of '*Proja dal*' (party of the subjects).

Military rule became highly unpopular in Khowai. Within a fortnight of his assumption of office, R. K. Roy (a Bengali I.C.S who became the first Chief Commissioner of Tripura on its formally joining India on October 15, 1949) began to enquire about the possibility of withdrawing military as it was failing to contain the movement. But the State police department ruled out that possibility,[14] and recommended the continuation of military rule admitting though that it had proved ineffective in changing the attitude of the people:

> Since the establishment of military administration in Khowai the situation has changed very little.[15]

So, military rule was retained 'in view of the continuing communistic activities of the Puran Tripura of Khowai division', and until the 'situation in the division' was 'reported to be fully normal'. The Chief Commissioner, on the basis of such recommendations, suggested opening more military camps in some other parts of the divisions, such as Teliamura. The government had since 1949 increased police powers; the Tripura State Security (1948) was extended to April 1951[16] in order to tighten up the repressive machinery. The military repression went on, and produced in its wake the Padmabil incident (April 1949) (Devbarma 1987: 50–2), when military personnel killed three tribal women, and the Ashrambari murder case (August 1949) in which an innocent man was shot dead by the military during a religious performance. No doubt, this justified the more and more violent course of the GMP movement.

From early 1950 the GMP, without abandoning the other relatively peaceful forms of protest like *hartal* and boycott, now resorted to open violence against the State in such a way as could in common parlance be cases of open armed encounter between its armed bands, both men and women, and the military: its resistance was turning into a full-scale rebellion. According to the Ministry of States, New Delhi, writing to the Chief Commissioner of Tripura:

> The latest reports from Tripura disclose very dangerous communist activities in the state.[17]

Setting fire to the houses of landlords and political opponents was part of GMP's class action. The GMP activists burnt down the houses of Ramkumar Thakur, a big Khowai landlord, and of another landlord at Campaknagar (Khowai).[18] There were many cases when traders procuring paddy from the villages were attacked and their money snatched away by the 'terrorists'. The GMP kidnapped Congressmen, and looted and burnt down their houses. The tactics of '*hartal*' and boycott were not however entirely abandoned in favour of violence. *Chiniha* reported that the 'underground communists' had been boycotting several markets for a month in protest against the killing of three tribal women at Padmabil. There was also a report that the GMP had called a State-wide *hartal* between Ashar 2 and 9, 1359 TE (July 1949) in protest against the arrest of Aghore Devbarma, the former secretary of the GMP in October 1949. In May 1950, the resistance of the GMP seemed to have reached its height when the GMP armed bands, men and women began street fighting with the military in Khowai. Quoting police source, *Chiniha* reported:

> On May 28, 1950 at about 2 pm when the military was patrolling on the street of Kalachhara in Padmabil, a band of armed Tripuris numbering more than a hundred, both men and women, attacked the military. The women severely injured two military personnel with choppers and snatched 2 rifles from the military.

The available information does not suggest the existence of GMP resistance in Kamalpur, a division further North of Khowai, before June 1949. But by June 1949, the movement in this region was found to be building bases. The distinctive feature of the movement in this region was that a predominantly Tripuri-led group was organizing the Reangs in this region was that the Reangs were giving shelter to the leaders were organizing the followers of Ratan Moni who all joined the party. Reangs were subscribing to the GMP Fund. The pattern of Reang mobilization by the GMP in this region revealed two features. First, the GMP focused its attention on the influential section of the community, chiefs and sardars. Second, the subscription to the GMP fund was collected not on individual basis, but per family, and the rate was fixed on a household basis too. In the social organization of the tribals, the family was the basic unit of life, and the most powerful loyalty of an individual tribal was to his family or clan. The GMP utilized this traditional loyalty of the tribals in building its organizational base.

This region followed in the footsteps of other divisions so far as the forms of political action were concerned. The State intelligence branch reported persistent secret meetings in the area, and continuous observances of *hartal* and boycott of *bazaars*. The above report also mentioned that the Tripuris had attended the GMP meetings and participated in the anti-government action. Particularly striking was the denial of State authority in this region in settling 'disputes by local panchayats'.[19] It was reported that Dasarath Devbarma had instructed his followers to form such panchayats comprising Tripuri youths with powers to settle disputes throughout Tripura. This was the first indication of an alternative government set up by the GMP.

As in Khowai, the GMP movement here began to take a violent form in early 1950. The SDO of Kamalpur summed up the situation:

> The internal situation has much deteriorated. It is reported that some miscreants from Khowai have entered here and are inciting the hill people against the government, and creating anti-Bengali feeling among them. They are holding secret meetings and organizing a movement. They are continuously boycotting the Kulai market which they intend to do for three weeks. They are organizing a procession to demonstrate against the government on May Day ... Many stray cases of looting and dacoity have occurred. A mob of hill people have attacked and raided the house of Mrityunjoy Das (a Bengali) and wounded him with bow and arrow.[20]

There were also reported cases of GMP highhandedness and intimidation in the drive to increase its membership. There was no evidence which could suggest that the GMP had given up its tactics of *hartal* and boycott entirely in favour of violence. On the contrary, there were reports of peaceful methods being pursued with renewed vigour. Class struggle of socialism was not on the top of the GMP agenda but the GMP placards urging 'Workers and Peasants Unite' suggest the strong communist influence on the movement. The GMP also demanded the release of Biren Datta and the trial for murder of the military personnel responsible for the deaths of the Muslim peasants of Sonatali and three tribal women of Khowai.

The available evidence suggests that the GMP-led armed struggle did not reach its peak in Sadar until the middle of 1949. This, the largest division, contained about 35 per cent of the total population and had the largest share of the State's flat and fertile lands. It had been in the forefront of the State's popular movements since late 1930s, and it was here that the GMP was born. At least part of the area became a stronghold of the JSS literacy campaign during 1945–48 and Aghore and Sudhanya Devbarmas built powerful bases of leadership in course of that campaign. Although Sadar was predominantly Tripuri, Agartala situated within it was the home of the Bengalis who comprised about 95 per cent of the capital's total population in 1951. The GMP movement initially built on the JSS mass base in this area, but did not turn violent until about June 1949. The State Intelligence Branch noted this change:

> After the incidents of Golaghati and Bhakathakurghat, Aghore's influence on the hill people more or less waned. But now, taking advantage of the famine situation, he is trying to regain his influence and spreading it among them by looting paddy and distributing it among the depressed people.[21]

Relief work by looting paddy and then distributing it among the famine stricken people was part of GMP's class action in the region. Since the time of the Reang rebellion, Tripura had experienced recurrent famines. To collect paddy, the GMP resorted to force and the threat of force and prevented the government from collecting any paddy from the people in the name of procurement.

The government responded to the growing GMP movement by tightening up its machinery and equipping itself with more powers to handle the growing 'communist menace'. The Commandant of the First Tripura Rifles ordered a 'strict census of guns among the hill people', and also recommended:

> A police station at once be established in Takarjala with a view to frightening the people that if they attend any of the meetings addressed by the communist leader, their landed property will be confiscated by the government.[22]

This barely contained the growing movement which was building bases not only among the sardars and teachers but also among the landless and poverty-stricken people. The intensity of mass mobilization by the GMP-led an intelligent officer to conclude:

> All the villagers of those [5] villages are members of the party.[23]

The GMP movement in Sadar undertook peaceful and violent methods of struggle simultaneously. It held *hartal* and boycotted different market places for quite a long period, and the State secret police recorded that such *hartals* were very successful. The GMP committed mayhem. Mass petitions complaining about the GMP excesses multiplied in the State's Home Department, and the secret police department was loaded with reports of looting of granaries, kidnapping of political opponents (mainly Congress workers), and intimidation for forcing others to join their ranks. Arms were displayed in demonstrations, and there was growing strength among the Muslims. As a response to this 'menacing situation', the government ordered the arrest of all the communists 'under relevant law', and the deployment of more military forces was strongly recommended.

Agartala, by contrast, presented a picture of passivity so far as the armed struggle was concerned. The movement failed to make any inroads in the city predominantly inhabited by the Hindu Bengalis who were tied to monarchy by patronage and privilege, and believed much of the government propaganda that the GMP movement was anti-Bengali. The GMP made no efforts to build a base in the city, or to dispel much popular misgivings about the movement.[24] The tiny State-unit of the CPI predominantly under the leadership of the Bengalis was moribund and made no effort to form public opinion in favour of the GMP movement. With the emergence of the GMP, a gap emerged between the urban-base communist movement, and the rural based GMP movement. Resolutions at the Secret CPI meetings asked middle-class youths to go to villages during their vacation to propagate the ideals and ideas of the Communist Party, but contained no indication that the local unit was aware of the GMP movement. Whatever existed of the communist movement in Agartala, did hardly survive after the arrest of its major leaders like Atikul Islam, Gouranga Devbarms and Saroj Chanda on April 10, 1949 under the Tripura State Security Act.

## *Armed struggle after August 1950*

August 1950 marked a dividing line in the history of the GMP-led armed struggle in Tripura. It was in August 1950 that the 'Rajeswar line' of the CPI reached Tripura. The local movement so far based on a synthesis of the Ranadive line and local experience, incorporated this new line, and entered a new phase. Those who brought the 'Rajeswar line' were Nripen Chakrabarty, later on, the Marxist Chief Minister of Tripura, (political trainer), Mohun Choudhury (real name Bipul Choudhury) an ex-soldier and guerilla trainer, Dr Bijoy Bose (doctor) and Shiva Ram (gun mechanic). They came to Tripura to help the local movement, to establish the leadership of the Communist Party over the local movement, and to rebuild the local Communist Party on the GMP movement. Their arrival in Tripura marked the more direct intervention of the all-India party in the locally developed GMP movement.

Rajeswar Rao (Andhra Pradesh) was the CPI's General Secretary between June and December 1950 replacing B.T Ranadive who had been the party's General Secretary from the Calcutta Congress (February 1948 to January 1950). This changed the Russian path of revolution advocated by Ranadive to the Chinese path broadly. The editorial of the Cominform organ *For a Lasting Peace, For a People's Democracy* (27 January 1950) highlighted the Chinese path of revolution for the colonial and ex-colonial countries, and contained a message foe the Indian communists. (Rao 1976: 611) Mainly on the basis of this editorial, the new CPI leadership advocated a rural based armed struggle to capture the countryside first, before liberating the cities. The party visualized a 'united front struggle' of workers, peasants and middle bourgeoisie and of parties and groups representing them based on a minimum programme of the party. This new line considered 'armed guerilla struggle as the principal form of struggle of this period and stage of revolution' (Rao 1976: 1075). It however advocated adoption simultaneously of all other conceivable forms of struggle, but stressed that armed resistance should be adopted as the principal form for the simple reason that 'armed counter revolution' could 'not be successfully resisted or defeated except through an armed struggle'. The party's Polit Bureau Draft Statement (November 1950) defined the communist struggle of the time as 'a peasant war under the leadership of the proletariat' (Rao 1976: 68–9). Quoting verbatim Mao's *Aspects of China's Anti-Jap Struggle*, this PB Draft Statement said:

> The total concept of this kind of struggle is guerilla warfare. It is the inevitable, and hence the best form of struggle in a backward, vast, semi-colonial country over a period of time by the People's armed forces.
> (Rao 1976: 68–9)

At the time Chakrabarty and his comrades came to Tripura and the communist rebels were prepared for a big attack. The government was strengthening its repressive apparatus. The West Bengal State Security Act, 1950 was introduced with modification in Tripura in August 1950. The basis of such action was the government report of impending danger:

> On the basis of secret communist documents and arms and ammunition seized by the police, it can undoubtedly be said that the communists were preparing for an open rebellion against the government.[25]

Large-scale arrest of suspected communists followed. *Chiniha* (No 20, 1950, 6) reported that the government has killed three communists and arrested 250 communists including four leaders. With the arrival of the Rajeswar Rao line, the local movement increasingly used organized violence against the government. The violent GMP/communist guerilla action now became exclusively offensive, although the other local forms of resistance like *hartal* and boycott were not entirely abandoned.

An important feature of armed struggle in Tripura after August 1950 was the communist attempt to recruit from the State's armed forces and police. The communists conducted propaganda urging the military to join their ranks.[26] State intelligent reports that after September 1950 there were an increasing number of desertions with arms and ammunition from the military and police. Mohun Choudhury added that the communists aimed at 'fraternization with army personnel' which paid them 'good dividends'.[27] Dasarath Devbarma has provided numerous names of those military police personnel and middle-aged ex-servicemen who joined the GMP and imparted military training to the GMP activists, and successfully conducted guerrilla raids on the military camps and police station. That most of those who deserted were Tripuris was a particular cause of concern to administration:

> As this conduct on the part of the Tripura Constables betrays their sympathy towards the Tripura communists, all Tripuri Constables are being withdrawn

from the army camps in the mofussils as a precautionary measure. The armouries have been placed in charge of Bengali personnel.

(Devbarma 1987: chaps 2, 4 and 5)

That the deserters, all Tripuris, were joining the ranks of the communists was particularly threatening to the authorities because the Tripura army was mainly composed of the Tripuris. The sympathy of Tripuri army personnel towards the GMP was related at least partially to the latter's politics which had not sought to abolish private ownership of land or to implement, as Aghore Devbarma had suggested, the slogan 'land to the tiller'. Many in the Tripura armed forces who were landowners had nothing to fear from the GMP (Devbarma 1987: 73–4).

As part of their offensive guerilla action, the GMP conducted several raids on military and police camps and stations, and looted arms and ammunition. In order to stop construction of new roads and to block road building, the communist guerrillas attacked several Public Works Department camps. The most daring and remarkable communist guerrilla action took place on March 1, 1951 when the communist guerrillas attacked Sidai (sadar) Police Station in broad daylight and looted arms and ammunition:

> A gang of communist Tripuris about 7 in number armed with stun and tommy guns attacked Sidai police station on 1.3.51 at about 2.10 p.m. They suddenly attacked the sentry and fired at random. One NCO, two Constables including the Sentry and a Chowkidar were injured. They took away 8 rifles (including the arms of the sentry), 450 rounds of 303 ammunition, 7 great coats and a few cardigan jackets, Constable belts, pouches, fatigue caps, khaki shirt and shorts. It was a hatbar (marketday), and there was a gathering of about 4 to 5 hundred people, but the raiders kept the crowd off at the point of arms and by firing at random in the air.[28]

Except for Mohun Choudhury who led the raid, most of those who took part in the raid were Tripuris including some army deserters.[29]

This organized armed struggle continued, by and large, until the end of 1951, although it had begun to recede after the Sidai raid. As the State Police Superintend wrote in his monthly report:

> [The] general situation is not so alarming as it was in the previous month. Except for the raid on Sidai P.S, and the attack on a small force (7) of Assam Rifles, there was very little evidence of violence.[30]

In May 1951 in his report to the chief commissioner of Tripura in connection with the information wanted for a question in the Indian parliament (CC's ref. No. D. 2973/H dated May 5, 1951), the Superintend of Police, on the basis of the materials available in the I.B. office, wrote:

> There has been some improvement so far as the anti-social and disruptive activities of the communists in this State are connected, and this is due to the

establishment of armed military and police pickets at different affected places and opening of the base camp at Chebri in Khowai for operational purposes.

(Devbarma 1987: 66)

According to Dasarath Devbarma, the government intensified repression with its devastating effects on people's life and property, the increase in military camps in the tribal areas and the decreasing scope for collection of arms created doubts among local communities about the prospect of continuing the armed struggle any longer. The other important factor taken into account in discontinuing the armed struggle was the Tripura movement's growing isolation from the communist movement elsewhere in India and Pakistan where similar movement had been withdrawn or suppressed.[31] The GMP armed struggle was not formally called off, but temporarily discontinued. (interview with Biren Datta in Agartala on 25 November 1986)

## Interaction between the GMP movement and all-India communism

For awhile after the beginning of armed struggle in early 1949, the GMP lost contact with the All-India headquarters of the CPI (then in Calcutta), but the link was re-established in jails (in Assam) mainly by Biren Datta (Rao 1976: 663).[32] All-India Communist Party sources show that by May 1950 Tripura's movement was in the party's knowledge and the new leadership (Rajeswar Rao PB) had its own understanding of the Tripura situation. In the new CC Letter of May 1950 (issued in June 1950) to all party members and sympathisers, the CPI admitted the indigenous character of the resistance movement in Tripura and other areas along the borders of India and East Pakistan (now Bangladesh), upholding them as heralding the emergence of the Indian democratic revolution. Analyzing these resistance movements, the document said:

> The people are already on the move "in their own way": they have been carrying on guerrilla warfare which can rightly be described as the beginning of the Indian Democratic Revolution.

(Devbarma 1987: 78)

The new PB entrusted Biresh Mishra (of the Assam Provincial Committee) with the task of keeping in touch with the Tripura situation, and Pranesh Biswas (Assam), a member of the PB, with that of assisting the movement in Tripura; the latter arrived there bringing with him a few copies of *For a Lasting Peace, For a People's Democracy* (January 27, 1950). In another report called *Left Deviations in Organizational Activities*, the new CC claimed that the resistance movements in Tripura, Manipur, Assam and the hill border regions of the Mymensingh district were entrenched in its 'strongholds' (Rao 1976: 75–7).

By the end of 1950, Tripura communism was taken seriously by the CPI. In response to party members' questions about the prospect of continuing armed struggle in different regions and under different conditions, the CPI PB cited the Tripura experience where the resistance movement had become possible. This document devoted considerable attention to the Tripura case where it promoted to the level of offering the party a model of armed struggle:

> For example, Tripura . . . where people had taken up arms in the recent period offers us one experience.
> 
> (Rao 1976: 75)

This showed that Tripura communism had left a powerful impact on the all-India communism as early as 1950.

The new PB sent Nripen Chakrabarty and others to Tripura in August 1950 in response to the party-level help sought by the local communists (interview with Mohun Choudhruy on 24 November 1986 at Agartala). They brought the Rajeswar Rao line of the CPI to Tripura. With their arrival, there took place significant changes in the local armed struggle in Tripura before the CPI intervention:

> Until our arrival, the style of operation was not strictly speaking offensive. The movement was locally determined and shaped; it was a real mass movement but spontaneous. The change of style from defensive to offensive took place after our arrival. We reorganized the armed struggle on the Telangana line. The party's intervention proved effective and it gave a great impetus to the movement.
> 
> (Rao 1976: 663)

Significant changes also took place in other more important areas of Tripura communism. In fact, the impact of all-India communism resulted in a substantial 'revision' of perspective among Tripura communists. The central idea of the new CPI line was a united front of the broad masses of the peasantry, the intellectuals, the petit bourgeoisie in the cities and the national bourgeoisie who suffered vexations and restrictions imposed by imperialism and its lackeys. The basis of the front would be the alliance of the workers and peasants under the leadership of the working class.[33] Born out of the Tripuris and developed in and through them, the GMP was essentially a Tripuri nationalist organization. Its base predominantly among the Tripuris was one of its limitations. It had made attempts on a smaller scale, to penetrate the Reangs. But now influenced by the CPI idea of building a broad-based united front, the GMP sought to transcend its own (single) 'tribal' power-base to penetrate other tribal communists. Its renewed appeal to the Halams, a small tribe (in 1931, they were 12,713) to join the GMP-led mass movement and to destroy the Tripura agents of Congress government has to be seen in this context.[34] In another GMP document, an appeal was made to the workers, peasants, students, government officials of all communists, patriotic forces, who were engaged in a movement for the destruction of the 'barbaric, exploitative, feudal-imperialist socio-economic order' to offer a powerful challenge to Tripura's Chief Commissioner rule, destroy the State apparatus and landlordism, and establish a peasant rule.

An analysis of a few important decisions of the GMP adopted between January 1951 and February 1952 (Devbarma 1952: 1) reveals the distinctive features of the GMP politics marks of influence of the all-India level party-line, and also the increasing ideological and political grip of the CPI over the local movement. In the Extended Conference of the Central Committee of the GMP, held on 22–23 Poush 1360 TF (Jan 1951), the GMP expressed serious concern for world peace, and appealed to all people irrespective of caste, religion and creed, to sign the peace appeals, and to come forward to form Peace Committees in villages and towns. In order to rebut government propaganda that the GMP was an anti-Bengali movement, it emphasized its 'broad-based nationalist character':

> The Tripura Rajya Gana Mukti Parishad is a democratic and revolutionary organization of Tripuris, Bengalis, Halams, Chakmas, Manipuris, Kukis, Jamatias, Reangs, all Hindus and Muslims. . . . It asked all to join "to make the GMP a broad-based anti-imperialist and anti-feudal democratic front" and assured them that the GMP would protect the nationalist interests of all.
> (Devbarma 1952: 1, 3)

The GMP's class perspective also underwent substantial modification. On the basis of its understanding that its resistance movement had resulted in a substantial retreat of Tripura's exploiters in many areas, and also in reduction of eviction of peasants from land, of rent and interest, and of the landlord's share of the produce, and an increase of wages of the agricultural labourers, the GMP redefined its class perspective:

> The GMP's anti-feudal struggle would not attack anybody except the non-cultivating big landlord. So the rich peasants, *jotedars*, and *mahajans*, talukdars, and even the small landlords have nothing to fear from the GMP. In its fight against exploitation . . . it wants cooperation of small landlords, *mahajans* and *talukdars*. The GMP wants to make it clear that for the sake of unity needed to fight imperialism, the conflicts [of interest] that may arise between peasants and small landlords, *jotedars*, *mahajans* and *talukdars* have to be resolved peacefully and reconcilably.
> (Devbarma 1952: 10)

The GMP's economic policies also underwent substantial revision. The age-old pernicious practice of *dadan* (advance) was the backbone of Tripura's feudal exploitation, and was a powerful factor in the tribals' loss of land to the Bengalis. The GMP had been, from its birth, anti-dadan, and campaigned against it, but it did not want to abolish this practice; it sought instead to reform it. It determined that the rate of *dadan* should not exceed 50 per cent, and in case of exchange in kind, not above 25 per cent of the capital. The GMP insisted that *dadan* be repaid on time. In the area where the GMP set up its own alternative government, it did not abolish private property in land, but reduced the rate of land tax by 50 per cent; it wrote off arrears of land tax preceding the year 1951 and cancelled all additional taxes collected by the talukdars and jotedars; it did not abolish the existing tenancy practices such as *Chuktibhagi* and *Adhibhagi*, but introduced *Tebhaga* (three-quarter share) for the peasants where different practices existed (Devbarma 1952: 107).

## Parallel communist government

In a two-day conference in an abandoned village (Patnipara in Sardar) held on 30-3 Chaitra 1348 TE (April 1950), the GMP arrived at the historic decision to form an undeclared parallel government in Tripura in order to take over the responsibility for Tripuri society. Such a decision was taken, Devbarma says, as a reaction to the high degree of repression let loose by the police and military in Khowai.[35] By June 1950 the existence of this alternative centre of authority was already posing a threat to its opponents and the government. The local Congress daily *Ganaraj* (20 Jaistha 1360 TF June 1950) wrote:

> Now the anti-socials have set up a parallel government in the Tripuri inhabited areas. They have their own office, courts police, military and even intelligent branch. They are inflicting severe punishment on those who do not cooperate with them.

While Congress seemed indignant at the emergence of this alternative centre of authority and considered the GMP as just 'anti-socials', Jairamdas Doulatram, the Governor of Assam (who was then in charge of Tripura as well), took note of the real situation in his report to S. V. Patel, then Home Minister of India: 'The latest reports show that they have set up a parallel government at Khowai and they are as good as administering as the Governor's Adviser here' (the Chief Commissioner).[36] This government was instituted much before the arrival of Chakrabarty et al. in Tripura in August 1950.

Little information is available for an analysis of this governmental experiment. On the basis of scant sources, it is possible to offer only an outline of the nature and working of this short-lived (1949–52) Tripura communist experiment with *power*. Nripen Chakrabarty has described its nature on the basis of first-hand information:

> The GMP declared the Congress government illegal in an area of four hundred thousand people. There it took charge of a democratic government where the Revenue and Forest Departments did not exist. The GMP committees distributed land among the landless tribals. People did not go to government office, courts and police stations. It was not simply the government of tribals, but also of Hindustani, Bengalis and women. The Shanti Sena maintained peace and order. This government established equal right of women and men to property and was engaged in social reform; it set up grain banks to help famine affected people.
>
> (Devbarma 1987: 72)

The government was based, for the execution of its decisions, on committees. A series of committees ran the day-to-day administration. There were two major sets of committees: People's Judicial Committees and Political Committees. Each set of committees was hierarchical, ranging from Central Committee to the village level. Thus, for instance, the People's Judicial Committees had four levels: at the lowest was the Village Committee to settle local disputes; above the Village Committee was the Anchal (Block) Committee consisting of two or more Village Committees to settle unresolved disputes of Village Committees; above the Anchal Committee was the Divisional Committee as the higher court of appeal; on top of that was the Central Committee which was the highest court of appeal. The President of the GMP delivered the final verdict on disputes. The Judicial Committees were partly elected by the people and partly nominated by the Central Committee.

In accordance with its decisions, the GMP made a series of civil and criminal laws. The committees of the GMP dealt with issues relating to wide-spread social reforms: abolition of polygamy, prohibition of child-marriage, control of dowry and related matters, control of untouchability practices by the Tripuris against the non-Tripuri Hindustani tea-garden workers of Tripura, land settlement, superstitions, land ceiling, *dadan* and wages of the agricultural labourers. The struggle for self-defence, on the one hand, and the reformation of Tripuri society, on the other, were, according to Devbarma, two major concerns of the GMP.

This government did not confiscate the landed property of the big landlords, but seized their *khas* land, and distributed it among the landless tribals and tea-garden workers. The *dadan* (advance) was reformed by determining a 'reasonable rate' of interest. This partial capitulation to the *mahajans*, Devbarma argues, was pragmatic: the *mahajans* were then the only source of credit, and the GMP was compelled to compromise with them (Devbarma 1987: 72).

The working of this government was instrumental in consolidating and further expanding the power base of the GMP. Its grip over area it ruled was total, and its decision were considered laws by the people. The progressive nature of this experiment was to be seen in the replacement of the old legal system and the social codes by new ones. The GMP became the embodiment of a new legality. Its strength was its mass base with a membership of 300,000 out of Tripura's total population of 700,000 in 1951. A Shanti Sena (village Defence Militia) consisting of 30–35 members under each GMP committee in each village maintained peace and protected people and their property from the attack of hostile forces. The Shanti Sena sheltered the GMP guerillas after the armed struggle had been discontinued, and put them to reconstructive work. Recognizing the demand for popular rule, *The Statesman*, March 3, 1951, wrote: The need for local self-government institutions such union boards or panchayats is also keenly felt (*The Statesman* Calcutta March 3, 1951, 2). The GMP fulfilled this popular demand partially, in its own way. The establishment of a government by the GMP as early as 1950 signified also the institutionalization of the communist movement in Tripura.

## Conclusion

The GMP communism of Tripura was a movement, although predominantly locally determined and shaped, which subsequently received powerful external influence. It was on the basis of its local strength that the GMP had asserted its autonomy and independence, and saved itself from the disorganizing effects of external forces initially by blatantly refusing Aghore Devbarma's plea to dissolve the GMP in favour of CPI. The GMP phase of Tripura communism, wherever organized, was a real mass movement. The GMP's success in dismantling established authority in some parts of the State, in setting up an alternative structure of power and in retaining it for quite some time indicated, in fact, a very higher level of mass mobilization by the GMP communists.

During the whole period of GMP communism, no reference was however made to the Reang rebellion (1943–45) (Chapter 5 above). This was a serious drawback in this phase of Tripura communism. But the language of the Reang rebellion and, for that matter, the tradition of Tripura's indigenous politics, was not entirely absent. The GMP communism combined, it can certainly be argued, indigenous idioms of mass politics with modern ones: its indigenous character was to be found in its spontaneity, and also in the particular ways violent and other non-violent methods of agitation were deployed. Moreover, the parallel government following the armed struggle was a local innovation, and fashioned by local considerations. The patterns of mass mobilization by the GMP were also local – its focus on the tribal chiefs and sardars as targets of the mass mobilization, and the utilization of collective identities of the tribal society (in providing for family-wise GMP membership and subscription to its funds) were what local considerations had dictated. The 'modern' elements or idioms of politics within this movement were the result of the impact of the all-India CPI line on the local movement, fundamentally consisting in a central hierarchical control over the movement, and the theoretical formulations accompanying this control.

In an inner-party document Nripen Chakrabarty described the GMP movement as follows:

> In the absence of working-class leadership, bourgeois leadership and ideology misguide the peasant movement. Nationalism, sectarianism, opportunism, terrorism, localism and tailism become predominant in the struggle, and therefore the movement fails to achieve its objectives. These are bourgeois ideologies, and one can not say for certain that they have not percolated Tripura's peasant war.
>
> (Quoted in Chanda 1983: 12)[37]

Whether they were bourgeois ideologies given the local situation or not is certainly a debatable question, but the movement had exhibited much of what he detected in it. An undefined (Tripuri) nationalism provided a powerful ideological impetus behind the growth of this movement; the movement was localized mainly in three sub-divisions out of ten; it used violence and terror as methods of struggle; it was sectarian in being confined predominantly to the Tripuris: the tailism (following on behind) could be seen in its allowance for spontaneity; and so on. Chakrabarty's real motive, in describing the movement in this way, as we will show later in this book, was to legitimize the GMP's subordination to the CPI authority, and the CPI's appropriation of the locally developed radical tribal ethnic movement.

The achievement of the GMP, from the standpoint of the development of communism in the State, was remarkable. In the course of armed struggle, the GMP recruited 300,000 members out of the State's total population, then, of 700,000. When nearly half the population opposed the regime, it was a moot question where legitimate authority lay. With the abandonment of the armed struggle, the GMP provided the local unit of the CPI with 800 dedicated and proven party members, and a few thousand sympathizers. The GMP was not dissolved, but the local unit of the CPI took over its entire platform. The State's communist movement was reborn out of the GMP armed struggle. When Pranesh Biswas (Assam) proposed in a GMP Central Committee meeting the reorganization of the Communist Party out of the GMP, his proposal was accepted without objections. The Tripura District Organizing Committee of the CPI was formed to rebuild the State Communist Party. The GMP gave Tripura communism its mass base in a very real sense.

As the GMP-led armed struggle grew, it received an increasingly powerful all-India CPI influence. The GMP adapted the national line of the CPI to the local environment, but in doing so, and particularly in expressing its politics in more precise terms, it began to use all-India political readings which demanded a series of adjustments with (the local) landlords and *mahajans*. The newly aroused Tripuri ethnic nationalist consciousness was subordinated to class theory and to the neo-Indian nationalism of the CPI. The GMP's politics in the end represented a combination of nationalist and class idioms, but this nationalism was Indian, and the classes were mainly alien to Tripura's mode of production. In Tripura's archaic agrarian structure, the CPI's class enemies were hard to find, but the local communists had to see in not only the royal family, but also the 'big' landlords, and the tribal chiefs, the class-enemies of Indian communism. While Tripura communism was integrating (since the early 1950s) with all-India communism, and the communists acquired their mass base in Tripura, the question of Tripuri ethnic nationalism born in revolutionary situations, as described above, remained unresolved. The theme was taken up since 1948 by a group of Tripuri intellectuals based in Agartala to formulate quite systematically a doctrine of Tripura ethno-nationalism against increasing Bengali ethnic domination in Tripura. This is taken up for detailed study in the chapter that follows.

## Notes

1 At the Second Congress of the CPI in Calcutta in 1948 with B. T. Ranadive as General Secretary, the CPI adopted the resolution to pursue an aggressive radical line which believed in the seizure of state power through armed urban insurrections. Internationally it was the so-called Zhadanov line after the leader of the former CPSU.

2  For more details on the Golaghati massacre, see Devbarma (1986: 49–51) and Dhar (1973: 16–25).
3  It was reiterated in the Congress thesis: 'For organizational weaknesses can never be a reason to abandon a basic slogan such as the abolition of autocracy' (p. 110).
4  Dev (-barma) said: 'After I and Datta got back from the Calcutta Congress, the most significant event that took place in Tripura was the isolation of a group of youths and students who had since 1946 been close to the party and rallied behind it; they got themselves isolated when they heard about the violent revolutionary programme of the party, witnessed the party declared illegal and the Preventive Detention Act promulgated' (p. 68).
5  *Jala*, a new magazine in Bengali, Jul-August 1974, p. 45.
6  Quoted in *Jala*, July-August 1974, 51.
7  He later admitted his mistakes. (pp. 81–4).
8  A note issued by the Military Administrator of Khowai (in Bengali) dated 15 Ashar 1355 TE (July 1949).
9  Secret Military Reports NO. 12/S/KpML, Office of the Khowai Military Administrator April 23, 1949. This was issued in reposne to confidential inquiry of the Commandant of the First Tripura Rifles, Tripura, Agartala NO. 4/MA/KH A. 66 April 18, 1949.
10  Secret Military Intelligence Report, as above.
11  Secret Report Khowai Sub-Division No. 186 dated 13 Baisakh 1359 TE (May 1949). This report contains a lot of seized materials of the GMP such as pamphlets, notices etc., calling for *hartal*.
12  Secret police Report Khowai dated November 17, 1949. The Khowai Congress Committee Resolution dated October 14, 1949 in which a point was raised for a change over to civilian authority (collected as proscribed materials in the Intelligence Report).
13  Extract from the I. B. report of the week ending on July 11, 1949.
14  Secret Military Report Confidential no. 35 M A/A-2 office of the Commandant Ist Tripura Rifles Agartala November 4, 1949. The seized GMP documents indicated the GMP sometimes used the cover of Proja Da; ie., the party of the subjects.
15  Captain G. J. Rana, Military Administrator in his fortnightly report ending on July 25, 1949. No. 12/S/K/MA Office of the Military Administrator.
16  The Superintendent of Police, Tripura in response to CC's inquiry NO. 1919/H/29 October 1949.
17  From the Superintendent of Police to Chief Commissioner dated November 19, 1949. See also Secret Correspondence between the Chief Commissioner of Tripura and the Adviser to the Governor, Government of Assam, Shilling NO. 1551/H/29 dated November 30, 1949.
18  Letter 'Immediate Secret' D O No. F-4 (12) C/49.
19  Secret Police report No. 439. S Kamalpur June 1949 p. 5 (copy forwarded to CID Agartala).
20  'Communist Troubles in Kamalpur' Political Department/Secret from D S P Kamalpur to S P, Agartala April 30, 1950.
21  I. B. report, Agartala (4 Ashar 1355 TE (July 1959).
22  Secret Urgent No 11/A-ID.H-6 Office of the Commandant Ist Tripura Rifles, agaratala dated June 22, 1949.
23  I. B. report July 1949.
24  Sarod Chanda, Tripura Darpan, Sharoad Issue (in Bengali), 1389 B E, p. 42. Chanda recalled: 'One has also to admit the weakness of the resistance of 1948–50. The movement was exclusively confined to the tribals. No attempt was made to attract the Bengalis to the movement. The main reason for that was the organizational weaknesses of the communist party which was so small that the greater section of the Bengalis remained outside the activities of communists'.
25  In a Press Note issued by the Home Department Government of Tripura dated July 26, 1950.

26 Fortnightly Confidential Reports ending on February 28, 1951 and March 15, 1951.
27 Mohun Choudhury in a written statement on November 6, 1986 to the author: 'There were many cases of desertions from the military. In the Fortnightly Confidential Reports of I B and C I D for the fortnight ending on October 31 1950 the Tripura Police Superintendent wrote under the heading 'political': Tripura Sepoys of the Ist Tripura Rifles of Shantinagr Military Camp deserted with the following arms and ammunition on 26–27 October 29150 at night: 2 Rifles with Beynets, and 2 Stenguns (303 rifles no. 145, 9 mm round 100 stenguns magazines Nos. 5, stengun fellen-1 and some money. [where does the extract end in this note?]
28 I. B. & C. I. D. reports March 15, 1951. Also see *Chiniha* No 48 (March 1951), p. 2.
29 Mohan Choudhru in a written statement corrected the above as follow: He said that only one Chowkidar was injured and five rounds were fired in honour of the communist party; party slogans were shouted and then dispersed at a double quick was ordered. To the list of raiders, he added another name – Sushen Devbarma.
30 Secret Political No.2528/F 162 May 8, 1951.
31 Devbarma (1987: 31).
32 See The CPI Central Committee letter after the CC meetings of May 20-June 1 1950.
33 A GMP pamphlet dated Jul 1950.
34 A GMP pamphlet july 1950.
35 See Patel's (1950: 2). See also Patel to Doulatram, Dehrudun, July 5, 1950, p. 1.
36 Patel's (1950: 1).
37 For details, 'Two unpolished documents of the communist movement in Tripura' (in Bengali) Chanda (1983).

# 8 Radical ethno-nationalism in Tripura, 1948–50

## Introduction

The term 'ethno-nationalism' or ethnic nationalism has since the 1960s, when it was introduced by Walker Connor (1993), acquired wider currency in the diverse discursive fields of knowledge such as political science, sociology and ethnic studies. The subject has also figured in the studies of ethnic conflict regulation with implications for policy. The term refers to a nationalism which is primarily defined by ethnicity, which entails a common heritage, ancestry, language and culture. In the larger literature on nationalism, this ethnic nationalism is different from political nationalism which aims at political power or a State for the large ethnic group; by contrast, ethno-nationalism is basically cultural in character with the main appeal to ethnic repertoire. Such nationalism can aspire for political power within the overall framework of the nation-state. While all nationalisms have had ethnic origins, as Smith would (1986) have us believe, in their manifestations, ethnic/cultural nationalism has emerged, historically speaking, in countries such as Germany and Italy where the so-called 'third estate' was relatively weak. In the reverse case, such as in England, France and the US, nationalism acquired profoundly a political character struggling to establish a nation-state. In the post-colonial contexts such as India nationalism remained heavily culture-oriented asserting the cultural sovereignty of the nation in the most period of its formation journeying into the more political form in the later days of colonialism (Chatterjee 1986, 1993). As argued by Chatterjee (1986), Indian nationalism took a particularly political turn in the writings of Jawaharlal Nehru post-1930s. Students of Indian politics and history will be aware of the rich tradition of cultural nationalism in India in the writings of such thinkers as Vivekananda, Aurobinda and Tagore.

According to Wallerstein (1991), the world took an ethnic turn since the 1970s, and the process was and remains intertwined with the contradictions of historical capitalism. He draws our attention here to the 'hierarchical reality of capitalism' which does not offend though the formal commitment of capitalism to legal equality (Wallerstein 1991: 84). In his own words: 'Ethnicization or peoplehood resolves one of the basic contradictions of historical capitalism – its simultaneous thrust of theoretical equality and practical inequality – and it does so by utilizing the mentalities of the world's working strata' (Wallerstein 1991: 84). But in the mainstream studies of ethno-nationalist movements and aspirations, the focus has been mostly on the construction of the discourse and the tenets of the same as the political strategies of the emerging middle classes, or their representatives for clearing the space for the ethnic group for contest for identity and power.

In the specific focus on the discourses of ethnicity, the scholarly debates have since been very rich and ongoing (Connor 1993, 1984; Balibar and Wallenstein 1991; Conversi ed. 2012; Parekh 2008; Horowitz 1985; McGarry and O'Leary eds. 1993; Smith 1979, 1981, 1986, 1995, 2003). Remarkably, despite the breakup of the USSR and former Yugoslavia into nation-states in the 1990s, the category ethnic rather than nation has acquired greater strength. The ethnic elements have asserted themselves more strongly in such old nationalist movements as the Basque, the Catalans, the Scots, the Irish and the Corsicans. The ethnic elements have also been globally acknowledged in such powerful hypothesis as the 'clash of civilizations' by Huntington (Huntington 1992). Huntington's subsequent work on national identity crisis, *What Are We: America's Great Debate* (Huntington 2004), the power of ethnic bonds has figured very powerfully in deconstructing and reconstructing identity as a challenge to established notion of national identity.

Baruah (2010) has used the term ethno-nationalism to cover a 'wider range of political phenomena' such as nationalism, separatism, secessionism, subnationalism, ethnic insurgency, ethnic militancy or even regionalism (Baruah 2010: 1). His definition of ethno-nationalism is thus very broad based because, for him, it requires basically a 'set of nation oriented idioms, practices and possibilities' (Baruah 2010: 1). With that minimum requirements of course many a movements and discourses would pass an ethno-national test but then it would do injustice to the very specific ethno-nationalist articulations. True in all cases he mentioned there would be present some ethnic elements or aspirations of one or more ethnic groups in despair but a systematic discourse formation in ethnic nationalism may lose out its value when clubbed together with regionalism, or ethnic insurgency. Can one, for example, group the nationalist doctrine of Bankim Chandra Chattapadhyay[1] with an ethnic insurgency or regionalism?

The Tripuri ethno-nationalism formulated in 1948–50 was a pioneer in the North East but remained neglected in the studies of ethno-nationalism in India in general and the North East in particular. In the very significant collection on the subject by Baruah (2010), the Tripura case suffered an undeserved neglect. In comparison with the other cases of ethno-nationalism in the region, the Tripuri ethno-nationalism was most systemic and coherent.

## Objectives

This chapter discusses how a radical Tripuri ethno-nationalist discourse was formed in Tripura at a very crucial historical juncture of the State when monarchy was dismantled and a new political regime was yet to emerge. The political and socio-economic situation in the State was rather volatile and contained radical possibilities. Tripuri ethno-nationalism was a tribal elite protest against non-tribal elite domination in the State. It emerged not against British colonialism *per se* because it was no longer there but against another group of Indians in the State. The ideology of Tripuri ethno-nationalism was to be seen as part, the intellectual part, of the ongoing India 'nationalist' movement in the State but, paradoxically, a challenge against it in order to redefine the nationalist cause in Tripura and to revitalize the movement with a new ideology. But, more importantly, it was a movement for tribal self-assertion. Here the Tripuri national identity formation took the form of a nationalist doctrine formulated by a group of disgruntled indigenous Tripuri elites who sought to articulate mass grievances against Bengali domination. The rise of Tripuri nationalism was synonymous with the growing conception of a Tripuri national identity.

## Indian debate

The existing literature on India nationalism and the nationalism question in India is not of much help in understanding the autonomous development of regional or local nationalisms in India. Such small-scale nationalism, needless to say, has no place in the nationalist writings of Indian nationalism which are preoccupied with the development of all-India nationalism and the Indian nation-state. Indian Marxist writings on Indian nationalism are also not free from this prejudice. Desai's (Desai 1976: 381–431) remains the classic Marxist study of Indian nationalism. Desai's idea of Indian nationalism is well known: the rise of Indian nationalism was organically linked to the development of capitalism in India during British rule. He believes that modern nations are 'the product of capitalist development of society'. In his analytical framework, the rise of regional nationalisms was 'problematic', and he views them as one of the 'outstanding problems of the Indian nationalist movement'. Adopting the standpoint of 'the united national movement', he argues that the rise of regional nationalisms was proof of the uneven process of Indian capitalism (Desai 1967: 381–432). A brief survey of literature on the national question in India over the last decades reveals that the dominant assumption underlying such studies is the organic link between capitalism and nationalism, 'great' pan-India and regional.[2] All these studies are based squarely on the assumption that nationalism in any form is a capitalist or bourgeois phenomenon, and its rise, therefore, is integrally connected with the capitalist transformation or a given society possible role of local factors which are not necessarily related to the emergence of capitalism in the autonomous development of nationalism at the regional level.

Chatterjee's (1986) is a neo-Marxist textual analysis of India nationalist thought in a global context, but it is not particularly helpful in understanding regional nationalism in India. He considers nationalism essentially as a political doctrine, and examines its construction in India. He argues that the construction of nationalist thought in India was inherently contradictory, but underlines the autonomous strength of such a project in the global context. Interestingly, the dimensions of regional (in this case Bengali) nationalism are apparent in his study, but are subsumed within his grand theory (Chatterjee 1986: 57–8, 65).

Despite Vanaik's (1988) provocative claim that India as a nation-state has solved the 'national question' in the classical Marxist sense, the 'national question' nevertheless remains one of the fundamental problematic of India politics. This question ultimately relates to the broader question of the uneasy relation between the Indian nation-state and Indian nationalism as its ideology. Paradoxically, in India there is national oppression without there being a single oppressive nationality, which makes the understanding of the question complex. Hugh Seton-Watson (1977) has provided a workable definition of nationalism:

> All that I can find to say is that a nation exists when a significant number of people in a community consider themselves to form a nation or behave as if they have formed one.
>
> (Quoted in Anderson 1983: 15)

Anderson translated the terms 'consider themselves' in the above definition to mean 'imagine themselves' in formulating his famous definition of nationalism as an 'imagined political community' (Anderson 1983: 25). In the case of Tripuri nationalism, the act of 'imagination' was performed by a group of middle-class Tripuris (a Marxist would prefer to call them 'petty-bourgeois') who occupied subordinate social and political positions in Tripura vis-à-vis the indigenous elites such as the '*Thakur*' and the '*Karta*' (Royal notables), but also, more importantly, relative to the alien elite – the upper-caste Bengali Hindus who enjoyed royal patronage and privilege and held powerful positions in Tripuri society. As a result of a series of social, economic and political changes from the late nineteenth century, Bengalis came to dominate Tripuri society, and by the 1940s Bengali domination over Tripuris was total. Tripuri nationalism, as it was formulated by this particular group of indigenous Tripuris, expressed the genuine concerns of the Tripuris as a whole, and was not simply elite manipulation of mass sentiments.

This chapter is based on original archival source mostly in Bengali, and so far unused. As the scope of Tripuri nationalism is far broader than a single chapter can possibly encompass, the present study does not claim more than to offer an analytical narrative of the broad contours of the development of Tripuri nationalism. This chapter therefore has two objectives: to trace the roots of Tripuri nationalism, and to analyze the doctrine and identify its major features. In conclusion, the relevance and implications of Tripuri nationalism are examined.

## Roots of Tripuri nationalism

The roots of Tripuri nationalism have to be traced to Tripura's historic transformation since the late nineteenth century. The key to the understanding of the rise of Tripuri nationalism lay in those changes which determined its growth and shaped its character. In the formulation of the doctrine of Tripuri nationalism the specific historical context was a rallying-point. Central to Tripuri nationalism was the existence of an acute awareness among its exponents of Tripura's historic transformation, and a resultant sense of deprivation and frustration about its consequence for the lives of the Tripuris. A perceived loss of identity in their own land remained a persistent element of Tripuri nationalism.

## Historical background

Tripura is a small hilly State in North Eastern India occupying an area of some 10,000 sq.km. An ancient tribal kingdom, Tripura came under British colonial rule in the late eighteenth century, and continued as a princely State until India's independence in 1947. For a long time, it remained a sparsely populated State. Although its tribal majority, especially in the rural areas, spoke, Tripuri (*Kok-Borok*), from the eighteenth-century Bengali was (and still is) the official language of Tripura. From the mid-nineteenth century, the princely rulers of Tripura incorporated many of the administrative and legal structures of colonial Bengal as part of their State-formation process. They also attempted to modernize Tripura, but this highly bureaucratic process was not accompanied by any mass movement. As a result of the incorporation of Tripura into the periphery of the Indian empire it became subject to major socio-economic change which laid the basis for the emergence of Tripuri nationalism.

## Demographic upheaval

The most powerful factor in the development of Tripuri nationalism was the dramatic demographic shift from a predominantly tribal society into a predominantly Bengali society over the span of a few decades. Tripura is the only State in India where successive migrations from neighbouring Bengal have totally upset the local demographic balance, and reduced its original tribal residents to a pitiful minority in their own land. The Tripura royal family had always encouraged Bengali settlement in Tripura. By 1872 when the first (inexact) census was held, the tribal proportion of the population had fallen to about 64 per cent. By the turn of the century, it was down to 53 per cent. In 1947), the indigenous people become a minority (34.55 per cent.) according to the census of 1951.

## The rise of a new mode of production

The migration of Bengalis, mostly landless and land-hungry peasants, brought about revolutionary changes in Tripura's tribal agrarian structure which had been market by shifting cultivation, locally known as *jum*. The rulers of Tripura gave favourable land grants to the Bengalis at the expense of the tribals. The migration of Bengalis and their eventual settlement in Tripura totally upset the local ecological balance, introduced plough technology and settled cultivation, and replaced the tribal communal mode of production with one based on the private ownership of land. One of the major effects of demographic upheaval in Tripura has been the emergence of a number of rural classes in society. The census categories are elusive but suggestive:

Table 8.1 Tripura's rural class structure (1931–51)

| Classes | 1931(%) | 1951(%) |
|---|---|---|
| Rent Receivers | 2363 (0.61) | 11918 (1.48) |
| Owner Cultivators | 39837 (10.41) | 382147 (59.18) |
| Tenant Cultivators | 2830 (0.73) | 55930 (8.66) |
| Agricultural Labourers | 7512 (1.96) | 30886 (4.78) |

Sources: *Tripuri Census Bibarani* (in Bengali), 1931, pp. 52–60; Census reports of India, 1951, The figures within brackets indicate percentage of total population.

The evolution of the new agrarian system in Tripura favoured the Bengali immigrants. For instance, by 1931 only 13.60 per cent of the tribal population had adopted plough cultivation (Ganguly 1983: 40). The tribal masses were largely deprived of whatever benefits the newly introduced agrarian system might have produced for them. Cultivable land in this hilly State was not plentifully available. The tribals had to surrender their land in many cases held communally, to the rulers and then to the Bengal 'Colonizers' in favour of settled cultivation. Thus, a new, more progressive, agrarian system emerged in Tripura at the high cost of large-scale alienation of tribal land to the Bengalis, who also had taken recourse to illegal means to grab tribal lands.

### *Alien and indigenous middle classes*

Significant number of middle-class Bengalis also migrated to Tripura. Unlike Bengal, Tripura did not witness the development of an indigenous middle class on any large scale. Men in the liberal professions, though small in number, were mostly immigrants. Under the impact of the Bengali Renaissance, Tripura experience its own Renaissance. But this so-called Tripura Renaissance was mainly brought about by what I would call *surplus bhadralok* (educated but unemployed middle-class professionals) from Bengal who enjoyed royal patronage. As a movement it did not go beyond the charmed circle of retainers. For obvious reasons, the Tripura Renaissance did not give rise to political contradictions between the Bengali middle classes and the monarchy.

There was some limited growth of literacy in Tripura which gave birth to a small new class of educated tribal youths who were to become the new leadership in Tripura politics. It also gave rise to nationalism. As an indicator of social change, the following table shows the growth of literacy in Tripura between 1911 and 1951.

The reason for the major difference between 1921 and 1931 is not known. The big increase of literacy between 1941 and 1951 was to be explained with reference to (a) the literacy campaign launched by the Jana Mongal Samity (Association for Mass Literacy) (1945–48) and (b) Bengali migration.

Table 8.2 Percentage distribution of literacy in Tripura (1911–51)

| Year | Per cent |
| --- | --- |
| 1911 | 4.76% |
| 1921 | 8.21% |
| 1931 | 3.43% |
| 1941 | 7.95% |
| 1951 | 15.61% |

Source: Ganguly (1983)

The Tripura rulers' discriminatory employment policy favoured Bengalis at the cost of their own subjects. They made it a policy to employ educated Bengalis from outside in order to staff and modernize the administration. The usual practice was to recruit retired civil servants and the educated unemployed from Bengal. For instance, in the 1940s, the top echelon of administration was filled by Bengals: Jyoti Sen (retired ICS) as the Chief Minister; Girija Prasad Dutta (retired Police Officer) as Tripura's Police Commissioner; Khagendra Chandra Nath (retired Barrister) as Chief Justice of the High Court, and so on (Devbarma 1986: 24–5). By contrast, local educated youths either had to be content with jobs at the lower levels of administration, or none at all. Many left the State, and those who did not, remained unemployed. Those educated tribal youths who came from rural areas could only find jobs in the King's Bodyguard Force or the First Tripura Rifles, which, being under control of the Nepalis (the rulers' maternal relations) were arguable not free from nepotism. Aghore Devbarma, a veteran Tripuri communist leader and himself a victim of such a situation in the 1940s, pointed out that those educated youths who formed the Tripura Rajya Jana Sikhya Samity in 1945 for eradicating illiteracy from Tripura and launching a mass literacy campaign were all unemployed (Devbarma 1986: 24–5). This prepared a breeding ground for anti-Bengali sentiment in Tripura. Not surprisingly, the issue of indigenous exclusion dominated much of the politics of the Proja Mondal which protested against employment of 'outsiders' in Tripura and raised the slogan of 'Tripura State for State subjects' (Roy/MS: 1948; Dutta 1982: 22–3).

Thus the emergence of a class of indigenous educated but unemployed youths remained at the heart of much of the tribal middle-class discontent in Tripuri nationalism.

## Disillusionment with Tripura politics

The development of Tripuri nationalism is unintelligible without a brief outline of major trends in Tripura politics from the late 1930s which created in the late 1940s disillusionment among the ranks of Tripuri nationalists who had participated in the political movement for 'responsible government', democracy and civil liberties. Modern political movements developed very late in Tripura. An absolute and autocratic monarchy, *bubagra* (a Tripuri word for the principle of divine right of kings) reigned supreme in the State as late as 1947 when monarchy formally ended in Tripura. In the early 1920s Tripura witnessed the birth of a 'terrorist' nationalist movement which, as an extension of Bengali nationalist-terrorist movements, sought to liberate India by committing individual acts of terror against colonial officialdom, but the political movement for civil liberties and responsible government in Tripura did not emerge until the late 1930s. Nationalist terrorism was locally embraced by the educated middle-class youth, both Bengali and tribal. The participation of Tripuris in anti-British (terrorist) activities was quite significant. Arguably, those Tripuri youths (and the further Tripuri nationalists) subscribed, however vaguely, to all-Indian nationalism when they joined the terrorist movement. Many of the Tripuri nationalists, most notably Probhat Roy and Bansi Thakur (both Tripuris), were former terrorists nationalists. These terrorists-turned local nationalists were actively involved in the local political movements from the late 1930s through the Jana Mongal Samity (Association for Public Welfare, 1938–42), the Jana Siksha Samity (Association for Mass Literacy, 1945–48) and the Proja Mondal (Subjects' Association for Public Welfare 1945–48). These regional political movements for responsible government, democracy and civil liberties became increasingly anti-Bengali in a State where real power was exercised by the princely bureaucracy, mostly staffed by the upper-caste, Bengali Hindu immigrants. From the 1940s Tripura's popular movement began to develop from a (still undefined) sense of Tripuri nationalism against Bengali domination. The Proja Mondal was openly based on the slogan of 'Tripura State for the State's subjects'. And yet, the movement, confined mostly to the State capital, predominantly inhabited by Bengalis, did not gather much strength and failed to realize its objectives.

Another important aspect of nationalist disillusionment with local politics was increasing communist control over the local movement, which was not accepted by the Tripuri nationalists. The State communist movement was founded in the late 1930s by a group of former nationalist-terrorists, mostly Bengalis of Tripura who had undergone an ideological transformation whilst in jail. The Tripura communists, from the beginning of the communist movement in the State, actively participated in local political movements through the JMS, JSS and PM, which they utilized as platforms for building mass bases. Congress nationalism was unable to establish itself effectively in Tripura. In the absence of powerful rival political forces, the communists increasingly began to control the local movements, and dwelt on the sense of Tripuri nationalism. The Tripura communists began to 'identify' themselves with the Tripuri nationalist cause against Bengali domination. In short, Tripura communism over the years developed in symbiosis with Tripuri nationalism, but it was an uneasy and tension ridden relationship. The local communist approach to the national question of Tripuris was predominantly tactical, if not manipulative. The communists, by and large, avoided the question. Aghore Devbarma, a veteran Tripuri communist leader – remained with the CPI after the party split – sums up the role the communists played with regard to the nationality question of Tripura tribals when he self-critically wrote:

> The question of the national self-determination of tribals was [in the past] avoided on the ground that it was alone in socialism that a solution to the nationality question was to be found. Therefore whatever was done for the tribes, was only partially so done. The communist party [Tripura] never launched any determined struggle for the national self-determination of Tripuris.
> (Devbarma 1986: 12)[3]

In May 1948 the Tripura Rajya Gana Mukti Parishad (known as the GMP) was born as a violent Tripuri nationalist organization to put up armed resistance to State repression against the local political movements. This organization soon engaged itself in an armed struggle which dismantled established authority in large parts of Tripura during 1949–51. But it developed under the increasingly powerful impact of the all-India level policies of the CPI into a broad-based (Indian) nationalist organization to incorporate into its fold not only the other tribal groups of Tripura, like the Reangs and the Halams, but even the Bengalis as well. In the GMP's own words:

> The Tripura Rajya Gana Mukti Parishad is a democratic and revolutionary organization of the Tripuris, Bengalis, Halams, Chakmas, Kukis, Manipuris, Jamatias, Reangs, All Hindus and Muslims.
> (Devbarma 1951: 3)

The GMP asked all of them to join it 'to make the GMP a broad-based anti-imperialist and anti-feudal democratic front', and assured them all that it would protect the nationalist interests of all (Devbarma 1952: 3).

This turn of events in Tripura politics created dissatisfaction among the nationalists who fundamentally disagreed with the communist approach to the Tripura national question, perceived a lack of sincerity on the part of the leadership of local movements, and formulated the doctrine of Tripuri nationlism in order to search for the identity of the Tripuris and to define their real problem (Devbarma 1952: 3).

## Major traits of Tripuri nationalism

Tripuri nationalism had several themes and features which could well be taken up in a separate study. Here we will discuss only the major aspects of the doctrine of Tripuri nationalism.

### *Protest against Bengali dominance*

Tripuri nationalism emerged fundamentally as a protest against Bengali dominance over the Tripuris. As a result of Tripura's historic transformation, Bengalis, especially upper-caste Bengali Hindus, came to occupy dominant positions in Tripura society, but there was very little indication that they identified with Tripura as such. The Tripuri nationalists deplored this attitude, and saw it as justification for the local people's disdain for the Bengalis as 'outsiders'. As Probhat Roy, one of the exponents of Tripuri nationalism wrote:

> A new Community gradually rose to power and position. It is the Bengali upper class Hindu community. These people were placed at the helm of State affairs, and were able to get hold of the economic field. Today almost all the officials down to peon are members of the Bengali Hindu community. All the banks, tea gardens and large commercial enterprises are owned by them. Their administrative and economic relations with the people apart, very few of the community cared to identify themselves with the State as their hearth and home, and this naturally reacted on the local people to look down upon them as "outsiders". Job-finding and fortune-seeking happen to be the core of their connection with the State.
>
> (Roy (MS 1948): 35–6)

This anti-Bengali stand of Tripuri nationalism was extended to denounce the existing leadership of popular political movements in the State and to highlight the need for a new kind of leadership:

> The 15-year-long "silent movement" in the State lacked momentum because of the absence of leadership of the Tripuris – the main basis of the State people. Formerly they could hardly put their faith in the words of those leaders whose fathers had been administrators and exploiters so long. . . . The 15th August 1947 marks the advent of a new born leadership that commands the confidence of all communities championing their cause against outsiders' domination and exploitation. The people demand their own rule by themselves.
>
> (Roy (MSS 1948): 36–7)

Tripuri nationalism was in part a critique of the Indian nationalist movement which achieved power for Indians but not for Tripuris. While Indian achieved self-rule, Tripuris did not, In Tripura little political change took place which could ensure Tripuri participation in the political and administrative processes of the State. With Tripura's accession to India in 1949, Tripura came under the rule of Indian and Bengalis. It was said sarcastically by one of the exponents of Tripuri nationalism: The land of the Tripura people [is] ruled by the Indian in general and Bengalis in particular.[4] In fact, this anti-Bengali attitude permeated the whole doctrine of Tripuri nationalism.

### Distinction between the proja and the oproja

Tripuri nationalism was also based on a distinction between the *proja* (subjects) and the *oproja* (non-subjects). In response to Tripura's transformation and as a protest against it, Roy felt the need to make such a distinction, which, he believed, would pave the way for defining a Tripuri nationality:

> The upper class Hindu Bengalis are well established in Tripura's economy and politics, and are dominating the State. But they do not consider themselves as belonging to Tripura, and always acted against the interests of the people. If the these [permanent/original] inhabitants of Tripura develop their unified nationalist consciousness, they can identify their exploiters. In order to develop the *jatiyo monobhab* [national consciousness] there is indeed need for distinguishing between the *proja* and the *oproja*.
>
> (Roy (MS 1948): 31–2)

Roy even went to the extent of blaming the *oprojas* (i.e. the Bengalis) for the relative failure of the Proja Mondal movement in the State. It is no wonder that the authority of the State, representing the interests of the upper-class Bengali Hindus, should be hostile to the Proja Mondal movement. The Bengali Hindu dominated local Congress for obvious reasons maintained the same attitude (Roy (MSS 1948): 39).

This distinction was one which was tenable in the specific context of Tripura. It was an attempt to identify the subject of Tripuri nationalism and to distinguish it from those who were not 'Tripuris'. It was different from the conventional Indian nationalist distinction between Indians and British; rather it was one between two groups of Indians. This doctrine did into amount to communalism because it was ready to include the poorer, peasant section of the Bengalis into its conception of a Tripuri: only the poorer section which adopts tilling as its sole occupation takes the sold as its homeland. It has neither the sense of racial and cultural superiority nor any scope for exploitation. So its identity merged with the common conception and outlook of the local people (Roy (MSS 1948): 36–7).

### *Critique of the Bengali cultural tradition*

Tripuri nationalists made a thorough criticism of Tripura's dominant intellectual tradition as created and dominated by the Bengalis. They criticized the Tripura Renaissance that began in the late nineteenth century on the grounds that it was led by immigrants from Bengal who thrived on royal patronage, and therefore could not give birth to any contradictions between the middle class and the monarchy. Inherently limited, the leadership of this movement could not feel the need for developing any political movement let alone leading one (*Chiniha*, No. 1, April 1949: 1). And yet, the consequences of this movement for Tripuri culture, they pointed out, had been tragic: it had created a hatred of and indifference to *ganabhasha* (people's language), and pave the way for the creation of a false history of the people of the State. Bengali culture, it was forcefully added, based itself on this falsified history of the State (*Chiniha* May 3, 1949: 17).

The criticism of the Tripuri Renaissance was extended to include the Bengali Renaissance of which the former was an offshoot. According to Tripuri nationalists, the Bengali Renaissance was a movement of the upper-class and upper-caste *bhadralok*, and its leadership, despite the fact that they had spoken about the lower-class and -caste, had nevertheless failed to communicate their message to the lower-classes because the language they spoke in was not the language of the masses. To the Tripuri nationalists, it was therefore hardly surprising that the culture created by these elites of Tripura for the aristocrats, royal notables and princes would be one-sided (*Chiniha*, May 3 1949: 17).

While the doctrine of Tripuri nationalism rejected the dominant tradition created by the Bengalis, it traced its roots to indigenous cultural tradition. Thus, the work of Col. Mahim Chandra (*Chiniha*, May 3, 1949: 17) was approved of and praised; and his limitations were overlooked. Mahim Chandra was a high-level princely official during the nineteenth century. Mahim's political ideas were reformulated. His political theory was that of benevolent despotism, but there was nothing wrong with that, the Tripuri nationalists argued. His long career in princely administration had convinced him that princely rule could prove better than of the British provided officials were honest and reliable. Mahim lamented the fact that, despite the growth of literature and culture, the gap between ruler and ruled had widened. The implication that Bengalis were responsible for creating such a gap was clear. He avoided such issues as existing feudal exploitation and inequalities, but he was exonerated on the ground that 'as a rich person himself and royal official, it was difficult for him to reflect on such issues' (*Chiniha*, May 3 1949: 17). That Mahim wanted to bridge the gap between ruler and ruled made him a cultural hero in the eyes of the Tripuri nationalists who assumed that he had played a glorious role in the Tripuri Renaissance.

The Tripuri nationalists did not, however, exonerate that indigenous elites, especially the Thankurs, for their indifference to native tradition and national cultural resources. The works of Radha Mohun Devbarma (a Tripuri ex-Commander) were cited to draw attention to such resources. Devbarma wrote three books – *Kok-Borok Ma* (*A Grammar of the Tripuri Language*, 1900), *Tripura Abhidhan* (*A Dictionary of Tripuri*, 1909) and *Tripurar Katha Mala* (*A Translation of the Tripuri Language*, 1919). Those books were written in Tripuri but in Bengali script. Yet, that did not appear as a limitation, for it was quickly added that there was nothing to be ashamed of the fact that Tripura did not have a script of its own. The history of the Bengali script, the nationalists pointed out, was not a long one. In fact, they accused the upper stratum of Tripuri society for its inability to understand the importance of its own cultural resources (*Chiniha*, September 20, 1949: 30–1).

## *Concern for political power*

Central to Tripuri nationalism was a desire for political power, a concern which was not only made clear by explicit or implicit reference but by making the demand of Tripuri self-determination based on language a political demand. A sense of political powerlessness, on the part of Tripuris vis-à-vis the Bengali outsiders, remained the main grievance of Tripuri nationalism. The Tripuri nationalists perceived in and through the demand for the Tripuri language 'a movement for national self-determination, a nationalist movement' (*Chiniha*, 37, January 1950: 246). It was thought to be a demand for 'full self-determination of the Tripura *jati* [nation], and for recognition of their political rights in their own land' (*Chiniha*, 37: 247). 'To miss the political dimension of the phenomenon', they argued, 'was to lose the whole thing'.[5] The Tripuri nationalists went as far as to argue that it was 'because of the absence of a powerful political consciousness, in the State that its cultural standards were so backward' (*Chiniha*, No.1, 1949: 5–6).

To drive home this point and to justify their claim to political power, reference was made back to Tripura's political history. Significantly, a particular period of monarchial rule in Tripura was glorified. In order to give a sense of historical continuity to Tripura's nationalism, a semi-historical essay mainly drawing on the chronicle of the Tripur dynasty was written describing the story of the expedition of King Bijoy Manikya in the sixteenth century and his victory over Bengal (*Chiniha*, No.: 5). The continuity was not sequential but thematic, the theme being the demonstration of strength, and the domination of Bengal (at least, part of it, and temporarily) by the King of Tripura. In order to provide legitimacy for this event, and to see it as not simply a figment of the imagination, passage from the *Rajmala*, the chronicle of the ruling dynasty, describing the royal expedition were extensively quoted. The description also served as interpretation:

> In order to conquer Bangladesh (Bengal) the great king Bijoy Manikya mobilized 24,000 infantrymen, 5,000 cavalry, quite a few artillerymen, 200 men carrying sword and shield, and 5,000 naval forces, and set out for the expedition. He easily conquered the nearby areas of Bengal and seized an enormous amount of wealth. Then he put down a number of rebellious Bengal zamindars, and conquered Shrihatta and the kingdom of Khasia, and thus expanded his territory.
>
> (*Chiniha*, No.1: 5)

Distortion in historical myth-making was unavoidable. The fathers of Tripuri nationalism quoted a passage from the magazine *Bengal: Past and Present* (October 1907, pp. 50–51): 'Here is the kingdom of Tripura, "naturally" fenced with hills and mountains and by that means hitherto defended against the Mughal Tartars, their bad neighbours with whom they have continued quarrels'. Interestingly, they interpreted the passage as demonstrating that Tripura had proved its strength historically by fighting with the great Moghuls and that the Tripura State existed today due to its historical strength (*Chiniha*, No. 1: 6).

Though Tripuri nationalists mentioned that there were a lot of Bengali soldiers in the expeditionary force, they were quick to stress that the number of Bengalis had been quite insignificant compared to the Tripuris:

> In all the cases the predominance of the hill tribes and the Tripuris was unimpaired. For the Tripura state was their motherland, and they had an

inseparable link with their ruler. The Tripuri *Jati* [nation] was the supreme physical strength of the state.

(*Chiniha*, No.1: 6)

Their 'reading' of the text was meant to show that Bengalis had once been under the dominance of the Tripuris, to exclude the Bengalis from Tripura's past power and dominance, and so to maintain the purity of the Tripuris as a nation.

In their practical programme the Tripuri nationalists aimed at political power within the Indian Union and not as a separate State. Princely Tripura acceded to the Indian Union on 15th October 1949, but there was wild speculation and uncertainty about its political future even within the Indian Union. Debates mainly focused on Tripura's merger with either neighbouring Assam or West Bengal. The nationalists strongly protested against this. They stated that the fundamental demand of the Tripuris was for national self-determination. which could be realized only within a politically autonomous Tripura, and not through its merger with any other region.[6] They asserted:

> What we see today in the demand for the Tripura language is nothing but the demand of the struggling people of a backward nation. Exploited and oppressed by the Bengalis, the nationalist movement of the Tripuris is basically manifesting itself in the language demand. This demand is as natural as the natural laws of history.[7]

In a letter to the Queen Regent of Tripura, Probahat Roy, it was insisted that Tripura wanted to participate in the Indian Union as an autonomous political unit based on the principle of self-determination, as a political entity were Tripuri would be the medium of instruction and one of the official languages, and where the structure of government would be democratic (*Chiniha* 37, January 1950: 246).

## *Language as symbol and argument*

In the formulation of the doctrine of Tripuri nationalism the Tripuri language was used both as a major symbol and as an argument for nationalism. Apart from letters and petitions, a series of essays appeared in the pages of *Chiniha* under the title 'Demand for the Tripuri Language' contributed by several authors, all Tripuris. Running through them were a series of arguments in favour of the symbolic use of the Tripuri language as a means of defining a Tripuri identity. First, the antiquity of the Tripuri language was emphasized as proof of the nation's antiquity. It was argued that the Tripuri language was an ancient one, belonging to the Tibetan-Chinese group. It was also claimed that this was one of the thirty sub-languages of the aboriginal people of India whose languages, it was pointed out, seldom remained unmixed. The disappearance of many languages had been recorded in history (*Chiniha* 24, September 1949: 164). But even under the impact of Hinduism and a hostile environment many of India's tribals had not abandoned their group language and hence their identity.

Second, and following from the above, the Tripuri language had survived despite the long-term domination of Bengali culture and language. Where, after all, had the language of the oppressed people developed, asked the Tripuri nationalists? Tripuri was still a living language: in the hilly areas where most Tripuris lived it was the people's language. It was also mentioned that on several occasions Tripuri had been used in official documents and gazettes.

The ideology of Tripuri nationalism was formulated in Bengali which was truly the language of the Tripuri's perceived enemies. This seemed a limitation of Tripuri nationalism. But the Tripuri nationalists did not consider it a limitation at all. On the contrary, they asked: why had the Tripuri language failed to develop as a written and literary language? The reasons, according to them, were basically economic and cultural exploitation: the subjugation and domination of the Tripuris for centuries had stood in the way of the development of their language. They also asked: had there been any historical instances when the language of the exploited people had developed in a condition of domination and exploitation? Drawing instances from Indian history, they argued that apart from a few cases, many languages like Santali, Oraon, Ho, Mundari, Khasi and Naga had failed to develop under long periods of alien domination.[8] They cited as counter examples to strengthen their case the many historical instances of languages undergoing changes, and losing identity, and sometimes completely disappearing from history.[9] Tripuris spoke Bengali, they were at pains to point out, under economic compulsion, for trade, business and exchange; yet their language had survived despite this hostile situation. That indicated, according to the nationalists, the vitality and strength of the Tripuris as a nation (*Chinhia* 24, September 1949: 164).

The central focus on language in formulating the doctrine of nationalism and in the formation of the Tripuris' identity was part of a general assumption made by the Tripuri nationalists:

> The cultural subjugation of a nation is worse than its general subjugation; it destroys the originality of the nation, eats into its vitality, and cripples it. The nation loses its power of invention, free thought and all-round development; nationhood evaporates into thin air.[10]

According to them, this cultural subjugation was linked to the political dominance of Bengalis which deprived the indigenous people of political power (*Chiniha* 19, September 1949: 132).

The nationalists' invocation of the Tripuri language was meant to evoke unity among the Tripuris, a cultural unity as a precondition for political unity. The language was used as a symbol of group identity and as a unifying force among the Tripuris. Significantly, Tripuri nationalists did not touch upon religion since Hinduism being the State religion, and also the religion of both Tripuris and most Bengalis, was not at all useful in unifying the Tripuris and excluding the Bengalis from the growing conception of a Tripuri identity. So the choice of language rather than religion as a major symbol of group identity was a conscious one.

Ultimately, Tripuri nationalism as expressed through demands for the Tripuri language aimed at a fundamental political objective. In the words of one of its exponents: 'This movement, in short, is the movement for establishing national self-determination for the Tripuris, a national movement against national oppression' (*Chiniha*, 24, September 1949: 14). This demand for the Tripuri language, they forcefully pointed out, was a political demand, a demand or a movement for recognition of the political right of the Tripuris to Tripura, their homeland.

## Conclusion

The rise of Tripuri nationalism was conditioned and shaped neither by capitalist transformations nor by British rule, not directly at least, but by factors which were apparently local. The conditions were the after effects of the British colonial rule in the late nineteenth century in India's peripheries. The Bengalis who migrated to Tripura belonged to different classes and castes. The upper stratum of Bengalis held high positions in society and wielded political power. Although few in number, a section of the Bengalis monopolized trade, commerce and middle-class jobs. The rest were peasants and agricultural labourers. It cannot be argued that the class content of Bengali domination was entirely absent in Tripura. But it needs more research to show whether Bengali domination was equivalent to capitalist domination. Tripuri nationalism was fundamentally a protest against Bengali domination, against the rule of one nationality by another. The nationalists sought to end this domination and to replace it with the rule of Tripura by the Tripuris themselves. This study suggests therefore a revision of perspectives in the existing understanding of the national question in India, and directs our attention to consider indigenous, local factors and autonomy in the rise and growth of such nationalisms in India.

The development of nationalism in Tripura was not a 'partial reflection' of Indian nationalism. In fact, the rise of Tripuri nationalism shows the failure of Indian nationalism to strike deep social roots in India. As Rajni Kothari observed, Indian nationalism's 'organizing reach was not that all-encompassing and it left out both major segments of society and quite a lot of territorial space' (Kothari 1988: 2223). This suggests the need for further studies of the local nationalisms which emerged in different parts of India at different times in the past, and of the potentiality for more which remain embedded in modern Indian society. Such studies might throw fresh light on the unresolved tension between Indian nationalism and the Indian nation-State, or what Chatterjee calls, the 'false resolution of the national question in India' (Chatterjee 1986: 168).

The mass character of Tripuri nationalism was limited in the sense that it represented predominantly the Tripuris, the major tribe, and excluded a substantial element of Tripura's indigenous population comprising different tribal groups like the Reangs, the Chakmas, the Kukis and so on who had a subordinate position in the social hierarchy of Tripura; the nationalist movement thus revealed a contradiction. While it sought to liberate Tripuris from the yoke of Bengali domination, it did not seek political power for the whole of Tripura's population, only for the Tripuris. As usual, the ethnic character of this doctrine was evident. It was exclusive in character.

Another limitation of Tripuri nationalism was its failure to develop the appropriate political organization 'to complete the process' by developing a vigorous mass movement on the basis of this new ideology. This relative failure of Tripuri nationalism should not be taken too far, and should be understood in the unique historical setting of Tripura in which the communists, in combination with another more powerful radical tribal force, i.e., the GMP, and with a qualitatively different approach to the national question, monopolized all political activity.

What then did Tripuri nationalism achieve? Tripura was not merged with any other region, and was able to maintain its separate historical and territorial identity albeit within the Union of India. But did that mean self-rule for the Tripuris? Did the Tripuris fulfill their fundamental right to rule themselves in their homeland? Tripura achieved Statehood within Indian federalism in 1972. Did that mean any progress towards Tripuris' self-rule? In the period since the early 1950s successive migration of more Bengalis to Tripura has further upset its demographic balance. Bengalis today constitute 68 per cent of Tripura's population with the original tribals reduced to a minority around 31 per cent. This has meant that Bengalis' domination has increased rather than decreased, and this is likely to continue in future. Tripuri nationalism and its aspirations, therefore, remain unfulfilled, and had occasionally found a distorted expression in and through such political agencies as the Tripura Upajati Yuba Samity (TUJS) (now defunct), the Tripura National Volunteers (TNV) (now defunct) and the Indigenous Nationalities Liberation Front of Tripura which formed opportunistic electoral pact with the Congress in Tripura, which is a party of the Bengali and urban based where few tribals live. But Tripura became a part of the Indian Union in 1949, something the Tripuri nationalist thinkers aspired. Tripura's Left radicals, however, took the cudgel and combined the concerns of the nationalists with that of the growing communist movement in the State – a subject discussed in greater detail in Chapter 9 that follows.

## Notes

1 Bankim Chandra Chattapadhyay was a famous Bengali administrator-writer and novelist in the nineteenth century who is considered as the first to articulate a systemic doctrine of Indian nationalism. (Chatterjee 1986; Kaviraj 1992).
2 See, *Social Scientist*, 4:1 (1975). This issue was entirely devoted to the nationality question in India; Chopra (1984: 3–14); Mishra (1972); Chandra (1985: 35–57); Guha (1980); Guha (1979); Annual Number, Kamat (1980); Namboodripad (1952); Roy (1967); Karat (1973); Vanaik (1988); B. Barua, Language and National Question in North East India (Gauhati, n.d.); Guha (1982); Alam (1981).
3 This view was definitely one-sided because it was the total involvement of the Communist Party and the GMP in Tripura with the emerging nationalist movements that brought them success subsequently.
4 *Chinihat* ('Our Country'), mouthpiece of Tripuri nationalists edited by Probhat Roy and Bansi Thakur (in Bengali, Sec No. 16, p. 111).
5 Ibid.

6 *Chiniha*, 18 August 1949, 'Incorporation or Self-Determination?' a letter from Chiniha to the Queen Regent in which the Tripura nationalists strongly protested against any move to merge Tripura with any other region or province, and advocated Tripura's autonomous political existence as a separate province on the basis of the popular demand for autonomy and self-detemination.
7 *Chinha*, 6, June 1949, p. 37; also Chinha, 36, January 1950, p. 240.
8 *Chiniha*, 25, September 1949, p. 168, and Chiniha, 12, September 1949, p. 80.
9 *Chinia*, 24, September 1949, p. 164.
10 *Chiniha*, 12, September 1949, 'Tripura Language and Tripura Government' by Probhat Roy and Bansi Thakur. In this article they criticized the Tripura government for not implementing the language policies of the government of India (as embodied in their Resolution No. D3791/48). This was an instance of how Tripuri nationalism developed also as a response to state politics.

# 9 Left radicalism turned parliamentary and institutionalized in Tripura

Appropriation of tribal ethno-nationalism

### Introduction: *Strange Theory, Strange Practice*

When placed in relation to the regional context of North East India, the GMP would have been an ethnic party to come out of its struggle, or insurgency, as the term came to be used nowadays, in post-1949 Tripura to usher in as a ruling party like its many counterparts in Nagaland, Mizoram and Meghalaya. This would have happened provided of course that democratic political process was available in the State to take power at the State level. Neither of the two happened, first, because the GMP developed a strong Left orientation; and second, the democratic process would not be available in Tripura well until 1972 when Statehood would be conceded to Tripura. The GMP would be integrated with Indian communism which would transform it not into an ethnic party *per se* but a tribal mass association under the leadership (and authority) of the Tripura unit of the CPI. Tribal ethnicity would be recognized only as a second order derivative of the Marxists' class perspective.

From 1950–52 Tripura's Left radicals (both the communists and the GMP) turned parliamentary, opted for the ballot instead of the bullet, decided to participate in the parliamentary democratic process under a process known in the writings on Indian communism as 'integration' of local traditions with 'all-India' communism (Fic 1969; Nossiter 1982, 1988; Singh 1994; Bhattacharyya 1999). This entailed, in effect, the subjugation of the locally developed GMP and Left movements to the authority of the all-India party. As Singh (1994) has pointed out, in great detail, the attempt in the case of the Punjab was disastrous because the Lal Communist Party, which had developed indigenously around a radical version of Sikh ethno-nationalism, had to give in, and in the wake it signaled the end of communism in the State very early on.[1] In Tripura, the GMP, in a way, was the Tripura version of the LCP but here 'integration' was possible, and the GMP was finally persuaded to submit itself to the authority of the State Communist Party, which effectively meant to toe the (internationally dictated) 'party line', as was received by the local unit from the all-India party. Locally it meant participation in the democratic political process as a legitimate political party, or its affiliate, and to engage itself in the parliamentary struggle. And yet, there was no local reason to call off armed struggle by the GMP cadres during 1950–51 – the local dynamics of the armed struggle (chapter 7) did not suggest as much.

Kaviraj argued, as we have seen in *Introduction*, that communism in India exhibited and still does, many 'strange practices' as a result of accepting uncritically the so-called 'universal theory' from the international arena. Our experiences so far do not show any such 'strange practices' in the case of Tripura. The reasons why the GMP had to call off armed struggle was because a theoretical party line (read, after Kaviraj, 'universal') arrived in Tripura and the local party (still reorganizing itself) had to apply that 'theory' to the case of the GMP-led armed struggle. I would prefer to call it a *strange theory* which would result in a series of 'strange practices' in Tripura, as perhaps elsewhere in India too, in the years to come. The acceptance of the *strange theory* would entail a series of strange idioms and concepts through which to fit the 'understanding' of the local situation. It meant in effect conforming to a theoretical paradigm which would displace the real world of struggle and the local situation by an imaginary one derived from the said paradigm.

Students of Indian communism are aware that Indian communism as a party and movement was subject to all the shifts and turns as a result of succumbing to the international policy lines dictated either from Moscow or Beijing (after 1949). This aspect has been adequately analyzed (Overstreet and Windmiller 1959; Fic 1969; Kautsky 1956; Nossiter 1982, 1988). The changes in leadership in the former CPSU and the resultant changes in policy lines has resulted, rather awkwardly, shifts and turns in the communist movements in India since its establishment in the early 1920s.[2] When the GMP's armed struggle was going on, there was a vague influence of the then Randive line[3] (in favour of guerrilla armed struggle) of the Second Congress of the CPI in Calcutta in 1948 through such leaders as late Biren Datta (who was a founding member of the GMP yet did not hold any organizational position) and late Aghore Devbarma. From 1950–51 the local Communist Party unit received the new party line – this time the so-called Rajeswar line (Andhra group of the CPI)[4] which advocated for peasant armed guerilla struggle. The editorial of the *Comminform* titled *For a Lasting Peace, For a Peoples Democracy* had changed the Russian path of revolution to the Chinese path for the colonial and ex-colonial countries and thus contained a message for the Indian communists. Three features of this 'theory' merit attention. First, the CPI decided to engage itself in rural based armed struggle to capture the countryside first before liberating the cities. Second, the party advocated for a 'united front' of workers, peasants and middle-class bourgeoisie as the primary form of struggle and the first stage of revolution. The other forms of struggle were not ruled out. Third, the communist struggle of the time was defined as 'the peasant war under the leadership of the proletariat' (Bhattacharyya 1999: 104–5).

Following this new 'theory', the All-Indian party (CPI) sent (the late) Nripen Chakrabarty as a political trainer, Mohun Choudhury (real name Bipul) as an experienced guerrilla solider (from the Telangana armed struggle), Shiva Ram as a gun mechanic and Dr Bijoy Roy as a doctor for intervening in the ongoing GMP-led armed struggle and helping it out. As I indicated above, it was a strange theory for the reality of GMP-led armed struggle. The GMP-led armed struggle was neither a peasant war led by the proletariat nor was there much of the cities to be liberated in Tripura. However, the arrival of those leaders along with the Rajeswar line in Tripura reinforced the armed struggle; the GMP guerrillas launched a virulent armed attack on the government. The government also arrested large numbers of suspected communists (Bhattacharyya 1999: 105). Before the local unit of the CPI could make full use of the Rajeswar line of rural armed struggle in Tripura, changes took place in the international line again; this time it came via the CPGM and its leader R. P. Dutt (read for the Moscow line), and a document titled the *Tactical Line of 1951*. This line did not openly discard violence and tilted towards other forms of action, most notably, legal ones. The so-called 'Partisan war of peasants' (Tripura included) were considered 'premature uprising and adventurist action of every type must be undoubtedly eschewed' (Bhattacharyya 1999: 130). The incoming India's first general elections of 1951–52 were no doubt the most important of 'legal possibilities', and therefore, the *Tactical Line* suggested strongly as much:

> It [the party] has to utilize the coming general elections for the extensive popularization of its programme, for mobilizing and unifying the democratic forces, for exposing the policies and methods of the government.
>
> (quoted in Bhattacharyya 1999: 130)

Although it was under Ajay Kumar Ghosh (CPI General Secretary from 1951–62) that the CPI was given a strong orientation to parliamentary and electoral politics, and constitutionalism, (following the Moscow line), there was an indigenous root to the line advocated by P. C. Joshi (CPI General Secretary during 1935–48) advocated that the CPI developed itself into the politics of 'loyal opposition' to the Congress. Joshi was removed from the General Secretaryship of the party in 1948 and expelled from the party in 1949.

## GMP's integration with Indian communism: identity and autonomy

An early attempt by Aghore Devbarma to dissolve the GMP (then called TRUGMP) in 1949 and form a Communist Party out of it and transform the GMP in to a peasant committee under the Communist Party was turned down by the main leadership of the GMP, particularly Dasarath Devbarma, who was the top leader of the GMP movement and known as the 'uncrowned king' of the tribals in Tripura. Aghore Devbarma resigned at the crucial time when the armed struggle was picking up in Tripura. The majority view represented by Dasarath Devbarma preferred to ignore Aghore Devbarma's proposal on tactical grounds: accepting the proposal would mean in effect surrendering to the authority of the Communist Party and losing the identity and autonomy of the movement. Dasarath Devbarma later recalled:

> It would be a tactical mistake to transform the GMP into a communist party. The struggle was being conducted in the name of an organization whose name

could not simply be changed. It would create confusion among the ranks of the GMP. Within the GMP there were hardly any hardcore anti-communists. Also it would be premature to persuade the activists to accept the communist party membership.

(Devbarma 1987: 74–5)

The GMP's refusal to merge itself in the Communist Party was based on its local strength and a sense of realism:

The class struggle cannot be imposed on the people; big landlords are hard to find in Tripura. The slogan of "land to the tiller" cannot be applied to Tripura. It will isolate the peasantry from the GMP. We have to wait and slowly persuade the GMP members to join the communist party.

(Devbarma 1987: 75)

The above statement of the top leader of the GMP was strongly suggestive of the hollowness of the alien theoretical paradigm, I have termed *strange theory*, that the all-India party was using to 'integrate' the GMP with all-India communism.

However, the irony of GMP's 'integration' meant that it was subjected to the two Rajeswar lines of the party – of 1950 and 1951. The first encouraged armed struggle but not in the way it had developed indigenously in Tripura centering around Tripuri ethno-nationalism, and the other was to push the local movement to the path of parliamentary politics keeping in view the upcoming general elections in India. Both were *strange theoretical practices* as far as the tenor of the GMP movement was concerned.

## Tripura party builds on the GMP

By the middle of 1950 the Tripura unit of the CPI, as such, was tiny with about half a dozen members altogether. The Assam Provincial Committee of the CPI was entrusted by the all-Indian party to shape the Tripura party unit. Around the middle of 1950 Tripura received a group of Assam communist leaders under the leadership of Rakhal Rajkumar (Secretary of the Assam unit) and a District Organizing Committee was formed in Boromura Hills consisting of 41 members; and it was in that meeting, as Dasarath Devbarma recalled, that the front-ranking leaders of the GMP got CPI membership (Devbarma 1987: 82). With the GMP recruits, the party membership grew to about a thousand in 1952. The moot question then remains: who should have integrated with whom? As a result of this 'integration', the GMP was not dissolved but kept as a tribal mass front of the party indicating that tribal ethnicity was recognized but only as a second order value to the principle of class struggle. But this organizational arrangement created a lot of confusion among the rank and file of the GMP regarding the real value of their organization and it identity and autonomy. The other relevant and very important question was the tradition of politics created by the GMP in Tripura. Those were construed as 'inner-party conflicts' to be resolved within the party by referring to what I have termed *strange theory*, i.e., a set of theoretical arguments that pointed out many pitfalls of the GMP, and stressed the 'right path' of revolutionary action.

Two inner-party documents in this regard proved instrumental. The first one[5] drafted by late Nripen Chakrbarty – the first Chief Minister of Tripura under the Left Front (1978–88); and the second one[6] drafted by late Dasarth Devbarma, the first Secretary of the Tripura State Council of the CPI and Deputy Chief Minister during 1983–88 and Chief Minister during 1993–98. Chakrabarty went to Tripura in 1950 as a political trainer and ideologue to implement the Rajeswar lines of the party. Devbarma emerged out of the indigenously developed GMP movement and the organization's top leader. The first document was a testimony to the imposition of the *strange theory* on the GMP pointing out its many pitfalls and directing it to the right path of political action. The issues are discussed in brief under the following five heads:

### *Spontaneity vs. organization*

Organization was a central problem of the CPI in Tripura and until (mid-) 1950 its membership was very small. The CPI leaders were rebuilding the party organization banking on the GMP. But the argument was strange: Marxism did not worship 'spontaneity'. So the Chakrabarty document asked to abandon 'spontaneity' in favour of the Communist Party organization. The communists were the party of the working class and its leadership was indispensable for the success of a historical mass movements. The GMP movement was thus explained away as 'spontaneous' and localized; it was termed 'a spontaneous peasant resistance against government onslaught'. Consider Chakrabarty's reasoning, with a set of alien concepts and idioms:

> Imperialism and native feudalism had been stumbling blocks to political, social and cultural progress of Tripura. In 1947 when the Nehru government took over Tripura, the crisis of the people only worsened. India's Partition destroyed Tripura's economy; its economy was taken over by India's big business communities like the Gujaratis, Marwaris etc. The Congress passed all sort of repressive laws, brought about the Golaghati massacre (chapter 7), and introduced military rule in Tripura. People became disillusioned with "Congress freedom", and took up arms to protect their lives and property from the onslaught of Congress police and military. There started spontaneously a peasant war in Tripura.
>
> (Chanda 1983: 12)

While imperialism and native feudalism being responsible for Tripura's backwardness had had a purchase but people's disillusionment with the Congress regime in Tripura was a far cry because there was no Congress regime there in Tripura in the first place. Second, calling the GMP movement a 'peasant war' fitted more to the CPI theory in 1950 than the ground reality in Tripura. Third, no political movement in the State since the 1930s was spontaneous; and the one started by the GMP was certainly not spontaneous. The GMP had had its own method of organizing resistance. Because there was no Communist Party to lead such movements would not be considered as a blemish on the part of such movements. But then Chakarbarty's objective was pre-defined.

## The GMP and its weakness

Chakrabarty evaluated the GMP movement. The GMP had organized all the agrarian classes around the common slogan of resisting the onslaught of the police and military of the Nehru government. It had generated a national upsurge among all the classes and tribes. But how far had the leadership, asked Chakrabarty, been successful in translating this mass upsurge, these anti-government popular forces, into a genuine anti-imperialist and anti-feudal struggle? Each class, continued Chakrabarty, while participating in the GMP movement, had aroused its own 'class aspirations'. The local leadership by not forming any other mass organization beyond the GMP had shown enormous weakness. For instance, he pointed out, the *talukdars* and *jotedars* while fighting police and military repression had joined hands with the poor peasants, but when the poor peasants had demanded *tebhaga* (three-quarter share of produce) there had developed class contradictions. The GMP could not resolve this contradiction. The peasants needed their separate organization, argued Chakrabarty, to fight for the abolition of landlordism and the practice of *dadan*, to stop their eviction from land, and to realize their demand for *tebhaga* and for increased wages. Without a separate peasant organization, the anti-feudal struggle could never be successful. He, however, pointed out that such a separate peasant organization was not to be antagonistic to the GMP; the GMP was the instrument of struggle of all classes, and a movement as well as a government in parts of Tripura. But he was quick to add: It would be a gross mistake to assume that feudalism could be done away with by the GM merely passing laws; feudalism could not be abolished without class struggle. The GMP therefore had remained weak, concluded Chakrabarty, so far as the anti-feudal struggle was concerned (Chanda 1983: 14).

As far as the trade union front was concerned the GMP betrayed similar weaknesses. There were about 15,000 small tea garden workers in Tripura, but the GMP had not formed any trade union organization. Those tea gardens numbering about 56 were owned by the small indigenous capitalists who, as a class, were the enemy of the communists, but had been the GMP ally and one of its financial support-bases. But they were vacillating and always placed their class interests above the interests of the people. Thus, when the tea garden workers demanded higher wages, they threatened them with police and military repression. In short, the GMP brought to the forefront the similar aspirations, doubts and questions of all classes, tribes and groups which, argued Chakrabarty, it had not been able to successfully actualize.

Another inherent weakness of the GMP movement, as pointed out by Chakrabarty, was that, confined predominantly to the Tripuris, it had given the State a propaganda advantage. The government had always branded the movement as anti-Bengali Tripuri-communalist, or a move of the Tripuris to establish their hegemony over the Reangs or the Halams – the other tribal groups in the State. A large section of both the Bengalis and the Halams had believed in that.[36] The GMP had failed to fight back by raising respective demands of different tribes and groups in the movement. 'First join the Muktiparishad (GMP), then we will settle our future' (Chanda 1983: 12) – this principle did not strengthen the national unity needed in the anti-imperialist struggle.

Chakrabarty explained the GMP's bafflement by showing how it punched all kinds of activities into its own agenda, instead of forming separate trade unions, and peasant organizations, and finding common grounds with tribal organizations. This decentralization was necessary for the purpose of drawing a large section of the people into the orbit of an anti-feudal struggle, and this is where the GMP had failed because the GMP 'had assumed the role of all: while working sometimes as a political party, sometimes as a united front, or sometimes as a peasant organization, it had now confronted an acute organizational impasse' (Chanda 1983: 16).

## *The communist party as Panacea*

What was the real status of the GMP? What was its exact relation with the Communist Party and other organizations? Why should the GMP not be sufficient when the same cadres worked both in the party and the GMP? In answering these questions, Chakraborty presented a series of arguments in favour of the need of the Communist Party and its leadership over the GMP.

First, the Communist Party as the party of the working class alone could lead the liberation struggle in the age of imperialism and proletarian revolution. Because the working class had nothing to lose in a revolution, its party could rightly claim 'to lead the masses in the liberation struggle' (Chanda 1983: 17).

Second, the Communist Party, though theoretically a party of the workers, was not to be composed of the workers alone. In an industrially backward State like Tripura, it was the peasants who had first organized themselves and started class struggle. But that did not mean that the Communist Party could not lead the liberation struggle in Tripura. To take an instance: despite the fact that the Chinese Communist Party was predominantly composed of the peasants, and the British Labour Party was predominantly composed of the workers, the former was a genuine Communist Party, while the latter was an agent of imperialism. So all that mattered was the ideology of the working class, which made a Communist Party genuinely communist. The Chinese case demonstrated that the peasants could make good communists. In this frame of analysis, therefore, a favourable condition existed in Tripura for building a genuinely effective Communist Party: all they needed was ideological indoctrination.

Third, the Communist Party was the leadership and guidance of the working class which, in a complex situation, could exercise 'a lot of flexibility' (Chanda 1983: 18).

Fourth, the Communist Party had a distinct ideology of its own based on dialectical and historical materialism which was the revolutionary ideology of the working class. The workers did not get this ideology spontaneously, but must acquire it through indoctrination:

> They have to know where to retreat, when to be peaceful and when to be violent, and when to draw into the struggle which allies.

Last, the Communist Party knew how 'to organize the unorganized, to unify the disunited, and to bring to the forefront the backward section of the people' (Chanda 1983: 18). These were not merely theoretical questions but practical questions of Tripura communism. Tripura communism under the GMP had experienced uneven growth: the GMP had not been able to organize all the people of all regions of Tripura; the peasants of Sadar and Khowai were more organized than those of Kailasahar or Bilonia. Localism thus had partially gripped the movement.

'Can the GMP perform all these tasks?' asked Chakrabarty (Chanda 1983: 22–3). He pointed out again that within the GMP were people with diverse interests and ideas, who had organized themselves around the GMP spontaneously. But without a Communist Party leadership how long could the GMP hold on to those forces? The existence of those forces inside the GMP made it all the more important to launch 'relentless inner-party struggle against bourgeois ideology by criticism and self-criticism' (Chanda 1983: 22–3).

## *What was to be done?*

Revolution or social movement or building up of an organization did not take place strictly according to the 'plan' of the leaders because, as Chakraborty pointed out, it drew larger number of people than the leaders had expected. Therefore, the most important task of the leaders was, he said, 'to master all the tactics and all the aspects of social activists, and to be ready to guide the revolutionary classes quickly from one tactic to another'. On the basis of the Tripura experience, Chakraborty wrote:

> A mass movement did not tread along a straightforward path. Sometimes secret, underground movement becomes dominant, while at some other time legalism becomes dominant; sometimes the revolutionary wave is at its low ebb, while at other times, it is at its high tide; sometimes confrontation is the main form of the struggle; at other times, it is to be avoided. A leadership which refused to tread this zigzag path, insisted on treading a plain road while climbing up the hills, could never hope to lead the masses.
>
> (Chanda 1983: 23)

Chakraborty's message to the GMP was thus clear. He was arguing in favour of adopting electoral tactics, legalism and peaceful means of struggle under the leadership of the communist party. Carefully avoiding any reference to violence in such a long inner-party document, he explained that it was time for the party to move to electoral politics: if a leadership which had carried guns now insisted on not carrying election posters it could not advance the cause of Tripura revolution. At present Congress was asking for popular votes, and the communists had to take advantage of this weakness of the enemy and utilize this opportunity intelligently.

## The Gana Mukti Parishad would not wither away

Chakrabarty went on to state that the GMP was the most powerful mass organization in Tripura, but it was not sufficient. It had given shelter to people of diverse interests which were necessarily contradictory. Class struggle had not ended because people had united for anti-feudal and anti-imperialist struggle. The Communist Party, Chakrabarty stressed, would form its own mass organization, and yet the GMP should remain as a voluntary front organization of all classes. He equated the period of the GMP communism with 'left sectarianism and opportunism', but wrote that the 'fighters for liberation in Tripura would learn from their past mistakes' (Chanda 1983: 28).

In terms of the Chakraborty thesis, the GMP would not wither away but assume a subordinate role under the leadership of the Communist Party. The Communist Party, he added, would have to act upon the foundation of the GMP, and the task of the communists would be, 'for the moment', also to expand the mass bases of the GMP. All things said and done, this document suggested that the GMP abdicate its leadership in favour of the 'modern prince', the Communist Party; and that was the price the GMP paid for the integration of Tripura Communism with all-India Communism.

## Left radicalism transits to electoral politics

Tripura's Left radical, to be precise, the GMP, took part in India's general elections in 1951–52 and won handsomely (details to be discussed later). The late Dasarath Devbarma, then the Tripura party's Secretary, prepared The *Draft* contained information for understanding Tripura communism during its transitional phase. This report spelt out the Tripura party's policy on violence and armed struggle. It announced that the Tripura party had called off violence and armed struggle 'for an indefinite period of time' (Chanda 1983: 31). It stressed that the party 'had to master all the tactics of legalism and to equip [itself] with the means and mechanisms of legal battle'. It asserted that 'parliamentary struggle was an integral part of the communist movement in Tripura at the present moment' (Chanda 1983: 35).

The *Draft Report* clearly suggested that there was internal opposition within the party to the new line. Not all members were convinced of the efficacy of the legal battle; they were cynical about the use of law courts and the judicial process, and the utilization of the 'minimum' opportunities available in the Indian constitution: What was the point of going to the State, laws, courts etc which are all organs of State power? The 'most vital weakness of the party' (Chanda 1983: 34–5), the Draft Report pointed out, 'was its failure to form the Committee for the Protection of Individual Liberty' which was thought to be vital to legalism and important to maintain the legal existence of the party, and to mobilize a wider section of the 'progressive' people. Devbarma, however, did not indulge in those 'sectarian attitude' of the party which, according to him, was the 'stumbling block to further growth of the movement'. He laid the blame mainly on the leadership which, he thought, 'had not been able to develop appropriate forms of struggle in accordance with the level of consciousness of the people' (Chanda 1983: 32). The party leadership, he continued, had failed to lead the masses through day-to-day struggle with appropriate party programmes, and this resulted in the reactionary forces taking advantage of the backwardness of the people. He was dismayed that party activists in many cases thought their job amply done when they had 'uttered a few revolutionary words and phrases' (Chanda 1983: 32).

The most controversial aspect of the transition of Tripura communism was the exact status of the GMP. Despite Chakrabarty's recommendations for maintaining the identity of the GMP, confusion remained inside the party. Was it a peasant organization? If so, why there should be two peasant organizations under the Communist Party? The GMP was working as a democratic front in the rural areas. Could it also be presented as the same in the urban areas? The question of the exact nature of the GMP was 'most urgent to the urban wing of the party' (Chanda 1983: 30) politically. The Draft Report did not find answer to most of the questions. The only thing it suggested was that it could not be used as a united front in the urban areas.

Another area where the party's weakness was most glaringly obvious to Devbarma was in the sphere of mass organizations. The party, he said, had failed to build these: wherever it had attempted to build one, it had not done it properly. For example, the party had built the trade union movement in the tea gardens in the manner of the peasant movement. The party had also failed to form organizations for the refugees. The Refugee problems had been discussed in the party, but nothing was effectively done. 'The party leadership', he believed, 'in a sense, betrayed its lack of thinking on the refugee problem'.[7]

Devbarma listed a series of weakness and flaws in the sphere of party organization. The District Committee (DC), for instance, did not work as a committee, and it did not function at all except as formulator of policy decisions; it did not have any "faction" in any mass organization. 'The work of the DC', Devbarma ruefully said, 'was mostly individualistic; self-criticisms were very rarely made; members of the DC did not make any attempt to educate the ordinary party members'. The secretary of the party, he wrote, himself acted as a party center leaving many of the functions of the party centre unfulfilled. In short, the flaws of the party centre had resulted in a number of harmful consequences for the party: individualistic activities rather than functioning as a collective unit; authoritarian mentality of the party members; excessive dependence on leaders; turning the party centre into gossip centres, thereby destroying the unity of the party; lack of attempts to recruit new members; and the lack of criticism and self-criticism among the older members; erosion of party discipline and the tendency to impose one's own opinion as the opinion of the masses, and tendency to conceal one's passivity, and the lack of contact of the members with the masses.

The above were some of the important inner-party crises that the Tripura unit confronted which, coupled with the complete lack of party ideological training, were pervading the party organization and putting the party into desperate situations. As Dasarath Devbarma said, in an earnest and open appeal 'to all party members', in the local party organ:

> With the expansion of the movement our tasks have increased. The leadership will not be able to build a powerful party in accordance with the *practical situation* and in *adaptation to changing consciousness*, if it has not educated itself in Marxism-Leninism. Our party comrades at present do not read our party programmes and decisions, let alone the Marxist literature. This is a serious crime and anti-party activity.
>
> [emphasis added][8]

The so-called problems listed by Devbarma were expected in the period of transition of a violent rural communism into an electoral force fighting for votes as a legal entity by playing by the rules of the game. Devbarma as the Secretary of the State unit of the party was in a more difficult situation to tame the armed cadres to give up arms and take up electoral posters.

## *Electoral performance*

The Tripura communists emerged as the most powerful electoral force in India's first general elections in Tripura in 1951–52. Locally, this election was a communist victory. The communists' share of popular votes in the parliamentary elections was 61.29 per cent and in the Electoral College (to elect one member to the *Rajya Sabha* from Tripura) 48.3 per cent. In India's first general elections, it was in Tripura alone that Congress was reduced to a minority with a share of popular votes of 25.58 per cent in parliamentary and 27.33 per cent in the Electoral College. The official report on the elections said: the Communist Party emerged as the largest single party in the State the only State where the CPI has been able to attain that position.

In the semi-legal conditions and under State repression, the achievement was indeed spectacular. The elections took place when the GMP movement, the main core of Tripura communism, was still underground. The task of taking the underground communist movement to the open, from armed struggle to legality, and to win the elections in the face of all conceivable hindrances, was not easy. What the Telangana, or the Punjab communists could not do, the Tripura communists did in Tripura with spectacular success.

## *Building the urban base*

If Tripura communism was to emerge as an electoral force engaging in legitimate political activity, it needed to be rehabilitated in Tripura, particularly for the urban electorate. This section of predominantly of upper-caste Bengali Hindus were believed to be hostile to Tripura communism. Biren Datta, much more than anybody else, played a leading role through the *Tripurar Katha* (local communist organ) in rehabilitating the GMP communism, in presenting an acceptable face of Tripura communism, and finally 'redefining' Tripura communism. In full conformity with the all-India CPI policy, Datta declared the new ideology of Tripura communism was neither socialism, nor classless society, but 'Peace, Progress and Democracy', and said that the party wanted to unite under its leadership all the progressive forces in a united front, and to help the progressive national bourgeoisie. In an article 'Criticism and Self-Criticism' published in the local communist organ, a historic apology was made for past mistakes and the party's commitment to liberal democracy was affirmed:

> Through criticism and self-criticism, through progressive activities, we shall try to understand our mistakes. We must frankly admit that we too were in the past trapped in the dangerous sectarianism and thus failed to achieve the support of the progressive classes. We must admit that we have not been able to understand scientifically Tripura's historical reality. We swear that we will try to keep in mind our past mistakes to understand Tripura's reality more patiently.[9]

As an index of its faith in the Indian constitutional framework, it said that the 'fundamental rights enshrined in the Indian constitution, however limited, [are] also applicable to Tripura', and the communists would 'utilize them for the benefits of people'. The *Tripurar Katha* declared 'New Democracy'[10] as the goal of Tripura communism, and translated it to mean locally the abolition of the Chief Commissioner's rule in Tripura. The Tripura communists could hardly hope to fight the electoral battle without taking the GMP with them. To do that would require first of all, legitimizing Tripura's 'peasant' communism without however advocating violence. It was emphasized that the movement in the hills (GMP) was also a movement for a responsible government in Tripura. Saroj Chanda, a Bengali communist and Datta's associate in electoral mobilization, said in a communist mass meeting: it [Communist Party] swears it will shake off all adventurism and rectify all past mistakes.[11]

The Tripura unit of the CPI formally took the decision in July 1951 to participate in the elections at a time when the GMP-led armed struggle was receding. The programme of the local unit of the party included demands, such as, abolition of landlordism without compensation, nationalization of British capital in India, protection of individual liberty, end of Chief Commissioner's rule in Tripura and the establishment of a responsible government in its stead, land to the tiller, rehabilitation of refugees and *jumias* of Tripura, withdrawal of arrest warrants, and the protection of the interests of the 'honest' businessmen from the monopolistic Marawaris. The Tripura Communist Party declared that it 'wanted to unify all the anti-Congress progressive forces in the ensuing elections', and in order to do so, sought to unite itself with progressive parties and individuals which, rather than classes, would be the unit of action. The local party unit indicated that anti-Congressism was going to be the *leitmotif* of its electoral politics, and the basis of a united front.

## First experiment with United Front tactics: the Agartala Municipal elections

The election for the 18-member Agartala Municipal Committee took place on November 5, 1951. Until then, elections of any kind were unknown to the people of Tripura. This was also the first election for the Agartala Municipal Committee since its birth in 1871. During this long period the Municipality had been ruled directly by the monarchs with the help of royal officials, mostly Bengalis. Despite the existence of a Municipality, Agartala had witnessed little or no development, and remained in the 1950s a backward medieval town.

The communists participated in the elections in alliance with the Progressive Bloc. Thus, the United Progressive Bloc (UPB), with the communists and other anti-Congress Progressive Forces combined, was in direct electoral competition with the Tax Payers Association (TPA) which was the local 'Congress in disguise'. The UPB took this election seriously. To defeat Congress became its single slogan. The Tripura unit of the CPI in a resolution[12] equated the defeat of Congress with the end of the Chief Commissioner's rule in Tripura, and said that the party should strive to unite all the progressive parties, groups and individuals, and will incorporate into the Bloc anybody who did not cooperate with Congress, and was not communal[76]. Avoiding any pure class-based analysis, the communists described this electoral battle as a fight between the progressive and the 'reactionary'. The UPB laid all blames on Congress for the backwardness of Agartala on the assumption that Congress was patronizing the forces of reaction and vested interests since independence.[77]

The UPB put up candidates in 17 of 18 Municipal Wards. Of those UPB candidates, ten were Bengalis (nine higher-caste Hindus and 1 Muslim), and seven tribals, a distribution which was more or less in keeping with the demographic balance of Agartala. The UPB candidates were local political leaders, businessmen, and professionals, whom the local communists described as persons from 'all classes and profesions'.[78]

The available information shows that the turn-out was as high as 60 per cent; was the victory went to the TPA which captured as many as 11 seats leaving only three seats for the UPB. The remaining four seats were won by the Independents (three) and the Businessmen's Association (one). This election was a setback for the UPB. The miserable performance of the UPB candidates showed that this Bengali-dominated State capital had rejected communism, and proved as early as 1951 that Tripura communism was not a 'Bengali communism in exile'. The Tripura communists admitted, in a post-election review of the situation, their 'organizational weaknesses' in this election.[79] The miserable performance of the communists in the Municipal elections was a pointer to the fact that the electoral battle of the communists in the ensuing general elections on their own was not going to be easy.

### Ganatantrik Sangha (GS): second experiment with United Front tactics[13]

The organization which helped the communists to play the drama out was the Ganatantric Sangha (Democratic Association), a platform which emerged on the eve of the general elections and which the communists utilized to their greatest advantage. This platform provided the communists with a ground for experimenting with their united front tactics, and with much of the background for transition to electoral politics, legality and legitimacy. Tripura communism's transition to electoral politics and constitutionalism in the 1950s will remain unintelligible without understanding the GS.

In origin, the GS was an urban middle-class political organization formed in 1951 to continue the fight for a responsible government in Tripura legitimately and peacefully, and if necessary, 'by consultation with the authority'. On the need for such an organization, Animesh Choudhury wrote: Tripura's Proja Mondal is dead; the communists and other Leftists are under the heavy watch of the State; the Tripura State Congress is non-existent (Chanda 1983: 27).

The GS therefore sought to utilize this political vacuum. It formed a Working Committee (WC) of 23 members, which was Bengali-dominated with only four tribal members. Most of the WC members were urban, middle-class professionals, and most of the Bengali members were upper-caste Hindus with only three Muslims. The WC's Bengali members included two communists, Biren Datta and Saroj Chanda, who represented the communists in the GS. The idea of forming such an organization to spread the party's influence in the "unorganized area" (urban area) had already been mooted. The WC of the GS had also three Congressmen from Tripura – Sukhomoy Sen Gupta, Anil Chakraborty and Priya Chakrabarty (all higher caste Bangali Hindus). This was both its strength and weakness. It gave birth to questions about the real nature of the GS. Was it anti-Congress? Was it pro-communist? Was it a Leftist organization? The communists coexisted in the GS with Congress, tactically, because it was the question of their survival in the urban area. The GS was then their lifeboat in the urban area. Interestingly, the local Congress's cohabitation in the GS even with the communists was an imperative for its survival too. The Tripura State Congress was a moribund organization of a few self-styled Congress leaders. These leaders aligned themselves with the GS for the establishment of a responsible government in Tripura. The Tripura State Congress (TSC), and its predecessor the Gana Parishad, had always wanted the abolition of monarchy in Tripura and the establishment of democracy in the State. The chief Commissioner's rule in Tripura was not a congress (party) rule. In this political-bureaucratic rule, the local Congressmen were not involved in sharing power and governance.

The presence of the communists in the GS was the cause of much concern to others, especially Congress. Saroj Chanda was the GS's secretary in charge of mass contact and organization, a position he 'utilized' for communist mass mobilization. As a result, the communists were bound to be organizing all the mass meetings of the GS, and not infrequently the GMP was found to be explaining its policy and programmes in typical GS mass meetings. As the general election drew nearer, and political polarizations developed, the edge of the anti-Congress stance of GS became sharper. Given the fact that the local political rule was maintained by the Congress party government in Delhi, the ultimate trust of GS attack had to be on Congress. The GS grew more and more anti-Congress, and as a result, the local Congressmen gradually withdrew from the GS. This gave birth to a bi-polar political situation: Congress versus the communists and other Leftists before the general election.

### Birth of the United Front

A United Front under the leadership of the communists was formed on November 15, 1951 comprising the communists, Tripura Ganatantric Sangha (GS), the GMP, the Forward Bloc, the Tripura Democratic Women's Association and other anti-Congress individuals as an anti-Congress Leftist electoral front. After its victory in the Municipal elections, the TSC decided to contest the general elections openly on its own, and contested the largest number of the Electoral College seats (24 out of 30), and the two Lok Sabha seats. The communist-dominated United Front (UF) launched a vigorous campaign against Congress throughout Tripura.

Many national-level communist leaders like S. A. Dange, Muzaffar Ahmed, Jyoti Basu and even the CPI General Secretary Ajoy Ghosh addressed many of the local communist election meetings. In an election meeting at Agartala on December 2, 1951, Jyoti Basu vehemently criticized the four years of Congress rule in India including Tripura, and declared that the CPI's 'sole objective would be to defeat Congress'.[14] In the same meeting, Dange denounced individual or group violence. The GMP fully endorsed the CPI programme and dedicated its whole organizational apparatus to electoral mobilization[84]. The GMP, still virtually underground, itself did not contest the elections, but those who stood for election in the name of the Communist Party were GMP members. This was one indication of the success of the integration of Tripura's rural communism with Indian communism, and particularly the urban wing of Tripura communism.

By contrast, the Left unity in the UF was not, however, sufficiently achieved. Initially, the UF was to contest all the 30 Electoral College seats: CPI (16), GS (five), and F. B. Ruikar Group (three), and communist-supported Independents (six). But just before the elections, the F.B. withdrew from the UF and decided to contest the elections independently.[85] In two constituencies in Agartala, the FB put up its candidates against the GS. This reflected, at least, partially the weakness of the UF. Another weakness of the UF was that it had supported a large number of Independents. The Independents stood for election in the area (i.e., northern- and southern-most sub-divisions of the State) where the communist movement had little following. Interestingly, as many as 30 Independents (six supported by the communists and two by Congress) contested the elections for the 30-member EC, a fact which indicated the volatility of Tripura's politics and also the weakness of its party system.

174  *Left radicalism turned parliamentary*

*Table 9.1* Ethnic composition of UF candidates in the Tripura Electoral College elections 1952 (total seats = 30)

| Parties | Bengali | Tribal |
|---|---|---|
| CPI | 7 | 9 |
| Tripura Ganatantrik Sangha | 3 | 2 |
| Neutral (Independent) | 4 | 2 |
| Forward Bloc | 3 | 0 |
| Total | 17 | 13 |

Source: Roy (1983)

A glance at the ethnic composition of the UF candidates (Table 9.1) shows that despite the significant proportion of tribal candidates (13 out of 30) in the UF and their predominance among the communist candidates (nine out of 16), on the whole, the Bengalis dominated the scene (17 out of 30). The Tribal dominance of communist leadership would be short-lived, but the Bengali dominance that emerged in the first general elections would remain as the most powerful factor in Left politics in Tripura, which in the case of the State Congress, would be equally and more powerfully true.

The Tripura State Congress (TSC) put up 24 candidates in the elections out of whom 18 were Bengalis, mostly upper castes.

An account of party electoral support in the 1952 elections must begin with a central methodological problem: imperfect and inadequate census data. The 1951 census data are unreliable. The 1961 Census reports are more reliable, but given the fact that between 1951 and 1961 Tripura received a huge influx of refugees from East Pakistan which totally upset Tripura's demographic balance, and that those refugees were unevenly distributed throughout Tripura, the treatment of the 1961 census data becomes fraught with difficulties. Moreover, census data are not collected for the benefit of the student of political sociology. While some categories (which are again changing over time) like the 'cultivator' are crude indicators of socio-economic reality, some others like 'castes' are not collected. No wonder, ethnic data are hard to find in the census reports. All this sharply contrasts with India's concrete social and economic reality marked by caste and ethnic division cross-cutting class divisions.

The communist-led UF swept the poll which took place on January 11, 16, and 26, 1952 to elect two members of Parliament and 30 members of the Electoral College, a non-legislative body to elect a member of the Council of States (Rajya Sabha). Tripura's 329,806 electorate (population 6,39,029)[15] exercised their franchise, in which the turn-outs were not high: 47.7 per cent (Lok Sabha) and 47.8 per cent (Electoral College). The UF's share of popular votes in the EC was as high as 56.01 per cent (CPI = 43.01 per cent; TGS = 4.83 per cent; communist-supported Independents = 8.17 per cent) with 19 seats (CPI = 12; TGS = three; Ind. = four). In the Lok Sabha elections, the CPI won both the seats with a big margin of popular votes (61.29 per cent).

*Table 9.2* Performance of political parties in EC (1952)

| Political Parties | Total Votes Polled | Percentage (%) | seats | unopposed |
|---|---|---|---|---|
| CPI | 55333 | 43.01 | 12 | 2 |
| TGS | 6221 | 4.83 | 3 | 1 |
| INC | 35197 | 27.33 | 9 | 3 |
| F. B | 2775 | 2.17 | nil | nil |
| Independent | 29156 | 22.6 | 6 | |

Source: Kogekar and Park (1956: 312) and Roy (1983: 17–20)

Note: of six successful neutral or Independent candidates, the CPI's share was four and Congress two.

*Table 9.3* Performance of political parties in Lok Sabha elections 1952 (total seats = two)

| Political Parties | Total votes polled | Percentage (%) | Seats obtained |
|---|---|---|---|
| CPI | 96453 | 61.29 | 2 |
| INC | 40263 | 25.58 | nil |
| Jan Sangh | 9663 | 6.14 | nil |
| Neutral | 10987 | 6.98 | nil |

Source: Roy (1983: 20)

*Table 9.4* CPI's comparative electoral strength in the State-level elections in India, 1952

| States | Percentage of votes polled |
|---|---|
| Tripura | 43.03 (with its allies 56.10) |
| Travancore-Cochin | 18 (with allied 23) |
| Malabar | 16 (with allied 29) |
| Madras | 12.96 |
| West Bengal | 10.76 (with allied 25.5) |
| PEPSU | 6.3 |
| Orissa | 5.68 |
| Punjab | 5.00 |
| Assam | 2.8 |
| Bihar | 1.13 |

Source: Kogekar and Park (1956, Appendix, 323)

The communist performance in the Tripura elections was commended in the official reports on the elections.[86] The Tripura communists' share of popular votes in 1952 was higher than that of the Kerala unit's 1957 achievement (35.28 per cent and with Independents, a further 5.45 per cent). As the Table 9.4 shows, in the first general elections, 1952, the State level, the Tripura unit of the CPI's share of popular votes was the highest. Kogekar and Park found the Tripura Communist Party 'to be very strong' (Kogekar and Park 1956: 314).

## An analysis of communist electoral support base

Who voted for the communists of Tripura in the 1952 elections? This is the central question in analyzing the electoral bases of the party. An answer to this question involves a number of other questions, such as, the regional concentration and the location of party support, class and ethnic dimensions of support, the relation between mass movement and electoral base and the extent of party support.

The very fact that the communists put up their candidates in 16 out of 30 Electoral College constituencies was an indication that their strength was geographically circumscribed. The candidates stood for election mostly in areas along the northwestern parts of the State covering the sub-divisions of Agartala (including the State capital) (largest sub-divisions with the largest concentration, ten out of 30, of EC seats), Khowai, Kamalpur, Kailasahar and Dharmanagar. The only sub-division in the south where the party had its candidates (two out of two) was Bilonia. The sub-division-wise distribution of CPI candidates was as follows: Agartala Sadar (eight, with its ally TGS, a further two), Khowai (three out of three), Kamalpur (one out of two), Kailasahar (one out of two), Dharmanagar (one, with its ally TGS, one more out of four) and Bilonia (two out of two). The CPI's ally TGS fought also in the southern parts of Tripura: Sonamura (one out of two) and Udaipur (one out of one). The CPI supported six candidates mostly in the northern parts of the State. The distribution of seats among the UF partners revealed one distinctive fact: the communists fought precisely in those acres which happened to be the GMP strongholds, leaving other unsafe areas to their allies. The notable exception was Bilonia (mostly Reang inhabited), but there the communists drew a blank.

The CPI-led UF won 19 seats, of which the CPI's won share was 12. Sub-division-wise, the CPI's electoral strength was largely concentrated in Agartala Sadar division (seven) and Khowai (three). The other two CPI seats were one each from Kamalpur and Kailasahar. Those areas again were GMP power-bases.

Voter turn-out provides one indication of the extent of party support. The overall turn-out was 47 per cent. What would explain the political apathy of non-voters? The most obvious reason seemed to be the low level of political organization. Despite the rise of a number of political parties in the State since the late 1930s, its party system remained largely fledgling. While the GMP was very strong in some areas, in others its influence was sparse. Organizationally, Congress had little influence over the people. In many cases, the tribal electorate *en bloc* abstained from voting. As it was reported: In Udaipur, (mostly Reang-inhabited), the tribal electorate have unitedly opposed the elections, their main argument of dissent being the absence of monarchy in Tripura.[16]

This rejection of elections in some areas was at variance with the discipline, maturity and organizational ability demonstrated by the electorate in the communist-controlled areas (Roy 1983: 17–20). Given the wide variations of electoral turn-out in different constituencies, the overall turn-out of 47 per cent hardly reflected the depth of Communist Party support in the State.

The available constituency-level electoral data (Chanda 1983: 29) strongly suggested that there was a clear correlation between communist mass base and higher turn outs. For instance, in seven out of the ten communist-won seats, the turn-outs were in the range from 50 to 74 per cent. In those constituencies, the communists share of popular votes polled was still higher (Agartala Sadar = 70.50 per cent; Khowai = 79.47 per cent). By contrast, the turn-outs in Congress seats were low from 20 to 43 per cent in four out of six contested seats. In the TGS seats also, the turn-outs were low: below 40 per cent on average. In the words of the local communist unit's organizational report, those areas were 'unorganized'. If the communists were more organized in the western part of the State than in the east, so was the turn-out higher in the western part in the Lok Sabha elections (West = 52 per cent; East = 44.27 per cent).

The CPI-led UF's performance and the pattern of its electoral support may be explained by reference to several factors. To begin with, Congress electorally was not powerful, and at the time of elections, 'not united' (Kogekar and Park 1956: 314) enough to 'face the electoral battle with full strength and enthusiasm' (Kogekar and Park 1956: 314). It had a negative image in the minds of the people, especially tribal people, for failing to offer a credible political alternative after the abolition of monarchy. The communists who had been nursing a mass base for the last few years skillfully utilized popular discontent and gave it an anti-Congress orientation. The Communists took the elections seriously and started their campaign from the beginning of 1951 when the GMP-led armed struggle was at its peak. The CPI observed May Day in different parts of the State and utilized the occasion for electoral mobilization. The CPI election-committees proliferated in large parts of the State, and its election meetings were addressed by its national level leaders. The TGS, the CPI ally, made inroads into many areas where the communists – because of their association with violence and class leanings – could not penetrate. By contrast, confusion prevailed among the ranks of Congress, particularly, because of changes made by the Central Parliamentary Board in the list of nominations submitted by the local Congress body.[17]

It was obvious that in a predominantly agrarian society as Tripura was (and still is) the Communist Party's electoral support-base must be largely rural. In 1952 the only urban area was the State capital with 3 EC seats, and where the voting turn-out was slightly higher (51 per cent). But as the results of elections revealed, the predominantly upper-caste Bengali-dominated (84.58 per cent) city did not totally reject communism. The CPI contested two seats and won one. The TGS contested the other one seat and won it. Despite the fact that the CPI had only one urban seat (with its ally, one more, its percentage share of votes, as the real index of support, in the urban area, a whole, was quite high [61.59 per cent]; with its ally, a further 4.58 per cent), and in the constituency where the communists won (i.e., Old Agartala), the communist share of popular votes was as high as 91.67 per cent. This suggests two conclusions. In contrast with their performance in the Municipal elections when the communists had been rejected by the urban electorate, they made in the general elections significant new inroads into an otherwise non-communist (if not anti-communist) urban electorate. Second, and this follows from the above, the communist votes in the 1952 elections were not simply tribal and Muslim votes – the high percentage of communist votes in the urban areas indicated that they had some support among the higher-caste Bengali Hindus too.

While commenting on the Muslim support base of the communists in the 1952 elections, the official report said: the largest single bloc in the population of Tripura is that of 130,000 Muslims who have migrated there.... now most of them are pro-communist.[18]

The number of Muslims of Tripura in 1951 was higher than the figure given above. There were 136,940 Muslims in Tripura in 1951, of whom only 5.53 per cent lived in the urban area of Agartala. The Muslims were mostly concentrated in the north-western parts of Tripura which accommodated about 65 per cent of Tripura's Muslims. The remaining Muslims lived in the south-eastern parts of the State. The Muslims supported by and large the GMP mass movement. The constituency-level electoral data suggested that there was a spatial association between the Muslims and the communist electoral support. Another indication of the Muslim base of communist support was that one-third of elected communist candidates were Muslims (four out of 12), and they were nominated for election from the Muslim-inhabited area. And yet, the Muslim votes for the communists were not communal because the communists in their appeal to the Muslims for votes promised not communal but socio-economic goods, such as the redistribution of lands of the landlords among the landless without compensation and equal rights with the Hindus. The Muslim votes for the communists were class votes.

The correlation, if any, between the socio-economic categories and Communist Party support is hard to establish. Tripura did not experience the development of economic class forces. The development of agrarian class forces in the State was uneven in terms of ethnic groups and regions. The census data show that in 1951 the Agartala sub-division had the largest share in the State of the four agrarian categories identified in the 1951 census: 30.49 per cent of all land-owning peasants, 22 per cent of tenants, 22.41 per cent of agricultural labourers and 42.17 per cent of landlords and rentiers.[95] Khowai, by contrast, had a relatively lower share of those classes (9 per cent, 14.6 per cent, 7 per cent and 9 per cent respectively). The relative levels of domination and subordination in Tripura's agrarian class-structure can be guessed from the proportion of each category in relation to others (see Chapter 4). But different socio-economic structures in different sub-divisions did not, however, produce any differential impact on the nature of Communist Party support, although the high concentration of agrarian classes in some areas must have been important in producing agrarian tensions.

## Conclusion

In this brief concluding section, we will comment on the effects of the so-called integration of Left radicalism on the growth and development of Tripura communism. We may begin by asking: what did the results of 1952 elections in Tripura distinctly prove for Tripura communism? Kogekar and Park who prepared the official reports on the Tripura elections commented: Tripura has fewer parties than its neighbour, Manipur. This fact helped in defining issues more clearly (Kogekar and Park 1956: 312). The electoral battle in the elections was fought essentially between Congress and the communists, but this bi-polarity was not a sufficient explanation for communist victory. The communists no doubt utilized this bi-polarity and channeled popular discontent against Congress. This paid them good dividends not in all areas but where the GMP had built bases. Kogekar and Park located the roots of massive discontent in Tripura in the poverty and landlessness of the people, and emphasized in their recommendations the 'urgent need' for land reform in the State (Kogekar and Park 1956: 315). Poverty and landlessness were important in explaining the roots of Tripura communism, but they did not simply translate into communist electoral support. While commenting on the electoral performance of the Indian communists at the all-India level in the 1952 elections, Overstreet and Windmiller said:

> The results of the elections appeared to provide exhilarating confirmation of the tactic of uncompromising opposition, for the party scored its greatest victories in precisely those areas where its struggle had been boldest or even most violent.
> (Overstreet and Windmiller 1959: 308)

It can equally be held to be true in Tripura. The electoral performance of the Tripura communists in the 1952 elections vindicated the way in which the communist mass-bases had been nursed for years. Despite the new inroads, particularly in the urban areas, with the help of their ally TGS, the Tripura communists largely failed to penetrate beyond the bases of the GMP.[19] Significantly, the all-India level party (CPI) assessment of the electoral performance of the communists counselled strong caution against associating communist electoral strength with violence or armed struggle, and preferred to link it with the whole history of the movement:

> Nothing will be more harmful than any attempt to explain the victories won by the party in the States of the south, in Bengal and Tripura, in Orissa and Punjab, by basing oneself on the events of the last 3–4 years alone or the events of any particular "period". Such explanation would lead to wrong conclusions and wrong practice.
> (Ghosh 1977: 331)

This was an instance of how a *strange theory* produced *strange practices*, or the worse, took the real centre of class struggle out of it real arena The root of the new CPI emphasis lay in the new understanding of the party led by Ajay Ghosh who 'believed that the country was not yet ready for armed insurrection and that the party should concentrate on constitutional opposition to the policies of the Nehru government',[20] and therefore, any attempt to associate electoral victories with violence must be discouraged. Such all-India-level assessment was evidently at variance with the ground reality in Tripura where the association of violent struggle of the GMP and the subsequent communist victory was strongly correlated.

Ironically, the local unit of the CPI toed the official line in assessing its performance in elections. The local party organ editorially wrote: 'the Communist Party (Tripura) openly declared that it does not support any individual *dacoity*, or other violent activities'.[21] Datta and (Dasarath) Devbarma, newly elected Members of Parliament from Tripura, emphasized in a joint press-statement that 'individual freedom was now the central concern of the party', and explained the communist victory in Tripura as a 'proof that the communists were committed to peace', a 'proof that the communists wanted to participate in the peaceful reconstruction of the country'.[22] Both the interpretations sharply contrasted with the real situation in which the communist victory was a vindication of Tripura communisms (or GMP's) most uncompromising and violent opposition to Congress rule.

Two more comments are in order. First, through its 'integration' with all-India communism, the tribal nationalism was appropriated by the Communist Party in building on the tribal bases, but subordinated to the authority of the CPI in Tripura. The price of this integration was painful for the GMP-led movement as a whole, for its indigenous tradition of politics and protest was subjected to too much condemnation by the CPI unit in Tripura. The GMP tradition of nationalist movement received only a left-handed compliment from the all-India party, or its local unit. Second, it was in this period (1950–52) that Tripura's Left radicalism (mostly the GMP) was given a strong dose of constitutionalism, parliamentary and electoral politics from which it would never turn back since. The State communist movement along with the GMP was to become a party and its mass associations to be intertwined with the specifics of institutional politics within the parameters of the Indian State. The future course of action of the Left in Tripura would be attuned to the political movement and campaign for sharing State power at different levels of India's federal polity.

## Notes

1 Singh argued that the Punjab case was a failed one, the failure of all-India 'official' party to recognize the original and historical contributions of the movement in the province and its persistence in attempting to subjugate it to the authority of the Official Groups (Singh 1994: chapter 4).
2 The same time the Communist Party of China was formed.
3 It was Indian communist edition of the Zhdanov line of the CPSU.
4 In 1950 Rajeswar Rao replaced Ranadive from the position of General Secretary (1948–50) of the party and followed the Chinese path of revolution. Rao was in that position from June to December 1950–1952.
5 It was titled 'Proceed to form the party and its Mass organizations' (1951) (in Bengali).
6 It was titled 'Draft Report of the First State Conference of the Tripura unit of the CPI' (in Bengal)) (1952) prepare after the first general elections in the state in 1952. These two inner-party documents remained unpublished until 1983 when late Saroj Chanda, a State-level leader of the CPI-M published them with an introduction.
7 This was understandable given the sensitive nature of the issue in Tripura, and the Pandora's box would open.
8 See *Tripurar Katha* (in Bengali meaning the story of Tripura), No. 52 (March 1952), p. 2 for details. *Tripurar Katha* was then the party organ.
9 *Tripurar Katha*, No. 1, February 1951), p. 1. (See Datta's Editorial).
10 Explicitly indicating that the Tripura party was adapting itself to the Chinese path of revoltuon through the so-called Rajeswar line.
11 *Tripurar Katha* May Day issue 1951, p. 4.

*Left radicalism turned parliamentary* 181

12 *Tripurar Katha* No. 29, October 1951, p. 1.
13 This *United Front tactics* were formulated by the Soviet leader Georg Drimitrov in the 1935 to fight Nazism and Fascism and then onwards transported to the communism worldwide. Lenin is said to have advanced the idea since 2014 [AU: 1914?] too.
14 *Tripurar Katha*, No. 37 November 1952, p. 1.
15 Compared to the size of the population, the number of voters was relatively smaller because of migration of refugees to Tripura, there were problems of issuing identity documents for voting.
16 *Chiniha*, No. 41 (January 1952), p. 1. *Chiniha* was a Tripura nationalist magazine.
17 Tripura Census Handbook (based on 1951 Census Reports) (Agrartala, 1955), pp. 162–325, 444–51.
18 *Tripura Census Handbook* 1955, p. 313.
19 Party (CPI) Letter No. 5 (April 1952) (HBPA).
20 *Tripurar Katha* No. 48, January 1953, p. 2.
21 Tripurar Katha No. 28, January 1953, p. 2.
22 Tripurar Katha No. 49, 1953 February 1953, p. 1.

# 10 The rise and decline of the TUJS in Tripura
Radical ethnic challenge to the left

**Introduction**

The rise of the TUJS in Tripura since the late 1960s was a challenge to the Left in Tripura and the latter's dwindling political fortune in the State during the same period. The TUJS was born in 1967 as a regional ethno-nationalist party and came up with a different nativist articulation of tribal identity in Tripura as opposed to that of the Left. In 1967 when the TUJS was born, the Left was not only not in power in the State but indeed passing through a major crisis in the wake of large-scale arrest of the communist leaders and activists following the Chinese invasion of India in 1962 and the party split in 1964, which resulted in the birth of the CPI-M. In Tripura, the party split occurred a year later in 1965 but then nearly the entire leadership of the CPI and of the future CPI-M were in jail. This created a new political opportunity structure for the TUJS to harvest by appearing as the true representative of the tribals in Tripura. The TUJS joined an electoral alliance with the Congress in 1983 in Tripura, an urban based party of the Bengalis and an arch rival to the promotion of any tribal causes, and shared State-level power with Congress during 1988–93[1] (when the Left Front led by the CPI-M lost power for the first and thus far the last time). The TUJS' electoral fortunes dwindled and it lost grounds among the tribals from the early 1990s. For instance, in the 1993 State Assembly elections the TUJS won only one seat in a house of 60 out of which 20 seats are reserved for the tribals. This was also the time when Tripura began to witness growing tribal insurgency. It finally merged with the Indigenous People's Front of Tripura (IPFT) to form a new party called Indigenous Nationalist Party of Twipra (INPT) in 2002, with ethnic nationalism as the sole goal. Mr Bijoy Kumar Hrangkahwl was the founding President (former TNV[2] leader), and arguably, under pressure from the National Liberation Front of Tripura (an underground tribal outfit) to use the INPT as its front organization. Paradoxically, when such tribal outfits grouped together as one tribal nationalist party, the Left has by then recovered its lost ground among the tribals.

Since its emergence in 1967 as a 'tribal party' the Tripura Upajati Juba Samity (henceforth TUJS), literally a youth association of the tribals, increased its electoral strength and expanded its social bases of support in Tripura. Its rise has profoundly altered the political scenario of Tripura. Its growth was immensely disturbing particularly to the Left in the State to whom it was a real challenge in their rural/tribal power bases. In rural Tripura, the TUJS's rise has transformed for some years the thus far communist monopoly of tribal support into a two-party system. Congress never had support among the tribals. At the State level the TUJS was the third force after the Left and Congress. The TUJS's achievement of State power as a junior partner in 1988–93 was a proof of its support among the tribesmen/women but more importantly this was to be understood as filling up a political vacuum caused by some erosion of support of the Left among the tribesmen.

## North Eastern context

If one keeps the political scenario of North East India in mind, the birth and growth of the TUJS would not appear to be anachronistic. It had, in fact, its parallels in almost every part of this region which experienced nearly similar historical transformation during the Raj and after. India's North East as a whole contains a large proportion of immigrants from other parts of India who have been able, over the decades during the Raj and after, to establish their sway over indigenous trade, commerce, economy, administration, culture and politics. Since independence, owing to a certain path of development in India under State guidance, this region experienced unevenness in development. This part of India has perennially suffered from a sense of deprivation and frustration. No wonder, India's North East contains a series of anti-immigrant ethnic parties and movements, some of them being extremist. Interestingly, the TUJS was born at about the same time the Shiv Sena in Bombay was born and when the anti-immigrant movement in Assam, though born much earlier historically, became sharpened (Weiner 1978). Weiner noted the overall pattern of development of such parties and movements in the late 1960s:

> The antiimmigrant political movements first became prominent in the late 1960s. They were most active in the eastern State of Assam, the western portion of the southern State of Andhra, the southernmost districts of Bihar, and in the cities of Bombay and Bangalore.
> (Weiner 1978: 12)

Unlike its North Eastern brethren, Tripura offers a most powerful and genuinely fertile soil for the rise of ethnic movements. Tripura underwent a set of historical changes which were devastating and dislocating for the original tribal inhabitants of the State. In Tripura, the immigrants outnumbered the original residents. In 1981, the ratio was 70:28 per cent; unofficially the tribals' share was even less than that (Bhattacharyya and Nossiter 1988). The demographic upheaval, the immigrants' control over the local State and the society was total. Those historic changes in Tripura would appear to suggest that the TUJS was the 'natural' party of the aggrieved tribals. But this was hard, if not impossible, to be. The reason was not far to seek. The communists in Tripura through intense tribal mobilization since the 1940s have made themselves the 'natural' party of Tripura's tribals.

They began campaigning for tribal rights and self-determination in the 1940s and by the 1950s their monopoly of tribal support through their tribal mass organization, the Gana Mukti Parished (GMP), was near complete. But the communists had their 'own' problem: combining class struggle with tribal nationality and ethnicity was always a hard task.

To be sure, the TUJS was a regional political force, regionally rooted with regionally specific aims and objectives expressing its politics in regional idioms and terms, and lacking any national vision. It was an anti-Bengali and anti-immigrant party. And yet, it is perforce mentioned and commented upon in the reports and political resolutions of its political rivals, especially the communists. Administrators and academics alike have felt the need to comment on it. The fact that the TUJS was able to enter into electoral alliance with a national level party and formed the government in 1988 was the other factor that drew considerable public attention to it. Indeed, it must be admitted, the boundary line between regional and national politics in India is always blurred, and regional idioms and terms are most often part and parcel of India's national politics (Mitra 1999; Bhattacharyya 2005). Regional politics, in many cases, cannot be truly understood without referring to some national political forces. The intimate connection between Assam's anti-immigrant ethnic movement and the Indian National Congress in that State, for instance, has been emphasized by authorities on the subjects (Weiner 1978; Baruah 2005; Das Gupta 1988, 2001). The existence of powerful regional interests in Congress itself is proverbial. The TUJS's rise nonetheless seriously posed the question of who was the 'real' and 'natural' party of the tribals in Tripura as well as in India.

This chapter, therefore, consists of three parts. In the first part, it presents some evidence showing the growth of the TUJS as an electoral force in Tripura. The second part reviews some approaches – CPI-ML, CPI-M, semi-academic, and journalist – to the understanding of the TUJS. The third part of this chapter assesses its merger into a new political party (INPT) as a vehicle of Tribal ethno-nationalism in Tripura.

## Social roots and objectives of the TUJS: internal colonialism challenged

The social roots of the TUJS so far as its leadership is concerned is to be traced to the birth of a new group of educated tribal youths who found no jobs, and a section of whom increasingly came under the impact of Christianity. And yet, the main leadership of the TUJS are Hindus. The strongly conflicting attitudes of the sections within the TUJS towards the Church are noticeable. The fact of the matter was that the rise of this new social group within the tribal society was instrumental in the birth of the TUJS. The State communist leaders admit in private that the problems of this new social group were never properly assessed within the party. All the party tried to do was 'tribal rehabilitation', believed Saroj Chanda, a State-level communist leader belonging to the CPI-M, but not organization among the tribals (interview on November 10, 1986). Despite the fact that the ethnic movement of the TUJS was exclusively rural, the same cannot be said of its leadership very few of whom really hailed from the rural areas. Its second ranking leaders are a valid proof of this: Harinath Devbarma was a graduate of Calcutta University and teaches in a government-aided private school; he stood for election for West Tripura Parliamentary constituency in 1977. The biodata of Bijoy Hrangkhawl (b. 1947) makes it more 'elitist': son of a Christian evangelist, he studied at Christian Mission School in Agartala, Jampui and Shillong, and was the editor of an English fortnightly; he stood for election from East Tripura Parliamentary constituency in 1977, and was a member of the Executive Committee of the party of the TUJS and later Vice-President.

The exclusive rural base of the ethnic movement of TUJS in Tripura is unique. Myron Weiner (1978: 9) has made a distinction between the 'geographic core' and the 'political core' in tracing the roots of the ethnic movements in Asia. With reference to the leadership of the emerging ethnic movements, he said: the new power elite is economically and socially subordinate to the ethnic group that dominates the urban center in which the capital is located (Weiner 1978: 9). The thrust of his argument is that the 'geographic core' and the 'political core' are held by different ethnic groups. His instances are: Rangoon with its Indian population; Kualalampur with Chinese migrants; Guwahati is Assam with Bengali and Marwari migrants; and Bombay with Tamil migrants. Weiner thus challenged the conventional understanding of the 'internal colony', and core-periphery hypothesis.[3] The hypothesis of 'internal colonialism' postulates that 'the dominant "core" population dominants the migrants from the periphery – the English in relation to the Welsh and Irish, the French in relation to Brittany' (Weiner 1978: 9). But Weiner argued that in much of post-colonial Asia, the picture is the reverse. Here the migrants who are dominant (Weiner 1978: 9). In post-colonial societies a different ethnic division of labour occurred which privileged the migrants over the locals who constitute the 'geographic core'. The politically strategic point indicated by Weiner (1978) needs some elaboration. Because of a variety of reasons, certain migrant groups came to be associated with the power structure in the urban centres, more particularly the capitals. This prior access to governmental power and trade and commerce went on benefitting the next generations of the same ethnic group ('political core') eventually marginalizing the geographic core, the majority in population. The situation in Tripura was not different where Agartala, the State capital, was and still now, held by the migrants (the Bengalis). As an instance, we may cite the following official statistics: in 1951, the Bengali speakers in Agartala were 94.46 per cent of the total population of Agartala town. The tribals' share in this respect was only 3.56 per cent. This was, it may be added, when the percentage of total Bengali speakers in the State was 58.68 per cent. This situation was not ever since changed much for the better. Agartala, the State capital, has been a Bengali city in a tribal land. We need here to add that Tripura's 'geographic core', owing to migrations again, is also held by the immigrants in the sense that in rural Tripura too the tribals have been reduced to a minority. In 1981, the tribals' share of the total population was 28 per cent. This above is cited for indicating the special paradox of the ethnic movement in Tripura. Agartala is not an 'explosive centre' with an insignificant tribal population. The Shiv Sena controls the Bombay Municipal Corporation. In Tripura the TUJS by contrast is not even able to stand for election to the Agartala Municipality. The contrast is clear. But the rural Tripura with the preponderance of Bengali population coupled with communist hegemonic control has not been an easy ground for the TUJS to build its electoral bases backed by a pro-tribal and anti-Bengali campaign.

From its inception the TUJS campaign has been pro-tribal and its demands have been expressed in local terms and idioms. The most central assumption of the TUJS was that the GMP (affiliated to the CPI-M) as a tribal organization had failed to serve the interests of the tribals. Its focus on the communist failure was significant in the context we have mentioned above. Its charter of demands, *inter alia*, included: tribal self-determination, unification of the cognate tribes, restoration of lands already illegally transferred to the non-tribals since 1960 to the tribals; formation of the District Councils in accordance with the Sixth Schedule of the Indian Constitution; closer relation among and between the tribes in North East India; Introduction of Inner Line (1873[4]) permit system in tribal areas to restrict the movement of outsiders; the use of Roman Script for the tribal dialect; reservation of more seats for the tribals in public bodies and in appointment etc. The mass organizations of the TUJS which popularized those demands were the Tripura Tribal Employees Association, the Tripura Students Federation, Tripura Sena and Tripura Sundari Nari (women) Bahini. The profoundly pro-tribal character of TUJS demands implied that Congress, not the communists in Tripura, was its real enemy. It was therefore not impossible for the communists and the TUJS to launch, at least, joint demonstrations and mass petitions. The communists received TUJS support on some very vital legislation too. When the Left Front government led by the CPI-M proposed to bring a bill, the TUJS supported it by passing a resolution in a meeting held on 19 March 1979. The TUJS's virulent anti-Bengali position must be understood in the context of the rise of a Bengali communal party of '*Amra* Bengali' ('We, the Bengali') on 27 September 1978.

## Tribal self-determination

Thus, from the late 1970s onwards, the TUJS's ethnic movement so far so its attitude and policies towards the Bengalis was concerned, took a sudden radical turn. The Tribal Students Federation (henceforth TSF) leader Viswa Devbarma provided the first clear hint in his speech in a TSF conference: 'When the whole of North East has united on the foreigner's issue, we cannot remain silent spectators' (*Chinikok* 28 February 1980).[5] In the same conference which was held in Taidua (Udaipur) the TUJS leader and MLA Nagendra Jamatia said: 'The tribals must unitedly fight for the tribal self-determination' (*Chinikok* 22 February 1980). Bibhu Devi, the former Regent Queen of Tripura, supporting the cause of the TUJS, offered a mythological rationalization of TUJS demands:

> The culture of the tribals of Tripura is five thousand years old. The tribals, who had once been independent, have now to fight for self-determination. The people of the advanced society are now coming forward to foil their attempt to secure self-government. Nothing could be more shameful.
> 
> (*Chinikok* 21 March 1980)

Sneha Kumar Chakma in his speech in the above conference traced the root of tribal discontent to nationalist exploitation in Tripura: Tribals today are exploited and oppressed by another nationality. Their prestige and self-respect are lost in their own homeland. The majority community maintains an attitude of hatred towards them. That is why there is so much discontent among the tribals (*Chinikok* 21 March 1980). Chakma blamed the communist and Congress policies for the plight of the tribals.

The Taidua Conference of TUJS was significant for another reason too. This was for the first time since its inception that the TUJS linked its fight for tribal self-determination with the deportation of those Bengalis who had come to Tripura after 15 October 1949, i.e. the date of Tripura's joining the Indian Union. The TUJS also linked its movement with that in Assam. As Shyama Charan Tripura, TUJS General Secretary said on 28 March 1980 in the North East Region Conference at Dibrugarh: The movement in Assam is spontaneous, and the root cause of that movement, like that in Tripura, is the fear of being swamped by the immigrants. We extend our support to the Assam agitation. The students of North East India are united and ready for action (*Chinikok* 21 March 1980). It may be noted in this connection that the TUJS took part in the infamous June 1980 riots in Tripura under the banner of the slogan – 'Deportation of Bengalis' (Karlekar 1985: 1428). The ethnic riots saw more tribes killed than the Bengalis.

## Perspectives on the TUJS

The rise of the TUJS in 1967 was something of a bull in a china shop, and it attracted naturally considerable attention from the opinion makers, rival political parties and academic. This is in contrast to other such regional parties as the Asom Gana Parishad and the Shiv Sena. The reasons was that in Tripura the Left, particularly the CPI-M and its various mass fronts, most notably, the GMP, held on to the tribal mass bases for many decades. The Left came to prove itself as the 'natural party' of the tribals in Tripura. The Left's successive victories in elections to the ADC since 1985 as well as most reserved seats to the State Assembly were proof enough confirming the Left's claim, as above. Therefore, the rise of the TUJS as a significant force to counter the Left and its electoral gains since 1983, and finally its ability to join as junior partner with Congress in a coalition government in 1988 was startling. We next consider the views and perspectives of different parties, media, academic and others which taken together provided an important window to observe and examine the importance of the TUJS in Tripura politics as well as the threat perceived by different stakeholders.

### *CPI-ML view of the TUJS*

The CPI-ML remains a small force in Tripura, its strength being 'still inadequate and unevenly developed' (Karlekar 1985: 1428). Nonetheless, its view is to be taken up seriously because it claims that the CPI-ML 'represents the highest development of class consciousness and organization' (Karlekar 1985: 1428). The basis of this discussion here is an article entitled 'The Tripura Riots,

1980: Problems of Marxist Strategy' by Ranajoy Karlekar, as he reflects, 'to an extent, the point of view of the Provincial Committee of the CPI-ML" (Karlekar 1985: 1428).

The CPI-ML's class view of the TUJS may be summed up as follows: the TUJS's rise is linked up with the 'revisionist' CPI-M in the State; the TUJS is the organizer and exploiter of communal sentiment and violence; it is, like the CPI-M, an elite organization which has an indigenous basis; its main leaders are Hindus and it is not to be equated with Christianity; its leadership is an amalgam of landlords, *Mahajans*, rich peasants and a new generation of Missionary elites; Congress has had a hand in its creation; the TUJS appropriated the popular slogans of the GMP; the TUJS leadership is chauvinist as well as communal as it fears the spontaneous radicalization of the own ranks; as an elite organization it seeks to control the '*pahari*' (hill) society as a homogeneous base, as a constituency from the top; its class basis would not allow or sustain a long-term mass strategy; and an uncompromising class line alone can isolate the TUJS (Karlekar 1985: 1428).

The CPI-ML's dogmatic class approach, clearly, did not recognize the TUJS as an ethnic force in any sense even though the party was sympathetic to the conspiracy theory and hence viewed the TUJS as secessionist. But its statement that Congress had had a hand in its creation smacks of the elements of conspiracy theory. Also, it fails to explain why Congress was interested in creating the TUJS. Even though the extreme Leftist view was ready to consider the indigenous basis of the TUJS, it failed to explain the rise of the TUJS and such other ethno-nationalist forces historically in the context of a certain pattern of distribution of political power as fall out of what Hechter (2017) would call 'international colonialism'.

## *CPI(M) view of the TUJS*

On the basis of its Marxist theory, the CPI(M) has always seen the TUJS as a 'secessionist', 'communal' and 'disintegrative' force (CPI-M Inner-party Document). While in the 1977 poll manifesto of the CPI(M), the TUJS was presented as 'solely tribal, anti-CPI(M) and pro-establishment force', (CPI-M 1980: 1), in the 1983 manifesto, the TUJS was described as 'against national integration and unity, and secessionist' (CPI-M Pamphlet). Earlier, in an inner-party document, the TUJS was explained away as a 'secessionist force linked to western imperialism'. In another CPI (M) document, meant to explain the significance of the TUJS-Congress(I) alliance, the Marxists described the TUJS as 'secessionist and anti-Bengali, communal from its birth' (Chakrabarty 1986: 44–52). The CPI(M)'s description of the TUJS smack of the communal stereotypes: from its birth it is anti-Bengali. Do not wear Bengali dresses. Do not write in Bengali scripts. Do not participate in Bengali *Pujas*. The leaders of the TUJS have spread all round hatred for the Bengalis (Chakrabarty 1986: 52).

The CPI-M's understanding has another facet. The TUJS is linked not only to western imperialism but also to political forces internal to India. In a State Committee level party document, it said: 'The *Amra Bengali* and TUJS are both children of Congress aiming at restoring Congress to power in Tripura and opposing communism'. Late Nripen Chakrabarty, a Polit Bureau member and former Chief Minister of Tripura during the Left Front regime (1978–88), recognized the magnitude of ethnic problem in Tripura in a recent article in the Party's theoretical journal *The Marxist*. Chakrabarty warned about the dangers the Congress(I)-TUJS alliance government in Tripura posed to Indian democracy, but quite predictably, his 'Marxist theory' almost totally bypassed the most burring issue of why the TUJS arose, why it grew in strength in the face of the communist power, and how it was to be related to Tripura's class structure. Chakrabarty's earlier pronouncement when he was the Chief Minister of Tripura seemed to have suspended any rigorous historical materialist analysis in favour of a kind of 'communal stereotypical-cum-conspiracy theoretical'. In his appeal in the context of the June 1980 riots, he said: 'No more blood'. The Upajati Juba Samity's propaganda is extremely Bengali-hating. The Bengalis are Hindus, therefore they quickly Christianize the tribals. 'Do not wear Bengali dresses, write in Bengali script, and get your *pujas* done by Bengali priests. Do not go to Bengali pujas' (Chakrabarty quoted in Karelakr 1985).[6] The extreme Leftist criticism of this approach emphasizes its commonness with the ruling class manipulation of stereotypes while playing on vague yet strong fear, fantasies, suspicions and preconceptions. The tenor of this criticism was that such an approach thrived on a suspension of critical thinking and fidelity to fact and evades clear definition and identification.

### *Emi-academic and academic comments*

The semi-academic commentary of Chakrabarty (1983: 115) partly shared CPI(M) view of the TUJS, and hence indulged in communal stereotypical analysis to be understood in such description of the TUJS as 'anti-Bengali, communal and anti-communist'. Chakrabarty said the TUJS meant Christianity: 'A Christian means(s) he is a member of the TUJS', and almost the 'whole leadership is Christian'. His understanding of the TUJS aim was based on simple communal stereotype: 'Bengalis are Hindus, therefore the whole of the tribals have to be Christianized'[7] (Chakrabarty 1983: 115).

While Gan-Choudhury's (1985: 59) comment on the rise of the TUJS was naïve in emphasizing the electoral defeat of the communist leaders in the 1967 elections as the so-called 'immediate factor' explaining the birth of the TUJS Singh (1987: 153), administrator-academic, followed a modernization approach in tracing the birth of the TUJS to 'land alienation in the state'. In our joint chapter, I and Nossiter (1988) attempted to trace the root of the TUJS support to the relative failure of the Left Front government 'to persuade the majority Bengali community to accept the claim of the tribals for the returns of lands alienated in dubious circumstances' (Bhattacharyya and Nossiter 1988: 162).

### *Journalistic approach*

In this section we will present evidence from both local- and national-level newspapers on the TUJS both during the June 1980 riots and since 1988 when it became a partner in governmental power. Riots provided an important occasion for understanding the most explicit behavioural manifestation of the parties involved. The TUJS was, beyond doubt, one of the principal actors in the June 1980 riots. *The Patriot* (12 June 1988) editorially blamed the TUJS for its active involvement in the riots stressing the 'dangerous activities of agent-provocateurs who were acting through the TUJS'. *The Statesman* (Kolkata) editorial of 12 June 1980 used the terms 'murderous terrorism mounted by the Tripura Upajati Juba Samity' to condemn its involvement in the riots. The Congress (I) was, however, not exonerated: 'The Congress(I) might succeed . . . by recklessly provoking the Tripura Upajati Juba Samity to further lawlessness'. While Dainik *Sambad* (Editorial 10 June 1980) wanted to see the rioters not simply as 'communal' but their action as 'plain rebellion against the state power', both *Vivek* and *Yugantar* (Editorials 11 June 1980); Yugantar (12 June 1980) stressed the 'secessionism of the TUJS' and the fact that the TUJS leaders were Christians. The local CPI(M) daily *Desher Katha* (Editorial 14 June 1980) also followed suit and saw secessionism in the TUJS action.

The TUJS in government since February 1988, however, received a sympathetic and defensive treatment from the press. It came to be known as representative of the tribals, as an ethnic force, and a 'disgruntled' partner etc. The *Telegraph* (26 December 1989) wrote: 'To worsen matters for the TUJS, its two years stint in power with Congress (I) has resulted in considerable erosion of its political bases in the tribal areas'.

The *Statesman* (6 March 1990) does no longer portray the TUJS as 'secessionist' but as an ethnic (tribal) force: 'The Inner Line Permit was first raised by the TUJS . . . almost a decade ago while the CPI(M) opposed it intransigently for the party identified it as a 'secessionist demand'. The *Statesman* (15 March 1990) wrote also: 'The Tripura Upajati Juba Samity, partner of the ruling Congress(I) government in the State, has criticized the functioning of the Administration and demanded a fair and corruption free government'. A historical treatment of its rise and growth was also attempted. 'The TUJS emerged in 1967 as regional outfit with tribal nationalism as its main plank. It grew in strength on the question of hill peoples' identity' (The *Statesmen*, 3 April 1990). However, the following criticism of *The Statesmen* (3 July 1990) of the alliance in Tripura contradicts the paper's earlier stand or fails to explain the real situation: 'The poll (ADC – July 1990) manifesto issued by the Congress (I)-TUJS-TNV alliance is evasive about the demand for greater tribal autonomy, tribal land restoration and effective step to check the influx from Bangladesh'.

The conspiracy theory and communal stereotyping dominated much of the journalistic writings on the TUJS particularly during 1967–88. As a result, its indigenous social base was not recognized. After 1988 its bad image improved to some extent when it came to be identified increasingly as an ethnic force. But a historically grounded theoretical analysis of not only the growth of the TUJS but also its alliance with Congress(I), later joined by the TNV, was a far cry in such approach. The journalistic approach reveals the increasing subordination of the TUJS to its alliance partner Congress (I), but did not explain its political implications.

## Electoral gains and losses

Over the years since 1971 the TUJS increased its electoral strength, and this was mostly at the expense of the Left. Its participation in Lok Sabha elections in 1971 (contesting only one seat) securing only 2.14 per cent of the valid votes cast was not presumably to win a seat but to test its strength and show its willingness to involve in and to integrate itself with the political process. In the elections to the 1972 State Assembly, however, it contested as many as 11 seats drawing a blank securing only 0.34 per cent of the valid votes cast. It contested 11 seats in the State Assembly elections in 1972, but did not win a single seat but gained some footing in some constituencies where its votes share went up to 15.75 per cent in reserved seat (Roy 1983). Interestingly, in the State Assembly elections in 1977 which brought the Left Front led by the CPI-M to power for the first time, this also witnessed significant gains for the TUJS. Of the 28 seats contested it won in '05 (three in-reserve seats [for ST] and two general seats). Its vote share increased too: 7.90 per cent (Roy 1983). Most importantly, the TUJS' vote share was above 10 per cent in as many as 18 constituencies. In the constituencies where it won it vote share was quite satisfactory: 30.8 per cent; 44.10 per cent; 44.29 per cent in reserved seats; and 22.38 per cent; 29.49 per cent and 32.48 per cent in general seats (Roy 1983).

In the next State Assembly elections in 1983 the TUJS improved its electoral position over its performance in 1972 by winning six seats (three in-reserve and three general) on the basis of 10.47 per cent popular vote share. Again, at constituency levels, it acquired significant popular support with vote shares ranging from 49.94 per cent to 61.77 per cent. In the general seats (four contested with three won), its vote share was remarkable: 42.88 per cent; 49.46 per cent; 50.77 per cent and 54.83 per cent (Roy 1983). This assumed added significance given the fact that it was post-Riot (June 1980) elections. It was clear that the party was able to encroach enough into the Left tribal support bases. The three seats it won from the general constituencies was an additional proof of its political credibility.

The TUJS performance in 1983 State Assembly elections was significant for more reasons than one. This election was held when the Left Front led by the CPI-M was in power. Second, in this election the TUJS for the first time entered into an electoral alliance with Congress although it contested alone 14. In the Tripura Tribal Autonomous District Council (ADC) elections the TUJS improved its position over the years since 1981: it won seven seats in 1981, ten in 1985 and 14 in 1990 out of 28. All these elections have been held in the post-June (Riot) 1980 period, but showed the riots had apparently little affected the TUJS' electoral fortunes. In the 1981 and 1985 ADC elections, the TUJS's overall share of votes was 37.53 and 33.46 per cent respectively. In 1981 in the seats won by the party, its percentage share of votes ranged from 47.89 to 66 per cent, and from 34.80 to 41.36 per cent where it lost (Roy 1983). The above data strongly suggest that the party had already gained the ground among the tribals. Significantly, in 1990 ADC elections held on 8 July, the TUJS for the first time won more seats than of the Left.[8] To be sure, the TUJS outstanding performance in the 1990s ADC

Table 10.1 Performance of political parties in the State Assembly elections in Tripura in 1988 (total seats 60)

| National Parties | Seat contested | Seats won | Votes polled (%) |
| --- | --- | --- | --- |
| BJP | 55 | 0 | 0.15 |
| CPI | 1 | 0 | 0.82 |
| CPI-M | 55 | 26 | 45.82 |
| INC | 46 | 25 | 37.35 |
| JNP | 10 | 0 | 0.10 |
| FBL* | 1 | 0 | 0.67 |
| RSP* | 2 | 2 | 1.60 |
| TUJS* | 14 | 7 | 10.52 |
| IND | 81 | 0 | 2.98 |

Source: Election Commission of India.

Notes: * State parties; INC and TUJS were in alliance and formed the government (1988–93).

elections should not read in isolation from the fact that during 1988–93 it was a junior partner in the coalition government in Tripura with Congress, and the State was in the grip of acute insurgency – encouraged, arguably, by the TUJS and other outfits, mostly underground. By 1993 the Left Front recovered its lost grounds under the new leadership of Manik Sarka (the Chief Minister since). While the Marxists won handsomely in this election, the TUJS was returned with only a lone seat although it improved its position marginally in the next Assembly elections in 1998 with four seats. In the State Assembly elections in 2003 the INPT into which the TUJS merged in 2002, won four seats but drew a blank in the next two State Assembly elections in 2011 (Roy 2011: 68–9, 2013) (*The Statesman* Kolkata 1 March 2013). The decline of the TUJS thus is a proof that a nativist solution (Weiner 1978)[9] to the problems of the tribals may not work always particularly when the political space is long occupied by the formidable Left in Tripura.

Even when the Left conceded defeat to the Congress-TUJS alliance in 1988 (Table 9.1) the alliance victory was very marginal; it got 32 seats while the Left Front (CPI-M and RSP) got 28 seats. So it was a one seat majority. In this election, the CPI-M came out as the largest party with 26 seats (with 45.82 per cent share of popular vote, and with the RSP, another, 1.60 per cent which taken together amounts to 47.42 per cent). Interestingly, the Congress-TUJS alliance total vote share was 47.87 per cent, the difference being less than half a per cent. Two features stand out from the electoral performance of political parties in this election. First, even though the Left lost the elections it retained its mass bases quietly strongly. Second, the victory of Congress-TUJS alliance proved that it was possible to challenge Left hegemony if the anti-Left votes are mobilized. As far the TUJS was concerned its electoral support bases began to dwindle.

A junior partner with Congress government during 1988–93, its vote share was 10.52 per cent. In 2002 it merged with the INPT which held on to the TUJS' support bases with some fluctuations. The INPT increased its vote share by about 2 per cent in 2003.

*Table 10.2* Electoral performance of political parties in the State Assembly elections in Tripura in 1993 (total seats = 60)

| Parties (National) | Seats contested | Seats won | Votes polled (%) |
|---|---|---|---|
| BJP | 38 | 0 | 2.029 |
| CPI | 2 | 0 | 1.35 |
| CPI-M | 51 | 44 | 44.78% |
| INC | 46 | 10 | 32.73 |
| JD (B) | 2 | 1 | 1.57 |
| FBL* | 1 | 1 | 0.80 |
| RSP* | 2 | 2 | 1.58 |
| TUJS* | 14 | 1 | 7.52 |
| AMB** | 42 | 0 | 1.46 |
| IPF** | 2 | 0 | 0.035 |
| IND | 297 | 1 | 6.16 |

Source: Election Commission of India.

Notes: AMB = Amra Bengali; IPF = Indigenous People's Front; TUJS = Tripura Upajati Yuba Samity; JD (B) Janata Dal (Biju); RSP = Revolutionary Socialist Party; CPI = Communist Party of India; CPI-M = Communist Party of India (Marxist); BJP = Bharataiya Janata Party; FBL = Forward Bloc (Liberation); INC = Indian National Congress.

\* denotes State parties;
\*\* registered unrecognized parties.

*Table 10.3* Electoral performance of political parties in the State Assembly elections in Tripura in 1998

| National Parties | Seats contested | Seats won | Votes polled (%) |
|---|---|---|---|
| BJP | 60 | 0 | 5.8 |
| CPI | 2 | 1 | 1.38 |
| CPI-M | 55 | 38 | 45.49 |
| INC | 45 | 13 | 33.96 |
| JD | 3 | 0 | 0.24 |
| FBL | 1 | 0 | 0.56 |
| RJD | 6 | 0 | 0.04 |
| RSP | 2 | 2 | 1.65 |
| TUJS | 10 | 6 | 9.43 |
| AMB | 24 | 0 | 0.32 |
| CPI-ML (L) | 2 | 0 | 0.03 |
| IND | 60 | 2 | 3.28 |

Source: Election Commission of India.

Notes: JD = Janata Dal; RJD = Rastriya Janata Dal

From 1993 onwards, Tripura's electoral politics went back, as it were, to the pre-1988 pattern when the Left Front maintains its dominance, but Congress remains as the minor Opposition with 13 seats out of 60, for example, in 1993 with a popular vote share of 33. 49 per cent (Table 9.2). In 1998 it remained more or less the pattern too when Congress increased its seats share to 13 while the

194  *The rise and decline of the TUJS in Tripura*

*Table 10.4* Political party performance in the Tripura State Assembly elections in 2003

| National parties | Seats contested | Seats won | Votes polled (%) |
|---|---|---|---|
| BJP | 21 | 0 | 1.32 |
| CPI | 2 | 1 | 1.54 |
| CPI-M | 55 | 38 | 44.82 |
| INC | 42 | 13 | 32.84 |
| NCP | 12 | 0 | 0.30 |
| AITC | 18 | 0 | 0.43 |
| INPT | 18 | 6 | 12.46 |
| RSP | 2 | 2 | 1.89 |
| CPI-ML (L) | 8 | 0 | 0.17 |
| FBL | 4 | 0 | 0.65 |
| JD (U) | 4 | 0 | 0.06 |
| AMB | 9 | 0 | 0.45 |
| LJNSP | 10 | 0 | 0.23 |
| IND | 52 | 0 | 0.84 |

Source: Election Commission of India

*Table 10.5* Political party electoral performance in Tripura in the State Assembly elections in 2008 (total seats = 60)

| National Parties | Seats contested | Seats won | Votes polled (%) |
|---|---|---|---|
| BJP | 49 | 0 | 1.49 |
| CPI | 2 | 1 | 1.48 |
| CPI-M | 56 | 46 | 48.01 |
| INC | 48 | 10 | 36.38 |
| NCP | 5 | 0 | 0.10 |
| AIFB | 12 | 0 | 0.16 |
| AITC | 22 | 0 | 0.35 |
| CPI-ML (L) | 14 | 0 | 0.28 |
| INPT | 11 | 1 | 6.21 |
| LJP | 9 | 0 | 0.16 |
| JD (U) | 2 | 0 | 0.06 |
| RSP | 2 | 2 | 1.69 |
| AMB | 19 | 0 | 0.31 |
| PDS | 1 | 0 | 0.11 |
| IND | 62 | 0 | 3.21 |

Source: Election Commission of India

CPI-M lost six seats, mostly to the successor of the TUJS, the NPT, which got six seats (Table 9.3). But then the INPT was a very minor electoral force in Tripura. The State politics began to repeat the bi-polarity from then on (Tables 9.3 and 9.4).

Table 10.6 Political party performance in the State Assembly elections in Tripura in 2013 (total seats = 60)

| National Parties | Seats contested | Seats won | Votes polled (%) |
| --- | --- | --- | --- |
| BJP | 50 | 0 | 1.54 |
| CPI | 2 | 1 | 1.57 |
| CPI-M | 55 | 49 | 48.11 |
| INC | 48 | 10 | 36.53 |
| NCP | 2 | 0 | 0.03 |
| AIFB | 1 | 0 | 0.70 |
| JD (U) | 1 | 0 | 0.02 |
| RSP | 2 | 0 | 1.95 |
| SP | 4 | 0 | 0.08 |
| AMB | 16 | 0 | 0.25 |
| CPI(ML) (L) | 10 | 0 | 0.16 |
| INPT | 12 | 0 | 7.59 |
| IPFT | 17 | 0 | 0.46 |
| SUCI | 6 | 0 | 0.05 |

Source: Election Commission of India.

Notes: NCP = Nationalist Congress Party; JD (U) Janata Dal (United); INPT = Indigenous People's Front; IPFT = Indigenous People's Front of Tripura; SUCI = Socialist Unity Centre.

## Final assessment of TUJS

The political biography of the TUJS was rather unusual. As it has been found out, the ethnic parties in India have rarely gone into the oblivion. The TUJS was born in the same year the Shiv Sena in Bombay (now Mumbai) was born. The Shiv Sena not only remains strong; it has been ruling over the Mumbai metropolis, and in power as a junior partner with the BJP in Maharashtra. The Asom Gana Parishad (AGP) was born in the early 1980s, got State power in 1985 and later lost it; but it remains as a regional ethnic party. In the elections to the Assam State Assembly in 2016 it entered into an alliance with the BJP, and is sharing State power again. The case of the TUJS in this perspective is rather tragic in the sense that although it was born as a strong tribal regionalist party and virulently anti-Congress, it never managed to establish enduring sway over the tribesmen. It joined an electoral alliance with its arch enemy in 1983 and tasted governmental power in 1988–93 as a junior partner. It even got itself involved in the ethnic riots in Tripura in May 1979 and June 1980. But with its merger with various extremist tribal outfits since 2002 and demanding self-determination right for the tribals which was suspected to be verging on secession. With the tribal heavily outnumbered in Tripura and pushed to the hilly terrain with little fertile land, secessionist self-determination would mean a political suicide that the tribals in Tripura chose not to commit. The TUJS was overall rejected by the tribals themselves.

Unlike the Left affiliated GMP with grassroots membership (family-wise) which now runs into four generations, the TUJS was basically an elite and urban based party, as the leadership profile of it shows. The TUJS' articulation of tribal ethno-nationalism was no match with the prudent accommodation of tribal ethno-nationalism with Left radicalism in Tripura. It was not merely an ideological and theoretical formula; in the ADC experiments since 1985, the Left has learnt to devolve powers further down the scale by instituting Village Committees by the method of direct elections. Tribesmen have elected the members of the GMP/Left into more than 527 such Committee. As I have examined in greater detail in my study of the ADC (2013),[10] the experiment has been very effective for preparing a new generation of tribal leaders into the dynamics of parliamentary democracy, its rules and procedures and in handling things for themselves. The ADC experiment is most successful compared to such other experiments in the North East, but a proof that an internal self-determination within the Indian Democratic Federation provides better scope for protecting their identity than going outside of India with barren hilly lands in the foot hills of the eastern Himalayan ranges in Tripura.[11]

## Notes

1 The State Assembly elections in Tripura in 1988 were held under heavy handed terror by the Centre government led by Rajiv Gandhi, the Prime Minister; the whole State was declared as 'disturbed' under Section 3 of the Armed Forces Special Powers Act. Despite this the CPI-L led Left Front got as many as 27 out of 60 Assembly seats leaving Congress (23)-TUJS (08) alliance with the rest to form the government.
2 It was a dreadful violent militant tribal organization, which forced the then-Prime Minister of India late Rajiv Gandhi to enter into an ethnic peace accord with them in 1988.
3 Weiner did not mention Hechter's (1975/paper back 1998) book titled *Internal Colonialism: The Celtic Fringe in British National Development 1536–1966* (Berkeley and Los Angeles: University of California Press) but rightly pointed out the exceptions to the thesis in Asia.
4 This was introduced by the British colonial authorities in the region in order to restrict entry to people coming from the mainland India. The system remains in force in a few States; there is a strong movement for introducing it again in Manipur.
5 *Chiniko*k (Our Voice) was the mouthpiece of the TUJS published from Agartala.
6 Karelkar quoted Chakrabarty's statement in a Press conference in New Delhi on 23 June 1980.
7 As if that was what the TUJS was propagating.
8 This election was held in conditions of insurgency in Tripura purportedly encouraged by the ruling Congress-TUJS government and utilized the opportunity by the underground tribal extremist outfits. Therefore, the fairness of these two elections is subject to doubt.
9 The relative failure of the AGP in Assam, now a small minority in the BJP led coalition government in Assam (2016), is another example that nativism may not be a lasting solution in a democratic country.
10 See, Bhattacharyya (2013: 1–140).
11 However, the political legacy of the TUJS is being carried on by the INPT which advocates for the policy of the 'sons of the soil' in Tripura and more protection of the tribal causes albeit within the parameters of the 6th schedule of the India Constitution. Its observance with a lot of fanfare the 31st '6th Schedule Day' on 23 August every year is a sign that the legitimacy of the constitutional arrangements of India for the tribals in the state has got a good purchase among the tribal rebels too (*Chinikok* 30 August 2015).

# 11 Marxists in power in Tripura
## Sub-State-level institutionalization of tribal identity

### Introduction

The fulfillment of tribal ethnic identity needs in Tripura has remained a very important and sensitive issue of governance in the State. The Marxists since the late 1940s have committed themselves to the cause of protection of tribal identity in the State. As I have argued elsewhere (Bhattacharyya 1990, 1999), the CPI, the parent party, developed in Tripura in symbiotic relation with tribal nationalism and insurgency in the late 1940, and subsequently built on it. The fulfillment of tribal identity needs in Tripura was not simply confined to the constitutional recognition of identity – non-territorial and territorial – but more sensitively the restoration of lands to the tribals, which were transferred to the settler Bengalis in often dubious circumstance in the wake of huge influx of post-Partition Bengali refugees from across the border which is now Bangladesh. The dilemma with the Left in Tripura was that with the major demographic transformation, the CPI/CPI-M[1] later also came to be dominated by the Bengalis. Given the delicate inter-ethnic relations in Tripura, it was a tight roping for the Left in power to restore land to the tribals in order to fulfill their commitment and pledge to the tribals but at the same time to not antagonize the Bengalis, the vast majority in population. The CPI-M led Left and Democratic Front (LFDG) in Tripura since 1978 sought to make use of the constitutional resources available within India's constitutional democracy as a legitimate means of responding to the tricky situation. The formation of the Tribal Autonomous District Council (ADC) in 1983 under the 5th Schedule of the Indian Constitution, and then from 1985 under the 6th Schedule has gone a long way to safeguard the tribal causes in the areas they inhabit.

This chapter examines the formation and functioning of the ADC in Tripura, and assesses it effectiveness within the appropriate historical, constitutional and political backdrop.

### Constitutional Resources

The Constitution of India provides for two main special institutional measures for the governance of what are known in India as 'scheduled areas' in States other than Assam, Meghalaya, Tripura and Mizoram (Art. 244 [1]) and 'tribal areas' in the States of Assam, Meghalaya, Tripura and Mizoram (Art. 244 [2]).[2] These are known respectively as the 5th and the 6th Schedules. The 6th Schedule is more empowering in terms of autonomy than the 5th Schedule. These institutional mechanisms have added to India's federalization by paving the way for further differentiation in the Indian Federation in favour of governance, and greatly served to ensure better protection of tribal ethnic identity.

The story of how these special constitutional measures providing for the District Councils as a sub-State-level governance for special areas inhabited by special communities, or tribal aboriginal people inhabiting particular territories, came into being is complex but makes for an interesting case of innovative regional governance. This was an illustration of the innovative capacity of the new political elites of India at the crucial re-formative stage of the Indian State. As Chaube pointed out, the District Council (DC) in the Sixth Schedule at once served to combine the hill men's demand for political autonomy with the need to integrate the tribal inhabited areas with the evolving political system of India.[3]

According to the provisions of the 6th Schedule, the tribal areas are to be administered as autonomous districts. Although such districts stay within the executive jurisdiction of the State concerned, the District and Regional Councils, as may be created, will have certain legislative, executive and judicial powers. As primarily representative bodies, to be elected by the people in the areas concerned on the basis of universal adult suffrage, their power of making laws include such fields as forest management (other than a reserved forest), inheritance of property, marriage and social customs and so on. The Councils will also have powers to assess and to collect land revenues and to impose certain specified taxes. Although the Governor's assent is required for all the laws passed by the Councils, the Acts of State Legislature shall not extend to such Areas on which the Councils have made laws. The Councils possess some judicial power, civil and criminal, subject to the jurisdiction of the High Court.[4]

The protection of identity of the State's tribals, and the Tribal District Council as a major institutional step were a long-standing demand of the State's Left movements, and was an electoral pledge of the CPI-M led LFDG in Tripura. The Left Front in Tripura contested the post-Emergency election in December 1977 with the following pledge:

> Reconstitution of Tribal Reserves with the areas inhabited by the tribals, and constitution of Autonomous Tribal District as per provisions of the Sixth Schedule of the Constitution; providing funds and delegation of requisite powers to such District Councils. The Central Government will be moved for introduction of the Sixth Schedule to the Constitution, in Tripura for formation of autonomous regions in the areas inhabited by tribals. Recognition will be given to Kok-Borok language as an official language along with Bengali in the State.[5]

Since Tripura was not originally in the 6th Schedule, the LDFG in Tripura demanded the extension of the more empowering 6th Schedule to tribal areas of Tripura, on the one hand, and made the move, in the meanwhile, to make the necessary legislative efforts within the competence of the State. Thus, the Tripura State Assembly (with the overwhelming majority of the CPI-M and its Left allies) unanimously passed on January 17, 1979, the Tripura Tribal Autonomous District Council Act, 1979 (the bill received the Presidential assent on July 20, 1979) by making use of the (entry 5 List 2) Seventh Schedule of the Constitution[6] which provided for a lot of safeguards and powers to the tribal minorities. The first ADC was formed on 18 June 1982 under the 7th schedule, but with the incorporation of Tripura's tribal areas in the Sixth Schedule by the 49th Constitutional Amendment Act in 1984, it was dissolved on April 1, 1985 long before the expiry of its normal term (i.e., five years), for making way for placing it under the 6th Schedule of the Constitution, and fresh elections were held for the formation of the second ADC on June 30, 1985. Since then, ADCs have been formed regularly at the interval of every five years, and today, the ADC is an indispensable part of Tripura's governing political institutions, particularly in the tribal dominated eastern but hilly areas of the State. To the tribals of Tripura, the ADC is like a State within a State.

The ADC thus has under its jurisdiction about two-thirds of the total territory of the State along the eastern side of the State, although in terms of population this amounts to no more than 30 per cent since the ADC areas were very hilly, inaccessible and sparsely populated. The tribals inhabiting the ADC areas are around 76 per cent, and the rest are non-tribal. Tribals live in non-ADC areas too. Thus, although in the ADC areas, the tribals are an overwhelming majority, around 25 per cent tribals of Tripura spread over and live in the non-ADC areas. Conceding most of the territory of the State to the authority of a sub-State-level institution is a remarkable instance of accommodation of diversity in a fragmented society.

The appropriate political accommodation of the tribal minorities of Tripura in the political process of the State, since the relative loss of their number in the wake of Tripura's demographic transformation, has remained the key to political order, governance and legitimacy in Tripura. The widespread tribal discontent, due to the loss of their power, and their sense of deprivation, has remained the basis of different forms of tribal insurgency, political extremism and violence. Bhattacharyya elsewhere has dealt with the complex relationships between the tribal identity and the State's communist movement, and analyzed the Left's mode of management of ethnic conflicts in the State.[7] For quite a long time from the late 1940s, the majority of the tribals of Tripura were the social bases of support for the communists although there were occasions when holding on to tribal support bases subsequently after Tripura's accession to the Union of India in 1949 has not been easy for the GMP and the CPI-M. The growth and development of the State's communist movement has also witnessed, as Bhattacharyya has argued, a growing Bengali domination over the movement and the government, and consequently a degree of *deidentification* of the tribals with the GMP and the State communist movement.[8]

The Tripura Tribal Areas Autonomous District Council (popularly known as ADC) in the predominantly tribal inhabited areas of Tripura formed under 1st, the 7th, and later the 6th schedule of the Indian Constitution (the latter being more empowering), has been the institutional response of great value and utility to the identity needs of the tribal minorities of Tripura. The ADC has also been an effective institutional method of containing minority secessionism and disintegration in Tripura. The introduction of this institution in Tripura in the early 1980s, after the CPI-M led LDFG came to 'power' (1978), was very challenging to political order and legitimacy in the State, but eventually it has turned out to be more stabilizing. The ADC, strategically speaking, has provided a political platform, a level and an institution for political participation for the newly emerging tribal elites of Tripura who are crucial to political order and governance especially in the vast tribal inhabited areas of the State. This innovative sub-State-level federal institution of India has been effective in the management of ethnic conflicts for political participation, political stability and governance.

First, a series of non-territorial measures for accommodation of tribal identity have been taken. 17 out of 60 (28.33 per cent) (Tripura) State Assembly seats have been reserved for the tribes of Tripura, which means that for those seats, the competition is restricted to the tribes alone. This is, more or less, in proportion to the percentage of the tribal people to the total population of Tripura. Second, one out of two Parliamentary (Lok Sabha, the popular chamber) seats has also been reserved for the tribals. Third, *Kok-Borok*, the language of the tribals of Tripura, has been recognized as one of the official languages for administration in Tripura. There are schools at primary and upper primary levels within the ADC areas for students of various tribal minority languages such as Manipuri, Halm Kuki and Kok-Borok.

## The land question, rural inequality and tribal identity

The question of land assumed special significance in Tripura although the land tenure system, as it took shape during the Raj, was somewhat similar to that of neighbouring Bengal. There took place large alienation of land from the tribals to the Bengali refugees in Tripura; the question of restoration of illegally held land to the original owners was a difficult task for the State government run by the Left headed by the CPI-M since 1978, for in the first three decades when (pro-Bengali) Congress was in power and the Bengali bureaucrats in administration and police, the tribal nearly lost all grounds. N. C. Devbarma (2005: 125) pointed out that the *Tripura Land Revenue and Reforms Act* in 1960 in Tripura the entire tribal reserve land was abolished to make way for the settlement of the Bengali refugees in the State. The landlord–tenant relations until was governed by a land of 1886. The 1960 Act dealt with a range of issues: abolition of intermediary interest in land; the rights of the cultivating tenants; land ceiling and the acquisition of any excess; proper maintenance of records and, above all, the prevention of the alienation of tribal lands. All transfer of land by tribals to non-tribals was disallowed, except where prior permission had been given by the District Collector (District Magistrate) in writing (Bhattacharyya and Nossiter 1988: 165).

For the privileged sections in an agrarian society, the Act was of more symbolic than substantive import. In practice, the ceiling for a family's personal cultivation turned out to be 150 acres. Not counting the scope of circumvention given by the exclusion of land used for non-agricultural purposes. Very little land was recovered for redistribution. The fact of the matter was that much and had been allocated to the refuges from East Pakistan, in small parcels, which was then sublet to share-croppers or other sub-tenants, mainly on verbal, not written, contracts. Both share croppers and tribals were at a grave disadvantage in securing their papers' rights. In fact, alienation of land continued unabated after the Act. Since the official figures rested on the clearly incomplete and dubious field index of rights, it was certain that their analysis seriously underestimated inequalities. Ten years after the land reforms Act (1960), 11 per cent of landholders were found to own 46 per cent of the total landholdings whereas 46 per cent of poor tenants owned only 11 per cent (with land less than .05 hectares). Thus, apart from the high ceiling and the holes in it, the growing pauperization of the rural population led to still more alienation of land from the tenants to the big land owners and money lenders. The various schemes for raising agricultural production that the government took since only served to further strengthen the position of the big farmers, even better placed to lease land from the refugees who could not afford to cultivate it. With very little achieved in terms of making much inroads into rural inequality, insecurity and exploitation, two more land reforms acts followed: 1974 and 1976 (Bhattacharyya and Nossiter 1988: 166). But the real land reform did not take place since the changes envisaged were only cosmetic. In between there was an amendment in 1969 which did not bar any aggrieved person from seeking redress in Civil Courts in relation to alienation prior to that date but the chances of a tribal succeeding in such an enterprise was as great as him flying to Delhi. The amendment of 1974 worsened the situation, as it repealed 1931 and 1943 Tribal Reserve Orders. It was modified in 1975 in order to give first right of purchase of land in the Scheduled Villages (tribal) to non-tribals. All in all, the number of landless tribals was getting swollen. One wondered about the prospects for the tribals through such land reforms legislations when the bureaucracy and the adjudicating courts were so close to the propertied (and the Bengalis). Land reforms were a success for the landed Bengalis and the refugees, not for the poor tribals and non-tribal Bengalis. What was required was a strong popular participation in land reforms through an organized party/movement which was not followed.

Land reforms in Tripura were never taken down to the level of popular participation through the party and its mass fronts. Even the pressing question of restoration of land illegally transferred from the tribals to the Bengalis – this was the crux of the land question in the State – and that too, in the absence of any record of ownership, particularly of the share-croppers but in the presence of a politically powerful Bengali vested interests, was not difficult for the party and the government already dominated by the Bengalis. The election manifesto of the LF in 1977 recognized this but its performance was far from adequate. The CPI-M's inner-party reports (1985) had only two scanty references to the issue: 'redistribution of land to 100,000 landless – or apologetic – restoration of alienated land to the tribals *to the extent possible*' (emphasis added) (Bhattacharyya and Nossiter 1988: 166–7). In the election manifesto for 1988 election to the State Assembly the *most remarkable achievement* of the LFG was the formation of the ADC in Tripura. Late Biren Dutta who was Land Reforms Minister in the first LFG in

Tripura said: the record of rights of the share croppers is far below the expectation of the exploited; in the first two years only 2,730 *bargas* were recorded and only 5,912 were granted land (Bhattacharyya and Nossiter 1988: 167). In an interview (on 21 November 1986 at Agartala) Datta complained:

> In my whole career as Land Reforms Minister I could not get the Agricultural Workers Wages Bill passed ... [because of] fear all round the party of losing the middle classes and absentee landlords' support. In 99 of cases we failed to record the share croppers' rights and we bypassed the Agricultural Workers Bill.

Reliable sources then suggested that only Datta and the then Chief Minister (late Nripen Chakraborty) did not possess any land. From the late 1980s, the party defined its main task as the 'struggle for the conservation of tribal rights' which, arguably, was not organically linked with the issue of restoration of land to the tribals.

That the issue of land reforms, particularly restoration of land to the tribals, in Tripura remains vexed, is proved among others that by 31 March 1990, about 100,000 petitions were received by the Land Records Department of the Government of Tripura from the tribals for land restoration. It was on record that only 4,300 petitions could be dispensed with. The Tripura Land Revenue and Land Reforms Act 1989 made unauthorized occupation of tribal land a punishable offence but high incidence of dispossession and reoccupation of tribal land by the 'outsiders' was reported (*Encyclopedia of North East India: Tripura*, 2001).[9] With the formation of the ADC under the 6th Schedule of the Constitution, the issue of land redistribution and restoration became further limited by the still limited amount of land available within the ADC's jurisdiction. Nearly 73 per cent land within the ADC areas became Reserve Forest on which the ADC could not exercise its powers. For the State as a whole, nearly 60 per cent are forests. Added to it is implementation of the Government of India's so-called Forest Rights Act 2005 (Scheduled Tribes: Recognition of Forest Rights), in the State to which there is much popular discontent.[10]

The land question in Tripura has been inextricably linked to the question of both tribal identity and the interests of the poor non-tribals too. Despite decades of land reforms, the agrarian society in Tripura is unequal in which landless agricultural labourers comprise as much as 24.06 per cent of the 'total workers', a census category which suggests the people who are engaged in any productive activity. To add salt to the injury, Tripura's population still remains mostly dependent in the sense that only about 37 per cent people are total workers, and about 62 per cent are dependent upon this 37 per cent (Government of Tripura 2015: 21). The agricultural laborers who comprise about one-fourth of the 'total workers' in 2015 have grown over the decades and are suggestive of the increasing concentration of lands in the few upper sections of rural society. The ADC's own official records say that the tribals in the ADC areas are 'mostly dependent on *Jhuming* practices and are landless and poor agricultural labourers' (ADC 2012; Annual Plan 2011–12: 1). The above official records coming from the ADC strongly indicate the precarious economic position of the tribals within the ADC areas, and the core issue in tribal identity.

Some restoration of land to the tribals did indeed take place. The Left Front government after assuming office implemented this to some extent. But giving adequate compensation to the 'land losers' (in this the Bengalis) was provided. The compensation was rather liberal: the government decided (19 April 1978) to grant two acres of lands plus Rupees 6900.00 to those who would become landless as a result. The detailed records of restoration of land to the tribals in the State especially those pertaining to the influx of refugees, require separate research in the sense that the experiences of land alienation from the tribals to the non-tribals (as well as tribals) remains continuous process – caused in later days (since 1969) due to mortgage of lands to the money lenders (Das Gupta 1988). The Government of Tripura's official records show that the process of land allotment in the State (an instance of land reforms) has been continuing: in 2010–11 the families (landless and homeless) who benefitted were 143, the figure went up to 304 in 2014–15 (Tripura At a Glance 2011: 17; Tripura At a Glance 2015: 19). Tribal beneficiaries of the above were not identified although one would assume that the tribals (since most of them are landless) constituted a good proportion. The GMP's (the tribal mass front of the CPI-M) 20th Central Conference on 9–11 November 2013 recorded satisfaction that until 2012 some 186533 families belonging to both the *jumia* tribal families and other landless families were resettled on government land amounting to 227053 acres of land (GMP 2013: 5).

## Political accommodation of identity: ethnic peace accords in Tripura

Another method used to contain secessionism in Tripura (as much as some other parts, most notably the North East, of India) resorted to by the Indian rulers since the 1980s is the signing, after some protracted negotiations, bipartite, or tripartite settlement of ethnic disputes between the federal government, the State government, and the ethnic forces. The 'Ethnic Peace Accords' (EPA), as they have come to be known in India, have been followed by the constitutional mechanisms in giving effects to the terms of agreement and thereby accommodating ethnic identity in the political process. The formation following the above two of a territorial authority has followed. In the rest of the region that has been the process but in Tripura the two ethnic peace agreements signed in 1988 and 1993 did not result in any major territorial concession because an autonomous territorial authority for the tribals of Tripura was a long-standing demand of the State communists, and the ADC for this purpose was formed way back in 1985 as per the amended 6th Schedule of the Constitution. These two ethnic agreements with the secessionist forces such as the TNV and the ATTF were encouraged when the Congress-TUJS was in power in the State and late Rajib Gandhi as Prime Minister was resorting to certain short-cut methods of 'achieving' peace. After 1993, insurgency in Tripura dissipated, and no such ethnic peace accords had to be signed. But then it was more due to the Left front which came back to power in 1993.

### 11.3.1 Memorandum of settlement, 1988 (TNV accord) (New Delhi)

This ethnic peace accord for the settlement of problems of the tribals was signed on May 4, 1988 in New Delhi by the representatives of the Governments of India, of Tripura, and the Tripura National Volunteers (TNV), an extremist tribal political organization demanding secessionism from Tripura and India.

1. In order to ensure greater share of the tribals in the governance of the State, legislative measures will be taken including those for the enactment of the Bill for the amendment of the Constitution. The Representation of the People Act, 1950 shall also be amended to provide for the reservation of 20 seats for the Scheduled Tribes in the Assembly.
2. Measures will be taken for the effective implementation of the law for restoration of tribal land, and stringent measures to stop fresh alienation.
3. To strengthen the Agricultural Credit System to provide for an appropriate agency with adequate tribal representation for easy operationalization of credit to the tribals.
4. Tribal-majority villages which now fall outside the ADC areas will be included in ADC area, and similarly placed non-tribal majority villages in the ADC areas will be excluded from the ADC areas.
5. Maximum emphasis will be placed on extensive and intensive skill-formation of the tribal youths of Tripura to equip them for various kinds of employment including self-employment.
6. Special intensive recruitment drives will be organized for police and paramilitary forces in Tripura with a view to enlisting as many tribal youths as possible.
7. In the ADC areas, rice, salt and kerosene oil will be given at subsidized rates during lean months for a period of three years.
8. Conscious efforts to be made for effective implementation of the provisions of the 6th Schedule to the Constitution as it relates to Tripura, and so on.[11]

### Memorandum of settlement, 1993 (ATTF accord) (Agartala, State capital)

This accord was signed on August 23, 1993 by the representatives of the All Tripura Tribal Force (ATTF), another secessionist extremist group in Tripura, in order to find solutions to the tribal problems within the framework of the Indian Constitution. This accord repeated many of the resolutions of the TNV accord relating to tribal land restoration, inclusion of tribal majority villages in the ADC areas, and so on. Additionally, it called for the introduction of the Inner-Line Permit System (ILPS) in order to check the entry of non-tribals to tribal inhabited areas, resolved to establish the Village Police Force (VPF) under the control of the ADC, increase in number of reserved seats for the tribals in the ADC (to 25 out of the total 28), to set up a Linguistic Commission for the development of *Kok-Borok* and tribal language, to rename again all villages and rivers which had originally tribal names (but subsequently changed!) are given back their tribal names.

Unlike other ethnic peace accords in the rest of the region ethnic peace accords in Tripura did not result in any territorial concessions to the rebels because even the rebels could not demand it. In 1982, the LFG had already established the ADC as a self-governing body for the tribals under the State law comprising about two-thirds areas of Tripura, which came to be under the amended 6th Schedule of the Constitution in 1985. Thus, quite early on the territorial issues had been resolved by the LFG in Tripura which minimized the scope of any further demand for territorial concession.

## Tribal identity and the ADC: multi-party competition

The inner-party documents of the State Committee of the CPI-M (2015) no longer were found concerned about the question of restoration of land to the tribals as part of protection of tribal identity. The LFG in Tripura headed by the CPI-M and led by Manik Sarkar (Chief Minister since 1998) has successfully distributed a whole lot of welfare benefits originating from the State government and those funded by the Union government schemes to the tribal people: provisions for stipends for the tribal students, and their residence; reliefs to distressed tribals, especially those still engaged in shifting cultivation; some special health care measures; self-employment schemes for the tribal youth, and so on. But such individualized measures, while of some help to and benefiting, some tribals, were not found to be enough as a guarantee for the protection of the identity of the disadvantaged tribals placed in unequal competition with the more advanced ethnic group i.e., the Bengalis.

As part of its pledge to protect the tribes in Tripura and prevent any further marginalization, the Left in Tripura since assuming power at the State-level in 1978, demanded appropriate constitutional reforms in favour of introducing the amended 6th Schedule of the Constitution to the tribals in Tripura, but then government at the Centre did not pay heed. The Left Front government by law in 1979 went ahead with formation by elections the Tribal District Autonomous Council for the tribals under its own powers (under the 7th Schedule of the Constitution. This sparked of discontent among the settlers Bengali who thought that this reforms measure was a means to take back the land from the Bengalis to the original owners. This was of a misconception that the Left failed to remove by prior campaign. The result was a huge Bengali backlash resulting riots in 1980 which killed a few thousand more tribals than the Bengalis (Bhattacharyya and Nossiter 1988: 144–70). However, in the first ever elections to the ADC in 1982, the Left swept the poll securing 21 seats out of 28 on a good share of popular votes of about 63 per cent (Table 11.1). However, in the first elections to the ADC under the 6th Schedule of the Constitution in 1985[12] the CPI-M lost significant ground to the party of the tribal youth (TUJS) which secured ten seats (with popular vote share [33.6 per cent]).

*Table 11.1* Party performance in the elections to the ADC in Tripura (1982–5) (28 seats)

| Political Parties | 1982 (Seats) | 1982 (% of votes) | 1985 (Seats) | 1985 (% of votes) |
| --- | --- | --- | --- | --- |
| CPI | 1 | 3.3 | 0 | 1.4 |
| CPI-M | 19 | 56.0 | 15 | 42.3 |
| INC | – | – | 3 | 14.3 |
| RSP | 0 | 1.2 | – | – |
| FB | 1 | 1.3 | – | – |
| TUJS | 7 | 37.5 | 10 | 33.5 |
| Ind | 0 | 0.1 | 0 | 1,8 |
| THPP | – | – | 0 | 7.2 |
| Total | 28 | | | |

Source: *Bhattacharyya and Nossiter (1988: 152)*

*Table 11.2* Performance of political parties in elections to the ADC (2010, May 3) (total seats to be elected 28)

| Political Parties | Seat won | % of votes polled |
| --- | --- | --- |
| CPI-M | 25 | 60 |
| AIFB | 01 | 1.79 |
| RSP | 01 | 0.05 |
| CPI | 01 | 0.91 |
| INC | nil | 21.09 |
| BJP | nil | .55 |
| AITC | nil | .28 |
| INPT | nil | 11.52 |
| Ind | nil | 2.51 |

Source: *State (Tripura) Election Commission, Agartala.*

The non-territorial measures, despite all their merits, are essentially individualistic in character. Apart from the language which satisfies, symbolically, to some extent, the identity need of the community, (this of course depends on the level of literacy among the community at stake!), the rest of the measures help equip only the individuals from among the tribal community.

In the last elections (4 May 2015) to the ADC the Left Front swept the poll winning all 28 seats for which elections were held on a high turn-out of 83 per cent. The CPI-M tally was 25, CPI, RSP and AIFB each one. The higher rate of popular participation of the electorate of Tripura has of course to be understood in terms of institutionalized and polarized political competition in the State. Despite the presence of many political parties in the electoral system of Tripura, a bi-party system (often broken by the rise of a third party such as the TUJS in the late 1960s although electorally not until 1988 when in alliance with the Congress it became a party of governance during 1988–93) has effectively characterized the electoral scenario. Thus, the CPI-M-led Left alliance versus the Congress has been the main pattern of electoral politics in the State.

## Performance of the ADC

The ADC has been empowered to make laws with respect to the allotment, occupation or use of land (excluding the reserved forest), regulation of shifting cultivation, water uses for agricultural purposes, inheritance of property, marriage and divorce, social customs etc. The 6th Schedule of the Indian Constitution empowers the ADC to establish, construct or manage primary schools, dispensaries, markets, cattle pounds, ferries, fisheries, village roads, waterways etc. The ADC has also financial powers to taxation. In short, it is seen as a governmental institution to deal with multifarious activities relating to the development and welfare of the tribals.

By performing multifarious activities particularly related to the welfare and development of the tribals, the ADC has been found to be heavily engaged in various developmental and empowerment programmes in its jurisdiction. Of the jobs received under the MNRWGA (Table 11.4), a high proportion constitutes the tribal families because the tribals are mostly poor and landless. Under various welfare and empowerment schemes including MNREGA until 31 December 2014, the tribal families benefitted were 93,183 and the sum spent for the purpose was INR 1332.8 million (Roy 2015: 191). Tripura's records in implementation of the MNREGA (100 days rural unemployment guarantee) place it at the very top scorers in the country. The literacy rate among the Scheduled Tribes in Tripura has increased manifold (from only 23.07 per cent in 1981 to 56.50 per cent in 2011) although this is far behind the high level of general literacy in the State (87.75 per cent, all India being 74.03 per cent). (Economic Survey, Government of Tripura 2013–14). The tribal population in the State began to increase from 1981. The decadal growth was 8–53 per cent in 1991 over 1981, 9.93 per cent in 2001 over 1991 and 11.66 per cent in 2011 over 2001 (Economic Survey 2013–14, 307, Government of Tripura).

The Government of India's records (Table 11.5) for the financial year 2015–16 corroborate the State government data contained in Roy (2015).

The ADC has appeared to be an effective institutional safeguard to the identity of the tribals. What the State government of Tripura could not do, the ADC did it. Within the first rather shorter term of its existence, the ADC restored some 2,946 acres of tribal land to some 3,006 tribal families.[14] The data in Table 11.3 give an indication of the various areas of activities of the ADC.

*The Scheduled Tribes and Other Traditional Forest Dwellers (Recognition of Forest Rights) Act 2006* (The Government of India's Ministry of Tribal Affairs, New Delhi) (effective on and from 31 December 2007) provides for the ensuring rights of the tribals and other forest dwellers the right to the forest, their home and livelihood to which they had no recorded legal rights. This Act was designed to recognize and vest the forest rights and occupation in forest land in forest dwelling Scheduled Tribes and other traditional forest dwellers who had been residing

Table 11.3 Public expenditure on tribal welfare (2011–12) (amount in INR @ 1 lakh (=100000)

| Name of Schemes | Approved ADC Budget | Physical Target |
|---|---|---|
| Rubber plantation | 140.00 | 1094 Hectares |
| Nucleus budget | 30.00 | 125 Fa |
| Tribal rest house | 25.00 | 04 Nos |
| Composite welfare and Relief Scheme | 19.50 | 1000 F |
| Total | 214.50 | |

Source: *Annual Plan 2011–12 (ADC, Khumulwng, Tripura, p. 26)*

Table 11.4 Governmental performances in implementation of MNREGA[13] (2006–7 to 2014–15)

| Year | Job seekers | Job received | Percentage |
|---|---|---|---|
| 2006–07 | 75067 | 75067 | 100.00 |
| 2007–08 | 425299 | 423724 | 99.63 |
| 2008–09 | 549145 | 549022 | 99.82 |
| 2009–10 | 577540 | 576487 | 99.82 |
| 2010–11 | 557413 | 557055 | 99.94 |
| 2011–12 | 567129 | 566793 | 99.94 |
| 2012–03 | 597437 | 596530 | 99.85 |
| 2013–14 | 605187 | 599531 | 99.00 |
| 2014–15 | 595862 | 571111 | 97.48 |

Source: *Roy (2015: 289)*

Table 11.5 Tripura's performance in implementing MNREGA in FY 2015–16 until 28th March 2016

| Physical and Financial | |
|---|---|
| Households provided employment | 5.70 lakh |
| Persondays generated | 535.65 |
| Women participation | 50% |
| Average Persondays per household | 94 days |
| House Holds completed | 2.98 |
| Total expenditure | 1338 crores |
| Wage expenditure | 889.3 crores |

Source: *http://164.100.129.6/netnrega/SRS_LB_Minutes.aspx (sighted on 16/2/17)*

in such forests for generations but whose rights could not be recorded. This Act also provided for developing a framework for recording the forest rights so vested and the nature of evidence required for such recognition and vesting in respect of forest. The performance of State governments has varied enormously in respect of implementing the provisions of the Act (http://economictimes.indiatimes.com/

Table 11.6 Benefits to tribal families under the Forest Act 2006 (up to 31 December 2014)

| Forest Rights | Families |
| --- | --- |
| Total families eligible | 123,293 |
| Tribal families | 123,291 |
| Total land received by them | 17,577,896 Hectares |

Source: Roy (2015: 191)

news/politics-and-nation/7-states-fall-short-of-forest-rights-act-implementation-government/articleshow/55647998.cms) (sighted on 16/10/17). The laggards are: Assam, Bihar, Himachal Pradesh, Tamil Nadu, Uttar Pradesh and Jharkhand. But the performance records of the Government of Tripura were found to be very satisfactory (Table 11. 5).

In the context of Tripura, the tribals' right to the forest assumes special significance connected very much to the question of their identity and its protection. The recording the traditional (customary) rights of the forest dwellers to the forest and its produce, by means of offering them *patta* (a piece of papers with the details of rights recorded), goes a long way to the fulfillment of their identity needs. In the elite interviews conducted in Tripura during 2014–15 with reference to the extent of implementation of FRA in Tripura, it was found out that of the 16 elites (a cross section of Minister; MLAs; former Ministers; Civil Servants; senior journalist and other officials of the ADC and the Government of Tripura), 12 responded positive and four negative – the latter category belongs to the Opposition party leaders: Congress and TMC. The responded who responded negative could not give any details though. Of the positive responses: most of them could provide some concrete figures and details. Mr Biswamani Devbarma, a top leader of the GMP was inchoate in his response but the indications were obvious: 'Yes, rehabilitation; pattas given the tribals but they cannot sell them; they can cultivate. About 1.19 lakh pattas were issued to the tribals' (interview dated 12/6/15 at Agartala). Other positive respondents mentioned at ease the range of success in giving *pattas* to the tribal families: 90–95 per cent.

The other kinds of benefit the tribals received included scholarship to tribal students in hotels (number was 230,585); pre-Madhyamik scholarship; Madhyamaik and post-Madhyamik scholarship; provisions for special coaching to tribal girl students; coaching for drop-out tribal students (26,059); supply of books free of costs to the tribal students (1,321,745); support to form Self-Help Groups among the tribals (1502 formed until 2014); 34 Tribal Rest Houses constructed; 17,320 tribal families have been trained and helped to engage in rubber plantation; and so on (Roy 2015: 188–9). The Government of Tripura recognized *Kok-Borok* as the second official language of the State way back on 19 January 1979, and 19 January is observed every year as the *Kok-Borok* day. The ADC's Language Cell (for all round cultivation of *Kok-Borok* language) had INR 22 *lakh* as its annual plan budget for 2011–12 (ADC Annual Report 2010–11: 18).

### Implications for governance

To the State's Marxists' rulers, the ADC symbolized a reconciliation of class and tribal ethnicity, a fulfillment of a long-standing aim of the democratic movement in the State. The ADC in Tripura is a sign that the force of tribal nationalism is recognized in the State, and 'not merely a second-order derivation of capitalism reducible in the last instance to economic distortion of true class consciousness'.

For our purpose, the ADC represents a major territorial institutional innovation and measure at the sub-State level for the accommodation of identity, and the management of ethnic conflicts. The tribal elites (elected officials at the ADC) as well non-elected GMP leaders interviewed in May-December 2015[15] recognized the (developmental) role of the ADC plus the determined political intervention by the GMP and the CPI-M to politically neutralize insurgency in the State. To be sure, the ADC was not an elite imposed device on the tribals, but a result of the institutional resource at the above combined with the popular political pressures from below for the establishment of such a decentralized political unit of tribal self-governance. The Tripura State government, it is true, had had to delegate and part with a lot of powers with the ADC (eight departments have been transferred), but then that helped in containing secessionism in Tripura, to a great extent. The State government has also shared with the ADC to a large extent (Table 11.7).

The ADC's own taxes bases are very limited, so it is heavily dependent on funding by the State government which makes the resources available through State Plans to the ADC. One must not, however, come to the conclusion that the ADC offered all the answers to the tribals' overriding need for protecting their identity and their well-being in Tripura. The ADC had problems, both structural and operational, to ensure what was termed 'meaningful autonomy'. As an institutional measure to supplement the ADC in its drive for 'meaningful autonomy', the Tripura State Assembly passed the Tripura Tribal Areas Autonomous District (TTAAD) (Establishment of Village Committee) Act, 1994 that provide for the formation of the Village Committees (VC) in the ADC areas as a step towards real, meaningful decentralization of power.[17]

The survey report by Bhattacharyya (2013a)[18] on the ADC showed that all tribal communities have been represented in the ADC; there is satisfaction over

*Table 11.7* State's sharing of taxes with the ADC Plans (2011–12)

| Tax Heads | Share in percentage (%) |
| --- | --- |
| Professional Tax | 25 |
| Land Revenue | 40 |
| Agricultural Income Tax[16] | 50 |
| Forest Revenue | 75 |
| Motor Vehicle Tax | 25 |
| Gas Royalty | 30 |

Source: *ADC Annual Plan (2011–12: 3)*

*Table 11.8* Satisfaction over the ADC's role (N = 26) (23 tribal and 3 Bengalis)

| | | |
|---|---|---|
| Relative satisfaction | Yes (19) | 73.07% |
| Relative satisfaction | No (7) | 26.93% |

Source: Survey Data.

Note: relative satisfaction is defined as 80 per cent and above.

the role of the ADC in regard to protection of tribal identity. The data in the following tables do not suggest a very optimistic picture, however. Despite the fact the ADC is a success story in Tripura, sub-State-level power-sharing and identity accommodation; there are areas of dissatisfaction, negative assessment and the evident lack of knowledge of the actual work done by the ADC for the five years (2005–10). However, the negative side of the story must not be blown out of proportions. The regularity of holding elections at the interval of five years in a free multi-party competition has meant the institutionalization of the self-governing body in the tribal dominated areas of the State.

The democratization even within ADC decisional process is not doubted by the INPT, the arch enemy of the CPI-M/GMP: 'apparently all decision are taken on the floor of the ADC, the implementation of such decision depends ultimately on the will of the State government' (INPT leader interviewed in Agartala on 10.9.11). Given the fact that the ADC funds from the Centre come via the State government, the latter naturally has a hand. But what is intriguing is the relatively higher cost of financing such a government (the ADC establishment). Of the knowledge and awareness of the Schedule that governed the ADC, 12 out of 15 leaders/elected officials of the ADC responded positive, only three negative.

No less the persons than the civil servants associated with the ADC admitted at the rate of 89 per cent (nine out of ten interviewed) that more than 80 per cent of ADC money goes to pay for the establishment – the cost of running the government at the ADC – leaving little for actual development works. But then, as Max Weber reminded us long back, more democracy results in more bureaucracy, inevitability and irony in a democracy. Nine out of 15 leaders/elected officials of the ADC were found to be aware of the ongoing activities of the ADC. Six had a negative response. *How effective was the ADC in protecting tribal identity?* 14 out of 15 responded 'positive'. 11 out of 15 could identify some concrete activities of the ADC over the last five years.

Be that as it may, the ADC experiment in Tripura has not failed unlike its neighbours; it has enabled the tribal folks of Tripura in the art of governance, to take part in debates in their own language (*Kok-Borok*) on the floor of the Council and thrash out vital issue such as land, rubber plantation, and schooling for the tribal children and so on. There is no doubt that the idea of self-government has been implemented in Tripura in the tribal inhabited areas under the jurisdiction of the ADC. The ADC in Tripura has proved that democracy can also be self-government. The next chapter will consider all the three States together and move in the direction of distilling the specific findings into more general conjectures.

## Conclusion

This chapter has provided a detailed, empirically based analysis of the specific historical background to the special aspects of tribal ethnic identity in Tripura as distinguished from Tripura's neighbours. In the rest of the North East except perhaps Sikkim, the sub-State-level experiment with ethnic self-government has not proved as successful as the ADC in Tripura. In Tripura the significance of the role of the ADC goes beyond tribal identity protection and promotion; the ADC is an example of democratic decentralization, but within the ADC there is further democratic decentralization in terms of the establishment of some 528 Village Committees which provide for real platform for grassroots participation to the tribal village folk, to decide on their own the issues of public affairs, development and empowerment. This chapter has also indicated the limits of the ADC in respect of the land question – restoration of illegally transferred land to the tribals. The records of the government at the State level as well as of the ADC show, however, some modest success. Above all, the ADC in Tripura has proved beyond doubt that ethnic radicalism and political secessionism could be moderated and managed within the contours of constitutional democracy through appropriate institutional reforms, and relative autonomy conceded to the stakeholders workable with the back up of a committed political party in power.

## Notes

1 With the party split in 1965 in Tripura, the overwhelming majority of the CPI went over to the CPI-M. For full details, see Bhattacharyya (1999), chapter 162–96.
2 See for details, Bakshi (2017: 427–8). Tripura tribal areas were brought under the ambit of the 6th Schedule of the constitution by the 49th constitutional amendment in 1984 by the Indian Parliament.
3 See for details, Chaube (1999), chapter 6 'The Sixth Schedule', pp. 91–06.
4 For details, see Bakshi (2017), asu, D D (1997), Op cit., pp. 179–81.
5 Quoted in Chakravarti (1986: 5).
6 See Bakshi (2017: 441–50). This relates to the welfare of the tribal communities, the matter on which a State has exclusive executive powers.
7 See his (1999) for a fuller account of the problem.
8 See Bhattacharyya (1999), especially the last chapter.
9 The issue of restoration of land to the tribals was facilitated among others by the lack of records of rights of the tribals to their land, as in such cases the ownership was secured by customary practices rather than by written records.
10 The Tripura Tribal Land Restoration Campaign Committee, has, for instance, been demanding rights of forest land and forest produce on behalf of the tribals and poor non-tribals too, and organized demonstration: www.oneindia.com/2007/10/01/land-reforms-politics-rocks-tripura.html (sighted on 13/2/17).
11 For further details on other aspects of the accord, see Datta (1995: 22–31).
12 The Tripura Tribal Areas Autonomous District Council was inserted in the Sixth Schedule by the Constitution (49th Amendment) Act in 1984 (w.e.f 1.4.85).
13 The Mahamta Gandhi National Rural Employment Guarantee Act 2005 (MNREGA) is the major flagship programme of the Government of India since 2005 that seeks to guarantee 100 days employment for the rural poor in the country.
14 Chakravarti (1986: 34).

15 This research was carried out as part of the International Network Research on 'Continuity and Change in Indian Federalism in the Age of Coalition Governments' funded by the Leverhulme Trust UK during 2014–17.
16 Tripura is one of very few States in India which has been charging taxes on agricultural income since 1952 (by application of the Bengal Agricultural Income Tax Act 1944) which includes income from tea also considered as partial agriculture.
17 Bhattacharyya (1999: 252).
18 Funded by the Indian Council of Social Science Research, New Delhi on *Asymmetric Federalism, Tribal Identity and the Left in Tripura: The Case Study of the Tribal UpajatiGanamukti Parishad and the Autonomous District Council* (2011–12).

# 12 Marxists in power in Tripura
Dilemmas of governance since the 1990s

## Introduction

The CPI-M led Left Front – effectively the CPI-M –[1] has been in power in Tripura from 1978 to 1988 and then again from 1993 to date. In the last elections held in 2013, the Marxist coalition was returned with a resounding victory. The Marxists are, beyond doubt, well-entrenched in the State – the only State that the CPI-M can boast of having acquired such a hegemonic position in India at the moment.[2] Elsewhere (Bhattacharyya 1999) I have offered critical examination of the electoral dynamics of the Left in Tripura up to the early 1990s. The crisis in the Left in the late 1980s which led to the loss of power to the Congress-TUJS alliance (1988–93) has also been explained (Bhattacharyya 1998: 13–30). As the chapters above on Tripura have shown, the Marxists have well-consolidated their political position since the early 1950s by converting themselves to an electoral force, as legitimate stakeholders in India's parliamentary federal system. Unlike West Bengal where the second split in 1969 that gave birth to the CPI-M (L) in the CPI-M weakened the parent party, the Tripura party did not witness such a split. Two institutional factors have been decisive in the consolidation of the CPI-M in Tripura. First, the party along with a plethora of mass fronts has remained engaged in liberal politics: democratic competition for power in multi-party competition; competition for power at all available level of the polity; peaceful, constitutional means of campaign and pretest against some policies of the Centre; and simultaneously engaging itself in delivering governance. Second, the party has not innovated any institutions but has decided to operate in and through the available federal democratic institutions. In the case of Tripura, like her regional neighbours, an asymmetric federal arrangement was provided for until 2014 which means greater access to federal funds that are not tied or conditional. In other words, Tripura enjoyed as a Special Category States (SCS) in Plan disbursement the facility of 90 per cent as grants and 10 per cent as loan from the Centre while for the General Category States, the loan portion was 70 per cent and the grant was for 10 per cent. Thus, winning the State-level government has enabled the Marxists to better nurse their constituency with the financial largesse. There is of late huge resentment against the withdrawal of this facility by the current NDA government in Delhi in 2014 among the elites in the region as a whole. In addition, Tripura received other funds from the Centre as a border region. However, the recent shifts in India's political economy to a neo-liberal (market-oriented) one has appeared as a 'radical' (Right) challenge to the Left in Tripura, and created uncertainty about the whether the State could continue to maintain current level of governance and development or not.

This chapter seeks, first, to provide a brief critical account of the CPI/CPI-M's engagement in liberal democratic politics as a liberal democratic force that has sought to build bases of support around the compelling issues of the day and gain in good political dividends in electoral politics. The second objective of the chapter is to examine the relative success in delivering governance in Tripura since the 1990s around a host of issues such as the rule of law, social inclusion, growth, development and empowerment. In this section I will also point out a dilemma though: a State within the Indian Federation can be better governed with growth, development and social empowerment without attracting any FDI, which is given priority in measuring development by the power that be at the Centre since the early 1990s.

## The CPI/CPI-M's liberal democratic politics in Tripura

From 1949 when Tripura acceded to the Union of India to 1972 when Statehood was conceded to Tripura, Tripura did not have political institutions for democratic governance. The CPI and its various mass front mounted protest and launched demonstrations and also submitted memoranda claiming democratic governmental structures and effective popular participation. *Tripurar Katha* (story of Tripura) (in Bengali), the mouthpiece of the party, has recorded such activities on a daily basis.

The CPI and later on the CPI-M kept up the pressure from below for democratization of the governing structures in Tripura including the movement for Statehood. In a pamphlet dated 1969, issued by the State Committee of the CPI-M and titled (in Bengali) 'Why we demand full Statehood and regional committee in the Tribal areas'?, laying all blames on the Congress (nationally as well as locally), it was stated:

> The Congress rulers do not believe in self-determination and full self-government; that was why the relations between the Centre and the States all over India are getting bitter by the day. It was because of non-recognition of linguistic self-determination that India is fragmented.
>
> (p. 10)

The CPI-M's political activities then concentrated on territorial issues – the territorial recognition of Tripura as a separate State within the Indian Federation. The party linked this claim to the tribal's self-determination.

When Tripura joined the Indian Union in 1949, it was made a Chief Commissioner's Province. Under the Indian Constitution, it was accorded the status of Part 'C' State. The Constitution of India, originally, provided for three categories of States – A, B and C – corresponding to their placement in the respective Parts of the 1st Schedule of the Constitution. This categorization implied different status and features, and powers for the units, and was necessitated as a first step towards the territorial reorganization of India. It must be acknowledged though that the territorial divisions of India during the British colonial rule were arbitrary, not always corresponding to the natural cultural (linguistic) boundaries of the people. India's national integration involved, as Morris-Jones argued, a lot of territorial reorganization. There was, first of all, the major task of integrating some 561 princely States of varying sizes and culture including Tripura, before the reorganization of States on linguistic lines was on the agenda. Morris-Jones aptly remarked: State's reorganization is best regarded as clearing the ground for national integration. The autocratic princely Tripura's transformation into a Part 'C' State within the Union of India did not mean, however, a democratic governance in the State because it meant that Tripura was to be ruled by a Chief Commissioner on behalf of the President of India, and internally, the State had only a 30-member Electoral College to be democratically elected by the people to elect one member from Tripura to the Rajya Sabha (Council of States, the parliamentary upper chamber). This remained the position until 1957 when by virtue of the States Reorganization Act, 1956, Tripura was upgraded to a Union Territory, with limited autonomy but as a centrally administered area governed by the President of India, acting through an administrator appointed by him, and issuing regulations for their good government under Articles 239–40 of the Indian Constitution. During 1957–63, the Union Territory of Tripura had a 30-member Territorial Council (under the Territorial Council Act, 1956) which was elected by the people on the basis of a universal adult franchise but whose legislative powers were very limited. Tripura received a State Assembly in 1963 with legislative powers, and was finally made a full-fledged State with a 60-member State Assembly with full legislative status from January 21, 1972, under the North Eastern States Reorganization Act, 1971 passed by the Indian Parliament. Like all the other States in the North East, Tripura was a 'Special Category State' for the purpose of the federal plan assistance, special federal measure which helps, no doubt, to facilitate the integration of the State (as much as its neighbours) with the political system of India.

Since the regime in Tripura from 1947–72 was a Congress regime, by default, the CPI/ and then CPI-M monopolized all political space of protest against what they termed 'Congress regime' in Tripura, and fought for democratization in Tripura. Aligned with the Left was the Tribal Upajati Ganamukti Parishad (GMP), the radical Tripuri nationalist organization. From the early 1950s onwards, the all-India party (then CPI) was giving an electoral orientation to the local movements, and tried to make use of all available issues to bank upon.

In elections in 1952 to form the 30-mmber Electoral College to select one member to the Rajya Sabha (the upper chamber of India's parliament), the CPI and its Left partners won 19 seats and sent its member to the upper chamber. In the elections for two seats to Lok Sabha (parliamentary lower house), the CPI and its front members obtained as much as 61 per cent of the votes cast and sent two CPI members to the house. The CPI's outstanding electoral performance in elections in 1952 entitles them to claim to have pre-empted the Kerala unit's 1957 achievement.[3]

The party kept up the movement for constitutional reforms, for establishing representative governing bodies instead of the Territorial Council, or the Union Territory which was, in the party's views, nothing but an authoritarian rule, and central rule. The CPI and its partners won 15 seats in the elections to the Territorial Council in 1957 (30-seat) but lost ground to the INC in 1962 by winning only 13 seats leaving the INC with 17. From the early 1960s to 1977, the CPI lost ground to the INC in the wake of the huge influx of Hindu Bengali refugees, which was a 'blessing to Congress' (Chakrabarty 1983: 77). With the Bengalis controlling the realm of government and administration that included refugee rehabilitation, the then CPI and GMP known as the pro-tribal party, had little to do with it but to mobilize for refugee rehabilitation. But the refugees supported the INC in power. Added to that was the Chinese invasion of India in 1962 which put most leaders of the CPI behind bars, and the party split in 1965 added to the further weakening of the party. The communist movement was in disarray. The post-split party was in effect the CPI-M but nonetheless both the CPI and the CPI-M fared very poorly in the first elections to the State Assembly in 1967: in the 30-member house, the CPI got only one seat and the CPI-M 2 (21.7 per cent vote share). In the elections to the (60-member) State Assembly after Tripura's Statehood in 1972, the CPI got only one seat but the CPI-M got 17 seats (8.6 per cent vote share) (Bhattacharyya and Nossiter 1988: 146–50; Bhattacharyya 1999: 165–6). During the Emergency (1975–77), all political activity was banned in the State as elsewhere.

However, the CPI fully participated in the deliberations of the Territorial College, raising issues of reforms for creation of representative bodies in Tripura, and pointed out many flaws of the Congress rule in Tripura. As I have discussed in detail (Bhattacharyya 1999: 166), late Nripen Chakrabarty, a top CPI/CPI-M leader and the first Chief Minister of the Left Front government in Tripura during 1978–88) as leader of the Opposition in the TC made skillful use of all available ways of highlighting the pitfalls of the regime, staged many walk-outs, and moved no-confidence matins; the same were highlighted in the party's press (Bhattacharyya 1999: 166). In Lok Sabha, Biren Datta, the father of communism in Tripura and elected Member from Tripura, and his colleague Dasarath Devbarma, the 'uncrowned king of the Tripuris', continued to highlight the regional problems of Tripura: refugee rehabilitation, increasing loss of tribal lands to the Bengali and the absence of democratic bodies in the State (Bhattacharyya 1999: 166).

When the CPI/CPI-M unit of Tripura was so much engaged in the dynamics of parliamentary and electoral politics – which was a proof of much moderated Left radicalism in any case – the inner-party self-critical understanding the CPI forewarned the party of the danger of pursing parliamentary politics at the cost of the real mass movements and class struggle. The late Saroj Chanda, the then-party Secretary wrote:

> For quite some time the Tripura party had over-emphasized the parliamentary work at the cost of the mass movement. Its best leaders have spent most of their time in the Parliament and Legislative Assembly. As a result, the middle-class intelligentsia without links either with the workers, or the peasants has come to occupy leading positions by showing off their strength in the doctrine of Marxism.
> 
> (Quoted in *Tripurar Katha*, May 27, 1960: 1)

Such self-critical assessment has been resorted to by the CPI-M subsequently. The party's national level assessment as to why the CPI-M had failed in the 1988 elections – first time so far – to a Congress-TUJS alliance – stated as much:

> election experience when self-critically reviewed shows that there has been a tendency on *rely on the ministry instead of relying on class struggle* and mass initiative. Independent mass activity and initiative suffered because of this *undue dependence on ministerial actions*.
> 
> (CPI-M 1988: 3; emphasis added)

Those were merely inner-party self-criticisms which carry little value for the party which had long abjured the method of radical political action and settled down deeply in the niceties of parliamentary politics and acquired governmental power at the State-level to govern. Since the early 1950s when the CPI had oriented itself to constitutionalism and parliamentary politics, neither it nor the CPI-M (born in 1964) ever looked back.

It was in 1977 State Assembly elections held in December 1977 that the Left Front under the leadership of the CPI-M won overwhelmingly by obtaining 53 seats (all by the CPI-M) with 49.2 per cent popular votes. The outstanding victory of the CPI-M in 1977 must also be related to the party's participation in two short-lived coalition governments in 1977 – first with Congress for Democracy (CFD) and then Janata. Large-scale defections from Congress took place (somewhat echoing the all-India events), and the Ministry headed by Sukhomoy Sen Gupta fell.[4] In April 1977 a CFD-CPI-M coalition under the leadership of Profulla Das was sworn in. This also fell in July and another Janata-CPI-M coalition government was sworn in under the leadership of Radhika Ranjan Sen Gupta. As a price of collaboration, the CPI-M got among others two very important portfolios of Finance and Home, which were very skillfully utilized: by publishing the failure of the rival parties and also by distributing some patronages to its supporters and sympathizers which helped build a platform needed for winning the next elections the same year. The party's victory in 1977 was a foregone conclusion. The CPI-M alone won 51 seats with a total vote share of 51.10 per cent (Table 12.8.4) and with its Left partners, a further 4.97 per cent. In a parliamentary and fast past the post-electoral system, winning more than 60 per cent of popular votes was a remarkable achievement indeed. The Left Front led by the CPI-M continued to maintain its political support bases in the State. Even when it conceded defeat to the Congress-TUJS alliance in 1988 it secured more seats than Congress.

## Multi-party electoral competition and the rise to power of the left in 1978

The multi-party competition in Tripura has been connected to federalism and governance. It has also marked the electoral struggle at the State and national levels (Tripura has two seats in the Lok Sabha, and one seat in the Rajya Sabha). It is remarkable that the political competition in Tripura exhibits a high degree of political institutionalization indicated among others by the negligible performance of the Independents, and greater degree of the party-oriented political loyalties in all the elections held since 1952 in the State.

Popular participation in elections should be considered as an important indicator of political integration. In the otherwise, isolated North East, this factor assumes added significance. Counterfactually, the deliberate non-participation in the electoral process by political parties and groups seems to indicate the boycott of the political process itself, and a radical opposition to it. Judged thus, Tripura's records are very satisfactory indeed. At the State level, beginning with a low 47.1 per cent in 1952 (Electoral College), the popular participation in the State has gone up: 64.6 per cent (1957), 71.2 per cent (1967), 65.6 per cent (1972), 78.4 per cent (1977), 81.7 per cent (1983) and 82.0 per cent (1988).[5] In the Lok Sabha (Parliament) elections too, the popular participation was very high. In the Lok Sabha elections in 1977, for instance, the turn-out was as high as 70 per cent. In 2013, the turn-out was as high as 91.82 per cent and in Lok Sabha elections in a year later it was 84.92 per cent.

But in the next elections in 1983 (post-riots), the CPI-M's strength shrank to 37 seats leaving six to TUJS and 12 to Congress. The party's vote share declined by

*Table 12.1* Performance of political parties in State Assembly elections in Tripura in 1977 (60 seats)

| Political parties | Seat won | Vote received (%) | Total votes received (%) |
|---|---|---|---|
| CPI | 0 | 4.94 | – |
| CPI-M | 51 | 47.00 | 51.10 |
| INC | 0 | 17.76 | 17.76 |
| Janata Party | 0 | 10.46 | 10.46 |
| FB-L | 1 | 1.04 | – |
| RSP | 2 | 1.66 | – |
| TUJS | 4 | 7.93 | 17.02 |
| IND | 2 | 4.11 | – |
| Others | 0 | 9.21 | – |

Source: *Election Commission of India (website) (26/7/17)*

about 3 per cent (Bhattacharyya and Nossiter 1988: 147). The relative decline in strength of the Left was certainly related to the LF government's poor handling of the June 1980 ethnic riots which gave a wrong message to the tribals as well as the Bengalis; the latter proved by the Congress' rise from zero seats in 1977 to 12 in 1983, and the TUJS's (a tribal party (1967–2002) better performance from four seats in 1977 to six in 1983. Emboldened by some rise in electoral strength, the Tripura Tribal Upajati Juva Samity (TUJS), a tribal youth organization (formed on 11 June 1967 but became defunct, and ceased to exist by 2003[6]), a pre-election coalition of the TUJS and Congress (led by Congress), thus far are arch-political rivals, came to power in the 1988 State Assembly elections and formed government. The declaration of the State as 'Disturbed Area' (under the AFSPA) just prior to the elections helped the coalition win.

When placed in relation to Left Front debacle in West Bengal since 2011, Left Front's record in Tripura is outstanding.

Since India's Statehood in 1972, the site of electoral contestation shifted to the State level. The competition was intense but took the standard institutional channel. While the LF has been winning majority in all State Assembly elections since 1977 (during 1972–77 Congress was in power) and governing the State, in 1988 the Left conceded defeat to Congress-TUJS alliance when LF won more seats (28) than Congress (25 seats) but with its alliance partner TUJS (seven), the Congress-TUJ alliance formed the government.[7] But since the 1990s the LF have continued to maintain its sway over the State Assembly. In the last assembly elections in 2013 the Left Front won 50 (CPI-M alone 49) out of 60 seats (Table 10.2 in Chapter 10).

The results of the State Assembly elections in 1993 show that the Left Front nearly fully recovered its bases of support winning 47 seats out of 60 leaving only ten to Congress, and a single seat to the TUJS. The Left's performance in this proved beyond doubt that the TUJS' so-called ethnic space was spurious, and Congress was not a force to reckon with in Tripura.

The Left Front has not only fully consolidated its political bases but left no space for the tribal outfits in 2013. The 7.59 per cent of popular votes obtained by the INPT is the traditional ethnic tribal base but the IPFT, a small break away outfit, which had merged in 2003 with the IPFT is far too negligible.

The CPI-M's successive electoral victory since 1993 is a proof of the party's deep roots among the tribals and the Bengalis. Second, this is also a solid confirmation of the better record of governance delivered by the Left government in Tripura. As we have seen in Chapter 3, comparatively Tripura has improved its governance records since 1981, although the post-1991 records have been very challenging. The late Dasarath Devbarma (1916–2014) was made the Chief Minister in Tripura in 1993, a post he served full term until 1998 (11 April 1993 to 10 March 1998) – [8] it was a recognition of the original tribal base of the party in the State and to reassure the tribals of their special importance to the CPI-M. This added to ensure better inter-community cohesion in the State. With a secure and reassured tribal base, Manik Sarkar took the baton in 1998 and continue to govern the State as a successful Chief Minister in a difficult State.

*Table 12.2* Political party performance in the State Assembly elections in Tripura in 2013 (total seats = 60)

| National Parties | Seats contested | Seats won | Votes polled (%) |
|---|---|---|---|
| BJP | 50 | 0 | 1.54 |
| CPI | 2 | 1 | 1.57 |
| CPI-M | 55 | 49 | 48.11 |
| INC | 48 | 10 | 36.53 |
| NCP | 2 | 0 | 0.03 |
| AIFB | 1 | 0 | 0.70 |
| JD (U) | 1 | 0 | 0.02 |
| RSP | 2 | 0 | 1.95 |
| SP | 4 | 0 | 0.08 |
| AMB | 16 | 0 | 0.25 |
| CPI(ML) (L) | 10 | 0 | 0.16 |
| INPT | 12 | 0 | 7.59 |
| IPFT | 17 | 0 | 0.46 |
| SUCI | 6 | 0 | 0.05 |

Source: *Election Commission of India*.

Notes: NCP = Nationalist Congress Party; JD (U) Janata Dal (United); IPFT = Indigenous People's Front; IPFT = Indigenous People's Front of Tripura; SUCI = Socialist Unity Centre.

## Globalization and governance in Tripura since the 1990s: new challenges

By the 1990s the governing political institutions in Tripura had taken roots; the political parties have learnt to play by the rules of the game; insurgency was nearly absent; and the Left, particularly the CPI-M, established its hegemonic control over the helm of affairs. But from the early 1990s India embraced macroeconomic reforms which opened the market for investment (indigenous and foreign), and encouraged more and more private capitalist investment. In the wake of the above, some of India's States such as Gujarat, Tamil Nadu, Andhra Pradesh and Maharashtra reaped the benefits and emerged as India's 'forward States' (Dua and Singh ed. 2003). The CPI-M nationally also tuned to the reforms (with its reserve of criticisms!) since 2004. In West Bengal where the CPI-M led Left Front governed (until 2011) began to acquire land for industrialization with the then Chief Minister Buddha deb Bhattacharjee re-christened 'the Brand Buddha'. In Tripura, nothing of the sort happened because the State did not have the required infrastructure, or the land to acquire for private investment. During the whole period of 1991–2015, no FDI flew into Tripura. As a party the State CPI-M had also to toe the all-India party line, and pointed out many blemishes of the macroeconomic reforms, and seemed to bank on the Left alternative models of development in some Latin American countries. (CPI-M State Committee Report Tripura 2015, unpub.) At the home ground, the Government of Tripura's Tripura Human Development Report (2007) was ready to go for some compromise: 'The

Government is willing to explore partnership with the private sectors in order to expand social infrastructure' (THDR: A Summary 2007: 33).

But what has been possible (and successfully) in the real realm of affairs to utilize the governmental machinery at State and sub-State levels for delivery of a whole range of public goods and services, mostly Central government's various social welfare programmes. In this respect, the State has remained perhaps the best governed State in the region. During 2006-07–2013-14, for example, in implementation of the MNRGA 2005 (100 days rural employment guarantee scheme), the largest flagship programme of the Centre in recent years, Tripura's success rates ranged from 97.48 per cent to 100 per cent. In 2012–13, one district (Unokoti) in Tripura received the best national award for creating the highest (100 per cent) work days; in 2012–13 the State as a whole achieved the first rank in the country implementing the above programme (Roy 2015: 279). The political crime as a result of insurgency activities has lessened to a large extent: insurgent event as the major indicator of such activities decreased from 184 in 2004–05 to only 7 in 2014 (Roy 2015: 293, 2011: 253). One would like to correlate the better delivery of public goods and service with better rule of law.

The important question is how we account for the above within the overall context of the region and India as a whole. Our first explanatory variable is the effective and committed political actors in government – the well-organized, disciplined and coherent leadership of the CPI-M, which has not experienced any split since 1964. The Chief Minister Mr Manik Sarkar is pragmatic in matters of implementing various social welfare programmes funded by the Centre and those of the State government's own. He is a CPI-M Polit Bureau member and a Marxist par excellence seemingly guarding the 'party line'. In Tripura he takes things in context, defends provincialism in the garb of 'unity-in-diversity' (inter-ethnic harmony) (interview on 20/2/15 at Agartala); and makes full utilization of all funds that are available from the Centre knowing well that the State is heavily dependent upon the Centre for funds. In West Bengal, the Chief Minister, Mamata Banerjee refused to greet the new Prime Minister Narendra Modi. In Tripura, Manik Sarkar extended a full red carpet welcome to him in Agartala and asked the media persons: 'What is wrong in inviting PM Modi? Every state has its own specific problems, characteristics, advantages and disadvantages; the decision is for every respective state to take on its own' (CNN-IBN dated 1/12/14). A Special Category State with heavy dependence on the Centre for funding projects, Tripura can hardly hope to ignore, let alone, antagonize, the Centre.

The second explanatory variable is continuity in policy thanks to enduring political stability except for a brief period.[9] In other States in the region, the fragile party systems, and factious political leadership fell victims to crash ethnic politics and contributed to political instability and chaos. In Tripura, the Communist Party regimentation has rather been functional in this respect in holding on to political stability. The Tripura State unit of the CPI-M is of course dominated by the Bengalis; demographic logic was unavoidable. But the CPI-M leadership which includes Bengalis and tribals has never reneged on tribal issues and the overriding need to protect their identity. While in the rest of the region, ethnic identity has remained very strong; in Tripura, the tribal comrades have recognized the value of tribal interests and identity but not at the cost of a 'class perspective'.

And yet, India's reforms have posed new challenges to Tripura as well as for other States in the region. For such Special Category States in the region (now defunct), what has mattered and served to ensure relatively durable order (in the midst of Baruah's over-stated concern of 'durable disorder') Baruah (2005), Tripura like her regional brothers and sisters, has failed to attract any FDI inflows. The following are the records of any FDI inflows in the region:

Assam: 2008 (42 million $); 2009–10 = 11; 2010–11 = 8; 2011–12 = I and 2012–13 = 0.02)

(Source: www.rbi.org.on/scripts/bs_view (20/2/16)

But the LFG in Tripura has already developed a more positive approach to development in tune with India's reforms. But what keeps the government concerned is the fledgling financial resources now that the earlier supports from the Centre/Planning Commission have been decreased. 'The government has failed to clear up the dues to many suppliers and contractors which has not happened before; such a problem is real' (Samiron Roy, Editor, *Tripura Darpan* in a telephonic interview on 28/10/16).

If governance is a matter of efficient and adequate delivery of goods and services – a yardstick much highlighted in the recent global understanding of the subject – the State' performance during 1981–2011, particularly from 1991, remains very high, comparable to many advanced States in India. Since the early 1990s, a lot of funds have flowed down to the States from the Centre for a number of welfare and empowerment programmes.

What all these policy effectiveness data suggest is that first, these States received various development and special grants from the Centre (Manor 2012) including the UPA government's Backward Regions Grant Fund (Bhattacharyya 2012), which is an area development programme. Second, they have a positive

*Table 12.3* Grants released (and utilized) under BRGF to the States in the North East (sum in crores = 10 million)

| States | 2005–06 | 2006–07 | 2007–08 | 2010–11 |
| --- | --- | --- | --- | --- |
| Arunachal Pradesh | 7.50 | 7.50 | 00 | 3.4 |
| Assam | 7.50 | 52.50 | 15.00 | 22.2 |
| Manipur | 15.00 | 15.00 | 00 | 23.39 |
| Mizoram | 7.50 | 15.00 | 00 | 6.0 |
| Meghalaya | 00 | 15.00 | 00 | 22.2 |
| Nagaland | 7.50 | 22.5 | 00 | 12.00 |
| Tripura | 7.50 | 15.00 | 00 | 2.73 |

Source: *Press Information Bureau (Government of India)* (www.pib.nic.in/newsite/erelease.aspx?relied=30298 (accessed on 20.3.15) and also (planningcommission.nic.in/reports/peoreport/peo/ser_brgf1206.pdf (accessed on 21.3.17).

impact on the relative decrease in violence, militancy and ethnic conflicts recognized as also in the official Punchi Commission Reports (2010).

The post-implementation evaluation of the programme by the Planning Commission's Study team (PEO Report No. 223) show implementation of the allocations of funds released to various States. In terms of ranking done on the performance of the States, the States in the region have done differently. In terms of percentage of utilization of funds, the following was the record of the States in the North East: Nagaland (91.67 per cent); Manipur (69.31 per cent); Mizoram (97.50 per cent); Tripura (67.3 per cent); Meghalaya (48.44 per cent); Assam (43.74 per cent) and Arunachal Pradesh (14.71 per cent) It is seen that some of the States have performed poorly (Assam and A. P., for example) but since this was to do with State capacity and the institutional arrangements of the agencies (such as the Panchayats and Municipalities), things have to be seen in perspective. We ought to keep in mind that the States are to implement other developmental and welfare programmes and schemes of the Central government. For instance, these States are also to implement the Border Region Development Programme (Table 12.5).

## Governance and public policy effectiveness

Tripura's relative political order and stability when placed in relation to the North East as a whole (except Sikkim incorporated in 2012) would seem on the face of it a little surprising. Since the Left Front was returned to State-level administration in 1978, the State has witnessed continuous institutionalization of political participation. Today in a land of some 3.7 million people, there is a (60-member) Legislative Assembly, one ADC (for the tribal dominated areas comprising two-thirds of the territory of Tripura) and 527 directly elected Village Committees of the ADC[10] (decentralization within decentralization) (total members 4,165), one 35-member Municipality at Agartala (State capital), 15 Nagar Panchayats[11] with the total members of 157, four District Councils (Zilla Parishad) (total members being 82), 23 Block Panchayats (total member 299) and 511 Village Panchayas (total members 5,295) (Roy 2011). The level of participation in elections, particularly at sub-State levels is very high. In the most recent elections to the ADC in 2015, the rate of popular participation was 83 per cent. The section above indicated the sustenance of party competition at State and the ADC levels despite some odds. Political stake holders including the erstwhile tribal insurgent groups such as the TNV have even forged electoral alliance with the arch rivals of the tribes such as Congress and joined as junior partner in coalition governments at State and sub-State (ADC) levels. In this Tripura is somewhat odd within the region in the sense that in this State, as distinguished from the rest of the region (except Sikkim) democratic and institutionalized political participation offers the only option for power-sharing. While the ADC itself is a decentralized governing body for the tribal dominated areas of Tripura, powers have been further decentralized through the passage of the Village Committee Act in 1994 when the State government was under the LF but the ADC was under the control of the IPFT

*Table 12.4* Tripura's growth of GSDP (2004–5 to 2013–14)

| Year | Amount in INR (Crores) |
| --- | --- |
| 2004–05 | 8903.53 |
| 2007-o8 | 11797.07 |
| 2011–12 | 19973.91 |
| 2012–13 | 22697 |
| 2013–14 | 26809.60 |

Source: *Economic Review 2013–14 (Government of Tripura)*

*Table 12.5* Per capita income in Tripura (2004–5 to 2013–14)

| Year | Amount in INR |
| --- | --- |
| 2004–05 | 24394 |
| 2005–06 | 24668 |
| 2006–07 | 29081 |
| 2007–08 | 31111 |
| 2008–09 | 35587 |
| 2009–10 | 39815 |
| 2010–11 | 46050 |
| 2011–12 | 50850 |
| 2012–13 | 57402 |
| 2013–14 | 69705 |

Source: *Economic Survey 2013–14 (Government of Tripura)*

(until 1995), a local tribal political outfit. The spurt in ethnic insurgency in the late 1980s and the early 1990s could not derail the much-entrenched democratic process in the State. Much credit goes to the Left for this. Tripura's better governance has been a function (among others) of this multi-level institutionalized political participation to which the Left in Tripura have remained committed.

Tripura's governance delivery, as we shall examine shortly, was accompanied by a steady growth (Table 12.4). During 2013–14 Tripura's growth rate was very good at 8.9 per cent (Economic Survey Government of Tripura 2013–14). The data on per capita income in Tripura further substantiate the claim that growth, governance and social inclusion can go together. Per capita income in Tripura has registered growth over the years since 2003–04. The data presented Table 12.4 and 12.5 reflects the second decade of India's reforms, and record relative prosperity.

What is the track record of Tripura in respect of public policy effectiveness in the last three decades or so, i.e. the period of India's reforms? How has the State coped with 'transforming' India? The Ministry of Development of North

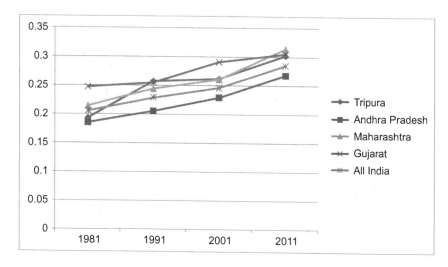

*Figure 12.1* Public Policy Effectiveness Index in Tripura compared to some Forward States in India (1981–2011) (PEI)

Source: Prepared on the basis of data in Malhotra (2014: 148–9)

Eastern Region (DoNER) in its report (2011) recorded satisfactory improvement for the States in the region in HDI scores, and showed that between 19993–94 and 2004–05, Tripura's record in HDI improved from 0.327 to 0.447 (DoNER 2011: 4–7). The report stated: 'the economic performance of States like Tripura and Sikkim in recent years take their per capita incomes (NSDP) well above those of other North Eastern States' (DoNER 2011: 6).

On the basis of more detailed and more up-to-date statistical analysis undertaken by Malhotra (2014),[12] we will examine Tripura's policy effectiveness in terms of a set of variables over the last three decades since 1981 in relation to other States in the region and some Forward States in India too. The Public Policy Effectiveness Index prepared by Malhotra (2014) is a composite index of some other variables which are composite themselves.

It is seen that between 1981 and 2011 Tripura improved its position; its level of performance in 2011 was above all-India, Andhra Pradesh and very close to Gujarat. Its index value of performance in 2011 0.302 was in the same league as Maharashtra and Gujarat.

The Rule of Law Index (ROLI) is a component of the Public Policy Effectiveness Index (PEI), but itself a composite index of four sub-indexes: law enforcement (police personnel per 10,000people), security of person and property and rates of crime under IPC and SLL (per 100,000persons) and crime against women. Overall these sub-indexes are suggestive of the level of administration of justice, legal redress to remedy and so on. Table 8.12 shows that since 1981, Tripura has performed well above all-India and three advanced States of Gujarat, Andhra Pradesh and Maharashtra. Of the other States the situation in Gujarat and Andhra Pradesh were abysmal.

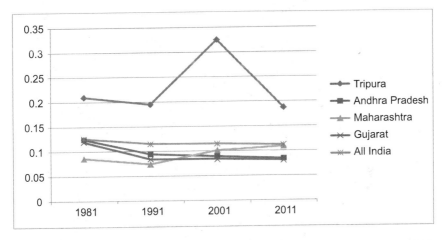

*Figure 12.2* Rule of Law Index in Tripura compared to India's Forward States (1981–2011)
Source: Prepared on the basis of data in Malhotra (2014: 148–9)

This raises a very interesting question that better rule of law and far better performance in other indexes of development do not correlate; also, that today those Forward States are considered better destinations for trade, commerce and investment when their track records in matters of rule of law were so abysmal (Table 12.9).

The development of infrastructure has attracted most attention in India in recent years thanks to the drives for reforms. Throughout India, all States and regions have registered improvement in this respect.

In Malhotra's study, the most important sub-index of PIDI is the access of household to electricity, water and toilets (Malhotra 2014: 55). While road connectivity and quality housing are important, particularly road connectivity, since the State is not fully responsible for proving housing to all. In the case of Tripura, it is seen that starting with a very low index (0.098 in 1981) there has taken place remarkable improvement over the next decades and in 2011 its performance value of 0.416 even placed it above Maharashtra.

The issue of social opportunity is part of a larger global debate centering on individuals' ability to live a 'socially meaningful life' (Malhotra 2014: 34). The writings of Sen and others, as well as the UNDP have focused on the means that ensure better social opportunity, the ones that build individual's capabilities in a world marked by larger extent of inequalities and discrimination (Dreze and Sen 2015). Malhotra has identified three sub-indices of SOI: education, health and income attributes. Each of them again is composite of other variables (Malhotra 2014: 34–5). Tripura's performance records in this regard again are not only above the all-India level but also above Andhra Pradesh and Maharashtra. In respect of LOI, Tripura's records were already better than that of all-India level and Andhra

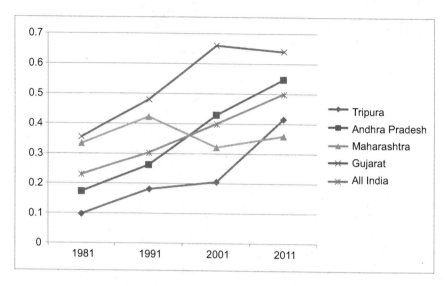

*Figure 12.3* Physical Infrastructure Development Index (PIDI) in Tripura compared to India's Forward States (1981–2011)

Source: Prepared on the basis of data in Malhotra (2014: 162–3)

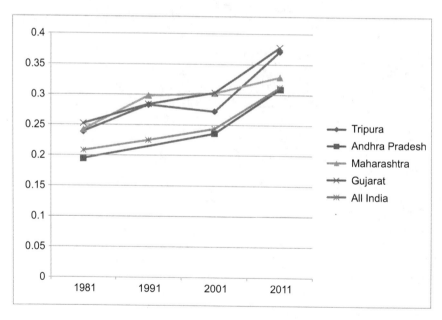

*Figure 12.4* Social Opportunity Index in Tripura compared to India's Forward States (1981–2011)

Source: Prepared on the basis of data in Malhotra (2014: 154–5).

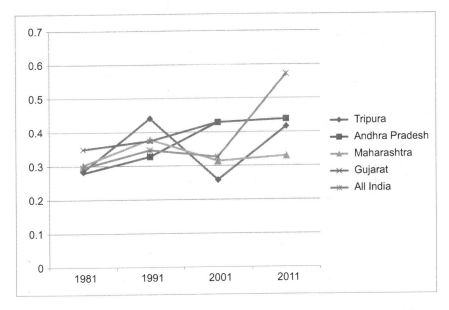

*Figure 12.5* Livelihood Opportunity Index in Tripura compared to India's Forward States (1981–2011)

Source: Prepared on the basis of data in Malhotra (2014: 152–3)

Pradesh. In 2011 its score of index value was 0.371 which was higher than that of Andhra Pradesh, Maharashtra and all-India level. Gujarat has the index value in 2011 of 0.378 which made it in league with Tripura (Malhotra 2014: 166).

It is seen that all the States in the region show improvement in 1991 over 1981 in PEI which in most cases are better than all-India average. It is also seen that although Tripura in the North East is not the highest scorer but its records in Physical Infrastructure Development Index, Social and Livelihood Opportunity Index and the Rule of Law Index places it in comparable position with India's advanced States, and in many cases above them.

## Political-organizational fall outs

The Left parties, to be particular, the CPI-M, are organization-driven and disciplined compared to the individual leader-centric parties across the country and the North East too. In the case of the CPI-M in Tripura, the better governance in the State and the active party organization remain correlated. The better governance in Tripura has produced better effects on the party organization too. The party factionalism that there is, is hardly, if ever, visible in public. The party has not experienced any split since 1965 and the leadership change has never raised many eye brows. In the last State Conference of the party in Tripura held on 25–28 February 2016, the party recorded growth in party membership from

76,636 in 2014 to 87,691 in 2016 (*People's Democracy* Vol. XL, No. 27 July 03, 2016). The rate of growth in party membership between 2011 and 2014 is stated to be very satisfactory at 12.61 per cent compared to West Bengal, where the party is yet to come of its crisis after conceding defeat to the TMC in 2011. The social composition of the Tripura party shows that there are 25.76 per cent women members including 265 Branch Secretaries from among them – which is double the all-India figure for the CPI-M as a whole. Of the total party members (excluding those vast numbers in various mass fronts of the party) the Scheduled Tribes constitute 35.69 per cent, which is some 6 per cent higher than their contribution to the total population. The Scheduled Castes constitute 19.36 per cent of the party members, and the OBCs 21.98 per cent (CPI-M Tripura 2015: 58). In terms of class composition of party membership, the Tripura State Committee of the CPI-M has overwhelmingly penetrated among the common people i.e. workers, landless agricultural labourers, poor peasants and middle peasants. The middle classes comprise 17.62 per cent (CPI-M 2015: 57).

The Tripura party and its various mass front continue to oppose the neo-liberal policies of the Centre and defend the social welfare State and public sector. It points out various pitfalls of withdrawal of public expenditure (which though on balance is not warranted!) but winning any elections in the State has remained the top most priority of the Left led by the CPI-M. In the (inner-party) Political Organizational report of the 21st State Conference of the party in 2015, which was held just before the elections to the ADC the following was the instruction to the party functionaries under a sub-heading 'Jump in for winning the ensuing ADC elections':

> Immediately after this conference the ADC elections is going to be held in May 2015. The whole party must jump in. The results of the elections are significant for the State's territorial integrity, peace and harmony and national integration. This is intimately connected with development in the ADC areas too. Some forces are trying to revive the insurgents and terrorists which have remained so far marginalized.
>
> (CPI-M 2015: 54)

This is outstanding proof yet again of the party's deep and all out electoral orientation as a liberal democratic force.

## Conclusion

The above detailed analysis of data supplemented by the documentary evidences suggest that an enduring cabinet stability, well-organized and discipline party (CPI-M in particular) and a cohesive political leadership, adherence to political practices of democratic political competition (multiparty) have combined to produce effective governance effects in Tripura. Tripura's relative success in identity accommodation through the instrumentality of the ADC compared with unresolved sub-State-level identity accommodation in West Bengal for the

Gorkhas in Darjeeling, and the creation of a separate State for the tribal in the form of Jharkhand out of Bihar is the best performer. The better indices of rule of law, social opportunity, livelihood opportunity and physical infrastructure which ensures better access to electricity, safe drinking water, toilets, road connectivity etc. Livelihood opportunity in our case entails such variables as labour force participation in the main economic activity, durability of employment, rate of employment etc. Finally the Social Opportunity Index, according to Malhotra (2014), includes such variables as access to education, health care, health care facilities at government hospitals, female literacy and schools per 1000 population. All in all, these are all indices of social inclusion by any sense of the term. In Tripura, then, better governance has been accompanied by better social inclusion although in terms of growth Tripura's records are far below India's. The Tripura is an important illustration for the Indian States that governance is possible despite many difficulties; ethnic conflict can be managed by appropriate constitutional reforms and power-sharing; and that when growth is accompanied by social inclusion, better governance is produced. As we have seen in Chapter 11 above, appropriate institutionalization of minority tribal ethnic identity in Tripura in the form of the ADC ever since 1985 – longest serving in India – which has added to the making of better governance in the State by further decentralization to the grassroots and power-sharing at the very bottom of society. The Left in Tripura is no longer a militant force – militancy was given up by the then CPI-in the early 1950s – but have performed (and continue to do), a very useful function in taking care of managing ethnic radicalism in the State by multi-pronged means – democracy, participation, institutionalized party competition and the delivery of public goods efficiently and effectively.

## Notes

1 In 2013, for example, the CP-M alone got 49 seats and the CPI a lone seat out of the Left Front's total of 50 Legislative Assembly seats.
2 It is further buttressed by the fact that the party holds political sway at the sub-State-level representative bodies and the student councils in the colleges where elections are held.
3 In 1957 the CPI along with its Left partner got itself elected to State-level government which made a history of sort as being the first democrtically elected Marxist government in the world (See Nossiter 1982 for a full account).
4 Observing the defections and political in-fighting, we described the situation as 'the law of the surrounding jungle encroaching on politics' (Bhattacharyya and Nossiter 1988: 149).
5 Bhattacharyya and Nossiter (1988: 147).
6 See Bhattacharyya (1991: 143–70) for the analysis of social basis of the TUJS up to 1993. The party increasingly lost ground and failed to make much inroads into the ethnic space in the State. In the 1998 Assembly elections in Tripura, the TUJS got four seats but left the ground. In 2003, the TUJS and the IPFT (Indigenous People's Front of Tripura) merged to form a new party called the INPT (Indigenous Nationalist Party of Tripura) which won four seats in 2003 but drew a blank in 2008.
7 This particular election was held under exceptional circumstances when the State was declared 'disturbed' under the AFSPA (1958); large violence and rigging were also reported.

8 He died on 14 October 1998 aged 82.
9 During 1988–93 a Congress-TUJS-TNC coalition government was in power. Two Cabinets with two different Chief Ministers had to take the oath. Party factionalism was rampant.
10 This is another institutional innovation by the ADC for further decentralization within the ADC by first legislating on the Village Committee Act in 1994 (when the INPT was governing the ADC 1990–95), but the LF was in power at the State level. The 527 Village Committees are since being elected regularly at the interval of five years. These are like the village panchayats to cater to the needs of local communities. The LF has won an overwhelming majority of 520 out of 587 (increased) in the elections held on 24 February 2016 (*The Shillong Times* 29 February 2016). After 2011 elections to the Vilage Committees of the total the women elected members some 1,662 held the office of chairpersons at the VC level; 3,652 tribal memebrs held the same positions and of the SC members, 20 held that positions in the VCs (ADC, Khumlung, Tripura 2011).
11 Definition needed.
12 Malhotra (2014).

# Conclusion

As the first ever in-depth, empirically-based and comparative study of radical politics and governance in India's North East, this research monograph has explored the main contours of radical politics – ethnic and Left – and the institutionalization of the same for participation and governance in the North East with particular reference to Tripura – the only State in the region which has sustained for over half a century a tradition of Left politics, and governance since 1978. As a new study in Indian federalism and State politics, the book has sought to pioneer the methodological grounds of studying the operational dynamics of federalism at the State level – the level which has become the centre of Indian politics since the days of neo-liberal reforms in India since 1991. The comparative grid of the study has gone beyond the North East to compare the governance performance of the States in the region to India's advanced or Forward States. On the face of it, Left radicalism may not compare with ethnic radicalism, but our study has shown that there are several grounds where an institutionalized ethnic radicalism meets an institutionalized Left radicalism: the Left radicalism decided on their own to abjure violence and participate in liberal democratic politics (from the early 1950s) and take charge of governance when the opportunity arrives; ethnic radicalism has been persuaded to participate in power-sharing and governance following a rather complex process of negotiation for power-sharing, territorial autonomy and other means of accommodation of identity. In both cases, yesterday's rebels have transformed themselves into the stakeholders for tomorrow and the day after. In the rest of the region, the heavy weight of ethnic identity politics has monopolized all political space; in Tripura, the heavy weight of Left politics has done so including containing ethnic identity politics within the discourse of Left politics and governance. The comparative governance records of the States between 1981 and 2011 (in many cases far better than India's Forward States) strongly militate against the existing hypothesis of 'durable disorder' (Baruah 2005, 2009), and the so-called 'insurgency' thesis advanced by many accounts of the region (e.g., Bhaumik 2009). India's North East is no longer India's 'insurgent country' although there are insurgent elements, which is perhaps unavoidable given the geographical location of the region and the complex ethnic mosaic in them.

The relative success of governance and participation in the region is also to be explained as the success of what I have termed elsewhere (Bhattacharyya

2015, 2017) *diversity-claims*, which has entailed recognition of ethnic identity; conceding territorial concession to ethno-regional groups; expanded scope of power-sharing through the existing constitutional mechanisms or the amended ones when so needed. As a result of many decades of meeting the *diversity-claims* in the region – bifurcation of existing territory; recognition of the languages as the official languages even when the scripts of the same are not developed and available for use officially; up gradation of the existing territorial status from the District Council via Union Territory to Statehood; and differential territorial arrangements such as the 'Associate Statehood'. The flexible State responses to ethnic militancy coupled with the various special financial arrangements (e.g., Special Category Status) for the States in the region has worked as the carrot, as it were, for the rebels to become the stakeholders. Our records of governance in the region suggest a positive correlation between the fulfillment of *diversity-claims*, on the one hand, and the relatively better governance performance, on the other. Nagaland, Mizoram, Meghalaya and Tripura are cases in point. Assam, the largest State in terms of population has borne the brunt of new State creation in the region; it has experienced continuous State contraction by way of the creation of Nagaland, Meghalaya and Mizoram which were all once parts of Assam. However, this has resulted in better ethnic homogeneity to the population of Assam, but the State remains nonetheless very diverse. The Bodoland Territorial Council (BTC) (2003) for the Bodos – imposed by the Centre on Assam – did not solve any problems but created more (Bhattacharyya et al. 2017). The amended constitutional provision (6th Schedule of the Indian Constitution) for the BTC has over empowered the minority Bodos (less than 30 per cent of the population in the BTC areas, at the cost of the vast majority of other ethnic groups, and has served to create the perennial grounds for inter-ethnic conflict and violence. The BTC is an instance of the short-sighted approach to meet the *diversity-claims* that deviated grossly from the well-tasted approach India has followed since 1956 to accommodate diversity by territorial re-sizing.

What have been the democratic effects of meeting the *diversity-claims* in the region? Has it meant that the elite got power and not delivered? Has ethnic empowerment made any difference to the lives of the people? In a democracy, this empowerment is challenging, not only politically but also democratically. Democracy does not embower the ethnic rebels-turned political party for its own sake. There is always the probability that the today's ruling party sits in the Opposition tomorrow. Therefore, the governmental performance, not simply confined to better law and order, but in respect of delivering a whole lot of public goods such as infrastructure; better livelihood and social opportunities; more social inclusion, etc. is nowadays competitive and measurable. This is reflected in the overall index of what Malhotra (2014) called the Public Policy Effectiveness Index (PEI, for short). Our data derived from Malhotra show that the States in the region have performed well: except Assam, which has improved, but the rest of the States' performance records are well above the all-India average and well above the so-called Forward States in India (Tables. 3.9 and 3.10). The achievement of social inclusion – with respect to better access of the Scheduled Castes and Scheduled Tribes to safe drinking water, sanitation and electricity – in the region has remained remarkable. Except Assam, the rates are higher in the rest of the States than that of the all-India average as well as the Forward States of India. Tripura's records on per capita (PPP) income have improved remarkably (see Chapter 12). In respect of delivering governance the performance of Left Tripura is comparable with its neighbours except perhaps the greater success achieved in Tripura in accommodation of minority tribal identity through the agency of the ADC. But then we do need more detailed researches and comparable data on the other such bodies operating in the rest of the region to arrive at any definitive conclusion. The basic point made here is that in governance terms the Left can hardly claim greater merit because it is found out that Tripura's records are comparable with her neighbours, and in some cases, are lesser than the latter.

This raises two pertinent questions. First, the Left in Tripura has been integrating itself with the liberal democratic political institutions since the early 1950s; it remained as an Opposition until 1978, and challenger to governance. But with its rise to power in 1978 the Left has been able to govern this difficult State. Its integration process since the early 1950s remains long drawn; as an electoral force it has engaged itself in the liberal democratic politics at any level of the polity although its terms of engagement are two-tiered; as a Marxist party (CPI-M) it has a higher-level political discourse with the ideological paraphernalia of People's Democracy punctuated with doses of universalism; at the day-to-day mundane politics, it operates, and has to do so, in local terms and idioms for popular mobilization for garnering mass support to win elections. The all-India categories that one finds in the party's documents apparently have little local resonance, but in the final analysis it is the regional/local issues that matter, and the relevant categories that will convey the message. However, the major ideological plank of the CPI-M in Tripura as much as in Kerala and West Bengal remains a deeply seated anti-Centrism in the dynamics of India's federal politics in which the regional moorings of the States are to be couched in the language of deprivation and neglect by the Centre (Bhattacharyya 2017: 91–115).

Second, the history of integration of the ethnic rebels with India's liberal democratic politics is chequered. As we have seen in Chapter 3 above, a long period of ethnic radicalism was followed by negotiations and ethnic peace accords in favour of power-sharing and participation. But then there were individual trajectories of such processes of the concerned ethnic groups and the States. One logical follow up of the above was the basis of political integration of the ethnic rebels with India's liberal democratic institutions and processes. Therefore, the longevity and degree of integration of the groups varied in different States. Some rebels are yet to be accommodated more so because of their demands which are, to use the phrase from Mitra (Mitra 1998, 1999), 'transcendental' rather than 'transactional'. For instance, the ULFA's demand for sovereignty of Assam out of India until 2010[1] was 'transcendental', not 'transactional'. Any concession, territorial or otherwise, which is not within the framework of the Indian Constitution, is ruled out. The difficulty of conceding to the demands of the Nagas for a greater Nagaland and also for sovereignty[2] lies in the transcendental nature of such demand. Pending that, however, the State of Nagaland is one of the best performers in India in governance terms and has maintained the best rule of law record in the North East as well as in India during 1981–2011. In the post-Statehood period, the records of the State's political participation in the State Assembly elections have been spectacular: 78.37 per cent in 1969 to 90.19 per cent in 2013 (Table 3.3).

What does the Tripura experience suggest for the prospects of radical politics and governance in the State? After about six decades of campaign for democracy (read liberal) preceded by very violent communist insurgency (from the late 1940s to 1951) and adaptation to the compulsions of the rules of the game, the communists in Tripura (in this case mostly the CPI-M) have been fully institutionalized and become a party of liberal democratic politics. With a disciplined and well-knit party organizations (that includes a plethora of mass associations affiliated to the party) spread over the civil society with extensive penetration among the tribals, winning elections, provided there is democratic environment, for the Marxists has remained a relatively easier task. With vigorous and continuing campaign for democracy and participation, the Left has proved itself functional for the system, in encouraging more and more popular participation in the elections to various levels of the polity – from the State level down to the villages – and minimized the scope of any radicalism, ethnic and Left. Since 1965 when the party (CPI) split took place in Tripura, the party has not experienced any split along more radical lines, unlike in West Bengal, which experienced a major split in the CPI-M in 1969, giving birth to the extremist CPI-ML. While the inner-party cohesion is an added strength of the party in the State, any innovative and radical institutional framework as an alternative to the any institutional arrangements of Indian constitutional democracy has still remained in short supply in the discourse of the party at the State level or at the national level. Ironically, there were evidences of alternative governments during the period of the Reang rebellion and the communist insurgency during 1948–51 in the State.[3] But with the new parliamentary and electoral orientations of the Left since 1950/51 and their full-scale adaptation to the norms of India's liberal democratic system, Left radicalism is now part of history. The CPI-M in Tripura as a party of government and governance is its present and, arguably, future too.

The ethnic/nationality question, (Chapter 1) remains vexing for the Left in Tripura as elsewhere. The Indian Communist Party's (then CPI) historical identification with various merging nationalities in other parts of India had helped them to build mass bases but with shifting party lines (dictated from outside) meant that the party's, or its mass fronts', deep engagement in and identification with the national causes received only negative assessment by the changing party leadership. This has resulted in de-identification with such identity movements. This has also meant, predictably, the loss of grounds built. The case of Tripura, as our detailed examination has shown, was more complex. The problem of the nationalities here was acute. But while the communist failed elsewhere in India (if not in other countries), the Left in Tripura successfully combined a class perspective with tribal ethno-nationalism. The resolute efforts of the Left, the CPI-M, if effect, in Tripura in association with the main organization of the tribals, i.e., the GMP, has institutionalized the question of tribal nationalism in the form of the ADC and allowed the representative of the tribals to take charge of their self-governance through the Autonomous Council, a 30-member body (28 elected and two nominated) and some 532 Village Committees, all elected, at the grassroots since 1985 (and the VCs since 1994). This has served to minimize the depth of inter-ethnic conflicts, and the State has not witnessed since 1980 any inter-ethnic communal riots. The sense of acuteness of the nationality/ethnic question, as Bhattacharyya and Nossiter (1988) recorded, is now passé. The educated tribal youths today are aware of their identity but more as modern employment seekers in the larger market beyond Tripura. There are also good records of self-employment of the educated tribal youths in transport, small scale business and rubber plantation in the State. That the Left has toned down its criticism of the market and neo-liberal reforms is to be read in getting greater benefits accruing from the market and investment. This remains a remarkable governance success of the Left in Tripura (Chapter 11). Tripura's governance success, when placed in the regional context, demands an additional mark because unlike the tribal ethnic States in the region, the issue in Tripura has remained balancing between the tribals, on the one hand, and the non-tribal (and advanced nationality), on the other hand, the unavoidable historical fact and cruel memory on the part of the tribals that the State once belonged to the tribals.

Finally, the question remains: how did the Left in Tripura overcome, if any, the so-called 'translation' problems in applied Marxism, that Thompson (1987) had indicated long back and Kaviraj (2009) highlighted? How did they grapple with the unresolved issue of the relation between Marxism and the national/ethnic question? To be sure, the Left's success in Tripura can never be explained without reference to the intricate balance in inter-ethnic relations. The earlier generation of leaders of the CPI and CPI-M in Tripura considered this to be central to the success of the Left in Tripura. With a down-to earth approach, with fidelity to the local situation, the Left highlighted the problems of Tripura in the State as well as the national level. The CPI and the CPI-M MPs in Lok Sabha and Rajya Sabha raised the issue of Tripura's specific problems with regard to the restoration of lands illegally transferred to the settler Bengalis as well as the miserable plight of the hapless Bengali refugees who crossed the border in the wake of India's Partition. The issue entailed the needs for rehabilitation of both the communities, and at the same time restoration of land illegally transferred from the tribals to the Bengalis. The Left in Tripura operated in and through their local idioms and categories within the overall all-India party line(s) (the 'universals') since the early 1950s. It was possible to do so for two reasons. First, since the early 1950s the all-India party line centred on peaceful, constitutional methods of struggle, participation in electoral politics and the struggle for democracy (read liberal). Any radical turn would have had a lot of displacement effects for the local party, displacement of the real arena of struggle for the sake of the sake of any policy shifts. This served to tame Left radicalism in Tripura from the early 1950s. By contrast, in West Bengal the Left failed to institutionalize appropriately the Gorkha identity issues in the extreme north of the State[4] due mostly to the party's (CPI-M) lack of catholicity on the ethnic identity issue, and half-heartedness to share power with the minority ethnic group. Critics would argue that the CPI-M, a party predominantly composed of and led by the Bengalis, always tended to read the power-sharing issue with the Gorkha as amounting to the division of Bengal so there was always an emotional element provoked and cultivated. The partisan considerations could not be ruled out. The current dispensation in Kolkata is no different. In Tripura, the tribals were the original bases of the Left, so the representatives of the tribals (the GMP and its legendary leaders such as late Dasarath Devbarma) were very much part of any method worked out for co-existence of the class perspective (if any) and the tribal ethno-nationalism in the party's discourse and the governmental practices.

## Notes

1 In January 2010 one faction of the ULFA decided to drop its sovereignty demand, and accordingly, a tripartite agreement was signed on 3 September 2011, between the Governments of India and Assam and the ULFA faction for Suspension of Operations (SoO) against ULFA.
2 In a very perceptive analysis on the future of the ongoing Naga talks, Patricia Mukhim, a very senior journalist and Editor of *The Shillong Times* pointed out the inherent weakness in the Naga demands for sovereignty: with 16 major tribes, each with a sense of nationality of its own and every tribe having its village republics which is a crucial part of their culture, there will be divergent 'national' narratives. Naga nationalism is both a sentiment and movement'. (www.thehindu.com/todays-paper/tp-opinion/gathering-the-tribe/article19971597.ece) (*The Hindu* dated 3/11/17)sighted on 3/11/17.
3 There were evidences as well of such innovations in self-government in Bengal in the wake of the famous Tebhaga movements (of the share croppers demanding three-quarters share of the produce. (Dhanagare 1983).
4 The CPI-M-led Left Front government in West Bengal (1977–2011) took initiatives and established the Darjeeling District Gorkha Council but placed it under the authority of the State government. Eventually it did not work. The TMC government that took over since 2011 did not do much, and the problems remain unresolved. See for more details, Mitra and Bhattacharyya (2018).

# Bibliography

Adas, M. (1979) *Prophets of Rebellion Millenarian Protest Movements against the European Colonial Order*, Cambridge: Cambridge University Press.
ADC Annual Report 2010–11, Khumlung: ADC.
ADC Annual Plan 2011–12, Khumlung: ADC.
Alam, J. (1981) 'Dialectics of Capitalist Transformation and National Crystallizations: Some Notes on the National Question in India' Occasional Papers No. 42, Calcutta: Centre for Studies in Social Sciences.
Alavi, H. (1989) 'Politics of Ethnicity in India and Pakistan' in Alavi, H. and Harriss, J. (eds.) *Sociology of Developing Societies*, South Asia, London: Macmillan.
Anderson, B. (1983) *Imagined Communities: Reflections on the Origin and Spread of Nationalism*, London: Verso.
Anderson, P. (1979) *Considerations on Western Marxism*, London: Verso.
Anderson, P. (1983) *In the Tract of Historical Materialism*, London: Verso.
An Inner-party report of the CPI-M (Tripura) (1988) (unpub), Agartala: CPI-M.
Balibar, E. and Wallerstein, I. (1991) *Race, Nation, Class*, London: Verso.
Bakshi, P. M. (2017) *The Constitution of India*, New Delhi: Lexis-Nexis.
Banton, M. (1994) 'Modeling Ethnic and National Relations', *Ethnic and Race Relations Studies*, Vol. 17, No. 1.
Barnett, A. D. (1963) *The Communist Strategies in Asia: A Comparative Analysis of Governments and Parties*, London: Mall Press.
Bartoszewicz, M. G. (2015) '50 shades of Radicalism: an analysis of contemporary Parties in Europe', *Journal for the Study of Radicalism* (https://www.degruyter.com/view/j/ipcj.2015.17.issue-1/ipcj-2015-0003/ipcj-2015-0003.xml sighted on 31.1.18).
Baruah, B. (1985). *Language and National Question in North East India*, Guwahati: n.d.
Baruah, S. (2005) *Durable Disorder: Understanding the Politics of North East India*, New Delhi: Oxford University Press.
Baruah, S. (ed.) (2010) *Ethnonationalism in India: A Reader*, New Delhi: Oxford University Press.
Basic Statistics of North East India. (2015) (http://necouncil.gov.in/writereaddata/mainlinkFile/BasicStatistic2015.pdf sighted on 31.1.18).
Bhattacharjee, P. N. (1983) *The Jamatias of Tripura*, Agartala: Tribal Research Institute, Government of Tripura.
Bhattacharyya, H. (1990) 'Communism, Nationalism and Tribal Question in Tripura', *Economic and Political Weekly*, Vol. 25, No. 39, September.
Bhattacharyya, H. (1991) 'The TUJS, Ethnonationalism and the State in India', *The Socialist Perspective*, Vol. 19, No. 3, 143–70.

Bhattacharyya, H. (1992) 'Deinstitutionalization of Indian Politics: A Micro-Critique', *The Journal of Socio-Political Studiers* (Burdwan University), Vol. 1, Nos. 264–85.

Bhattacharyya, H. (1998) 'The Communist Movement in Tripura since the 1980s: Governmentalisation of the Movement and the Problem of Deidentification', *The Socialist Perspective*, Vol. 26, Nos. 1–2, June–September, 13–30.

Bhattacharyya, H. (1999) *Communism in Tripura*, Delhi: Ajanta.

Bhattacharyya, H. (2004) 'The CPI-M: From Rebellion to Governance' in Mitra, S. K. et al. (eds.) *Political Parties in South Asia*, Westport, CT: Praeger, 76–103.

Bhattacharyya, H. (2005) 'Federalism and Regionalism in India: Institutional Strategies and Political Accommodation of Identity', *Heidelberg Papers in South Asian and Comparative Politics*, Working Paper No. 27, May 2005, (ISSN 1617–5069) (Online Journal: www.hpsacp.uni-hd.de).

Bhattacharyya, H. (2008) 'Ethnic and Civic Nationhood in Inida: Concept, History, Institutional Innovations and Contemporary Challenges' in Saha, S C ed. *Ethnicity and Sccio-Political Changes in Africa and Other Developing Countries: A Constructive Discourse in State Building*, Landham, US: Lexington Books, 169–194.

Bhattacharyya, H. (2009) 'Globalization and Indian Federalism: Re-Assertions of States' Right' in Lofgreen, H. and Sarangi, P. (eds.) *The Politics and Culture of Globalization: India and Australia*, New Delhi: Social Science Press, 99–112.

Bhattacharyya, H. (2010) *Federalism in Asia: India, Pakistan and Malaysia*, London and New York: Routledge.

Bhattacharyya, H. (2012) 'UPA (2004–) and Indian Federalism A paradigm shift?' in Saez, L. and Singh, G. (eds.) *New Dimensions of Indian Politics The UPA in Power*, London: Routledge, 26–39.

Bhattacharyya, H. (2013a) *Asymmetric Federalism and the Left in Tripura* (unpublished report based on detailed research on the subject funded by the ICSSR, New Delhi, pp.1–146).

Bhattacharyya, H. (2015a) 'Indian Federalism and Democracy: The Growing Salience of Diversity-Claims over Equality-Claims in Comparative and Indian Perspective', *Regional and Federal Studies*, Vol. 25, No. 3, 211–27.

Bhattacharyya, H. (2015b) 'Political Parties and Democracy in South Asia: The CPI-M in India's Liberal Democracy' in Wolf, G. O. et al. (eds.) *Politics in South Asia: Culture, Rationality and Conceptual Flow*, Heidelberg: Springer, 1–16.

Bhattacharyya, H. (2017) 'West Bengal against the Centre: Continuity in Anti-Centrism in Indian Federal Politics' in Jain, S. K. (ed.) *Indian Federalism: Emrging Issues*, New Delhi: Kalpaz, 91–115.

Bhattacharyya, H. and Koenig, L. (eds.) (2016) *Globalization and Governance in India: Fresh Challenges to Society and Institutions*, Abingdon, Oxon: Routledge.

Bhattacharyya, H. and Nossiter, T. J. (1988) 'Communism in a Micro State: Tripura and the Nationalities Question' in Nossiter, T. J. N. *Marxist State Governments in India*, London: Pinters, 144–70.

Bhattacharyya, H. et al. (eds.) (2010) *The Politics of Social Exclusion in India: Democracy at the Crossroads*, London: Routledge.

Bhattacharyya, H. et al. (2017) 'Indian Federalism at the Crossroads: Limits of the Territorial Management of Ethnic Conflict', *India Review*, Vol. 16, No. 1, March, 149–78.

Bhaumik, S. (1996) *Insurgent Cross-fire: North East India*, New Delhi: Lancer Books.

Bhaumik, S. (1999) 'North-East India: The Evolution of a Post-Colonial Region' in Chatterjee, P. (ed.) *Wages of Freedom*, Delhi: Oxford University Press, 310–27.

Bhaumik, S. (2009) *Troubled Periphery: Crisis of India's North East*, New Delhi: Sage.

Bitner, E. (1968) 'Radicalism' in *The Encyclopedia of Social Sciences*, Vol.13, edited by Sills, D.L. London: Macmillan, 294–99.

Bottomore, T. (1979) *Political Sociology*, London: The Hutchinson.
Bottomore, T. et al. (eds.) (1983) *A Dictionary of Marxist Thought*, Oxford: Basil Blackwell.
Brass, P. R. (1990) *Ethnicity and Nationalism Theory and Practice*, New Delhi: Sage.
Brass, P. R. and Franda, M. F. (1973) *Radical Politics in South Asia*, Cambridge, MA: MIT Press.
Calhoun, C. (2009) 'Radicalism' in Kuper, A. and Kuper, J. (eds.) *The Social Science Encyclopedia*, London: Routledge.
Callinicos, A. (ed.) (1989) *Marxist Theory*, Oxford: Basil Blackwell.
Chakladar, S. (2004) *Sub-Regional Movements in India*, Kolkata: K. P. Bagchi & Co.
Chakrabarty, J. (1983) *Tripura Trish Theke Ashi (in Bengali) Tripura from 1930 to 1980)*, Agartala: Barnamala.
Chakrabarty, S. (1986) *Identity and Autonomy A Study of the Tripura Tribal Areas Autonomous District Council*, Kolkata: Ekushe.
Chakravarti, N. (1991) 'Note on Semi-Facists Terror in Tripura in the Background of Srrtius Ethnic Problem', *The Marxist*, Vol. 9, No. 1, 44–52.
Chanda, S. (ed.) (1983) *Duti Aprakashito dalil* (Two unpublished Documents), Agartala: Tripura Darpan.
Chandra, P. (1985) 'The National Question in Kashmir', *Social Scientist* Vol. 13, No. 6, 35–57.
Chatterjee, P. (1986) *The Nationalist Thought and the Colonial World: A Derivative Discourse*, London: Zed Books.
Chatterjee, P. (1993) *The Nation and Its Fragments*, Delhi: Oxford University Press.
Chaube, S. K. (1999/1978) *Hill Politics in India*, Hyderabad: Orient Longman.
Chiniha (Our Country) the Mouthpiece of the Tripura Nationalists edited by Bansi Thakur and Probhat Roy.
Chopra, S. (1984) 'Marxism and the National Question: An Overview' *Social Scientist* Vol. 12, No. 1, 3–14.
Cohen, G. A. (1978) *Karl Marx's Theory of History: A Defence*, Princeton, NJ: Princeton University Press.
Cohen, G. A. (1989) 'Reconsidering Historical Materialism' in Callinicos A.ed. *Marxist Theory*, Oxford: Oxford University Press.
Cohen, G. A. (1989) *History, Labour and Freedom*, Oxford: Oxford University Press.
Cohen, S. P. (1988) 'The Military and Indian Democracy' in Kohli, A. (ed.) *India's Democracy*, Princeton: Princeton University Press, 99–144.
Concise Oxford Dictionary (2011, 12edn), Oxford: Oxford University Press.
Concise Oxford Dictionary, 35th edn (2011).
Connor, W. (1984) *The National Question in Marxist-Leninist Theory and Strategy*, Princeton: Princeton University Press.
Connor, W. (1993) *Ethnonationalism: A Quest for Understanding*, Princeton: Princeton University Press.
Conversi, D. (ed.) (2002) *Ethnonationalism in the Contemporary World: Walker Connor and the Study of Nationalism*, London: Routledge.
Copland, I. (2002) *The Princes of India in the End Game of the Empire 1917–47*, Cambridge: Cambridge University Press.
CPI-M 'Why is Congress-TUJS Alliance and in Whose Interests?' (in Bengali), a pamphlet, Agartala: CPI–M.
CPI-M (2012) *Political Organizational Report of the 20th Party Congress* (Unpublished).
CPI-M (2015) *Political Organization Report of the 21st State Conference* 25–28 February (Unpublished) (in Bengali), Agartala.
Dange, S. A. (1951) *India: From Primitive Communism to Slavery*, Bombay: People's Publishing House.

Das, N. K. (2010) 'Identity Politics and Social Exclusion in India's North East: The Case for Redistributive Justice' in Bhattacharyya, H. et al. (eds.) *The Politics of Social Exclusion in India: Democracy a the Crossroads*, London: Routledge, 33–48.

Das Gupta, J. (1988) 'Ethnicity, Democracy and Development in India: Assam in a General Perspective' in Kohli, A. (ed.) *India's Demopcracy*, Princeton, NJ: Princeton University Press, 144–69.

Das Gupta, M. (1991) 'Land alienation among Tripura Tribes', *EPW*, Vol. 26, No. 36, September, 2113–2118.

Das Gupta, J. (2001) 'India's Federal Design and the multicultural national construction' in Kohli, A. (ed.) *The Success of India's Democracy*, Cambridge: Cambridge University Press, 49–77.

Datta, P. S. (ed.) (1995) *Ethnic Peace Accords in India*, New Delhi: Vikash Publishing House Pvt.

Davis, H. (1978) *Toward a Marxist Theory of Nationalism*, New York: Monthly Review Press.

Desai, A. R. (1976/1948) *The Social Background of Indian Nationalism*, Bombay: Popular Prakshan.

Devbarma, A. (1981) *The Riots in Tripura: A Survey*, Agartala: Tripura Darpan.

Devbarma, A. (1986) *The Primary Stage of the Communist Party and Democratic Movement in Tripura*, Agartala.

Devbarma, D. (1952) 'Some Important Decision of the GMP' (unpub.).

Devbarma, D. (1987) *Gnamuktiparihader Itihas* (A History of the Gana Mukti Parishad) (in Bengali), Calcutta: National Book Agency.

Devbarma, N. C. (2005) *History of The Land System and Land Management in Tripura (1872–2000)*, Agartala: Manjushree Publications.

Devbarma, N. and Devbarma, R. K. (2005) *Kokborok LIpi bitarka* (debate on the kpokborok script), Agartala: Tripura Darpan.

Dhanagore, P. N. (1983) *Peasants Struggles in India, 1920–50*, New Delhi: Oxford University Press.

Dhar, B. (2007) *Antorer aborodh* (in Bengali), (Inner Conflict), Agartala: Tripura Darpan.

DoNER (Department of the North Eastern Region), a separate Ministry set up in 2002.

Dreze, J. and Sen, A. (2015) *An Uncertain Glory India and Contradictions*, London: Penguin.

Dua, B. (1979) 'Presidential Rule in India: A Study in Crisis Politics', *Asian Survey*, Vol. 19, No. 6, June, 611–26.

Dua, B. and Singh, M. P. (eds.) (2003) *Indian Federalism in the New Millennium*, New Delhi: Monohar.

Dutta, B. (1982) *My Reminiscens of the Communist and Democratic Movement in Tripura* (in Bengali), Calcutta: Nabajatak.

Dutta, B. (1986) *Tradition of Popular Movements and Present Responsibilities*, Calcutta: Nachiketa Publications.

Economics Survey 2008–09, Government of Tripura, Agartala.

Economics Survey 2010, Government of Tripura, Agartala.

Economics Survey 2013–14, Government of Tripura, Agartala.

Ernst, W. and Pati, B. (eds.) (2007) *India's Princely States: People, Princes and Colonialism*, New York: Routledge.

Fic, V. M. (1969) *Peaceful Transition to Communism in India: Strategy of the Communist Party*, Bombay: Nachiketa.

Gagnon, A-G. and Tully, J. (eds.) (2001) *Multinational Democracies*, Cambridge: Cambridge University Press.

Gan Chaudhry, J. (1983) *The Reangs of Tripura*, Agartala: Tripura Darpan.

Gan-Choudhury, J. (1985) *A Political History of Tripura*, Agartala: Tripura Darpan.

Ganguly, J. B. (1983) *The Benign Hills*, Agartala: Tripura Darpan.

Ghosh, A (1977/1952) 'Some of our Main Mistakes' in For a lasting Peace, for a People's Democracy' (Cominform journal) published as a pamphlet.

Giddens, A. (1994) *Beyond Left and Right: The Future of Radical Politics*, Cambridge: Polity Press.

GMP (2013) *9th Central Conference of the Tripura Rajya Gana Mukti Parishad* 9–11 November 2013 (Unpublished) (in Bengali), Khowai.

Gramsci, A. (1971) *Selections from Prison Notebooks*, London: Lawrence and Wishart.

Guha, A. (1979) 'Great Nationalism, Little Nationalism and the Problems of Integration: A Tentative View' *EPW* No. 14.

Guha, A. (1980) 'Little Nationalism turned Chauvinist: Assam's Anti-Foreigners' Uprising, 1979–80 Economic and Politica; *Weekly October* (Special issue).

Guha, A. (1982) 'Indian National Question: A Conceptual Framework', *Occasional Paper* No. 45, Calcutta: Centre for Studies in Social Science.

Guha, R. (1982) 'On Some Elementary Aspect of Historiography of Colonial India' in Guha, R. (ed.) *Subaltern Studies: Writings on South Asian History and Society* Vol. 1, Delhi: Oxford University Press.

Guha, R. (1983) 'Counter-Insurgency Prose' in Guha, R. (ed.) *Subaltern Studies* Vol. 2, Delhi: Oxford University Press.

Hardgrave, R., Jr. and Kochanek, S. (2000) *India: Government and Politics in a Developing Nation*, Connecticut: Harcourt Publishers.

Hassan, S. (2010) *Secessionism in Northeastern India: Identity or Crises of Legitimacy?*, Delhi: Oxford University Press.

Hechetr, M. (2017/1975) *Internal Colonialism: The Celtic Fringe in British National Development*, London: Routledge (rev edn).

Hill, C. (1947) *Lenin and the Russian Revolution*, London: Hodder and Stoughton Ltd.

Hiltz, J. (2003) 'Construction of Sikkimese National Identity' (http://himalaya.socanth.cam.ac.uk/collections/journals/bot/pdf/bot_2003_02_04.pdf sighted on 11/10/17).

Hobsbawm, E. (1992) *Nation and Nationalism since 1780*, Cambridge: Cambridge University Press.

Horowitz, D. (2000) *Ethnic Groups in Conflict*, California: Berkeley: University of California Press.

Hunter, W. W. (1876) *Imperial Gazetteer of India*, New Delhi: Government of India.

Huntington, S. P. (1992) *The Clash of Civilizations and the Remaking of World Order*, London: Touchstone Books.

Huntington, S. P. (2004) *America's Great Debate: Who Are We?*, London: Penguin.

Jeffrelot, C. (ed.) (2001) *Hinduism a Reader*, New Delhi: Permanent Black.

Jeffrey, R. (ed.) (1979) *People, Princes and Paramount Power: Society and Politics in India's Princely States*, Delhi: Oxford University Press.

Jeffrey, R. (ed.) (1981) *Asia the Winning of Independence*, London: Macmillan.

Jenkin, R. (1984) 'Rethinking Ethnic Identity: Categorization and Power', *Ethnic and Race Relations Studies*, Vol. 17, No. 2, April 1994.

Kamat, P. (1980) 'Ethno-linguistic Issues in Indian Federal Context', *EPW* Vol 15, 14–21.

Karat, P. (1973) *Language and Nationality Politics in India*, New Delhi: Orient Longman.

Kallen, H. (1959) 'Radicalism' in *The Encyclopadia of the Social Science*, Vols 13–14, London: Macmillan, 51–54.

Karlekar, R. (1985) 'The Tripura Riots (1980): Problems of Marxist Strategies', *Economic and Political Weekly*, No. 34, August.

Katzenstein, M. and Weiner, W. (1981) *India's Preferential Policies*, Chicago: Chicago University Press.

Kautsky, J. (1956) *Moscow and the Communist Party of India*, New York: Wiley.

Kaviraj, S. (1992) 'Marxism and the Darkness of History', *Development and Change*, Vol. 23, No. 3.

Kaviraj, S. (2009) 'Marxism in Translation: Reflections on Indian Radical Thought' in Bourke, R. and Geusa, R. (eds.) *Political Judgment: Essays for John Dunn*, Cambridge: Cambridge University Press.

Khilnani, S. (2004) *The Idea of India*, New Delhi: Penguin.

Kogekar, S. V. and Park, R. L. (eds.) (1956) *Report on the Indian General Elections 1951–56*, New Delhi: Government of India.

Kothari, R. (1988) 'Integration and Exclusion in Indian Politics', *EPW*, 22 October.

Kohli, A. (ed.) (1988) *India's Democracy: State- Society Framework*, Princeton, NJ: Princeton University Press.

Kohli, A. (1990) *Democracy and Discontent: India's Growing Crisis of Governability*, Cambridge: Cambridge University Press.

Kumar, S. (2016) *Police and Counter-insurgency*, New Delhi: Sage Publications.

Laushey, D. (1975) *Bengal Terrorism and the Marxist Left: Aspects of Regional Nationalism in India 1905–42*, Calcutta: Firma KLM.

Loadenthal, M. (2017) 'Eco-Terrorism: An Incident Driven History of Attack (1973–2000)' *Journal of the Study of Radicalism*, Vol. 11, No. 2, Fall, 1–33.

Mackenzie (1888) Quoted in Bhattacharyya 1999 p. 35. See note 7

Maheshari, S. R. (1977) *State Governments in India, (2000)*, New Delhi: Macmillan.

Majumdar, R. C. (1963) *History of Freedom Movement in India* Vol. 3, Calcutta: Firma KLM.

Malhotra, R. (2014) *India's Public Policy Report 2014*, New Delhi: Oxford University Press.

Manor, H. (2016) 'Indian States: The Struggle to Govern', *Studies in Indian Politics*, Vol. 49, 1–14.

Manor, J. (2012) 'Did the central government's poverty initiatives help to re-elect it?' in Saez, L. and Singh, G. (eds.) *New Dimensions of Politics in India: The United Progressive Alliance in Power*, London: Routledge, 13–26.

Marx, K. (1975) 'Letter to Ludwig Kugelmann Dated November 29, 1869' in *Selected Correspondence Marx and Engels*, Moscow: Progress.

Marx, K. and Engels, F. (1972) *Ireland and Irish Question*, New York: International Publishers.

Marx, K. and Engels, F. (1948) (1975) *The Communist Manifesto*, Moscow: Progress.

McGarry, J. and O'Leary, B. (eds.) (1985) *The Politics of Ethnic Conflict Regulation*, London: Macmillan.

Menon, H. (1959) 'Radicalism' in Seligman, R. A. (ed.) *Encyclopedia of the Social Sciences*, Chicago: Macmillan Company.

Mishra, K. K. (1972) 'Linguistic Nationalities in India' *Social Scientist*, 1(3).

Mitra, S. K. (1999) *Culture and Rationality: The Politics of Social Change in Post-Colonial India*, New Delhi: Sage.

Mitra, S. K. (2012) 'Measuring the Mosaic: Caste, Class and Sentiment in Making the Citizen in India' in Bhattacharyya, H. et al. (eds.) *The Politics of Citizenship, Identity and the State in South Asia*, New Delhi: Samskriti, 42–67.

Mitra, S. K. and Bhattacharyya, H. (2018) *Politics and Governance in Indian States: Bihar, West Bengal and Tripura*, Singapore: World Scientific.

Mitra, S. K. and Singh, V. B. (2009) *When Rebel become Stakeholdwers*, New Delhi: Sage Publications.

Morris-Jones, W. H. (1987/1964) *The Government and Politics of India*, Cambridheshire: The Eothen Press.

Namboodripad, E. M. S. (1989) *A History of Indian Freedom Struggle*, New Delhi: Social Science Press.

Nin, Andre (1935) Austro-Marxism and the National Question (https://www.marxists.org/archive/nin/1935/xx/austromarx.htm sighted on 26/1/18).

Nossiter, T. J. N. (1982) *Communism in Kerala: A Study in Political Adaptation*, London: Hurst & Co.

Nossiter, T. J. N. (1988) *Marxist Sate Governments in India*, London: Pinters.

Overstreet, G. and Windmiller, M. (1959) *Communism in India*, Berkeley: University of California Press.

Padmanavian, K. (1987) 'Communist Party in Tamil Nadu', *The Indian Journal of Political Science*, Vol. 48, No. 2, June, 225–50.

Parekh, B. (2008) *A New Politics of Identity Political Principles for an Interdependent World*, Basilstroke: Palgrave Macmillan.

Parulekar, G. (1978) *Adivasi's Revolt* (in Bengali), Calcutta: National Book Agency.

Ram, M. (1971) *Maoism in India*, New Delhi: Vikash.

Ram, M. (1973) 'The Communist Movement in Andhra Pradesh' in Brass, P. and Franda, M. (eds.) *Radical Politics in South Asia*, Cambridge, Mass.: MIT Press, 281–324.

Rao, M. B. (ed.) (1976) *Documents of the History of the CPI 1948–50* Vol. 7, New Delhi: People's Publishing House.

Rasul, A. (1974) *A History of All India Kisan Sabha*, Calcutta: National Book Agency.

Roy, A. (1967) 'Some Aspects of the National Question in India', *Marxist Review* (Calcutta) No. 1, 41.

Roy, P. (1948) *Private Manuscripts* (Unpublished), Agartala.

Roy, S. (1983) *Tripoura Darpan: Facts and Directions*, Agartala: Tripura Darpan.

Roy, S. (2011) *Tripura Darpan: Facts and References (in Bengali)*, Agartala: Tripura Darpan.

Roy, S. (2013) *Tripura Darpan: Facts and References (in Bengali)*, Agartala: Tripura Darpan.

Roy, S (2015) *Tripura Darpan: Facts and References (in Bengali)*, Agartala: Tripura Darpan.

Roy Choudhury, N. R. (1978) *Tribal Uprisings in the Second Half of the Nineteenth Century* (Unpublished D thesis: Calcutta University), Calcutta.

Saha, S. B. (1980) *A Socioeconomic Study of the Noatia Tribes*, Agartala: Tribal Research Centre, Government of Tripura.

Saigal, O. (1980) *Tripura: History and Culture*, New Delhi: Concept Publisher.

Saez, L. (2002) *India: Federalism without a Centre*, New Delhi: Sage Publications.

Sardar Patel's Correspondences with Doulatram 28 June 1950, Shimla: Government of India.

Sen, T. (1971) *Tripura in Transition*, Agartala: Author.

Sen Gupta, B. (1972) *Communism in Indian Politics*, New York: Columbia University Press.

Sen Gupta, B. (1979) *CPI-M: Problems and Prospects*, Madras: Young Asia.

Sen Gupta, S. (2009) *Radical Politics in Meghalaya: Problems and Prospects*, New Delhi: Kalpaz.

Sen, M. (ed.) (1977) *Documents of the History of the CPI, 1951–56*, New Delhi: People's Publishing House.

Seton-Watson, H. (1977) *Nations and States: and the Politics of Nationalism*, Colorodo: Boulder.

Singh, G. (1994) *Communism in Punjab*, Delhi: Ajanta.

# Bibliography

Singh, B. P. (1987) *The Problem of Change: A Study of North East India*, Delhi: Oxford University Press.
Singh, K. S. (1982) *Tribal Movements in India*, 2 vols., New Delhi: Monohar.
Smith, A. D. (1979) *Nationalism in the Twentieth Century*, Oxford: Robertson.
Smith, A. D. (1981) *The Ethnic Revival in the Modern World*, Cambridge: Cambridge University Press.
Smith, A. D. (1983) *Theories of Nationalism*, 2nd edn, London: Duckworth.
Smith, A. D. (1986) *The Ethnic Origins of Nations*, Oxford: Basil Blackwell.
Smith, A. D. (1994) 'The Problem of National Identity: Ancient, Mediaval and Modern', *Ethnic and Race Relations Studies*, Vol. 17, No. 3.
Smith, A. D. (1995) *Nations and Nationalism in a Global World*, Cambridge: Polity Press.
Smith, A. D. (2003) *Nationalism*, Cambridge: Polity Press.
Stalin, J. V. (1913) *Marxism and the National Question*, Calcutta: National Book Agency. (reprint 1975).
Statistical Abstract of Tripura 2014–15, Agartala: Government of Tripura.
Statistical Abstract 1992, Agartala: Government of Tripura.
Thompson, E. P. (1987) *The Poverty of Theory and Other Essays*, London: Merlin Press.
Tillin, L. et al. (eds.) (2015) *The Politics of Welfare: A Comparison Across Indian States*, New Delhi: Oxford University Press.
Tremblay, R. (2003) 'Globalization and Indian Federalism' in Dua, B. and Singh, M. P. (eds.) *Indian Federalism in the New Millennium*, New Delhi: Monohar, 335–50.
Tripura At a Glance (2011) *Directorate of Economics and Statistics*, Agartala: Government of Tripura.
Tripura At a Glance (2014–15) *Directorate of Economics and Statistics*, Agartala: Government of Tripura.
Tripura Human Development Report (2007) Agartala: Government of Tripura.
Tully, J. (2001) 'Introduction' in Gagnon, A.-G. and Tully, J. (eds.) *Multinational Democracies*, Cambridge: Cambridge University Press, 1–35.
Turley, W. S. (1980) *Vietnamese Revolution in Comparative Perspective*, Colorado: Westview.
Vanaik, A. (1988) *The Painful Transition: Bourgeois Democracy in India*, London: Verso.
Wallerstein, I. (1991) 'Construction of Peoplehood: Race, Nationalism and Ethnicity' in Balibar, E. and Wallerstein, I. (eds.) *Race, Nation, Class: Ambiguous Identities*, London: Verso, 71–86.
Weber, M. (1948) *From Max Weber: Essays in Sociology*, eds. Gerth, H. H. and Mills, C. W., London: Routledge & Kegan Paul.
Weiner, M. (ed.) (1968) *State Politics in India*, Princeton, NJ: Princeton University Press.
Weiner, M. (1978) *The Sons of the Soil: Migration and Ethnic Conflict in India*, Princeton, NJ: Princeton University Press.
Weiner, M. and Katzenstein, M. (1981) *India's Preferential Policies*, Chicago: Chicago University Press.
Winter, M. (1992) 'Politics and States in a New Ethnic Order', *Third World Quarterly*, 13.2.1992.
Yadav, Y. and Palshikar, S. (2008) *Ten Theses on State Politics in India* (http://www.india-seminar.com/2008/591/591_y_yadav_&_s_palshkar.htm sighted on 26/18.

# Index

adivasis 32
Agartala Municipal elections 171–172
Ahmed, Muzaffar 173
All Assam Students Union (ASSU) 54, 57, 61
All Assam Tribal League 53
All Bodo Students Union, 53–54
All-India Kisan Sabha (Peasant Organization) 103
All-Indian party (CPI) 160
All Tripura Workers Union 105
Analytical Marxism 27–28
Anderson, Benedict 144
Andhra 31, 32
Andhra Pradesh 31, 63, 221, 226, 227, 229
Anusilan Samity of Tripura 104
Arunachal Pradesh 1, 17, 37, 40, 47, 69
Asom Gana Parishad (AGP) 40, 43, 49, 54, 61, 66
Aspects of China's Anti-Jap Struggle (Mao Zedong) 130
Assam 1, 17, 34, 37–38, 44, 53–54, 61, 66, 67, 234
Assam Accord 54, 57
Assam Kachari Association 53
Austro-Marxists 24

Baidesahik Amla (foreign bureaucracy) 113–114
Bandopadhyay, Mamata 12
'Bangal Kheda' (Drive away the Bengalis) movement 111
Bangladesh 1, 34, 37–39, 42, 57, 72, 74–76, 88
Bankim Chandra Chattapadhyay 142
Barnett, A. Doak 29
Baruah, Sanjib 52
Basu, Jyoti 173
Bauer, Auto 24

Bengal 9, 73, 75, 103–105, 107, 145–147, 151, 153, 179, 200
Bengalis: anti-Bengali stand of Tripuri nationalism 110–111, 129, 134, 144, 149–150, 156–157, 165; in Assam 40; communist 103–108; critique of cultural tradition 151–152; economic structure 83; GS and 172; land question 201, 237; language 73; leadership in PM 113–114; migration of 15, 39, 42, 74, 75, 88, 91; settlement in Tripura 75–80; social structure 80–82; TUJS attitude and policies towards 186–187, 188–189
Bentham, Jeremy 5
Bhadur, Ram 97
Bharatiya Janata Party (BJP) 54
Bhaumik, Subir 37; 'Insurgent Cross-fire' 52; 'Troubled North East' 52
Bhutan 1, 37, 38
Bodo Accord 57–58, 61
Bodo community 53
Bod Sahitya Sabha (The Bodo Literary Association) 53
Bose, Bijoy 129
Buddhists 47, 77–78

Calcutta Congress 120
Canada 18
Capital (Marx) 8
Chakrabarty, Nripen 98, 99, 129–130, 133, 135, 137, 160, 163–167, 189
Chakrabarty, Priya 172
Chakraborty, Anil 172
Chanda, Saroj 129, 172
Chandra, Mahim 152
Chatterjee, A. B. 118
Chatterjee, Partha 141, 143–144, 156
Chaudhury, Prarnanshu 104
China 1, 18, 37, 38, 48

Choudhury, Animesh 172
Choudhury, Mihir 119
Choudhury, Mohun 129, 131, 133, 160
Choudhury, Tarbang 94–95
Christians 42, 47, 77–78
The Civil War in France (Marx) 8
class 19–20, 22, 45
The Class Struggles in France, 1848-1850 (Marx) 8, 31
Cohen, G.A. 27
communism: GMP integration with 161–162; impact on JSS 111–115; influence over tribal mass mobilization 117–138; rise of movement in Tripura 102–106
Communist Manifesto (Marx) 19–21, 30
Communist Party of India (CPI): Agartala unit of 105; Assam Provincial Committee 162; electoral support base 176–178, 179–180; influence in Tamil Nadu 33; liberal democratic politics in Tripura 215–219; national question and 30–35; organization and membership in Tripura 163–164; as panacea 165–166; radical tribal nationalism movement of 9; role of GMP under leadership of 167; success in Kerala 32; support for Marathi self-determination 32; support in Maharashtra 32; in Tripura 104
Communist Party of India (Marxist) (CPI-M): governance in Tripura 4, 79, 86; influence in Assam 17; influence in Maharashtra 33; influence in Tamil Nadu 33; liberal democratic politics in Tripura 215–219; political-organizational fall outs 229–230; political participation 59; State Assembly elections 191; view of TUJS 188–189
Communist Party of India (Marxist–Leninist) (CPI-ML) 187–188
Connor, Walker 141
Constitution of India: Article 356 10; Article 371-A 55–57; challenges to 10–11; Eighth Schedule 47; ethnic peace accords 55–58; fundamental rights enshrined 170; non-recognition of religion in 42; power-sharing allowances 52, 54; recognition of tribal identity in 197–200; reforms 107–109; Sixth Schedule 2, 44, 47, 186, 199; STs recognized in 39

dacoits party 94, 97, 179
Dainik Sambad (journal) 190

Dange, S.A. 30, 173
Datta, Biren 104, 105, 108, 110, 113, 119, 120, 127, 132, 170, 180
Datta, Santi 104
De, Ananta 104
Desai, Akshay Ramanlal 143
Desher Katha (journal) 190
Devbarma, Aghore 105, 110, 119, 147
Devbarma, Akhil Chandra 98
Devbarma, Dasarath 110–111, 118, 119, 120, 127, 130, 132, 162, 163, 167, 180, 220
Devbarma, Hemanta 110
Devbarma, Hredoymoni 124
Devbarma, Jitendra Mohun 98
Devbarma, N.C. 200
Devbarma, Nimai 104
Devbarma, Radha Mohun: Kok-Borok Ma 152; Tripura Abhidhan 152; Tripurar Katha Mala 152
Devbarma, Shri Kumara Nandalal 98
Devbarma, Sudhanya 110, 127
Devbarma, Thakur Hara Chandra 98
Devbarma, Thakur Ram Kumar 122
Devbarma, Usha Ranjan 98, 104, 105
Devbarms, Gouranga 129
*diversity-claims* 53, 58, 234
Doulatram, Jairamdas 135
'Durable Disorder' (Baruah) 52
'durable disorder' hypothesis 70
Dutta, Biren 98
Dutta, Girija Prasad 147

East Bengal see Bangladesh
East Pakistan see Bangladesh
economic structure 82–85
electoral support base 176–178
Engels, Friedrich 5, 19, 23–24, 31
ethnic conflicts 75–80
ethnic diversity 37–42
ethnic identity: Analytical Marxism and 27–28; class, nation and 19–20, 45; definition of 20–21; Marxism opposition to 21–22; national question and 19, 236–237; recognition in Constitution 197–200; religion and 42; tribal ethnicity and 9–10, 14
ethnic mobilization 53–55
Ethnic Origins of Nations (Smith) 20
ethnic radicalism: conceptual issues 6–9; ethnic mobilization and 53–55; institutionalization of 52–70; in Tripura 88–99
ethno-nationalism 141–142

F. B. Ruikar Group 173
foreign direct investment (FDI) 11, 12
foreign policy 12
Forward Bloc 173

Ganatantric Sangha (GS) (Democratic Association) 172–173
Gandhi, Indira 10, 54, 58
Gandhi, Rajiv 55, 58
Ghosh, Ajoy 173
Giddens, Anthony 6
Golaghati peasant massacre 119
Goswami, Dharani 107
Gramsci, Antonio 99
Gujarat 221, 226

Hayek, Friedrich 5
Hill Districts 37
Hills State People's Democratic Party 34
Hindus 47, 77–78, 82, 178, 189
Hunter, W.W. 83
Huntington, Samuel 142
Hyderabad 9

India from Primitive Communism to Slavery (Dange) 30
Indigenous Nationalist Party of Twipra (INPT) 192, 194, 220
'Insurgent Cross-fire' (Bhaumik) 52
internationalism 28–29
Islam, Atikul 129

Jana Mongal Samity (Association for Public Welfare/JMS) 148
Jana Mongal Samity (JMS): background 106–108; ideology 108–109; terrorism and 148
Jana Shiksha Samity (Association for Mass Literacy): background 106–108, 110–111; impact of communism on 111–115

Kadem, Kaji Samsuddin 103
Kangleipak Communist Party (KCP) 34
Kashmir 38, 48
Kaviraj, Sudipta 8–9, 28, 160
Kerala 2, 31–32, 63, 235
Keynes, John Maynard 5
Khowai 124–127, 178
Kisan movement 103
Kok-Borok 80–82, 200
Kok-Borok Ma (A Grammar of the Tripuri Language) (Devbarma) 152

Lal Communist Party (LCP) 159
Lal Party 9
land question 200–203, 237
Land Revenue and Land Reforms Act 202
language 40, 42, 73, 80–82, 106, 154–156, 200
For a Lasting Peace, For a People's Democracy (Cominform organ) 129, 132, 160
Left Front Government (LFG) 2, 79, 191–192, 201–203, 205
left radicalism: background 6–9; conceptual issues 6–13
Lenin, Vladimir 8, 21, 24–25, 29
Lohe, Z. 44

Mackenzie, Alexander 74
Maharashtra 32–33, 63, 221, 226, 227, 229
Malhotra, Rajeev 63
Manipur 1, 17, 34, 37–42, 59, 63, 69, 178
Maoist Communist Party of Manipur (MCPM) 34
Mao Zedong 130
Marxism: Analytical Marxism 27–28; ethnic identity and 27–28; formation of 5–6; national question and 19, 22–24; nation, nationalism and 19–20; opposition to ethnicity 21–22; overview of national question/ethnic in India and 29–35; 'translation' problem in 8–9
Marxism and the National Question (Stalin) 26
The Marxist (journal) 189
Marx, Karl 5, 19, 23–24, 27–28, 31; Capital 8; The Civil War in France 8; The Class Struggles in France, 1848-1850 8, 31; Communist Manifesto 19–21, 30; Proclamation on the Polish Question 23
Meghalaya 1, 17, 34, 37–42, 47, 58, 59, 63, 65, 69, 159, 234
Memorandum of settlement, 1993 (ATTF accord) 55, 204–205
Mishra, Biresh 132
Mizo Accord 49, 55, 57
Mizo National Front (MNF) 49, 54–55
Mizoram 1, 17, 34, 37–42, 44, 47, 58, 59, 63, 65, 69, 159, 234
Mohanta, Prafulla K. 44
Moni, Chinta 97
Moni, Ratan 93–96
Muslims 42–43, 47, 77, 82, 178
Myanmar 1, 37, 38, 48

Naga-Akbar Hydari Ethnic Peace
   Accord 48
Naga Club 53
Nagaland 1, 17, 34, 37–42, 44–45, 47, 55,
   59, 63, 65, 69, 159, 234
Namboodripad, E. M. S. 31
Nath, Khagendra Chandra 147
nation 19–20
nationalism: class, ethnic identity and
   19–20; ethno-nationalism 141–142;
   Indian debate 143–144; Tripuri 144–157
national question: CPI and 30–35; ethnic
   identity and 19, 236–237; Leninist
   'strategy' on 25; Marxism and 22–24;
   post-Marxist positions 24–27; Stalin's
   'theory' of 25–27
Nehru, Jawaharlal 55
Nepal 38
Noaties 90–92, 96

*oproja* (non-subjects). 150–151

Parulekar, Godavari 33
Patel, S. V. 135
The Patriot (journal) 190
peace accords 48, 55, 203
Plains Tribal Council of Assam (PTCA) 53
political participation 58–61
political violence 61–63
power-sharing 55–61
Pradesh, Andhra 31
President's Rule 10
Proclamation on the Polish Question
   (Marx) 23
Proja Mondal movement 111, 147–148, 172
Projar Katha (JMS publication) 108–109
proja (subjects) 150–151
public policy effectiveness 63–65
Punchi Commission 12
Punjab 9, 36

radicalism: concept of 4–5; ethnic 6–9;
   Indian left 6–13; left and right 4–6;
   religious movements 5; State politics
   and 10–13
radical tribal nationalist movement 9
Rajkumar, Rakhal 162
Rajmala (chronicle of Tripur dynasty) 73
Ram, Mohan 31
Ram, Shiva 160
Ranadive, B.T 129
Rao, Rajeswar 129, 132
Reang rebellion: assessments 97–99;
   conceptual issues 89, 102, 106;
   counter-insurgency operation 93–97,
   236; GMP communism and 137; rise of
   93–97; roots of 90–93, 97–98
religion: religious diversity 42–43, 47;
   religious movements 5
Renner, Karl 24
Revolutionary Socialist Party (RSP) 192
Roy, Bijoy 160
Roy, Probhat 104, 107, 110, 113, 148, 154
Roy, R. K. 125
rule of law 65–67
rural inequality 200–203
Russia 24–26

Sangma, P.N. 44
Sarkaria Commission on the Centre State
   Relations 10
Scheduled Castes (dalits) 67, 77
Scheduled Tribes (STs) 67–69
Sen, Benu 105
Sen, Chitra 97
Sen, Debaprosad 104, 105, 123
Sen Gupta, Bhabani 31–32
Sen Gupta, Nalini 104
Sen Gupta, Sukhomoy 172
Sen, Kanu 104, 105
Sen, Nabin Chandra 74
Sen, Rabi 104
Seton-Watson, Hugh 144
share-cropping 83–84
Sharma, Ganga Prosad 107
Sikkim 1, 37–42, 45, 63, 65, 69
Simon Commission 53
Sino-Indian border conflict 55
Smith, Anthony 20
social inclusion 67–69
socialism 6
social structure 80–82
Soviet Marxism 6
Stalinism 6
Stalin, Joseph 24
State Assembly elections 191–192
State politics 10–13
Statesman (journal) 190
Sundarayya, P. 31

Tamil Nadu 33, 63, 221
Tamilnand 32
Tax Payers Association (TPA) 171
Telangana 31
Telegraph (journal) 190
territorial issues 43–45
terrorism 103–104, 148
Thakur, Bansi 104, 148

# Index

Thakur, Ramkumar 126
Thatcher, Margaret 5
Thompson, E.P. 28–29
Todd, H. J. 74, 97
Tour Impressions (Todd) 74
Tribal Areas Autonomous District Council (ADC) 2, 70, 82, 191, 196, 199–200, 202–203, 205–212
Tribal Autonomous District Council Act 199
tribal ethnicity 9–10, 14
tribal ethnic States 44
tribal identity: ADC and 205–211; land question and 200–203
tribal self-determination 186–187
Tripura: ADC 2, 70, 82, 191, 196, 199–200, 202–203, 205–212; background 1–4; CPI/CPI-M's liberal democratic politics in 215–219; demographic upheaval 75–80; dilemmas of governance 214–231; discriminatory employment policy 147; disillusionment with politics 147–149; diversity-claims 234; economic structure 82–85; ethnic conflicts 75–80; formation of parallel government in 135–136; formation of State 73–75; globalization and governance in 221–229; globalization and governance in since 1990s 221–229; governance and public policy effectiveness 224–229; impact of communism on JSS 111–115; industrial base 85; institutionalization of tribal ethnic identity 70; linguistic diversity 40, 42; literacy rate 79–80; location 72–73; major traits of nationalism 149; Marxists in power in 197–231; multi-party competition in 219–221; multi-party electoral competition and the rise to power of left 219–221; new agrarian system 145–146; parallel communist government 135–136; peace accords 48, 55, 203–205; political-organizational fall outs 229–230; political participation 59; population 39, 76–77, 90; princely State of 73–75; radical ethno-nationalism in 141–157; Reang rebellion in 88–99; rise and decline of TUJS in 182–196; rise of communist movement in 102–106; rise to power of left 219–221; roots of radical politics in 72–86; rule of law 66; second phase of development of communism in 106–111; social inclusion 67–68; social structure 80–82; terrorism in 103–104

Tripura Abhidhan (A Dictionary of Tripuri) (Devbarma) 152
Tripura Democratic Women's Association 173
Tripura Rajya Gana Mukti Parished (Tripuri Nationalist Liberation Organization) 99
Tripura Rajya Jatiyo/Gana Mukti Parishad (GMP): achievement of 138; armed struggle 123–132, 138, 160–161; electoral support base 179–180; formation of parallel government in Tripura 135–136; Golaghati peasant massacre and 119; ideology and autonomy 122–123, 137–138; imposition of strange theory on 163–167; integration with Indian communism 161–162; interaction between all-India communism and 132–135; organization 120–122; organization of 163–164; participation in general elections 167–169; rise of 117–119, 149; role under leadership of Communist Party 167; status of 165–166; weakness of 164–165
Tripura Rajya Mukti Parishad (Liberation Council) 119
Tripura Rajya Proja Mondal (The Tripura State Subjects Association) (PM) 112–115
Tripura Rajyer Kotha (communist weekly) 113, 124, 170
Tripurar Katha Mala (A Translation of the Tripuri Language) (Devbarma) 152
Tripura State Congress 172, 174
Tripura Upajati Gana Mukti Parishad (GMP) (Tripura Tribal Liberation Council) 75
Tripura Upajati Juba Samity (TUJS): CPI-ML view of 187–188; electoral gains and losses 191–195; final assessment of 195–196; journalistic approach 189–190; multi-party electoral competition and 219–221; North Eastern context 183–184; perspectives on 187–191; PI (M) view of 188–189; rise and decline in Tripura 182–196; semi-academic and academic comments 189; social roots and objectives of 184–186; tribal self-determination 186–187
Tripuri nationalism: anti-Bengali stand of 149–150; background 145; critique of Bengali cultural tradition 151–152;

demographic shift 145; desire for political power, 152–153; development of 156–157; disillusionment with Tripura politics 147–149; language issues 154–156; major traits of 149–156; middle-class discontent and 146–147; proja and oproja distinction and 150–151; roots of 144–145
'Troubled North East' (Bhaumik) 52

Udayachal 53–54
United Front: Agartala Municipal elections and 171–172; birth of 173–175; GS and 172–173; tactics 171–173
United Liberation Front of Assam (ULFA) 40, 43, 54
United Progressive Bloc (UPB) 171

Vanaik, Achin 144
Vietnam 18, 30
Visalandhrala Praja Rajyam (Sundarayya) 31
Vivek (journal) 190

Wallerstein, Immanuel 7, 21–22, 141–142
Weber, Max 21, 26–27
Weiner, Myron 11
West Bengal 2, 12, 63, 154, 214, 220–222, 230, 235–237
West Bengal State Security Act 130
What Are We (Huntington) 142
Working Committee (WC) 172

Yugantar (journal) 190

zamindary 74, 77, 103